MW00795498

The Dispersion of Egyptian Jewry

CONTRAVERSIONS
Critical Studies in Jewish Literature, Culture, and Society
Daniel Boyarin and Chana Kronfeld, General Editors

The Dispersion of Egyptian Jewry

Culture, Politics, and the Formation of a Modern Diaspora

Joel Beinin

UNIVERSITY OF CALIFORNIA PRESS
Berkeley · Los Angeles · London

University of California Press
Berkeley and Los Angeles, California

University of California Press, Ltd.
London, England

Library of Congress Cataloging-in-Publication Data

Beinin, Joel, 1948—.
    The dispersion of Egyptian Jewry: culture, politics, and the formation of the modern
    diaspora / Joel Beinin.
        p.   cm.   (Contraversions; 11)
    Includes bibliographic references and index.
    ISBN 0-520-21175-8 (alk. paper)
        1. Jews—Egypt—History—20th century.   2. Jews—Egypt—Politics and govern-
    ment.   3. Operation Susannah.   4. Karaites—Egypt.—5. Jews, Egyptian—Israel.
        6. Arab-Israeli conflict.   7. Egypt—Ethnic relations.   I. Title.   II. Series.
DS135.E4B45   1998
    962'004924—DC21   97-28043

Printed in the United States of America
9   8   7   6   5   4   3   2   1

An earlier version of Chapter 2 appeared as "Egyptian Jewish Identities: Communi-
tarianisms, Nationalisms, Nostalgias," *Stanford Humanities Review* 5 (no. 1, 1995).
    An earlier version of Chapter 4 appeared as "Nazis and Spies: Representations of Is-
raeli Espionage and Terrorism in Egypt," *Jewish Social Studies* 2 (no. 3, 1996).
    An earlier version of the first half of Chapter 6 appeared as "Exile and Political Ac-
tivism: The Egyptian-Jewish Communists in Paris, 1950–1959," *Diaspora* 2 (no. 1, 1992).
    A slightly different version of the interview with Jacques Hassoun in the Appendix
appeared in *MERIP Newsletter* (Winter 1997).

To Miriam, my life partner

Contents

Acknowledgments

I am deeply indebted to the many Egyptian Jews in Egypt, Israel, Paris, and San Francisco who shared their memories, papers, and hearts with me in the course of my research for this book. Without their assistance, this book would have been an entirely different and inferior product. Their names are listed in the Bibliography.

Many Egyptian Jews as well as other friends and colleagues saved clippings from the Israeli and Egyptian press for me, allowed me to copy personal papers, or gave me books, magazines, and other materials that were invaluable sources for this book. Among them were Raymond Aghion, Ada Aharoni, Shlomo Barad, Esther and Gilbert Bar-On, Henriette Busnach, Yusuf Darwish, Marcelle Fisher, Karim al-Gawhary, Yitzhaq Gormezano-Goren, David Harel, Anda Harel-Dagan, Jacques Hassoun, Reuven Kaminer, Mourad El-Kodsi, Yoram Meital, Doris and Henry Mourad, Remy and Joe Pessah, Sami Shemtov, Ted Swedenburg, and Robert Vitalis. Ninette Braunstein and Gabi Rosenbaum suggested the names of people I should speak with. Roger Kohn, curator of the Judaica collection at the Stanford University Library, was always willing and often successful in acquiring materials I needed. He kept my research interests in mind during the course of this project and passed on to me several items I might otherwise have missed.

Saba Mahmood, Remy Pessah, Aron Rodrigue, Mohamed Sid-Ahmed, Robert Vitalis, and Jane Zimmerman graciously read and commented on portions of the typescript and made many valuable suggestions. Zachary Lockman and Nancy Reynolds each painstakingly read a late draft of the book and offered incisive, detailed critiques. I have not been able to respond adequately to all of their points, but the text has, nonetheless, been significantly improved because of the attention they lavished on it. Much of my thinking and development as a scholar is inextricably bound up with my long friendship and collaboration with Zachary Lockman. It is an enormous source of satisfaction and pleasure to be able to benefit from the intellectual acumen of Nancy Reynolds, the first doctoral student in Middle East history at Stanford University in many decades.

This project was conceived and came to fruition during the period of my association with Stanford University's Program in Modern Thought and Literature, an interdisciplinary doctoral program in cultural studies. Teaching the first-year graduate students the required course in "The Modern Tradition" has been a welcome challenge that provided me the opportunity to think systematically about many issues I might otherwise have avoided. My colleagues in Modern Thought and Literature and in the faculty seminar in cultural studies that met for several years in the 1980s and early 1990s have influenced my thinking in ways too numerous and subtle to catalog. The interdisciplinary Seminar in Empires and Cultures sponsored by the Stanford Humanities Center, which Richard Roberts and I co-convened for three years, has also been a source of stimulating discussion of the ideas that have shaped my approach to this book. I also wish to acknowledge my debt to Stanford's Department of History. In addition to providing supplementary financial support for this project at critical points along the way, the department has long fostered an atmosphere that has allowed me to take many intellectual risks without a second thought. This is as it should be but is, unfortunately, all too rare.

Research for this project was funded by a Fulbright Research Grant in 1992–93 and a Social Science Research Council Advanced Research Grant in 1994. The Department of Middle Eastern and African History at Tel Aviv University hosted me when I was a Fulbright grantee during 1992-93.

As always, my wife, Miriam, and son, Jamie, have been supportive and tolerant of my physical and emotional absence for extended periods during my work on this book. My debt to them can never adequately be redeemed.

CHAPTER I

Introduction

Since the conclusion of the peace treaty between Israel and Egypt in 1979, subjects that transverse the border between the two countries have become feasible research agendas as well as new sites of contention in the Arab-Israeli conflict. The Egyptian Jewish community is situated in this cross-border zone. This book examines the history of this community after 1948, pursuing three areas of inquiry. Part 1 examines the life of the Jews who remained in Egypt after the 1948 Arab-Israeli War (mainly until the aftermath of the 1956 Suez/Sinai War). Part 2 explores the dynamics of the dispersion and reestablishment of Egyptian Jewish communities at selected sites in Israel, France, and the United States. Part 3 surveys contending revisionings of Jewish life in Egypt since Egyptian President Anwar al-Sadat's visit to Jerusalem in 1977 and the subsequent conclusion of an Egyptian-Israeli peace treaty in 1979.

The best comprehensive work on the history of Egyptian Jewry in the twentieth century, Gudrun Krämer's *The Jews in Modern Egypt, 1914–1952*, demonstrates that no single experience was shared by all Egyptian Jews because differences of class, ethnic origins, rite, and political outlook all tended to erode Jewish communal solidarity without completely effacing it. Krämer challenges the tendency of Zionist historiography to view the state of Israel as the teleological fulfillment of the history of Egyptian Jewry as well as the traditional Egyptian nationalist argument that all would have been well were it not for Zionism. She concludes that "a Jewish question as it emerged in nineteenth-century Europe did not exist in twentieth-century Egypt. Jews were not discriminated against because of their religion or race, but for political reasons." Egyptian Jews experienced "neither uninterrupted persecution and terror nor uninterrupted harmony."[1] These judicious assessments are the point of departure for this book.

According to Krämer, some 50,000–55,000 Jews remained in Egypt at the time of the Suez/Sinai War in 1956. Nonetheless, she unwittingly reinforces the prevailing assumption that the creation of the state of Israel in 1948 marked the end of the Egyptian Jewish community because, despite the nominal end date of her book, it contains only a minimal discussion—a mere six pages—of events and issues after 1948. The continued existence of this community in Egypt after 1948 apparently contradicts the Zionist assumption that there could be no normal life for Jews anywhere but Israel, all the more so in an Arab country in a state of war with Israel. The ultimate departure of the great majority of the remaining Jews after 1956 seems to confirm this assumption, albeit belatedly. This book begins on the uncertain terrain delimited by these two moments.

THE JEWS OF EGYPT

The Egyptian Jewish community was formed by a distinctive process of historical accretion. At its core were indigenous Arabic-speaking Rabbanites and Karaites with a Judeo-Arabic culture, including some who claimed to trace their residence in the country to the pre-Islamic era. They resided primarily in Cairo's Jewish quarter, in the port district of Alexandria, and in several provincial towns. Indigenes composed perhaps 20,000 of the 75,000–80,000 Jews in Egypt in 1948 (only 65,639 were recorded in the 1947 census, but this is commonly regarded as an undercount).

Because the Karaites are a relatively unknown group, I say a bit more about them in introducing the Egyptian Jewish community than I say about its other component elements. The Karaite Jews of Egypt were part of a small minority within Judaism who reject the validity of the Talmud as a source of Jewish law.[2] Karaites date the beginnings of their community to the late second temple period and identify with non-Pharasaic (Essene and Sadducee) currents of religious thought and practice of that era. The term Karaites (*kara'im*) was first applied to followers of 'Anan ben David (ca. 754–75), who broke with the leadership of the Jewish community in Mesopotamia and established himself in Jerusalem. By the ninth century, when the Karaite rite was consolidated, the community was well established in Fustat (subsequently incorporated into Cairo). The Karaites have had a difficult and often antagonistic relationship with Rabbinic Judaism since the Egyptian rabbi and scholar Saʿadya ben Yosef al-Fayyumi (882–942) declared their doctrines heretical. However, before the modern era, disputes between the two rites were regarded as internal to the Jewish community. Egypt has long been an important Karaite center. During the medieval Tulunid (868–969) and Fatimid (969–1171) periods, the Karaites were a particularly robust and vibrant community, at times even stronger than the Rabbanites. Subsequently, their numbers dwindled sharply. There were only some 5,000 Karaites in Egypt in 1948.

In the modern era, the estrangement between Karaites and Rabbanites intensified after Lithuania and Crimea, where Karaites had settled since the twelfth century, were conquered by the Russian empire. In 1795, Catherine II exempted the Karaites from the double tax imposed on Jews and allowed the Karaites to own land. In 1827, the Crimean Karaites, like their Tatar neighbors, were exempted from military service. Because the Karaites were not subjected to the discrimination and oppression directed against Rabbanites in imperial Russia, they eventually came to be seen as a separate non-Jewish community.

The distinction between Karaites and Rabbanites sharpened in 1939, when the German Ministry of Interior declared that the Karaites were not Jews after consulting with orthodox Rabbanite authorities, who may have been motivated by the desire to save the Karaites from destruction by the Nazis. Karaite rabbis concurred with this conclusion, and they too may have been seeking to avoid persecution. During the Nazi era, the Karaites of Poland, Lithuania, and Crimea were not treated as Jews.[3]

Despite ambiguities about the Jewish identity of the Eastern European Karaites in the modern era, in Egypt there was never any doubt that the Karaites were Jews. There were certainly tensions between Karaites and Rabbanites over questions of religious law and practice. Traditionally, both communities banned marriages between the two rites. The last Karaite chief rabbi of Egypt, Tuvia Babovitch (r. 1934–56), was personally committed to the view that Karaites who married Rabbanites thereby excluded themselves from the community. He also upheld the ban on conversion to Karaism against the wishes of some members of the community.[4] In contrast, Murad Farag (1866–1956) and his proteges among the young Karaite intelligentsia openly called for intermarriage and closer Karaite-Rabbanite relations. Though they did not succeed in formally changing Karaite religious law, they did influence the Karaites to strengthen their ties to the Rabbanite community.

The general tendency during the twentieth century was toward closer cultural and social relations between the two Jewish communities. The traditional Cairo neighborhoods of the Rabbanites and Karaites—*harat al-yahud* (the Jewish quarter) and *harat al-yahud al-qara'in* (the Karaite Jewish quarter)—were adjacent to each other. Rabbanites and Karaites worked in some of the same trades in the surrounding neighborhoods. Dr. Musa (Moshe) Marzuq, a Karaite executed for his role in Operation Susannah (see "Operation Susannah" later in this chapter), worked in the Rabbanite hospital, which many Karaites used because their community did not operate its own medical facility. The Karaite community made an annual contribution to support this hospital. Maurice Shammas, a protege of Murad Farag, wrote for the Rabbanite Arabic newspaper *al-Shams* (The sun) between 1946 and 1948 and then for the Karaite biweekly *al-Kalim* (The spokesperson) before he emigrated to Israel in 1951. Neither the state authorities nor the members of the two Egyptian Jewish communities ever considered the Karaites anything but Jews.

The beginning of the Sephardi (Spanish Jewish) community in Egypt is associated with the arrival in 1165 of Maimonides, who was then fleeing from the intolerant al-Muwahhid regime in Spain and Morocco. After their expulsion from Spain in 1492, many Sephardim were welcomed in the Ottoman Empire, and some settled in Egypt. In the modern era, Sephardim made their way to Egypt from the Ottoman cities of Tunis, Aleppo, Damascus, Izmir, Istanbul, Salonika, and even Jerusalem to take advantage of the economic opportunities generated by the cotton boom of the 1860s and the opening of the Suez Canal in 1869.

Among the Sephardim, there were social distinctions among those who had passed through Corsica, Italy, or the Ottoman territories on their families' journeys from Spain to Egypt. Sephardim were the most prominent elements of the Jewish social and business elite. The largest single section of the Egyptian Jewish community—"the confused Jewish masses," as one Israeli historian called them—was composed of Sephardim of the middle strata.[5] They were politically quietist, concerned primarily about the well-being of their families, and generally satisfied with their relatively comfortable lives in Egypt.

The Ashkenazi (Eastern European Jewish) Egyptian community was entirely a product of the modern era and the arrival of Jews fleeing persecution in Europe in the nineteenth century. From 1865 on, the Ashkenazim of Cairo maintained a separate communal organization. They were geographically concentrated in the Darb al-Barabira quarter, where Yiddish was spoken in the streets until the 1950s. The community maintained

a Yiddish theater group and a Yiddish program on the Egyptian state radio until the 1950s.[6] The more established and generally wealthier
Sephardi community looked down on the Ashkenazim as social inferiors.

The multiplicity of religious rites does not exhaust the heterogeneity
of the Egyptian Jewish community. In any case, most were not scrupulously observant, though most observed the traditional festivals and the
rites of passage. Many Jews were multicultural and multilingual, but
some social status was attached to speaking Arabic, Judeo-Spanish, Italian, Yiddish, or French at home. The cosmopolitan character of the Jewish community, especially its commercial middle and upper classes, is
captured by the casual remark of a son of an upper-middle-class Sephardi
family holding Italian citizenship that emigrated from Anatolia to
Alexandria in the nineteenth century in describing the ambience of his
family: "We spoke French and English in school, Italian at home, Arabic in the street, and cursed in Turkish."[7] Alexandrines were typically
more cosmopolitan than Cairenes. However, there were also thousands
of indigenous, poor, Arabic-speaking Jews in Alexandria whose existence has generally been ignored because the cosmopolitan and commercial elements of the community were so prominent. Even in Cairo,
except in *harat al-yahud,* where the language of the school and the home
was Arabic, it was rare to find monolingual Jews. Among cosmopolitan
and Europeanized middle- and upper-class Jews, intermarriages with
Christians and Muslims were not uncommon.

AUTHENTICITY AND COSMOPOLITANISM

This survey of the component elements of the Egyptian Jewish community draws attention to both its internal diversity and its openness to a
variety of Egyptian, Middle Eastern, and European cultural influences.
The canons of nationalist historiography would direct us to reconstruct
from this heterogeneity an originary, authentic Jewish identity separable
from an originary, authentic Egyptian identity. We might then engage in
an analysis of the extent to which these distinct and self-contained cultural essences interacted—how each influenced the other, what elements
of the twentieth-century practices of the Egyptian Jewish community
could be identified as having Jewish or Egyptian origins, and whether
Egyptian Jews saw themselves and were seen by others as "Egyptians"
or as "Jews." We might then try to define the essential characteristics of
the Egyptian Jewish community and note how its members adapted to
the various sites in which they sought refuge after leaving Egypt. These

efforts are meaningful only if the categories of nationalist discourse are already accepted as given.

This book seeks to denaturalize these categories and adopts the view that ethnonational identities are historically and socially constructed. Its title intentionally inverts Zionist imagery by suggesting that Egypt can be considered a center of Jewish life from which a diaspora was generated. But I am not seeking to discover and memorialize an originary, authentic Egyptian Jewish identity. The Jews of Egypt were always already a heterogeneous community of cosmopolitan hybrids. This was both a strength of the community and one of the factors in its ultimate demise.

Heterogeneity is not a characteristic peculiar to Egyptian Jews. Although nationalists take pride in Egypt's long history as an identifiable cultural and political entity, this has been constituted by Semitic and African ethnic elements; pagan, Muslim, Christian, and Jewish religious cultures; the Arabo-Islamic high cultural tradition; and lively popular-colloquial forms. Egypt has absorbed Greek, Roman, Christian, Arabo-Muslim, and modern European cultural elements without becoming any less "Egyptian" as a result.

The heterogeneity of the Egyptian Jewish community was not random. Certain aspects of its cosmopolitan character in the late nineteenth and twentieth centuries can be easily historicized: the use of French in the community schools as a result of the proselytization of the Alliance Israelite Universelle; the legal privileges attained through relationships with European merchants, bankers, and diplomatic personnel; kinship and commercial relations with extended family members living throughout the Mediterranean basin. Cosmopolitanism is often regarded as a distinctively Jewish characteristic, an adaptive mechanism for a persecuted people without a homeland or political power who always had to be prepared to uproot themselves and move on to another refuge.

Cosmopolitanism is also deeply rooted in the classical Arabo-Islamic cultural heritage. Egypt's geographical location at the nodal point of Africa, Asia, and Europe has always made it a commercial entrepot and intellectual center traversed by merchants and scholars of many ethnicities and cultural traditions. In the medieval period, Fatimid gold dinars circulated in a geographical range bounded by Muscovy, Scandinavia, Spain, Sudanic Africa, and India; and *shari'a* law was the merchant's law of the Mediterranean basin and beyond. In the last third of the nineteenth century, Cairo emerged as the premier intellectual center of the Arab world (rivalled only by Beirut). Lebanese, Syrian, Palestinian, and Algerian intellectuals and political leaders have all been headquartered in Cairo; and their presence has contributed to the formation of contemporary Arabo-Egyptian culture. The cosmopolitan ambience and Egypt's deep self-confidence in its historical identity rendered it particularly tolerant of the Jewish presence.   *tolerant ?*

Egyptian Jewish identity was constituted by apparently contradictory and incongruent elements and the changing configuration of those elements over time. Jews were "different from" Muslim and Christian Egyptians because of their historically established association with a particular set of religious beliefs, cultural symbols, social practices, and institutions commonly identified as aspects of the Jewish tradition. At the same time, Jews were "the same as" their non-Jewish neighbors in many respects, sharing languages, newspapers, novels, poetry, the nation-state and its political structure, trades, professions, investments, markets, neighborhoods, foods, films, and other forms of popular culture. Egyptian Jewish identity was informed by historical, cultural, and political forces beyond Egypt. Yet Egyptian Jews, for all their diversity, also shared communal structures, historical memories, and contemporary attachments that distinguished them from French or even Syrian Jews with whom they could have communicated relatively easily in French or Arabic.[8] Individuals and groups of Jewish and non-Jewish Egyptians held a wide range of ideas about the diverse elements constituting Egyptian Jewish identity, the priority of their importance, and what they signified. It is also important to remember that most of them probably did not think consciously about such issues at all. Egyptian and Jewish cosmopolitanism complemented and nourished each other until the conditions that supported them were radically altered by the struggle against the British occupation, the establishment of the state of Israel, and the Arab-Zionist conflict.

INTERDISCIPLINARY RENEGOTIATION OF HISTORY, DIASPORA, AND MEMORY

The task of representing the heterogeneity of the Egyptian Jewish community has led me to compose this book somewhat unconventionally. It is a self-consciously interdisciplinary text structured not by an overarching linear historical narrative (though several of its chapters are historical narratives), but by the themes of identity, dispersion, and the struggle over retrieval of identity: In what ways were Jews part of yet still a discrete element within Egyptian society? What forces shaped their distinctive culture and identity? What were the forms of Jewish attachments to Egypt? How did those attachments become undone and redone as the community was dispersed and resettled in its several diasporic locations? Why did the Jews of Egypt emerge as a subject of historical knowledge after 1979, and what are the parameters of the contest over that history? I address these questions with a historically informed approach to cultural studies, attentive to critical social and cultural theory without slavishly following its current fashions. The calculated genre mixing in this book seeks to challenge the limits of traditional positivist history while affirming the value of critically informed historical knowledge.

Dipesh Chakrabarty, reflecting the more recent outlook of the Indian subaltern studies school, has argued that history as a category of knowledge is inseparable from the coerced imposition of modernity on non-Europeans in the colonial era:

> If the capitalist mode of production and the nation-state were the two institutions that nineteenth-century Europe exported to the rest of the world, then it also exported two forms of knowledge that corresponded to the two institutions. "Economics" embodies in a distilled form the rationality of the market in its imagination of the human being as *homo economicus;* "history" speaks to the figure of the citizen. "History" is one of the most important ways in which we learn to identify ourselves with the nation and its highest representative, the state. . . . [P]ositivist historical narratives . . . are integral to the institutions and practices of power of the modern bureaucracies we are all subject to, particularly those of the state. Just consider how the court of law functions. It wrings positivist historical narratives out of you.[9]

James Clifford makes a similar critique of positivist history in his perceptive investigation of the identity claims of the Mashpee Indians of Cape Cod, Massachusetts. In the court case Clifford described, the central issue was whether the residents of the town of Mashpee constituted an Indian tribe. He suggested that "the trial can be seen as a struggle between history and anthropology."[10] Just as Chakrabarty would have predicted, the court relied on positivist forms of historical evidence in ruling that the Mashpee community was not a tribe because in the course of its historical evolution, the group did not always possess the attributes legally required to claim tribal identity. Therefore, its claims to land and recognition were denied. The Mashpee community shared a more anthropological sense of culture, one that privileged its common sentiment and shared experience of struggle. These, it felt, merited legal recognition of the community as a tribe and the economic benefits this would entail.

Arguing, like Chakrabarty, that positivist history is aligned with the oppressive power of states, Clifford proposes that a more dynamic, anthropological conception of culture, privileging shared sentiment and experience, would support the rights of the oppressed (the Mashpee community). Or, to stretch the point some at the risk of losing some of Clifford's nuances, social and historical determinants disenfranchised the Mashpee community while their discursively constructed "anthropological" sense of themselves was a vehicle for empowerment. Clifford offers a sensitive and sympathetic representation of the cultural politics of the Mashpee community that the legal procedures failed to appreciate. I would insist that the historically formed social sources of the court's power are as much a part of Mashpee identity as the community's discursive self-representation.

The movement of postcolonial cultural studies offers another strategy for escaping from the oppressions of history: imaginative literature and cultural criticism, especially that produced by Western-educated émigrés from the former colonies to the metropolitan centers. Salman Rushdie acknowledges that the physical alienation of émigré writers from their places of birth impedes them from reclaiming precisely what was lost and compels them to create "imaginary homelands." However, he believes that this confers on them a special advantage enabling them "to speak properly and concretely on a subject of universal significance and appeal."[11] Similarly, Edward Said sees diasporic postcolonial intellectuals as occupying a uniquely creative position enabling them to overcome the limits of narrow national culture and history.[12] Paul Gilroy favors expressive culture over writing in his appreciation of the African diaspora, but the thrust of his work is allied with the arguments of Rushdie and Said.[13]

Gilroy's conception of "the Black Atlantic" and his critique of ethnic absolutism are especially relevant to this book's project of valorizing the Jewish diaspora. Despite the many strengths of Gilroy's work, it also illustrates the limits of discursive analysis detached from historical specificities. Gilroy acknowledges his borrowing of the diaspora concept from Jewish history in order to explore "the relationship between blacks and Jews in radical politics." He suggests that "modern Zionism provides an organizational and philosophical model for twentieth-century Pan-Africanism." Although Gilroy acknowledges the "obvious problems and differences," this does not deter him from seeking the pragmatic "gains involved in setting the histories of blacks and Jews within modernity in some sort of mutual relation."[14] He is willing to speak of the "zionist aspirations of American blacks" and seems amenable to Harold Cruse's call for black intellectuals to practice a cultural nationalism "equivalent to that which has made Jewish intellectuals a force to be reckoned with in America."[15]

These arguments detach the abstract ideas of Zionism from the concrete history of the Zionist project's historical alliance with British imperialism in the Middle East from 1917 to 1939 and with U.S. hegemony in the region from the mid-1960s to the present. Among the reasons that American Jewish intellectuals have been able to wield the cultural power that Gilroy admires is that Jews succeeded in defining themselves as "white" after World War II. Christian Zionism (often concomitant with anti-Semitism, a point Gilroy misses in his discussion of Edward Wilmot Blyden), the consecration of Jews as the quintessential victims of the Nazi era, the demographic and financial weight of Jews in the Democratic Party, and the strategic value of Israel as an ally of the United States— all of which are unavailable to African Americans and other blacks—are major ingredients of the power and prestige that Israel and American Jews have enjoyed in the second half of the twentieth century.

I accept the arguments of Chakrabarty, Clifford, and many postcolonial intellectuals that the category of history is to some degree complicit with modern structures of domination, especially the nation-state. Therefore, in sympathetically representing the experiences, memories, and aspirations of subaltern groups, anthropological and literary techniques can be of great value. There is no single "proper" way to combine these genres. Assia Djebar's historical novel, *Fantasia,* deploys archival research into the atrocities of the French colonial conquest of Algeria, oral history interviews with female veterans of the independence struggle, and a complexly structured fictionalized narrative to insert the presence of Algerian women into a history in which they had previously appeared primarily as reified symbols for both the colonizers and the nationalist elites. Yael Zerubavel's *Recovered Roots: Collective Memory and the Making of Israeli National Tradition* examines three central Israeli national historical myths: the mass suicide at Massada (73 CE), the Bar Kokhba Revolt (133–35 CE), and the Battle of Tel Hai (1920) that connect a glorious ancient Jewish past in the land of Israel with the heroic origins of modern Zionist settlement. She draws on canonical literary works, political and historical writing, children's literature, school textbooks, newspaper articles, popular jokes, cartoons, and interviews to document the social construction of the public memory of these events using the techniques of textual analysis, literary history, and historical criticism to challenge the hegemonic version of Israeli national history.[16]

In very different ways, Djebar and Zerubavel ally literary and ethnographic techniques with historical knowledge as a strategy for overcoming the limitations of history. At the same time, they are willing to engage history on its own terrain, gathering empirical evidence and marshalling arguments about causes and effects to challenge hegemonic historical representations. This is a viable strategy not only because, as Chakrabarty declares, "to deny now, in the name of cultural relativism, any social group—peasants, aboriginals, Indians—access to the 'post-Renaissance sense of the past' would be to disempower them."[17] History can also temper and refine textualist poststructuralist theorizing by insisting on the relevance of the temporal and social context of ideas and cultural currents.

In its most extreme form, textualist poststructuralism confuses cleverness and anarchy with realizable social projects. For example, Gilles Deleuze and Félix Guattari adopt a similar line of argument as Chakrabarty and Clifford in asserting, "History is always written from the sedentary point of view and in the name of a unitary State apparatus, at least a possible one."[18] Their strategy for liberating humanity from history is "Nomadology, the opposite of history" and a "rhizomatic" model of identity in which "any point connects to any other point. . . . [T]he rhizome pertains to a map that must be produced, constructed, a map that is always detachable, connectable, reversible, modifiable, and has multiple entryways and exits and its own lines of flight."[19] At a very high level of abstraction, this is an attractive approach celebrating the unlimited potential for liberatory change. But it has little relationship to the social structures of any contemporary societies, hence little capacity to affect them either. This was poignantly expressed by Ines, the mother of the central character of Ronit Matalon's novel recounting an Egyptian Jewish family history, *Zeh 'im ha-panim eleynu* (The one facing us): "A person does not need roots, he needs a home."[20] Thus, Ines reluctantly abandoned her roots in Egypt to move to Israel in the 1950s, but rhizomatic connections and a life of nomadism were not alternatives she or others in her circumstances could embrace.

In configuring "new maps of desire and attachment"[21] after their dispersion from Egypt, Jews were constrained by their passports (or lack thereof), wealth, languages, education, the location of relatives and friends, occupational opportunities, and religious or political precommitments. These historically formed social and cultural factors as well

as the events and structures of international relations and political economy—the role of the Jewish business elite in Egypt, the Palestinian-Israeli
conflict, the decolonization of Egypt, Arab socialism, pan-Arabism,
Egypt's military defeats by Israel in 1948, 1956, and 1967, and the
Egyptian-Israeli peace treaty of 1979—were the determinants of the ma-
trix in which the repertoire of possibilities for Egyptian Jewish life after
1948 were played out. I have tried to account for these factors in a non-
deterministic way that leaves considerable space for the relative autonomy of culture, politics, and economics while avoiding idealization of
exile through textualist utopias like nomadology and rhizomatics.

In the same essay in which he seeks to privilege the insights of emigre
writers, Salman Rushdie asserts that "description is itself a political act"
and "redescribing a world is the necessary first step towards changing
it."[22] I have sought to redescribe the world of Egyptian Jews while remaining cognizant that the great diversity of their life in Egypt and their
diasporic trajectories precludes the possibility of establishing a consensus version of Egyptian Jewish social memory, although Zionist historiography has nonetheless attempted to create one. Therefore, I have not
aspired to retrieve the collective memory of Egyptian Jews and to constitute it as a coherent countermemory in resistance to the hegemonic
forms of collective memory promoted by nationalist historiography in
Israel and Egypt. Countermemory can be oppositional and subversive,
and I have tried to highlight these possibilities. But countermemory is
rarely sustained and nourished by the array of financial support, social
institutions, ideological apparatuses, and ultimately coercive power that
reinforce hegemonic collective memory. Countermemory tends to be
fragmentary, dispersed, and disunited. It usually cannot, in and of itself,
constitute a counterhegemonic project.

This is certainly the case for the countermemories I have sought to retrieve in this book, especially in part 2, where I have employed ethnographic vignettes to draw attention to the experiences of individuals and
small groups of Egyptian Jews that would inevitably be lost in a grand
historical narrative. In parts 1 and 3, I have used imaginative literature
as a way to highlight aspirations and understandings that are marginalized by nationalist discourse as well as literary expressions and historical writing complicit with it. But I do not argue that these literary expressions constitute a coherent counterhegemonic project any more than
the countermemories of part 2.

Each of the three sections of this book emphasizes a different method
of analysis and exposition. Part 1 consists of social, political, and cultural

history. Part 2 is based on ethnographic investigation and oral history. Part 3 emphasizes cultural and social history and literary analysis. In addition, autobiographical segments are dispersed throughout the text as they relate to its several topics.

As in much of my previous work, I have made extensive use of oral history. Writing a history of Egypt in the second half of the twentieth century invites the use of oral evidence because archival materials are generally not available for this period. For example, researchers are not permitted to read the papers of the Cairo and Alexandria Jewish community that remain on shelves in the offices of the chief rabbinates of those cities. In May 1993, I spoke to Emile Risso, acting president of Cairo's Jewish community, to inquire about whether I might see these documents. I introduced myself as an American Jewish professor writing a history of the Jews of Egypt, to which he immediately responded, "*Ma lish da'wa bi'l-ta'rikh*" (I have nothing to do with history).

In some important sense he was right. His personal safety and the security of the remaining tiny Jewish community in Egypt could very well be undermined by historical investigations that might highlight episodes of the community's past that the Egyptian state authorities or the leaders of the Jewish community would regard as problematic. "History" had already created difficulties for Egyptian Jews because part of the archive of the Jewish community of Cairo had previously been illegally removed from Egypt. It is currently designated the "Jamie Lehmann Memorial Collection: Records of the Jewish Community of Cairo, 1886–1961" and housed at Yeshiva University in New York. This, too, may have influenced Emile Risso to avoid having anything to do with this project.

About the same time that I spoke to Emile Risso, I interviewed an elderly Muslim merchant in Cairo's Suq al-Hamzawi quarter, a major textile market near *harat al-yahud*, where many members of the Jewish community had shops. Many of his business associates in the textile trade had been Jews, and I wanted to ask him about his memories of the community. He told me that the *mukhabarat* (security police) had visited him and instructed him not to speak freely about such topics. While we were chatting, one of the three Jewish women who still lived in *harat al-yahud* passed by the shop. After some conversation, she began to tell me about her career as a dancer and actress. My host became agitated, tried to stop her, and rudely contradicted her. I could not decide what to make of the woman's story. She appeared somewhat demented. My host insisted that she exaggerated grossly, but he was very likely motivated, at least to some extent, by concern not to be identified with information about Jews given to a foreigner.

Here were clear instances in which the subaltern could not speak. Although Egyptian Jews have, in many ways, been impeded from narrating their own history because of political considerations in both Egypt and Israel, I did not write this book in order to "speak for" them as individuals or as a group. Some may appreciate my efforts to examine their past; others may reject it. I assume full responsibility for my role as the interpreter of the memories of my interlocutors and the other evidence I have gathered. I also acknowledge that my intentions in writing this text and offering these interpretations have no capacity to limit the readings they may be subjected to.

THE NEO-LACHRYMOSE CONCEPTION OF JEWISH-ARAB HISTORY

Bat-Ye'or (Daughter of the Nile, pseudonym of Giselle Littman) is an Egyptian Jew living in Switzerland since 1956 and a leading exponent of what Mark Cohen has termed "the neo-lachrymose conception of Jewish-Arab history": a gloomy representation of Jewish life in the lands of Islam that emphasizes the continuity of oppression and persecution from the time of Muhammad until the demise of most Arab Jewish communities in the aftermath of the 1948 Arab-Israeli war.[23] Bat Ye'or was one of the earliest authors to adopt this perspective as a comprehensive understanding of the history of the Jews of Egypt, which she first presented in a short book, *Les juifs en Egypte: Aperçu sur 3000 ans d'histoire*.[24] An expanded Hebrew version of the book was published in 1974 by Ma'ariv Library and the World Jewish Congress "on the initiative of the [Israeli] Ministry of Education and Culture with the participation of the Department for Sephardic Communities of the World Zionist Organization."[25] The imprimatur of major institutions of the state of Israel, the Zionist movement, world Jewry, and the publishing house of a mass circulation newspaper signified the consecration of Bat-Ye'or's neo-lachrymose perspective as the normative Zionist interpretation of the history of Jews in Egypt.

Prior to 1948, leading individuals and institutions of the Jewish community, including those who considered themselves Zionists, proudly embraced a more positive view of the long history of the Jews in Egypt. The neo-lachrymose historical perspective of Bat-Ye'or and others was expounded as a conscious challenge to this earlier self-image. Drawing its authority from Bat-Ye'or's claim to authenticity as an Egyptian Jew, this historical vision has won broad acceptance among both scholars and the general public in Israel and the West.[26] The prominence and credibility of the neo-lachrymose view of Egyptian Jewish history were enabled, at least in part, by the near silence observed by Egyptian Jews about their lives in Egypt from 1948 until the late 1970s.

Building his argument around the role of Bat-Ye'or, Mark Cohen argues that the neo-lachrymose thesis was generated by popular works published by Jews living outside Israel. But Cohen minimizes and homogenizes two distinctly Israeli sources of the neo-lachrymose perspective: Zionist concern to counter the claims of the resurgent Palestinian nationalist movement after 1967 and the desire of Middle Eastern Jews to redress the discrimination and mistreatment they suffered as new immigrants in Israel during the 1950s and 1960s.

Palestinian Arab claims of dispossession by Israel, relegated to the bottom of the international agenda since the mid-1950s, began to receive considerable international attention once again after the 1967 war. The neo-lachrymose interpretation of Jewish Arab history distracted attention from Palestinian claims by constructing a narrative focusing on the eternal suffering of Jews under Muslim rule. Some adherents of this approach suggested that even if it were true that the Palestinian Arabs had been dispossessed, a roughly equivalent number of Middle Eastern Jews had fled their homes and lost their property. Consequently, the Palestinians had no valid claim against Israel.[27]

Middle Eastern Jews living in Israel (commonly agglomerated as Mizrahim, or Orientals, sing. Mizrahi) generally shared the objective of reinforcing the Zionist case against the Arab world, but they also had their own agenda. A narrative emphasizing the unrelenting suffering of Jews in the Arab world established the claim of these Jews to a status in Israeli society comparable to the Ashkenazi survivers of the mass murder of European Jewry. Affirming their victimization in the Arab world allowed Mizrahim to distance themselves from any Arab cultural attachments, which are widely regarded in Israel as symptoms of backwardness. Sometimes the transformation of attitudes toward the Arab world was quite self-consciously understood as the price of admission to Israeli society. For example, at a demonstration protesting a racist assault on Palestinian Arabs living in the Ramat Amidar neighborhood of Ramat Gan (colloquially known as Ramat Baghdad because of its high concentration of Iraqi Jews), one woman spontaneously remarked to me, "In Baghdad we got along fine with the Arabs. But here we have to fight them."[28]

The neo-lachrymose interpretation of Jewish Arab history also allowed Mizrahim to claim a role as active members of the Zionist movement and thereby assert their full participation in the mainstream of Jewish national history as presented in the Zionist narrative. Until the 1970s,
the dominant school in Israeli and Jewish history portrayed Zionism as
the achievement of Ashkenazi Jewry. Minimal participation in the Zionist movement was considered yet another expression of the backwardness of Mizrahim. But if Mizrahim had their own long history of diasporic oppression, this could logically be linked to a claim to have
independently arrived at the Zionist solution to the Jewish problem. Asserting that Zionism was not merely a narrative about the crisis of European Jews and its resolution and that there had also been an independent Middle Eastern Zionist movement provided Mizrahim in Israel with
a lever to reverse the negative evaluations of their history and culture
that predominated during the years of MAPAI (Israeli Workers' Party,
subsequently the Labor Party) rule and buttressed their claims to equal
status with Ashkenazim.

Another important Israeli source for the neo-lachrymose perspective
was the work of Yehoshafat Harkabi. Shortly after the 1967 Arab-Israeli
war, he published a book arguing that the Arabs completely rejected any
negotiated resolution to the conflict with Israel (in fact, they rejected resolutions on terms acceptable to the activist current in Israeli politico-
military thinking promoted by Israel's first prime minister, David Ben-
Gurion).[29] Although Harkabi addressed only Arab-Israeli relations since
1948, his cataloging of instances of Arab anti-Semitism and his insistence that the Arabs viewed the conflict as a fundamental clash of des-
tinies that allowed for no compromise encouraged his audience to believe that a conflict so intense must have deep historical roots. Although
this was not his primary purpose, Harkabi's work inclined Israelis and
others to imagine the intense conflict over Palestine as one more instance
of Arab and Muslim enmity toward Jews.

The broad political and cultural context for the translation and sub-
sidization of Bat-Ye'or's work by the Israeli government in 1974 is the
emergence of a new school of Israeli historical writing that integrates the
previously marginalized history of Middle Eastern Jews into the Israeli
national narrative. The two central themes of that narrative are the re-
lentless oppression and suffering of Jews in the diaspora and the modern secular redemption of Jews by Zionism. When Israeli public culture
began to consider accepting Mizrahim as something other than primi-
tives who should assimilate to Ashkenazi and *tzabar* (native Israeli)

norms, the neo-lachrymose conception of Jewish Arab history provided a readily acceptable basis for acknowledging the history and culture of Middle Eastern Jews as a permanent, though not fully equal, element of Israeli society.

ALTERNATIVES TO NEO-LACHRYMOSITY

The mirror image of the neo-lachrymose interpretation of the history of Arab Jews is the common Arab claim that Jews were always well treated in the lands of Islam. Many educated Egyptians are aware of the prominent positions of Ya'qub Ibn Killis and other Jews in the Fatimid era, Maimonides's choice of Cairo as a safe haven, the waves of Jewish refugees who were welcomed in Egypt from the Spanish expulsion to the pogroms of Russia in the nineteenth and early twentieth centuries, and the wealth and economic influence of many Jews from the late nineteenth to the mid-twentieth centuries. In support of its claim that Jews had never experienced mistreatment of any sort in Egypt, an official publication of the Egyptian government maintained, "Egypt, throughout its history, has been the shelter of persecuted Jews—no matter where they came from."[30] In recent years, both Arab nationalists and Islamists have asserted with increasing vehemence that despite the warm welcome they received and the wealth they attained, the Jews betrayed Egypt by collaborating with imperialism to undermine the national economy and embracing Zionism. In Chapter 9, I present a critique of this argument and offer an alternative approach.

Despite Bat-Ye'or's claims, there is nothing in medieval Jewish Arab history that can reasonably be compared to the expulsion of Jews from Spain. Many scholars would agree that Jews were generally better treated in Muslim lands than in Christian Europe during the medieval era. And nothing in modern Jewish Arab history can reasonably be compared to the Nazi mass murder. But communities and individuals live in specific moments, not broad historical tendencies. Even if we do not judge by the standard of civic equality, which was not an operative ideal in the premodern Muslim world any more than it was in pre-Enlightenment Europe, there have been more than occasional instances of socially structured discrimination against Jews in Egypt. In the twentieth century, they were inextricably linked to the processes of colonization and decolonization, the nationalist struggle to expel the British troops who occupied Egypt from 1882 to 1956, and the intensification of the Arab-Zionist conflict.

During and after the outbreak of the nationalist uprising of 1919, many Jews identified with and supported the Egyptian nationalist movement. Leading members of the Jewish business elite such as Yusuf Cicurel Bey and Yusuf ʿAslan Qattawi Pasha, like many of their Muslim and Coptic compatriots, were wary of the populism of Saʿd Zaghlul and his Wafd Party—the popular leaders of the mass movement. Nonetheless, they regarded themselves as nationalist Egyptians. Decolonization followed a convoluted course, and the pot of gold at the end of the rainbow never materialized. Unable to negotiate with the militant Wafd, the British overlords unilaterally granted Egypt nominal independence in 1922, and a constitutional monarchy was established. But the palace and the British Embassy, backed by a very large garrison of imperial troops, retained substantial power in the country. They connived to dismiss each government formed by the Wafd, which won every democratic election from 1923 to 1952 (except the two it boycotted because they were obviously rigged). The scope of Egypt's sovereignty was augmented by the Anglo-Egyptian treaty of 1936, but many nationalists maintained that as long as British troops remained in the country, independence was a fraud.

Even under the monarchy, there were clear signs pointing to the impending decline in the status of foreign nationals and the *mutamassir* minorities—permanently resident Greeks, Italians, Armenians, Syrian Christians, and Jews—in postcolonial Egypt. The abolition of the Capitulations in 1937 ended the tax immunities of foreign nationals. The Company Law of 1947 set quotas for the employment of Egyptian nationals in incorporated firms. The abolition of the mixed courts in 1949 established a unified legal system for resident foreign nationals and Egyptian citizens.

On July 23, 1952, a military coup led by Gamal Abdel Nasser and the Free Officers overthrew the monarchy. The Free Officers were motivated by humiliation over their ignominious defeat in the 1948 Palestine War, revulsion from the corruption and excesses of privilege flaunted by King Faruq and the large landowning elite, resentment over the grossly unjust distribution of Egyptian national wealth, and a burning desire to end the British occupation. The military regime further eroded the privileges of foreigners and *mutamassirun* and in practice impinged on the status of non-Muslim citizens as well. The markers of this trajectory were the October 1954 Anglo-Egyptian agreement on the evacuation of British military forces, the abolition of the communal courts in 1955, the nationalization of the Suez Canal in 1956, the confiscation of the property of British and French nationals and Jews in 1956 and

Belgian nationals in 1960, and the nationalization of large sectors of the economy in 1961–62, which affected many *mutamassir*-owned firms along with enterprises owned by Muslim, Coptic, and Jewish citizens. Listing these measures in chronological succession creates the impression of an inexorable trend, but this was not the perception of most contemporary observers.

OPERATION SUSANNAH

The most salient symbol of the transformation of the status of Jews in Egypt was Operation Susannah. In July 1954, Israeli military intelligence ordered an espionage network of Egyptian Jews it had formed three years earlier to launch Operation Susannah—a campaign to firebomb the main Alexandria post office, the United States Information Service library in Cairo, the Cairo train station, and several movie theaters in Cairo and Alexandria. The saboteurs (today they would be called terrorists, especially if they were Arabs or Muslims acting against Israel or the United States) were quickly apprehended and brought to trial in December 1954. The verdicts and sentences delivered in January 1955 spanned the full range of options. Sami (Shmu'el) Azar and Musa (Moshe) Marzuq were sentenced to death along with the Israeli handlers of the network—John Darling (Avraham Dar) and Paul Frank (Avraham Seidenwerg)—who were not apprehended and were tried in absentia. Marcelle Ninio and Robert Dassa were condemned to life in prison. Victor Levy and Philip Natanson received fifteen-year prison sentences. Me'ir Meyuhas and Me'ir Za'fran were sentenced to seven years in prison. Caesar Cohen and Eli Na'im were acquitted. Max Binnet, a major in Israeli military intelligence apprehended with the network but not directly involved in its operations, committed suicide in jail. Armand Karmona, the lodger of Marcelle Ninio, was interrogated by the Egyptian authorities and, though apparently not involved in Operation Susannah, either committed suicide or was beaten to death by his interrogators.[31]

One possible objective of Operation Susannah was to convince the British government, then engaged in negotiations with Egypt over the withdrawal of the British garrison from the Suez Canal Zone, that Egypt was an unstable, radical, nationalist state and therefore that British forces ought not to be evacuated. It is also possible that the activist elements in the Israeli military and the Ministry of Defense loyal to David Ben-Gurion, who retained great influence despite having temporarily retired as prime minister during 1954, intentionally initiated and then exposed Operation Susannah in order to break up secret Egyptian-Israeli negotiations then going on and eliminate the possibility of a face-to-face meeting between Israeli Prime Minister Moshe Sharett and Egyptian President Gamal Abdel Nasser, which was under consideration.[32]

Many of the documents pertaining to Operation Susannah have apparently been destroyed by the governments of Israel, the United States, and Britain or are unavailable to researchers. No Egyptian government documents for the 1950s are yet available to researchers. Consequently, it is impossible to construct a traditional political history of the operation addressing the perennial question in Israeli politics: "Who gave the order?"[33] In 1960, when some of the details of Operation Susannah were revealed in Israel, this question became the focal point of a protracted political scandal labeled the "Lavon affair" or, in the sanitized discourse of Israeli national security, *ha-'esek ha-bish* (the dirty business), commonly further obscured by English translation as "the mishap."[34]

Knowing who gave the order might shed new light on military-civilian relations in Israel and strengthen ongoing revisionist assessments of the possibilities of peace between Israel and Egypt from 1949 to 1956.[35] But the lack of evidence, indeed the high likelihood that important rele-vant evidence has been intentionally destroyed or falsified, has led me to focus on the discursive aspects of Operation Susannah in Chapters 2 and 4. Although imposed by necessity, this strategy is justifiable in its own right because Operation Susannah has become an important symbolic marker connecting the fate of the Egyptian Jews to the course of the Arab-Israeli conflict. The uncertainty of many of the facts of the case has perhaps even augmented the power of Operation Susannah as a recurrent theme in the popular political culture of Egypt and Israel.

FROM PILLARS OF THE COMMUNITY TO COMPRADORS

The Jewish community as a whole was identified with the cosmopolitan culture, international business connections, and foreign citizenship of many of its wealthiest and most prominent members. Many Jews, in addition to the business elite, were passive beneficiaries of or active collaborators with colonialism. Insofar as Jews, like other *mutamassirun*, were identified with foreign interests and culture, their status was undermined by decolonization. In addition, from the late 1930s on, the increasing intensity of the Arab-Zionist clash in Palestine also generated a dynamic that affected the Jewish community specifically. Most members of the *mutamassir* communities left Egypt after 1956, which suggests that a large proportion of the Jewish community might have left Egypt in the 1950s whether or not there had been an Arab-Israeli conflict and regardless of any specific measures the Egyptian authorities directed against Jews.

Asking if the emigration of the Jews was inevitable or assuming that it was are not particularly fruitful points of departure for a history of the Jews of Egypt. Therefore, I propose a more open-ended, critical approach to the demise of the Egyptian Jewish community rooted in three propositions: (1) Only a small minority of Jews were active Zionists, even after 1948. (2) Most Jews who left Egypt after 1948, especially those with enough resources to have a choice, did not go to Israel. (3) Wherever Egyptian Jews did go, including Israel, many of them reconstructed forms of communal life and collective practices that preserved a link between them and Egypt. This approach contests the Israeli nationalist narrative, which situates the experiences of Egyptian Jews wholly within the trajectory of the Zionist project and insists on their absolute and total alienation from the land of their birth.

Nonetheless, it does not conform to the Egyptian nationalist narrative, which accounts for the demise of the Egyptian Jewish community in terms of Zionist machinations. Any critical account of the emigration of the Jews and other *mutamassir* communities must take into account the development of the Egyptian political economy and political culture in ways that excluded Jews and other minorities from the political community. For example, the Company Law of 1947 required that 75 percent of all salaried employees, 90 percent of all workers, and 51 percent of the paid-up capital of joint stock companies be Egyptian. To monitor compliance, firms were required to submit lists of their employees stating their nationalities and salaries. They were thus forced to answer the question: "Who is an Egyptian?" There can be no unequivocal, transhistorical answer to such a question. Both the question and its answer are historically and socially constructed cultural categories, as the fate of the department store chain of Les Grands Magasins Cicurel et Oreco, owned by the prominent Jewish Cicurel family of Cairo, illustrates.

To protest the rearrest and deportation of Saʿd Zaghlul to the Seychelles, the Wafd called on Egyptians to purchase only at "national stores" in 1921–22. The Cicurel department store near Cairo's Opera Square was specified as an approved shop.[36] In a 1948 memorandum submitted to the Ministry of Commerce, the Cicurel firm described itself as "one of the pillars of our [Egyptian national] economic independence."[37] Nonetheless, the Cicurel store was firebombed during the 1948 Arab-Israeli War, probably by supporters of the Society of Muslim Brothers, and it was burned as a symbol of European influence in the Cairo fire of January 26, 1952. Both times the store was rebuilt with the support of the government. The Cicurel store did have a European cultural character because of its largely Jewish staff, its expensive and largely imported merchandise, and the use of French by employees and customers on the shop floor. Even many of the Egyptian-born Jewish members of the Cicurel staff did not hold citizenship papers and were classified as "stateless." Cicurel's contradictions could not be balanced indefinitely. At the outbreak of the 1956 Suez/Sinai War, unlike in 1948, the Cicurel firm was placed under sequestration. The Cicurel family soon ceded its majority holding to a new group headed by Muslims, and in 1957 Salvator Cicurel, who had managed the firm, left Egypt for France. Between 1919 and 1956, the entire Egyptian Jewish community, like the Cicurel firm, was transformed from a national asset into a fifth column.

MIDDLE EASTERN JEWS (MIZRAHIM) AND THE ZIONIST NATIONAL NARRATIVE

Many Mizrahim in Israel felt excluded and neglected by the labor Zionist governments of the 1950s and 1960s led by MAPAI and its successor, the Labor Party. Labor Zionism was a self-consciously European ideological synthesis that emerged in response to the crisis of Eastern European Jewry in the late nineteenth and early twentieth centuries. It proposed to "normalize" the Jewish people by transforming them from a persecuted minority disproportionately composed of economically marginal petty merchants and craftsmen into citizens and productive workers and peasants: the proper subjects of a nation-state and what labor Zionists hoped would become a socialist economy. Secularism, socialism, redemption through physical labor, and a reformation of Jewish identity in national-political terms were the core elements of the labor Zionist solution to the Jewish problem. This ideology was articulated and implemented through highly centralized political parties—MAPAI, MAPAM (the United Workers' Party), and Le-Ahdut ha-'Avodah (Unity of Labor)—that created the institutions that dominated the prestate yishuv (Jewish settlement) and the early state of Israel—the Histadrut, the kibutzim, the Haganah, and the Palmah.

Most Mizrahim shared little of the history in the diaspora or in the yishuv that informed the theory and practice of labor Zionism. Except for the descendents of the pre-Zionist "old *yishuv*" and several thousand Yemenis who were brought to mandate Palestine by Zionist authorities seeking Jewish workers who would work for Arab wages, only a small minority participated actively in the Zionist project before 1948.[38] The leadership of the Zionist movement and the early state of Israel was overwhelmingly Ashkenazi.

After open Zionist activity became impossible in Nazi-occupied Europe, all the Zionist parties of the *yishuv* began to send emissaries to Egypt, Iraq, Tunisia, Morocco, and elsewhere in the Middle East and North Africa. There had been small Zionist organizations in these countries before World War II. The combination of the emissaries' work, the reception of the news of the mass murder of European Jewry, and the more precarious conditions of Middle Eastern Jews due to the intensification of the Palestinian-Zionist conflict made Zionism a significant, though still a minority, orientation for Middle Eastern Jews after the war.

Some Mizrahim became active in the labor Zionist movement, but most had no links to the labor Zionist establishment and its key institutions. Hence, they had no patrons to ease their way into Israeli society. When they arrived in Israel in large numbers in the 1950s, their customs and lifestyles were commonly discounted as "primitive," and they were expected to adopt the modern, healthy, *tzabar* culture. By a conscious decision of the state and Zionist authorities, large numbers of Mizrahim were settled in "development towns," *moshavim* (cooperative agricultural villages), or in the former homes of recently departed Palestinian refugees in cities such as Jaffa, Jerusalem, Haifa, Acre, and Tiberias. Their role in the Zionist project was to establish a Jewish population in territories and neighborhoods previously inhabited by Palestinian Arabs and to occupy the bottom ranks of the Jewish labor force. The immigration of the Mizrahim was vital for the demographic and economic stabilization of the Jewish state, but they were settled on the margins of Israeli economic, political, and cultural life.[39]

Alienation from the political ideology, cultural and social norms, institutions, and economic benefits of labor Zionism drove many Mizrahim and their children to provide the votes that brought the first Likud government to power in Israel in 1977. The new regime made extensive efforts to find places for its supporters in the official national culture and historical narrative. Dozens of scholarly and popular books, articles, television programs, and public symposia revised the formerly Eurocentric history of Zionism, asserting that there had been a Zionist movement in Middle Eastern Jewish communities and that Mizrahim had contributed substantially to establishing the state of Israel. The inflection of Israeli public culture was transformed as the Middle Eastern origins of about half its Jewish population at last received public and official acknowledgment. Mizrahi Hebrew accents began to be heard on the radio and television news, and Arab-accented Hebrew music found its way to the top of the popular song lists. In response, Labor and other political parties began to promote "their" Mizrahi figures and to rediscover and revalorize the role of Mizrahim in the history of labor Zionism. The reassertion of Egyptian Jewish identity examined in Chapter 8 is both an expression of this broad movement of Mizrahi self-assertion and a particular phenomenon related to the course of Egyptian-Israeli relations.

ENCOUNTERING EGYPT

In part 2 of this book, I invoke and celebrate the diversity of the Egyptian Jewish community and the rich texture of its identities, practices, and commitments by presenting three case studies of subcommunities of Egyptian Jews who made new lives for themselves outside Egypt after 1948: (1) the graduates of ha-Shomer ha-Tza'ir (The Young Guard) who settled in Kibutz Nahshonim and Kibutz 'Ein-Shemer in Israel, (2) the communist Jewish émigrés in Paris, and (3) the Karaites who settled in the San Francisco Bay Area. They have been chosen not because they are representative of the Egyptian Jewish community as a whole. Two of these subcommunities, the Zionists and the communists, are expressly atypical because of their high level of political consciousness, and the Karaites constituted only a small minority of Egyptian Jews. Nonetheless, I offer these case studies because in addition to their intrinsic interest, they confirm, as I believe any closely researched social history or ethnographic study of an Egyptian Jewish subcommunity would, that neither the Israeli nor the Egyptian national narrative offers an adequate framework for comprehending the modern experience of Egyptian Jews.

My choice of these three groups is largely due to accidents of my own life experiences, which have made certain connections and understandings more available to me. Although I am not an Egyptian Jew, I cannot claim to be a disinterested party with respect to the many contentious issues addressed in this book. My personal, political, and intellectual commitments have shaped a specific relationship to the subjects of this book, many of whom I regard as friends and colleagues. Because I will be revealing much about them, it seems fair, and I hope not overly self-indulgent, to reveal something about how and why I came to know them.

—◦◦◦—

Egypt in the summer of 1969 had a grey and forbidding face. The public mood was suspicious and depressed after the crushing military defeat of 1967. Artillery duels over the Suez Canal and deep Israeli bombing raids maintained a wartime tension long after the official cease-fire was signed. The population of Isma'iliyya was evacuated to Cairo, where windows were painted blue to maintain a nighttime blackout. Small red brick walls lined the downtown streets, strategically placed in front of each doorway to shield buildings in case a bomb fell in the street. These devices, too flimsy to render effective protection, constantly reminded the public that the country was in a mortal struggle with the Zionist enemy. These unwelcoming external signs severely strained the personal warmth and hospitality so common among Egyptians.

My apprehensive reaction to all of this was magnified by my being a young Jewish American with very limited Arabic skills visiting for the first time a country at war. I had come to Cairo to study Arabic at the American University in Cairo (AUC). After three years of Arabic study at Princeton University, I could not understand the most basic street conversation because my training had consisted entirely of grammar, reading, and translation of standard Arabic texts. Like most students of that era, I had studied Arabic as if it were a dead language, like Latin. I do not recall my teachers explaining clearly the extent to which the language I was learning was unusable for daily affairs. Inability to converse despite years of Arabic study intensified my feeling that Egypt was a difficult and potentially dangerous place.

Before departing, I worried that being Jewish would be a problem in Egypt. My teachers assured me that it would not. The previous year Rabbi Boruch Holman had been a student in the same program, and his religious needs were accommodated by providing him with kosher food. The administrators of the Arabic program considered this evidence of Egypt's profound civilization and tolerance. So I obeyed instructions and wrote "Jewish" in the space on my visa application asking for my religion, though I have never regarded my Jewishness as a matter of religious faith.

I don't remember how I met Ahmad.[40] It may have been while drinking a soda at a kiosk near AUC on Shaykh Rihan Street. We struck up a conversation, and he was interested in the American student movement, the new left, and other such things I could tell him something about. We met several times and had long discussions about politics, the current situation in Egypt, and the Arab-Israeli conflict. When it felt comfortable, I told him that I was a Zionist, a member of ha-Shomer ha-Tza'ir, that I was planning to move to Israel the next year to live on a kibutz, and that I favored reaching an accommodation with the Palestinian Arabs. One day Ahmad did not come to a meeting we had arranged. I tried to find him, but could not. It was close to the end of my stay, and I began to be preoccupied with preparing to return to Princeton to begin my senior year.

A few days before my departure, I was notified that I had been summoned to be questioned in the Mugamma'—an ugly and imposing Stalinesque structure in Tahrir Square where many government offices are concentrated. A representative of AUC accompanied me to the meeting, where I was asked by an official whose precise title I do not recall ever being told, "Why did you put down that you are Jewish on your visa application?"

After some hesitation, I could think of no better answer than "Because I am."

"I see."

Sensing that this encounter might become difficult, my chaperon quickly intervened, "It's okay. He is leaving the country in two days."

"Oh, I see," said the official with obvious relief in his voice. "Then write down on this paper the date you are leaving and the flight you are leaving on."

"I am leaving Egypt on whatever day it was in August on whatever TWA flight it was," I wrote.

The official examined my affidavit and made one further request: "Put down 'for good.'"

I complied and, after completing the formalities, left the office without ever being told what had prompted the inquiry. Everyone seemed satisfied, and I did leave Egypt as scheduled with no further incident. But I wondered if Ahmad had turned me in to the authorities.

Several years later I came across an article Ahmad had written and concluded that this was improbable. The note identifying the author described him as a communist student activist living in France. It is unlikely that someone who belonged to an illegal organization would risk attracting suspicion to himself by turning me in, especially because the Egyptian security apparatus had long promoted the notion that Zionism and communism were part of the same antinational conspiracy. It is more likely that Ahmad was under surveillance by the *mukhabarat* or that our meetings had been noticed by one of the many street informers in the internal security system who thought it suspicious that an American and an Egyptian were in regular contact. I hope that Ahmad was not arrested because of his association with me.

I came to Egypt convinced that Israel had to reach a rapprochement with the Palestinians. This conviction was reinforced by my meetings with Palestinian students at AUC, though I was still not able to articulate fully how this should happen. The students I met considered themselves members of a national community and supported the Palestine Liberation Organization. They took me to visit the Cairo office of the PLO, where I met people who had been trained in the People's Republic of China. I was convinced that they were sincere and that Israel would have to find a way to accommodate their national aspirations.

When I returned home after my summer in Cairo, I lectured about Egypt to the older members of ha-Shomer ha-Tza'ir in New York. Our Israeli emissaries tried to undermine or reinterpret my meaning. I tried to limit myself to reporting my experiences because I did not then know a political language to advocate a program that diverged from the positions of MAPAM, our party in Israel. It seemed to me then that the differences between us were due to my having seen and heard Palestinians firsthand. It did not occur to me that certain "facts" are political and that most Israelis would not then have allowed themselves to be in a position where they would be exposed to hearing Palestinians express themselves freely.

After completing my degree at Princeton in 1970, I went with about sixty other graduates of ha-Shomer ha-Tza'ir to live on Kibutz Lahav in Israel, as I had told Ahmad I intended to do. Soon after arriving I realized that my own trajectory was moving in the opposite direction of the political winds in Israel, including the kibutz and MAPAM. Most Israeli Jews were then convinced that considering Palestinian Arabs as a national collective entity was no more than an anti-Semitic intrigue. The arrogance of victory after the 1967 war made accommodating Arab demands of any sort seem like a ridiculous proposition.

I had come to Israel intending to be politically engaged. Because this was virtually impossible for a new member of a kibutz hours away from a major city, and the kibutz was antagonistic to my views in any case, I soon found my way to the student new left at the Hebrew University. A period of intense activity during which I was jailed several times for doing no more than participating in demonstrations brought me to revise most of what I had believed in since I was a child. With profound emotional pain, I concluded that I was no longer a Zionist and that I could not serve in the Israeli army and enforce the occupation of the West Bank and the Gaza Strip.

I returned to the United States in 1973 with my face turned away from Israel. Having experienced a pervasive fear and disdain for everything

Arab in Israel, I was determined to learn to feel comfortable in an Arab environment. My most transformative experiences during the years I devoted to attaining this goal were working in auto plants in the Detroit area and helping to produce and distribute the Arabic section of a workers' newspaper directed at the large Arab community, mostly Lebanese, Yemenis, and Palestinians, in the greater Detroit area. Though the Arabic section of the newspaper was crudely produced, and my translations were often clumsy, we easily sold many copies of the paper and enjoyed a wide network of friends and contacts in the South End of Dearborn and southwest Detroit. The Arab community was pleased to learn that there were Americans who supported both the national rights of Palestinians and the rights of Arab workers in the auto plants. I attended many events sponsored by Palestinian nationalist organizations and sometimes delivered solidarity messages in the name of the newspaper. The Palestinian brothers who owned a grocery store on the corner of the street where I lived in southwest Detroit became my friends and collaborators in translating articles for the newspaper.

These experiences taught me more than anything I had learned previously in a university and at the same time convinced me that I would be more effective in publicly addressing the issues that mattered to me most if I returned to the university. With great ambivalence and feelings of guilt for choosing an easier life, I decided to pursue a Ph.D. and write a doctoral dissertation on the emergence of the Arab working class in Palestine during the British mandate period. Richard P. Mitchell, my mentor at the University of Michigan, agreed that this was an acceptable topic. But he added that if I wrote about Israel or Palestine, I would probably not get a teaching job when I completed my degree. "Why not write about Egypt instead?" he proposed. I agreed, and I have been engaged with Egypt ever since.

The first Egyptian Jews I met were members of the communist organizations established in the 1940s. I came to know them through researching my doctoral dissertation on the Egyptian labor movement. Both they and I were aware of each other as Jews, but reluctant to examine what that meant, partly because there were more "important" things to do on our agendas. For better and for worse, those agendas have been superseded. I embarked on this study in the hope that a sympathetic exploration of ways of being Jewish that have been marginalized in both the Zionist and the Egyptian national narratives may suggest alternatives for the future.

PART ONE

Discourses and
Materialities of Identity

CHAPTER 2

Communitarianisms, Nationalisms, Nostalgias

Operation Susannah was the most salient political event in the life of the Jewish community of Egypt from 1949 to 1956. The involvement of Egyptian Jews in acts of espionage and sabotage against Egypt organized and directed by Israeli military intelligence raised fundamental questions about their identities and loyalties. These issues are explicitly addressed in the apology for the operation offered in the name of four members of the Operation Susannah network—Robert Dassa, Victor Levy, Philip Natanson, and Marcelle Ninio—by Aviezer Golan, in their authorized collective memoir.[1]

After fourteen years in Egyptian jails, the four reached Israel in the prisoner exchange following the 1967 Arab-Israeli war. Their presence in the country was an official secret until 1971, when Prime Minister Golda Meir announced her intention to attend Marcelle Ninio's wedding. Not until March 1975, when the four told their story publicly for the first time on national television, did the Israeli government acknowledge that they had been trained and directed by the Israeli army. Nonetheless, Aviezer Golan explained that their actions did not constitute treason against Egypt because

> [t]he foursome—like all the other heroes of "the mishap"—were born and brought up in Egypt, but they never regarded themselves—nor were they ever regarded by others—as Egyptians. . . . They were typical members of Egypt's Jewish community. . . . It was a community with shallow roots. The Jews reached Egypt during the second half of the nineteenth century or the beginning of the twentieth. . . . [T]hey could not read or write Arabic, and spoke

no more of the language than was necessary for the simplest daily needs. . . . All of Egypt's Jews could have been considered Zionists—or, to be more precise, "lovers of Zion."[2]

Speaking for Dassa, Levy, Natanson, and Ninio, Golan emphasized the lack of Jewish affinity to Egypt. In contrast, at the press conference convened to announce the arrest of the saboteurs, Egyptian Minister of Interior Zakariyya Muhyi al-Din stressed that the majority of Egyptian Jews were loyal citizens like all other Egyptians. He claimed that some Jews approached by Israeli agents had refused to act against their homeland and that those who did succumbed to trickery or coercion.[3] He vowed that the government would deal harshly with the minority of Jews who committed espionage and sabotage on Israel's behalf while continuing "to treat the non-Zionists with the kindness and respect due to every decent citizen."[4] Fu'ad al-Digwi, the prosecutor at the Cairo trial of the network, reiterated the official view of the status of Egyptian Jews in his concluding statement: "The Jews of Egypt are living among us and are sons of Egypt. Egypt makes no difference between its sons whether Moslems, Christians, or Jews. These defendants happen to be Jews who reside in Egypt, but we are trying them because they committed crimes against Egypt, although they are Egypt's sons."[5] Photo essays on the trial in the popular weekly *al-Musawwar* and daily reports of the proceedings in *al-Ahram* repeated that the accused were not being tried as Jews, but as spies and saboteurs, while loyal Jewish citizens continued to live peacefully and without discrimination.[6]

These contradictory representations of the identity and consequent obligations of Egyptian Jews are products of the national narratives of Israel and Egypt. Both national projects required Jews to identify unequivocally with one or the other. Any ambivalence was an unacceptable betrayal of the nation-state and its imperatives. But until the dispersion of the community after the 1956 Suez/Sinai War, Egyptian Jews maintained more complex multiple identities and loyalties than can be accommodated by either of the contending national narratives. Their responses to the demands for loyalty from the emerging national states of Egypt and Israel were inflected by differences of class, ethnic origin, religious rite, educational formation, political outlook, and personal accident. Yet few could embrace fully the options of official state-centered identities. Forced to decide between Egypt and Israel, most chose to make new homes in other diasporas. Decades after the liquidation of the community, some Egyptian Jews have reclaimed their Levantine cosmopolitanism through nostalgic literary reconstructions of Egypt that challenge the canons of Zionist discourse and simultaneously resist the discourse of Egyptian nationalism.

BETWEEN TWO HOMELANDS: EGYPTIAN JEWISH REPRESENTATIONS OF EGYPT

The Jewish connection to Egypt, even if partly mythological, is ancient. The biblical stories of Abraham, Joseph, and the Exodus incorporate Egypt into the sacred geography of the Jewish tradition, and these narratives were regularly invoked. The 1942 *Annuaire des Juifs d'Egypte et du proche-orient,* whose editor, Maurice Fargeon, openly declared his Zionist sympathies, proudly reviewed the Jewish bond to Egypt:

> The history of the Jewish people has been linked, since the remotest times, to that of Egypt. Already in the time of the pharaohs of the first dynasties we find Joseph sold by his brothers becoming, because of his great wisdom and profound judgment, a powerful minister in the valley of the Nile. . . . [T]he children of Israel went to Goshen (a province of Egypt) at the call of Joseph. . . . Moses, the most sublime figure of Israel, the first legislator, emerged from the womb of Egypt. . . . Thus the first *halutzim* [pioneers] of history were the Jews of Egypt led by Moses and then Joshua.[7]

According to Fargeon, some Jews did not leave Egypt at the time of Moses but remained and moved to Asyut, where they formed a tribe of warriors. They were later joined by refugees, including the prophet Jeremiah and his secretary, Barukh, fleeing the Babylonian conquest of Judea.[8] The 1945–46 edition of the *Annuaire des Juifs d'Egypte et du proche-orient* reiterated the historic link between Jews and Egypt and risked offending religious sentiment by suggesting that the source of Jewish monotheism was the ancient Egyptian cult of Ra. The anonymous author of this article (probably Maurice Fargeon) claimed that many Jewish rituals, symbols, and precepts—circumcision, the candelabrum, the altar, the design of the pillars of the temple, even several of the Ten Commandments—derived from ancient Egypt.[9] These assertions are based on Ernest Renan's *Histoire du peuple d'Israël,* a popular text among rationalist Francophone Jews. The questionable evidence supporting them does not diminish their significance in the construction of Egyptian Jewish identity and self-presentation. As Renan himself noted, "Forgetting . . . and even historical error are an essential factor in the creation of a nation."[10]

Recapitulating these stories affirmed the ancient bond of Jews with Egypt, hence the legitimacy of their residence there. This history implicitly disputed the positions of Young Egypt and the Society of Muslim Brothers, who were, by the late 1930s, antagonistic to the Jewish presence. These organizations embraced what might be regarded as a romantic-reactionary vision of the Egyptian nation based on its Islamic (and for Young Egypt also its pharaonic) past. They opposed the secular-liberalism of the Wafd and vigorously fought the Marxist political currents that emerged in the middle of World War II and that attracted many Jews to their banner. Hierarchically structured and militarized, the Muslim Brothers and Young Egypt adopted fascist organizational techniques and were sympathetic to the Axis powers during World War II. They were not fascist groups in the same sense as contemporary European movements, but that is how many liberal and left-leaning Egyptians, including most of the Jewish community, regarded them.

Fargeon's narrative of Egyptian Jewish history also contested the validity of the Zionist goal of "negation of the diaspora." Referring to Egyptian Jews as pioneers did link them to the Zionist settlement project in Palestine. But Fargeon undoubtedly knew that only a small minority of Egyptian Jews were political Zionists. Perhaps by noting their contribution to the pioneering effort over 3,000 years ago he meant to excuse them for neglecting this enterprise in the twentieth century. Moreover, as even in the time of Moses some Jews remained in Egypt, it would be unreasonable for Zionists to expect them all to emigrate to Palestine in the twentieth century.

Between the two world wars, many Jews felt no contradiction between Zionist and Egyptian national commitments. In an open letter to Haim Nahum Effendi, the chief rabbi of Egypt, the editor of the Arabic/French pro-Zionist periodical *Isra'il/Israël,* Albert D. Mosseri, asked the rabbi to "Please explain to our brothers that one can be an excellent patriot of the country of one's birth while being a perfect Jewish nationalist. One does not exclude the other."[11] Rabbi Nahum, a consistent anti-Zionist throughout his tenure in office (1924–60), did not accede to this request.

Several Egyptian Jews did participate in both national movements. Léon Castro conducted propaganda for the Wafd Party in Europe after the 1919 nationalist uprising and founded and edited a pro-Wafd French language newspaper, *La Liberté,* after returning to Egypt. At the same time, he was the head of the Zionist Organization of Cairo. In the 1940s, he served as the representative of the Jewish Agency for Palestine in Egypt. Félix Benzakein was a member of the Wafd, a deputy in parliament, a member of the Alexandria rabbinical court, and president of the Zionist Organization of Alexandria. Despite his Zionist commitments, Benzakein remained in Egypt until 1960, when he emigrated to the United States.[12]

The intensification of the Arab-Zionist conflict in Palestine during the Arab Revolt of 1936–39 strained such dual commitments. And they became nearly impossible after the 1948 Arab-Israeli War. Yet as late as 1965 Shlomo Kohen-Tzidon, a native of Alexandria who emigrated to Israel in 1949 and eventually became a member of the Knesset, published a book memorializing Shmu'el Azar—one of the two Jews executed for their roles in Operation Susannah—whose central argument, in sharp contrast to prevailing opinion in Israel, was that accommodation and understanding between the Egyptian and Israeli national movements were possible and desirable.[13]

For Zionist historiography, the creation of the state of Israel and the 1948 Arab-Israeli War signal the end of the Egyptian Jewish community. When Egypt invaded Israel on May 15, 1948, hundreds of Zionist activists were interned in Huckstep, Abu Qir, and al-Tur (along with the other major opponents of the regime—the communists, including some 300 Jews, and the Society of Muslim Brothers).[14] The property of those suspected of Zionist activity was sequestered, pro-Zionist Jewish newspapers were closed, and Zionism was declared illegal. The government did little to protect Egyptian Jews and their property from bombings and other attacks generally attributed to the Muslim Brothers during the summer of 1948. The regime was not necessarily ill-disposed to the Jewish community, but it feared confronting the Muslim Brothers, who did not distinguish between Jews and Zionists. Vigorously defending the rights of the Jews of Egypt during a war against the Jews of Palestine would have been difficult for an unpopular regime to explain to the public. During 1949 and 1950, about 20,000 Jews left Egypt, of whom 14,299 settled in Israel; the others went to Europe, North America, and South America.[15] Conditions began to improve when Ibrahim 'Abd al-Hadi became prime minister at the end of 1948. Husayn Sirri, a business partner of several of the wealthiest Jewish families, rapidly succeeded 'Abd al-Hadi in the premiership. His government issued a political amnesty in July 1949. By the time the Wafd returned to power in January 1950, all the prisoners had been released from internment, and many Jews felt it would be possible to return to life as it was before the war.

A Zionist activist who left Egypt in late 1949 reported to the Jewish Agency's Department for Middle Eastern Jewry that many of his compatriots felt there would be peace between Egypt and Israel sooner or later and that neighborly relations would be resumed. He affirmed the historic Jewish link to Egypt in the same terms used by the *Annuaire des Juifs d'Egypte et du proche-orient*: "The Jewish people has taken root in Egypt and the most beautiful Jewish figures resided in that country or came there seeking refuge: Joseph, the first minister of supply in history, our great legislator Moses, Philo of Alexandria, Sa'adya ha-Ga'on, Maimonides. . . . Our Torah, the most beautiful achievement of the spirit, the charter of humanity, was given to us on Mt. Sinai, land of Egypt."[16]

A few months later Haim Sha'ul, a clandestine Zionist emissary sent back to his native Egypt by the Jewish Agency to organize immigration to Israel, reported that an important Jewish community would continue to live in Egypt and that it was necessary to think about how to organize it.[17] As late as 1961, when fewer than 10,000 Jews remained in Egypt, longtime Zionist activist Félix Benzakein believed that "one day [Jews] . . . will come back in peace to resume our unalterable friendship with the [Egyptian] people."[18] Ultimately, perhaps 45 percent of all Egyptian Jews resettled in Israel; others reestablished their communities in Europe and the Americas.

MILLET, MINORITY, AND CITIZENSHIP

Aviezer Golan's desire to justify Israeli-inspired espionage and sabotage led him to overlook much that was significant, yet not easily contained by the Israeli national narrative. But the Egyptian national narrative is similarly flawed because the secular-liberal conception of the Egyptian nation invoked by Zakariyya Muhyi al-Din and other Egyptian officials during the trial of the perpetrators of Operation Susannah has never been fully realized. Until 1914, Egypt was a part of the Ottoman Empire, and its Jewish residents were juridically a religious community protected by a Muslim state. Community affairs were governed by autonomous institutions in accord with the Ottoman *millet* system, and members consisted of those who accepted the authority of Jewish law (*halakhah*) as interpreted and applied by rabbinical courts, though by the twentieth century few Jews resorted to these courts except for matters of personal status: marriage, divorce, adoption, burial, and inheritance.

This millet identity can be termed communitarianism: the worldview and self-perception of Jews (and other non-Muslims) living in a multiethnic, multiconfessional empire. There was a high level of toleration, communal autonomy, and cultural symbiosis among Muslims, Christians, and Jews. Individual Jews achieved high positions in the political and economic arenas in late Ottoman and monarchical Egypt. But Muslims occupied the leading military and political positions, and their right to do so was not seriously challenged.

The Ottoman political field was defined by a hierarchical relationship among religious communities that the installation of the formal apparatus of representative democracy and a nation-state promised to abolish. Secular-liberal nationalist political theory defined all citizens as equal members of the nation. But by dividing citizens into a "majority" and "minorities," secular-liberalism created new and somewhat less transparent forms of hierarchy.[19]

The secularist slogan of the 1919 nationalist uprising—"Religion is for God and the homeland is for all" (al-din li'llah wa'l-watan li'l-jami')—invited Jews to claim their place as citizens of the Egyptian nation, and some did so. Yet even in the 1920s, the hegemony of secular-liberal nationalism was challenged on two fronts by the persistence of colonial privilege and by Islamic conceptions of the polity. From 1876 to 1949, foreign citizens residing in Egypt had the right to have their legal affairs adjudicated in mixed courts, which Europeans commonly regarded as more "advanced" and modern than the indigenous legal system. Preserving a zone of legal separatism reproduced elements of Ottoman-style community autonomy that undermined secular-liberal notions of citizenship.

However, the legal autonomy of non-Muslims was not solely a product of colonialism. Until 1955, Egypt recognized the communal courts of all its religious communities. The state colluded in undermining its own sovereignty for over three decades because the authority of the Muslim *shari'a* courts derived from the same conceptual order that sustained the non-Muslim religious courts. Until Gamal Abdel Nasser, no political leader commanded sufficient authority to challenge it.

By the late 1930s, the limited character of the independence achieved in 1922 and the inevitable reaction against it eroded secular-liberal, territorial conceptions of the nation. British collusion with the monarchy in undermining parliamentary democracy, the continuing British military occupation, the privileged position of Europeans, the intensifying Arab-Zionist conflict in Palestine, and the rise of fascism and communism in Europe led many Egyptians to reject secular-liberal conceptions of the nation and to rearticulate their nationalism in either pan-Arab or Islamist terms. These had long been elements of the cultural repertoire from which Egyptians drew their self-conceptions.[20] The leading

organized expressions of these tendencies were the Society of Muslim
Brothers and Young Egypt. Their orientations excluded Jews from mem-
bership in the nation, either because they were not Muslims or because
they were not "real" Egyptians. Jews could not accept the militant anti-
Zionism that was commonly associated with pan-Arabism or the pro-
Axis sentiments of some Arab nationalists.

At the turn of the twentieth century, autochthonous Jews who would
be entitled to Egyptian citizenship by the 1929 nationality law and its
successors made up at least half of the Jewish community.[21] But in 1948,
only 5,000–10,000 of Egypt's 75,000–80,000 Jews held Egyptian citizenship. Some 40,000 were stateless, and 30,000 were foreign nationals.[22] Many of the 10,000 poor, Arabic-speaking residents of the Rabbanite and Karaite Jewish quarters (harat al-yahud and harat al-yahud
al-qara'in) in the Gamaliyya district of Cairo or the 15,000 residents of
the port district (harat al-liman) of Alexandria were among the stateless.[23] Jews with foreign citizenship typically bought it from European
consular representatives seeking local proteges as commercial agents or
levers to intervene in Egyptian affairs during the colonial era. At that
time, the category of Egyptian citizen did not exist. Egypt was a province
of the Ottoman Empire, and its residents were the subjects (reaya) of the
sultan/caliph. Jews who obtained foreign citizenship did not usually regard this as impugning their identity as Egyptians; most other Egyptians
felt otherwise.

Establishing citizenship, like many other transactions between the
Egyptian state and its subjects, was a cumbersome procedure. Until the
enactment of the Company Law of 1947 requiring firms to employ fixed
quotas of Egyptians, those who did not travel abroad had no need for
a certificate of citizenship and rarely bothered to obtain it. Chief Rabbi
Nahum encouraged eligible Jews to apply for Egyptian citizenship during the 1930s and 1940s, but despite the nominally liberal language of
the law, their applications were often subjected to bureaucratic delay
and rejection.[24] Such practices were not directed specifically at Jews.
Members of the other non-Muslim, mutamassir communities long resident in Egypt—Syrian Christians, Greeks, Italians, Armenians—were
similarly treated.

Egyptian Jews, like others trapped by the false promises of liberalism,
blended elements of communitarianism and nationalism in practices and
worldviews shaped by the European presence in the Middle East yet incompatible with the logic of the nation-state. In what follows I examine
sectors of the Egyptian Jewish community—the Karaites, the haute bour-

geoisie, the young radicals of the Francophone middle class—whose outlooks and activities resist incorporation into the national narratives of Egypt and Israel.

THE KARAITES: AN ARAB JEWISH COMMUNITY

The Karaites lived in Egypt for over 1,000 years, mainly in Cairo's *harat al-yahud al-qara'in*. They were integrated into Cairo's ethnic division of labor, typically working as goldsmiths and jewelers. Remnants of their historic role persist in the Karaite family names of firms in Cairo's gold market, like al-Sirgani, though no Karaites remain in the trade and few Egyptians are aware of the origin of these names. In the twentieth century, wealthier Karaites began to move to the middle-class districts of 'Abbasiyya and Heliopolis and to adopt elements of bourgeois, Francophone, cosmopolitan culture. But in all respects except religious practice, the daily lives of the Karaites of *harat al-yahud al-qara'in* were indistinguishable from those of their Muslim neighbors, celebrated by Naguib Mahfouz as the quintessential traditional Cairenes in his Cairo trilogy.

In March 1901, the Karaite communal council was organized and recognized by the Egyptian state.[25] The somewhat archaic Arabic name of this body (*majlis milli*) expresses the Karaites' self-conception as an ethnic-religious Ottoman millet.[26] The editor of the community newspaper explained, "Our community's existence is based on religion so it is our first duty to preserve our religion and to behave in accord with the law of our lord Moses" (*shari'at sayyidina musa*).[27] When the shaykh of al-Azhar died in 1945, Karaite Chief Rabbi Tuvia Levi Babovitch attended the funeral, and the community newspaper extended condolences "to the Egyptian nation and the Eastern countries" (*al-umma al-misriyya wa'l-aqtar al-sharqiyya*)—a formulation implying that Egypt was a Muslim country, not a secular-liberal state in which religion was irrelevant to citizenship.[28] The same conception motivated the congratulations offered to "the Egyptian people" on the Muslim feast of *'id al-adha*.[29] Similarly, the community greeted "the Christian peoples" (*al-umam al-masihiyya*) on the occasion of "the foreign new year" (*ra's al-sana al-ifranjiyya*).[30]

The Karaites' historical narrative legitimated their presence in Egypt with reference to its Islamic history and the protected status of Jews according to Islamic law. One account claimed that Karaites resided in Egypt when it was conquered for Islam by 'Amr Ibn al-'As, who gave them a plot of land at Basatin (near Ma'adi) as a communal cemetery and exempted them from paying the *jizya* tax. Another traced the Karaite presence in Egypt to the time of ʿAnan ben David in the eighth century. Both versions affirmed that, except during the reign of the Fatimid Sultan al-Hakim, Karaites enjoyed good relations with their Muslim neighbors.[31]

These linguistic usages and historical narratives are imbedded in the categories of Arabo-Muslim culture. By the 1940s, most Karaites had only partially assimilated the secular-liberal notions of citizenship and nationality recently introduced to Egypt. They saw themselves as a protected religious minority in a Muslim country, employed concepts and institutions derived from the Islamic cultural and political tradition, and regarded themselves as Egyptian in those terms.

At the same time, educated Karaite youth, responding to the mass murder of European Jews and the widespread hopes for a new world in the post–World War II era, began to feel constrained by the limits of communitarianism. Some were not particularly interested in religion, did not pray regularly, did not observe the Sabbath scrupulously, and used Passover *matzah* (unleavened bread) baked by Rabbanite Jews.[32] The Young Karaite Jewish Association (YKJA) was formed in 1937 by educated youth seeking to establish a modern identity for their community. They published an Arabic bimonthly, *al-Kalim* (The spokesman, the Arabic term refers to Moses), which appeared regularly until 1956 and promoted a program of communal reform, including the study of Hebrew and modern forms of sociability such as the Karaite boy scout troop, the Karaite youth orchestra, theater performances, sports activities, and outings of young men and women to the Pyramids, Saqqara, the Barrages, and Maʿadi. *Al-Kalim* also campaigned to improve the status of women.[33]

The reform orientation of the YKJA demonstrated considerable strength when the organization challenged Rabbi Babovitch and the community council by supporting a slate of candidates in the council elections of 1946. Seven of its ten candidates were elected.[34] Except for the particularity of Hebrew (which has its parallel in Muhammad ʿAbduh's efforts to reform the study of Arabic), the activities encouraged by the YKJA were similar to those embraced by secular-liberal Egyptian nationalists seeking to create modern, bourgeois citizens, though conducting them within the Karaite community reinforced communitarianism as much as it promoted nationalism.

In this spirit, an editor of *al-Kalim,* Eli Amin Lishaʿ, criticized the Karaites' social isolation. He reproached Rabbi Babovitch for failing to visit the newly appointed shaykh of al-Azhar in 1946 or to greet King

Faruq when he returned to Cairo from Alexandria and urged the community to participate in Egyptian national holidays "because our Egyptian citizenship requires this." This would win the affection of "our Egyptian brothers" and increase their sympathy for the community.[35] Lisha's appeal to assume the responsibilities of national citizenship acknowledged that Karaite practices and outlooks were still largely communitarian. Moreover, his concern for the community's image in the eyes of other Egyptians is itself a form of communitarian sentiment.

The editors of *al-Kalim* linked the project of communal reform to the Egyptian national revival and regarded Karaite Jews as Egyptians in all respects. The newspaper's front page often featured the cartoon figure of "Abu Ya'qub"—the Jewish counterpart of "al-Misri Effendi," who symbolized the modern, educated Egyptian nationalist. Sometimes the two were shown walking arm in arm; sometimes Abu Ya'qub appeared alone, accompanied by an article on his Egyptian character. *Al-Kalim* repeatedly referred to Karaites as *"abna' al-balad"* (sons of the country), a populist term connoting native Egyptians. Language, dress, and gender relations were commonly cited as markers of the Karaites' authentic Egyptian identity.

The language of instruction in the Karaite communal schools was Arabic. *Al-Kalim* proudly noted that Karaite dialect and usage were indistinguishable from those of other Cairenes.[36] Even in referring to contested localities for which Jews and Arabs used different names, *al-Kalim* used Arabic not Hebrew terms—"Nablus" (Shkhem), "al-Quds al-sharif" (Jerusalem), and "Filastin" (the land of Israel).[37]

Because the Karaites spoke native Arabic and used it in all of their affairs except religious liturgy, they were fully integrated into Arabo-Egyptian culture. *Al-Kalim* often published poetry in colloquial Egyptian (*zagal*), an art commonly considered a marker of cultural authenticity.[38] The poet laureate of the community, Murad Farag, composed both colloquial *zagal* and standard Arabic *qasidas*. His style was said to resemble that of Ahmad Shawqi, a leading twentieth-century, Egyptian poet.[39] *Al-Kalim*'s editor-in-chief, Yusuf Kamal, was the son of Da'ud Husni (1870–1937), a major figure in modern Arabic music. Each year on the anniversary of his death, *al-Kalim* celebrated Husni's artistic accomplishments, sometimes reprinting articles from other Arabic publications affirming the nationalist contribution of his music.[40]

According to *al-Kalim*, Karaite men historically wore *sharawil* (baggy pants) and *tarabish* (fezes) like other Egyptians, and there was "almost no difference in outward appearance between the Karaite woman and her Muslim friend."[41] Eli Amin Lishaʿ regarded the Karaites as "Eastern" and "conservative" in their social customs, unlike their Rabbanite brothers. He acknowledged that Karaite women participated in mixed cultural and sports clubs, but he believed that this was legitimate because it encouraged marriage and did not violate propriety because women of other communities had already done the same.[42] Thus, Lishaʿ acknowledged changes in Karaite gender relations while affirming the norms of Middle Eastern patriarchy and a communitarian outlook. He emulated the Egyptian nationalist movement in assigning to women the burden of cultural authenticity while promoting moderate reforms in their status so that they could become proper companions for male citizens.

The relationship between the Karaite community court and the Egyptian state illustrates the unstable amalgam of communitarianism and the demands of citizenship shaping Karaite practices by the 1950s. Like all the non-Muslim religious communities, the Karaites opposed the abolition of communal religious courts despite the nationalist criticisms of this institution. *Al-Kalim* reprinted an article in *al-Ahram* arguing that these courts were not an Ottoman innovation (hence not properly Egyptian), but a valid Islamic institution established in the time of the Prophet.[43] Each year the link between the Karaite court and the state was renewed when the governor of Cairo confirmed its members, who were required by law to be Egyptian citizens. In October 1949, the judges who had served the previous year were reappointed by the community council. An official of the governorate sent to certify the citizenship of the judges rejected their claims to be Egyptians and demanded that they obtain certificates of citizenship. This official admitted that he, like most Egyptians, did not have such a certificate. Jacques Mangubi, the head of the communal council and a senior employee of Bank Misr, then explained, "It is known that we are Egyptians. The government must determine if we are foreigners or Egyptians. And as long as we are not foreigners, then we are Egyptians." Yusuf Kamal affirmed that the members of the court were Egyptians but that it was difficult for them to obtain certificates of citizenship "for reasons not hidden from anyone." He advised the government to expedite the procedures for certifying citizenship and to facilitate granting certificates to all Egyptians regardless of religion.[44] This was an unusually bold criticism of the government and a departure from the loyalist quietism typical of the Karaite community.

Most Karaites were entitled to be and wanted to be Egyptian citizens, but they met with official resistance to their claim. Yet a low-level state official might well be uncertain about the identity of even this most

Egyptian of all Jewish communities. As Eli Amin Lishaʿ acknowledged, "some have French or Russian citizenship even though they and their fathers have never left the country, and this is because citizenship used to be sold, and a Karaite may have bought it though he is 100 percent Egyptian" (*wa-huwa masri lahman wa-daman*).[45] This incident indicates, in a small but crucial way, that even Jews who regarded themselves as fully Egyptian and who eschewed political Zionism were not treated exactly like other Egyptians, as the government and the press claimed during the trial of the Operation Susannah conspirators.

There is probably a measure of defensiveness in *al-Kalim*'s representation of the Karaite community because articles stressing its Egyptian character appeared after events threatening the status of Jews in Egypt, such as the anti-Zionist demonstrations on the anniversary of the Balfour Declaration on November 2, 1945, that degenerated into anti-Jewish riots and the start of the first Arab-Israeli war on May 15, 1948. But many such articles were unconnected to any crisis.[46] Even if its insistence on the Egyptian identity of the Karaites was strategically motivated, *al-Kalim* was an Arabic publication and the only organ of the Karaite community from 1945 to 1956, giving substance to the claim. The Karaite community was deeply imbued with Egyptian Arab culture while remaining fully Jewish in its own terms.

This included a religiously based love of Zion but no organized involvement with political Zionism.[47] The he-Halutz (The pioneer) Zionist youth movement tried to organize Karaites and Rabbanites in *harat al-yahud,* but with limited success. The Cairo Zionist Federation had no ties with Karaites, and few residents of *harat al-yahud* belonged to the Zionist youth movements.[48]

Murad Farag, the leading intellectual of the Karaite community, had long advocated closer relations between Karaites and Rabbanites. He encouraged some of the educated youth around *al-Kalim* who were unsatisfied by the communitarianism of their elders to seek contacts with the Rabbanites, who were considered more "advanced." Stepping beyond the boundaries of their community exposed these Karaite youth to the full range of political orientations of the post–World War II era, and some became Zionists. Several hundred young Karaites emigrated to Israel between 1948 and 1956 against the advice of Chief Rabbi Babovitch.[49]

The best-known Karaite involved in organized Zionist activity was Moshe Marzuq, the commander of the Israeli espionage network in Cairo, who was executed for his role in Operation Susannah. He was a member of he-Halutz and the underground self-defense (Haganah) organization established by emissaries from Palestine in 1946 before becoming a spy and saboteur for Israel. Marzuq's older brother, Yosef, had been arrested as a Zionist activist in May 1948, although he was one of the first to be freed because of the intervention of the French Consulate (his grandfather had bought a Tunisian passport from the French Consulate). Yosef Marzuq emigrated to Israel in 1953.[50] This family background and the fact that Moshe Marzuq was employed as a doctor in the Rabbanite Jewish hospital meant that his social and cultural milieu was not limited to *harat al-yahud,* and this may explain his receptivity to Zionism. Marzuq's arrest and execution had a chilling effect on the Karaites. Because of his status as a doctor, he was well known and respected, though not even his older brother suspected he was engaged in espionage and sabotage on behalf of Israel.[51]

Nonetheless, a significant proportion of the Karaites remained in Egypt until the 1960s. Because most Karaites were thoroughly Arabized and defined themselves in terms rooted in their experience as an Ottoman millet, they tended to remain in Egypt longer than Rabbanites. But ultimately, they could not resist the forces reshaping the Egyptian political community in ways that effectively excluded Jews.

COSMOPOLITANISM AND EGYPTIANISM: THE JEWISH HAUTE BOURGEOISIE

If Karaites regarded themselves as Egyptians on the basis of their long residence and Arabic culture, the Jewish haute bourgeoisie did not believe that their lack of these attributes made them any less Egyptian. The Qattawis and the Mosseris, powerful Cairene Jewish business families in the interwar period, were longtime residents of Egypt. But many families of the Jewish business elite were Sephardi immigrants from other parts of the Ottoman Empire who had arrived in Egypt in the nineteenth century seeking economic opportunities. As Ottoman subjects, they were not juridically foreigners. They were Arabic and, occasionally, Turkish speakers. Their "Eastern" culture allowed them to acclimate easily.

Kinship connections throughout the Mediterranean basin, a long tradition of diasporic commercial activity, and participation in the local cultures of the Levant and overseas French culture enabled Jewish businessmen to function as commercial intermediaries between Europe and the Ottoman realms, often obtaining foreign citizenship in the process. In the shadow of British colonial rule, from 1882 to 1922, several

Sephardi families established business enterprises on their own and in collaboration with European partners. In the 1920s and 1930s, they expanded their network of business relationships to form partnerships with Muslim Egyptians. These alliances became prominent institutions of the modern capitalist sector of the economy during the first half of the twentieth century and linked the prosperity of the Jewish haute bourgeoisie to Egypt and its future.

Yusuf ʿAslan Qattawi (Cattaui) Pasha (1861–1942), president of the Sephardi Jewish Community Council of Cairo from 1924 to 1942, was the most visible Egyptian Jew of the interwar era, not only because of his leadership of the community, but perhaps even more so because of his extensive business and political activity.[52] He studied engineering in France, returned to Egypt to work for the Ministry of Public Works, and then left to study the sugar refining industry in Moravia. Returning again to Egypt, Qattawi Pasha became a director of the Egyptian Sugar Company and president of the Kom Ombo Company, which developed and cultivated sugar on 70,000 acres of desert land in Aswan Province. Building from this base in the sugar industry, the Qattawis established several industrial, financial, and real estate enterprises in collaboration with the Suarèses and other Jewish families, amassing considerable economic and political power.

Talʿat Harb, the apostle of Egyptian economic nationalism, began his career in the employ of the Suarès and Qattawi families, first at the Daʾirah Saniyeh Company and then as a managing director of the Kom Ombo Company.[53] He acknowledged his debt to the Suarèses and Qattawis and maintained close relations with the Cairo Jewish business elite. Two prominent Jewish businessmen, Yusuf ʿAslan Qattawi and Yusuf Cicurel, collaborated with Talʿat Harb on the Executive Committee of the Egyptian Chamber of Commerce and the Commission on Commerce and Industry. Both these institutions promoted the economic and industrial development of Egypt and served as incubators for the doctrine of economic nationalism popularized by Talʿat Harb. In 1920, when Talʿat Harb established Bank Misr—widely acclaimed as the embodiment of Egyptian economic nationalism—these Jewish colleagues accepted his invitation to join him as founding directors; Qattawi became vice-president of the board.

The Qattawi family claimed residence in Egypt since the eighth century, and Yusuf ʿAslan Pasha identified himself as an Egyptian of Jewish faith. Under his leadership, the Cairo Sephardi Jewish Community Council adopted a consistent non-Zionist position.[54] Though his

grandfather apparently acquired Austrian citizenship, Yusuf ʿAslan Qattawi must have been an Egyptian citizen because this was a condition
for membership on the board of Bank Misr. His French education was
not a marker of otherness or a political liability. It was a prestigious symbol of modernity and progress common to the sons of the landed elite,
the business community, and many leading intellectuals of the early
twentieth century, Muslims and Christians as well as Jews.

The Qattawi family's Egyptian identity was reinforced by its ties to
the royal family and political activism. Yusuf ʿAslan received the title of
pasha in 1912. He was an appointed deputy for Kom Ombo from 1915
to 1922, and his parliamentary colleagues elected him to the committee
that drafted the 1923 constitution. He served as a minister in the
promonarchist governments of Ziwar Pasha in 1924–25, though he was
forced to resign because he maintained a respectful personal relationship
with the leader of the antimonarchist Wafd, Saʿd Zaghlul. King Fuʾad
appointed Qattawi Pasha to the senate in 1927. His wife, Alice (née
Suarès), was chief lady in waiting to Queens Farida and Nazli. Though
he was a monarchist and never supported the Wafd, Yusuf ʿAslan Qattawi considered himself an Egyptian patriot. His nationalism was socially conservative and business oriented.

His sons, ʿAslan Bey (1890–1956?) and René Bey (1896–?), succeeded
him in both the political and business arenas. Both were educated in
Switzerland, but like their father they vigorously asserted their Egyptian
identity and cultivated the family's relationship with the royal family.
When Yusuf ʿAslan Pasha retired from the senate in 1938, King Faruq
appointed ʿAslan to take his father's place. The same year René was
elected deputy for Kom Ombo. Both retained their positions until 1953,
when the parliament was dissolved by the regime of the Free Officers.

René Qattawi inherited his father's leadership of the Cairo Sephardic
Jewish community. He urged Jews to see themselves as an integral part
of the Egyptian nation and in 1935 encouraged the formation of the Association of Egyptian Jewish Youth, whose manifesto proclaiming
"Egypt is our homeland, Arabic is our language" called on Jews to take
part in the Egyptian national renaissance.[55] In 1943, the Arabic language
Jewish weekly newspaper al-Shams (The sun) supported René Qattawi
for the presidency of the Cairo Sephardi Jewish Community Council as
the candidate best able to promote the Arabization and Egyptianization
of the community.[56] He was elected and served until 1946.

René Qattawi aggressively opposed political Zionism, which gained
significant support for the first time during World War II. In November

1944, he and Edwin Goar, vice-president of the Alexandria Jewish community, sent a "Note on the Jewish Question" to a meeting of the World Jewish Congress in Atlantic City arguing that Palestine could not absorb all the European Jewish refugees and noting Egypt's exemplary treatment of its Jews.[57] In late 1944 and early 1945, Qattawi carried on a barbed correspondence with Léon Castro demanding that Castro close the camps operated by the Zionist youth movements. Qattawi was unable to impose his will on the Zionist elements of the community council, and this was apparently the cause of his resignation in August 1946.[58]

The Qattawi family maintained extensive business relationships with all the leading Muslim families in the emerging Egyptian bourgeoisie of the interwar period. Such intercommunal business alliances were common among wealthy and powerful bourgeois Jews, including the Adès, Aghion, Goar, Mosseri, Nahman, Pinto, Rolo, and Tilche families. Other bourgeois Jewish families, especially the elites of the Karaite community, operated within an "ethnic economy": Their business associates and customers were mostly other Jews.[59]

The Cicurel family business operated midway between the fully integrated business activities of the Qattawis and similar haut bourgeois families and an ethnic economy model. Moreno Cicurel had migrated to Cairo from Izmir in the mid-nineteenth century, when both cities were part of the Ottoman Empire. The Cicurel family held Italian citizenship at the time. After working for several years in a Jewish-owned haberdashery shop in the Muski and then purchasing the shop from its owner, in 1909 Moreno Cicurel opened a large department store on what is now 26th of July Street in the heart of the European section of Cairo.[60] Moreno's second son, Yusuf Cicurel Bey, born in Cairo in 1887, was a member of the Cairo Chamber of Commerce and one of the ten original members of the board of directors of Bank Misr in 1920, by which time the family must have acquired Egyptian citizenship. Yusuf Cicurel also participated in several of Bank Misr's ventures in the 1920s, but the family's participation in the broader sectors of the economy beyond its store declined after the 1920s.

Moreno Cicurel's youngest son, Salvator, was educated in Switzerland and worked for the family firm continuously after completing his studies in 1912, eventually becoming managing director and chairman of the board. He shared a business-oriented conception of the national project with Tal'at Harb and the Qattawis and like them became a member of the Executive Committee of the Egyptian Chamber of Commerce in 1925. At the request of non-Wafd governments, he served on the Supreme

Council of Labor and participated in an economic mission to the Sudan. Salvator Cicurel was also a patron of sports, a prominent component of bourgeois nationalist modernity in Egypt. He was the national fencing champion and the captain of the 1928 Olympic fencing team. These contributions were recognized in 1937, when he received the title of bey.

In addition to his management of the family business, active sports life, and service to the Egyptian state, Salvator was a leader of the Jewish community. He served on the Cairo Sephardi Jewish Community Council in 1927–28 and from 1939 to 1946, and in 1934 he became a founding member of the Friends of the Hebrew University in Jerusalem. He probably considered this a philanthropic activity because Salvator Cicurel does not appear to have been a political Zionist, though he was less adamant in his opposition to Zionism than René Qattawi.[61] He succeeded René Qattawi as president of Cairo's Sephardi Jewish community from 1946 to 1957.

The Cicurel store developed into Egypt's largest and most fashionable department store chain: Les Grand Magasins Cicurel et Oreco. Cicurel specialized in ready-to-wear men's and women's clothes, shoes, housewares, and notions, much of which were imported from Europe. It had an excellent reputation for high quality and was a purveyor to the royal palace during the reigns of Kings Fu'ad and Faruq. The Oreco branch of the firm consisted of thrift stores serving the lower middle classes.

The Cicurel stores had a foreign cultural character due to their largely noncitizen Jewish staff, their exclusive and largely imported merchandise, and the use of French by employees and customers on the shop floors. Nonetheless, the Cicurel family regarded themselves as Egyptians and saw their business activities as contributing to the Egyptian national economy. The products they purveyed in their department stores and the cultural ambience they promoted were widely considered by the elite and upper-middle strata to be proper accoutrements of modern culture completely compatible with nationalist ideals and aspirations as they were commonly understood until the mid-1950s.

Because it was favored by the royal family, unlike the other major Jewish-owned department stores, the Cicurel firm was not placed under government administration during the 1948 Arab-Israeli War. The main Cairo store was damaged by a bomb on July 19, 1948, most likely the work of the Muslim Brothers, but it soon reopened. The building was destroyed in the Cairo fire of January 26, 1952, another indication that militant nationalists regarded the Cicurel store as a foreign institution. But it was rapidly rebuilt with the support of General Muhammad

Naguib after the military coup of July 23, 1952. Despite the favor shown to the Cicurel firm by the new regime, by 1954–55 the two non-Cicurel family members left the board of directors and were not replaced. At the outbreak of the Suez/Sinai War, unlike in 1948, the firm was placed under sequestration. The store was quickly reopened, but the Cicurel family soon ceded its majority holding to a new group headed by Muslim Egyptians. In 1957, Salvator Cicurel left Egypt for France.

Regardless of the character of their business activity, most of the older Jewish haute bourgeoisie embraced loyalist, Egyptianist sentiments—a natural accompaniment to their comfortable lives and prominence in many sectors of the Egyptian economy. Because of their comfortable and privileged position, most of the Jewish haute bourgeoisie elected to remain in Egypt after 1948. I was able to identify 892 Jewish names in the 1947 edition of The Egyptian Who's Who. A large minority, 43.5 percent, left Egypt after the 1948 Arab-Israeli War. In 1952, 504 Jewish names were still listed in The Egyptian Who's Who. After the initial departures, most of the remaining Jewish elite continued to reside in Egypt, at least until the 1956 war. Over 37 percent of those names I could identify as Jews in the 1947 edition of The Egyptian Who's Who were still listed on the eve of the 1956 war. Some of those listed in 1947 had died in Egypt, and 170 new Jewish names that had not appeared in 1947 were added to the directory during the 1950s. So in 1956, a total of 472 Jews were listed in The Egyptian Who's Who, 52.9 percent of the number listed in 1947. As late as 1959, at least 251 Jews were listed.[62]

Despite the clear decline in numbers, the listings of Jews in The Egyptian Who's Who affirm that between the Arab-Israeli wars of 1948 and 1956 a substantial portion of the Jewish elite remained in Egypt and continued to occupy positions in its economic life in numbers far greater than their proportion of the Egyptian population, though their role was gradually diminishing. Moreover, the Jewish elite did not, in the main, immigrate to Israel after leaving Egypt. Like Jews throughout the Middle East in the 1950s who abandoned their countries of origin with the intensification of the Arab-Israeli conflict, most of those who had a choice went to Europe or the Americas.

FRENCH CULTURE, RADICAL POLITICS, AND MIDDLE-CLASS JEWISH YOUTH

In 1860, the Paris-based Alliance Israélite Universelle embarked on a Jewish "mission civilisatrice" to uplift and modernize the Jews of the

Middle East by imbuing them with French education and culture.[63] French opposition to British imperial policy in Egypt throughout the nineteenth century allowed many Egyptians, not only Jews, to embrace French culture as an acceptable form of European modernity. By the late nineteenth century, French was the lingua franca of the entire Egyptian business community. Knowledge of a European language was virtually a requirement for a white-collar job in the modern private sector of the economy and constituted significant cultural capital. Therefore many Egyptian Jews willingly underwent de-Arabization.

Children of the haute bourgeoisie, Muslims and Christians as well as Jews like ʿAslan and René Qattawi and Salvator Cicurel, were often educated in boarding schools in France or Switzerland. A few Anglophile elite families sent their children to England or to Victoria College in Alexandria, where they also learned French. Upper-middle-class children typically attended a French lycée or a Catholic missionary school in Egypt. Victor Sanua, the product of such an education, estimated that more than half the students in the Catholic schools of Cairo were Jewish.[64] A large proportion of the others were Muslims and Copts; it was not uncommon for children of very prominent Muslim families to be educated in such schools. Children of the Jewish lower middle class populated the schools of the Jewish community, where the language of instruction was French, but Hebrew and other Jewish subjects were part of the curriculum.

The political inflection of a French education in Egypt was often toward the left. Many French teachers, even in the Catholic schools, were leftists participating in a national-secular program of cultural imperialism—the *mission laique* (lay mission). Jacqueline Kahanoff, the daughter of an upper-middle-class Cairene Jewish family, explained why the radical ideas she absorbed at school were embraced by Christians, Jews, and elite Muslims whose families had abandoned strict religious observance and no longer lived as members of millets but were neither fully European nor fully Egyptian:

> We thought ourselves to be Socialist, even Communist, and in our school yard we ardently discussed the Blum government, the civil war in Spain, revolution, materialism, and the rights of women, particularly free love. The only language we could think in was the language of Europe, and our deeper selves were submerged under this crust of European dialectics, a word we loved to use. . . . We blithely dismissed everything that was not left as reactionary. . . . Revolution, which would destroy a world where we did not have our rightful place, would create another, where we could belong. We wanted to break out of the

narrow minority framework into which we were born, to strive toward something universal, and we were ashamed of the poverty of what we called "the Arab masses," and of the advantages a Western education had given us over them. . . . Revolution and Marxism seemed the only way to attain a future which would include both our European mentors and the Arab masses. We would no longer be what we were, but become free citizens of the universe.[65]

Marxism entered the Jewish schools through French teachers or emissaries from Palestine, where socialist Zionism was hegemonic. These schools became centers of the Zionist youth movements, which advocated that Egyptian Jewish youth transcend what they were by becoming Jewish nationalists. The largest and most active of these movements was ha-ʿIvri ha-Tzaʿir (The young Hebrew), the Egyptian branch of ha-Shomer ha-Tzaʿir (The young guard) that sought, usually unsuccessfully, to blend Zionism and internationalism. The youth movement was affiliated with ha-Kibutz ha-Artzi (The national kibutz federation) and, after 1948, with the MAPAM, which had a strong pro-Soviet left wing who strove to minimize the differences between their Marxist Zionism and Soviet-style Marxism-Leninism.[66]

A second Marxist Zionist youth movement formed in 1949–50: Dror—he-Halutz ha-Tzaʿir (Freedom—the young pioneer). Dror was the youth organization of ha-Kibutz ha-Meʾuhad (The united kibutz federation), which was, until 1954, mainly affiliated with MAPAM. Dror established a strong base at the Lycée de l'Union Juive pour l'Enseignment of Alexandria, where, according to one graduate, the dominant ideology was Marxism-Leninism. Students learned dialectical and historical materialism in geography class from Alexandre Roche; and Ms. Mizrahi had her nine-year-old pupils conduct monthly sessions of criticism and self-criticism.[67]

In preparation for MAPAM's second party congress in Israel, Dror members began to discuss the positions of the party's two kibutz movements on the Palestinian-Israeli conflict and other political issues such as democratic centralism. The left wingers concluded that the kibutz was not a revolutionary institution at all. Many of them adopted communist positions. After a year and a half of ideological ferment, Dror's leadership decided to liquidate the movement in June 1952. Most of the senior members became communists in Egypt, Israel, or France. Others joined ha-Shomer ha-Tzaʿir.[68] Similar debates raged in ha-Shomer ha-Tzaʿir, though because it was a highly disciplined formation with a long organizational and political tradition, the movement was not threatened with ideological liquidation.[69]

The indistinct boundary between fractions of the middle class and the accidental factors influencing a family's choice of school produced a large zone of intersection between the social and cultural milieux of communist and socialist Zionist Jewish youth. In the early 1950s, the boundary between communism and socialist Zionism was permeable. The same French cultural influences and the political ferment of the post–World War II era attracted some Egyptian Jewish youth to Zionism while their brothers, sisters, and cousins embraced communism.[70]

Except for the Zionist minority, the Francophone children of the Jewish middle classes, especially the Marxists and other leftists among them, generally saw themselves as part of Egypt. They were conscious of a difference between themselves and "the Arab masses," but they believed that it would be gradually overcome through education and social progress. The Marxists, especially the followers of Henri Curiel (see Chapter 6), consciously sought to Egyptianize themselves, though not very many succeeded by the standards of the post-1952 regime.

A large proportion of the educated Jewish middle-class youth was highly politicized, but the lives of many, perhaps the majority, like those of their parents, revolved around their families, their sporting clubs, and their future in business. Those who embraced Zionism and communism were undoubtedly sincere and deeply devoted to their chosen political ideology. These commitments entailed very different consequences in Egyptian politics. Nonetheless, Zionist nationalism and communist internationalism, which was in practice the left wing of the Egyptian nationalist movement, were both strategies for resolving the contradictions of being Jewish in Egypt that relied on the same modernist political categories. Parents and older relations were often just as displeased by youthful political activism whether it was Zionist or communist.

NOSTALGIAS: BEYOND NATIONALISM?

Rahel Maccabi's autobiographical memoir, *Mitzrayim sheli* (My Egypt), was one of the first Hebrew books to portray Jewish life in Egypt for an Israeli audience. Maccabi grew up in an upper-middle-class family in Alexandria, but her life history is exceptional. After several visits with her family, she emigrated to Palestine in 1935, joined a kibutz of ha-Shomer ha-Tza'ir, and became an officer in the Haganah and then the Israeli army. These pioneering Zionist credentials authorized her to write about her youth in Alexandria of the 1920s and 1930s.

Maccabi's childhood milieu was almost entirely isolated from everything Arab or Egyptian. She made only the slightest effort to learn Arabic in school; even her knowledge of colloquial Egyptian was minimal, as is evident from the errors in simple Arabic words in her text. She knew of a neighborhood in Alexandria where Jews spoke Arabic, but never went there.[71] At an early age she "came to the conclusion that the world of the Egyptians is frightening."[72] Her father's family, originally from central Europe, Arabized rapidly after her paternal grandfather married into the Qattawi family and settled in Cairo. Her father was educated in Arabic and had worked for the Qattawi family in the sugar industry. Rahel and her mother avoided Cairo and her father's family, whose members they regarded as Egyptian others.

Rahel Maccabi's mother became a Zionist in 1904 by reading the British *Jewish Chronicle.* She belonged to a wealthy Baghdadi family that emigrated to Bombay to trade in precious stones and then moved to Egypt at the time of Napoleon's invasion. Though she was far more deeply rooted in the Arab world than her husband's family, Rahel's mother had learned to regard everything Arab as dirty, foreign, and barbaric. Internalizing this message, Rahel perceived "an unfathomable distance that separated Cairo of those days, with its Jews dressed in Eastern style and living in a quite traditional, patriarchal, primitive world, from the atmosphere in which mother grew up."[73] For Maccabi, everything Egyptian was unreal, inferior, or frightening except for her exoticist memories of flowers, food, and rose water.[74]

Mitzrayim sheli affirms the Zionist national narrative: Some Egyptian Jews became good Zionists even before 1948; they were unaffected by contact with anything Arab, and their Jewish identity was preserved by leaving Egypt as soon as possible. In the triumphalist atmosphere following Israel's overwhelming victory in the 1967 war, the publishing house of ha-Shomer ha-Tza'ir easily found a market for this image of Egypt and its Jews. Conquest of a substantial piece of Egyptian territory in that war stimulated a desire for knowledge about Egypt that explained military victory as a consequence of civilizational superiority.

The first chapters of *Mitzrayim sheli* were written in 1965 and appeared as essays in *Keshet,* the journal of the Canaanite movement, which rejected Zionism and the concept of a worldwide Jewish people in favor of a native Hebrew identity rooted in the Middle East. In Israel of the 1950s and 1960s, it was rare to find any literary recognition of the fact that a high proportion of Jewish Israelis were born in Muslim countries of the Middle East or were children of those born there. Rahel

Maccabi's acknowledgment of her birthplace was apparently sufficient for *Keshet*'s editor, Aharon Amir, to find her writing of interest. He dubbed her essays *Mitzrayim sheli*. She disliked the title's suggestion of a sentimental attachment she did not feel toward Egypt and would have preferred "Qantara-West"—the last train station in Egypt on the way to Palestine. This title would clearly proclaim her Zionist trajectory, but the reference was too obscure to market to the Israeli public.[75]

Jacqueline Kahanoff, like Rahel Maccabi, was also raised in an upper-middle-class family and educated in French schools where Zionism was a rarity among the Jewish pupils. Many of her essays, including her signature piece, "The Generation of Levantines," were written in English, translated by Aharon Amir, and published in the late 1950s and early 1960s in the first issues of *Keshet,* whose outlook was far more congenial to Kahanoff than to Maccabi. Unlike Maccabi, Kahanoff felt a strong positive connection to Egypt, noting with pride that her schoolmates were "pro-nationalist as a matter of principle," though their parents were "pro-British as a matter of business and security."[76] Sensitive to her location in a potentially explosive cultural and political border zone, she consciously sought a creative Levantine synthesis:

> [E]ven though we sympathized with the Muslim nationalists' aspirations, we did not believe them capable of solving the real problems of this society, and for this they could not forgive us. As Levantines, we instinctively searched for fruitful compromises, feeling as we did that the end of the colonial occupation solved nothing unless western concepts were at work in this world, transforming its very soul. We knew that Europe, although far away, was inseparably part of us because it had so much to offer. These radically different attitudes toward Europe and towards our conception of the future made the parting of our ways inevitable.[77]

Although they wished to identify with Egypt, Kahanoff and her schoolmates had no doubt that European culture was more advanced and should be the dominant component in the Levantine synthesis she aspired to. She "wondered how those young Muslims intended to change conditions in Egypt if they did not realize that learning what the Europeans knew was the most important thing of all."[78] Until 1956, she could have found many Egyptian nationalists who agreed with her. Decades after formal independence, Egypt's upper classes continued to regard the European imperial powers as cultural models. The Suez/Sinai War initiated a new phase in the process of decolonization in which bourgeois European culture was widely repudiated.

Because they felt they could not be full participants in the Egyptian national movement, Kahanoff and her Jewish friends tried to realize their youthful ideals by starting a clinic in *harat al-yahud*. Despite their initial success, they had to abandon the project because the head of the Jewish community in the *hara* accused them of advocating birth control and Zionism. They responded that the second allegation was a lie. Blocked in both the Egyptian national arena and in the Jewish community, Kahanoff left Egypt in 1940. "I loved Egypt, but could no longer bear to be part of it, however conscious I was of its queer charm, its enchantment, its contrasts, its ignoble poverty and refined splendor," she recalled.[79] After living in the United States and Paris and publishing a novel in English, Kahanoff moved to Israel in 1954.[80]

Keshet was a highly regarded literary journal, though very few Israelis embraced its cultural politics. Kahanoff's celebration of Levantinism was abhorrent to the dominant Ashkenazi Zionism that required the mass migration of the Middle Eastern Jews to Israel to populate the country but detested their culture and regarded Levantinism as a curse to be avoided at all costs. Critics praised Kahanoff's sensitivity and emotional range, but Levantinism was not an idea that could elicit a serious response from the militantly Eurocentric Israeli cultural establishment. One critic who tried to consider Kahanoff's cultural formation dismissed her youthful aspirations as "fruitful illusions"—"an interesting addition to the psychology and sociology of one more exile."[81]

Until Egyptian President Anwar al-Sadat's visit to Jerusalem in 1977, the centrality of Egypt in the Arab confrontation with Israel made it difficult for Egyptian Jews to say anything positive about Egypt or their lives there. The al-Sadat visit created a receptive audience in Israel that enabled Jews from middle-class backgrounds in Cairo and Alexandria to contest Rahel Maccabi's representation of the Jewish experience in Egypt. Remembering Egypt in a positive light allowed them to reclaim their places as cultural, and in some cases economic, intermediaries. Post-1977 memories of Egypt generally reject Maccabi's colonialist Orientalism and insist that there was much that should be valued in Jewish life in Egypt. For this generation, Jacqueline Kahanoff's work is a point of departure. In the hopeful atmosphere following al-Sadat's visit to Jerusalem, her essays were collected in a warmly received book, *Mimizrah shemesh* (From the east the sun). A review in an avant garde literary magazine endorsed her revalorization of Levantinism.[82] Such critical receptivity, though far from unanimous, was encouraged by the soaring hopes for peaceful normalcy in Israel.

Yitzhaq Gormezano-Goren's *Kayitz aleksandroni* (An Alexandrian summer), a semiautobiographical novel recalling his family's last summer in Alexandria before they emigrated to Israel in December 1951, also appeared during the post-al-Sadat visit euphoria. Like Kahanoff, Gormezano-Goren relishes the hybrid Mediterranean identity of Egyptian Jews. His story begins with a sardonic lesson in cultural geography: "Yes, precisely Mediterranean. Perhaps it is by virtue of this Mediterraneanism that I sit here and spin this tale. Here, in the Land of Israel, which lies on the shores of the Baltic Sea. Sometimes you wonder if Vilna is really the Jerusalem of Lithuania or if Jerusalem is the Vilna of the Land of Israel."[83]

The novel is suffused with unstable dualities and shifting identities. The narrator is and is not Robbie, the ten-year-old son of a midlevel employee of the Ford Motor Company. The middle-class propriety of Robbie's Jewish family is undermined by homoeroticism, which his mother identifies as Arab.[84] The Muslim servants of the family speak French. Many of the central characters of the novel are not exactly who they seem to be and slip easily in and out of ostensibly incompatible roles. The retired jockey, Joseph Hamdi-'Ali, is a Turkish Muslim who has converted to Judaism. His son, David Hamdi-'Ali, is also a jockey but does not have his father's single-minded passion to win. David's rival, Ahmad al-Tal'uni, embodies Muslim Egyptian aspirations and resentment of the privileged foreigners and minorities. The competition between them ignites chauvinist rioting. Yet al-Tal'uni is not a typical Egyptian, but a bedouin favored by the wife of the British consul. Because of al-Tal'uni's appetite for victory, Joseph Hamdi-'Ali regards him as his spiritual heir and a more worthy successor than David. Rabbi Ferrara consistently refers to Joseph by his Muslim name, Yusuf. Toward the end of his life, Joseph Hamdi-'Ali worries that Allah may punish him for converting. In the style typical of the rationalist intelligentsia of the Iberian convivencia, the one God shows different faces to Muslims, Christians, and Jews.[85]

Kayitz aleksandroni received several positive but patronizing reviews that avoided engagement with the themes of the book and treated it as a light and pleasant diversion or background to current political developments.[86] Reviewers who noticed Gormezano-Goren's valorization of Mediterraneanism were distressed by it. One did not understand the passage about Vilna and Jerusalem and wondered if it could mean that Israel was a foreign implant in the Middle East.[87] Another found nothing at all positive in Gormezano-Goren's memories of Alexandria and concluded, "if this is Mediterraneanism, then it is better for us for now to remain on the coast of the Baltic Sea."[88]

Perhaps in response to such arrogant Eurocentrism, the second volume of Gormezano-Goren's projected Alexandria trilogy, *Blanche,* has a more sharply anti-Ashkenazi tone. Unlike Jacqueline Kahanoff, Gormezano-Goren is not sure that Europe should be the dominant element in the Mediterraneanism he advocates. But he is not naive, and *Blanche* directly engages the historical processes that led Jews to "leave the flesh pot of Alexandria in exchange for the food ration books of the early 1950s in Israel." But Gormezano-Goren is equally conscious of the loss of his community's distinctive heritage. Raphael Vital, who sang in the taverns of Alexandria, lost his voice "in the desolate desert between Alexandria and Be'ersheba."[89] Although modulated by years of accommodation to Israeli Euro-Zionist discourse, the reassertion of Middle Eastern Jewish identity following the 1977 electoral victory of the Likud and the peace with Egypt enabled Yitzhaq Gormezano-Goren to attempt to retrieve this Egyptian Jewish voice.

Blanche was not well received by reviewers. The influential Dan Miron dismissed it as "Alexandrian kitsch" and pronounced the whole genre of Mediterranean Jewish writing to be "an entirely marginal phenomenon" in Hebrew literature.[90] Tamar Wolf also denounced *Blanche* as "Alexandrian kitsch" (perhaps one of these critics was less than entirely original) and, with unwarranted self-confidence, she scolded Gormezano-Goren for anachronistically inserting Flash Gordon and Superman cartoons into Alexandria cinemas of the 1940s.[91] She apparently believed that, like so much that is valued and recognized by Israeli yuppie culture, they were a commodity of the 1980s.

I suspect that one element of *Blanche* that offended the critics, though none of them dared to refer to it, is the portrayal of Zionist activity in Alexandria in the late 1940s as a dilettantish and ineffectual Ashkenazi-initiated project with no appeal to the young members of Robbie's family except for cousin Rosie and the superficial and flighty Raphael Vital. Characters in *Kayitz aleksandroni* and *Blanche* acknowledge that there is no future for Jews in Egypt, but Gormezano-Goren is ambivalent about the Zionist resolution of their problem. In an interview after *Blanche* appeared, Gormezano-Goren ridiculed the heroic pretensions of Zionism: "Operation Susannah in 1954, during which Jews were arrested and hung in Egypt, revealed the infantile Zionist base there."[92]

And so we return to Operation Susannah—the Israeli-led campaign of espionage and sabotage—with which we began. Robert Dassa spent fourteen years in an Egyptian prison for his role in that fiasco. In 1979, eleven years after his release, he returned to Egypt as a journalist for the Arabic service of Israeli television to cover Prime Minister Menahem Begin's visit to Alexandria. Thirteen years later he finally wrote about his memories of Egypt in his own name.[93] *Be-hazarah le-kahir* (Return to Cairo) is a report of his twenty-some return trips since 1979 interwoven with a recapitulation of the events of Operation Susannah, the trial of the conspirators, and their experiences in Tura prison. Publication of this book by Israel's Ministry of Defense permitted both a long overdue payment of a debt to the author and supervision over its contents.

Did Dassa, once he was permitted to speak in his own voice about his identity, confirm Aviezer Golan's assertions about the identity of Egyptian Jews with which this chapter began? Dassa oscillates between recapitulations of well-worn elements of the official narrative—the Cairo judicial proceedings were a show trial;[94] Paul Frank was a double agent who betrayed the network;[95] Dassa felt no connection to Egypt[96]—and disclosures that undermine it. Dassa grew up in a mixed Alexandria neighborhood with no apparent anti-Semitism.[97] His parents, both twentieth-century immigrants to Egypt, were Middle Eastern Jews from Jerusalem and Yemen. Zionism was "quite an exceptional thing in the Egyptian Jewish community."[98] No other members of his family were Zionists. His sister married a Muslim Egyptian and lived with him in the fashionable Muntazah district of Alexandria as of the writing of his book.[99]

Dassa's central preoccupation is his repeated accusation that Israeli military and political authorities never assumed full responsibility for the operations he and his colleagues undertook on behalf of the state. He accuses the mythic figures in the history of Israel's security establishment—David Ben-Gurion and Moshe Dayan—of failure to request their release in the prisoner exchange following the 1956 war because they were a political embarrassment, causing them to spend twelve more years in jail unnecessarily.[100] By focusing on such issues, Dassa's charges reinforce the discourse of national security regulating discussion of the Lavon affair in Israel. Dassa never asks, What was the purpose behind the orders he executed? Was it justified to endanger the entire Egyptian Jewish community by ordering him and his colleagues to bomb civilian targets in Egypt? What does this activity imply about Israel's policy priorities? What was the effect of the Lavon affair on Israeli-Egyptian relations?

Dassa's confessions that he craves connection with Egypt undermine the many normative elements in *Return to Cairo*: "I do not come to Egypt as a tourist. I never was and never will be a tourist there. I come to it as a free citizen, and only there can I express the full feeling of liberation."[101] Throughout his years in jail, Dassa yearned for Alexandria, and after leaving Egypt, he dreamed and hoped for the moment he would return.[102] When he did revisit Alexandria, he felt as though he had never left it. Dassa concludes his account of his travails by revealing, "In order to feel complete freedom, I need to walk freely in the streets of Cairo. Only there do I feel that I really have been released."[103]

Robert Dassa's admission that he requires continuing contact with Egypt is a sharp repudiation of Aviezer Golan's endeavor to contain Operation Susannah within the boundaries of the Zionist national narrative, which views Jewish authenticity and security as possible only in Israel. Dassa, even as he justifies his acts of espionage and sabotage against Egypt, like Jacqueline Kahanoff and Yitzhaq Gormezano-Goren, acknowledges that his well-being requires him to maintain a strong tie to Egypt. In fact, Dassa seems schizophrenic in a modern political universe defined by the proposition that individuals must identify with only one state.

The writings of Robert Dassa, Jacqueline Kahanoff, and Yitzhaq Gormezano-Goren attest that the currently prevailing exclusivist conceptions of national identity and national sentiment are a relatively recent construction. They do not conform to previously existing forms of political community in Egypt. And they fit uneasily in contemporary Israel.

Aviezer Golan's attempt to impose the Zionist representation of Jewish identity on the "heroes" of Operation Susannah obliterates the complex multivocality of Egyptian Jewish identities and histories. Both the Zionist vision of Jewish identity and the rearticulation of Egyptian identity in nationalist terms ultimately excluded Jews from membership in the Egyptian political community. Operation Susannah illustrates one of many instances in which Israel was actively complicit in that exclusion. Golan also shares the common Ashkenazi expectation that the Jews of the Middle East would abandon their identities and cultures in order to be absorbed into a more modern, dynamic Israel. Egyptian Jewish writing since Jacqueline Kahanoff contradicts this expectation and reveals the inadequacy of essentialist, state-centered discourse and conceptions of the nation and citizenship in both Egypt and Israel.

CHAPTER 3

Citizens, *Dhimmis,* and Subversives

If Arab blood is shed in Palestine, Jewish blood will
necessarily be shed elsewhere in the Arab world despite all
the sincere efforts of the governments concerned to prevent
such reprisals.[1]

> *Muhammad Husayn Haykal, Egyptian delegate*
> *to the United Nations (November 24, 1947)*

Soon after the outbreak of the 1948 Arab-Israeli War, the Israeli government and diaspora Jewish organizations such as the World Jewish
Congress, the American Jewish Committee, and B'nai B'rith began issuing alarming reports about the treatment of Jews in Egypt and elsewhere
in the Arab world.[2] They were outraged by internments, sequestrations
of property, physical attacks by urban crowds, and discriminatory measures directed against Jews. Jewish and Israeli spokespersons also objected when Egypt banned Zionist activity, which had been legal until
1948, suggesting that it was an inalienable human right of Jews to engage in political activity on behalf of a state at war with Egypt.

These public condemnations of violations of Jewish rights were framed
by the secular-liberal discourse of citizenship and rights that developed
in Europe between the Enlightenment and the French Revolution. They
assumed, or affected to assume, that Jewish life in Egypt could and should
remain uninfluenced by the Arab-Israeli conflict. According to the principle that the nation-state represents all its citizens who share equal rights
and obligations, it was unjust to mark Jews for discriminatory treatment.

The Zionist project justified itself in terms of the same post-
Enlightenment discourse of citizenship and rights. But Zionist discourse
also drew on illiberal, organicist conceptions of the nation because it did
not seek to represent actually existing Jews, but the "new Jewish man"
(often defined in explicitly masculine terms) who would be created in the
Jewish state. Israel's treatment of its own minority population was no
better, and arguably worse, than Egypt's treatment of its Jews from 1948

to 1956. Most of the Palestinian Arab citizens of Israel were subjected to a military government until 1965, and their lands were subjected to large-scale expropriations for development projects such as "Judaizing the Galilee." Arab citizens were denied membership in Israel's leading trade union (the Histadrut) and consequently often employment as well, in accord with the labor Zionist principle of Jewish labor ('avodah 'ivrit).[3] Thus the Zionists who called Egypt and other Arab states to task for failing to apply consistently liberal principles in the treatment of their Jewish residents were also inconsistent in their own ideology and practices. International public opinion generally failed to note this incongruity because after World War II, denial of Jewish rights was widely recognized as a crime against humanity and a symptom of fascist politics, while denial of Palestinian Arab rights, when it was acknowledged at all, was typically regarded as an accidental and inconsequential side effect of making the desert bloom.

Zionist criticism of Egypt's treatment of its Jewish population had multiple purposes. It was an expression of concern for the fate of fellow Jews; it was a propaganda weapon in the conflict with Israel's Arab adversaries; and it was a demonstration of the correctness of the Zionist solution to "the Jewish problem." The catalogs of violations of Jewish rights compiled by Israel and Jewish organizations certainly contain a measure of truth, but they are fundamentally flawed as characterizations of the circumstances of Jewish life in Egypt. Informed by a neolachrymose fatalism about diasporic Jewish life and exaggerated fears of an imminent recurrence of Nazi-style persecution, they rarely provide the historical and political context necessary to judge the import and seriousness of violations of Jewish rights.

Anti-Semitic sentiment and action in Egypt are distinctly twentieth-century phenomena that became factors of public consequence because of the exacerbation of the Arab-Zionist conflict in Palestine and sympathy for Italy and Germany in certain political circles (especially the officer corps) whose members understood fascism primarily as a challenge to British imperialism. From the late 1930s on, anti-Zionism and anti-Semitism were increasingly indiscriminately commingled. But not all political tendencies were equally culpable. Anti-Semitism was concentrated in political groups with an Islamist or ultranationalist orientation, most notably the Society of Muslim Brothers and Young Egypt. In contrast, many politically influential Egyptians, including most supporters of the Wafd and its major rival, the Liberal Constitutionalist Party, continued to endorse secular-liberal conceptions of the national community.

No discussion of the status of the Jews in Egypt after 1948 can be convincing without acknowledging that from 1948 to 1979 Israel and Egypt were in a state of war. It is simply not credible to assert that Egypt's invasion of Israel on May 15, 1948, was motivated by anti-Semitic malice. The strife between Egypt and Israel was part of a regional political and military conflict that grew out of the clash between Zionist settlers and indigenous Palestinian Arabs over the land and the labor markets of Palestine/Eretz Israel.[4] In the course of the conflict, both camps engaged in racist denigration of the other side, a common aspect of the propaganda of twentieth-century warfare. Egyptian Jews were contradictorily interpellated by their status as citizens or noncitizen permanent residents (legally defined as "local subjects" without citizenship), their status in Islamic civilization as *dhimmis* (*ahl al-dhimma*—a "protected" people possessing a recognized holy book), and the real or imagined security threat they posed to the Egyptian state. Ultimately, the pressures of war, defeat, and scandals that discredited the entire regime rendered Jews a convenient other against whom Egypt's postcolonial political culture was defined.

The epigraph of this chapter is excerpted from the speech delivered by the Egyptian delegate to the United Nations General Assembly days before that body voted to partition Palestine into an Arab state and a Jewish state. As a leading member of the Liberal Constitutionalist Party, Muhammad Husayn Haykal could credibly present himself as a secular nationalist who regarded the Jewish citizens of Egypt as full members of the national community. Even in the midst of the 1936–39 Palestinian Arab Revolt, his party's weekly magazine had insisted on distinguishing between the Zionist settlers in Palestine and the Jews of Egypt. *Al-Siyasa al-'usbu'iyya* (The political weekly) defended the loyalty of Egyptian Jews and affirmed their solidarity with the rest of the Egyptian public on the Palestine question.[5] Nonetheless, Haykal correctly predicted that the Arab-Zionist conflict over Palestine would inexorably involve the Jews residing elsewhere in the Arab world. In contrast to the Jewish and Israeli tendency to deny the relationship between the Arab-Zionist conflict and the fate of the Jews of the Arab world, Haykal acknowledged that connection and adduced it as an argument against the partition of Palestine.

Haykal's statement of concern for the welfare of the Jews of the Arab world was also a veiled threat. Pointing to their vulnerability constituted an admission that the security and status of Jews were conditional and could be adversely affected by factors unrelated to their loyalty to the countries where they resided. If the physical security and welfare of a certain category of residents of Egypt could be threatened because of political developments in a neighboring country over which they had no control (and that many of them opposed), then they were obviously marked by a difference that conferred a status inferior to those not so threatened. Thus, Haykal inadvertently revealed that the government's official proclamations that Egypt did not discriminate against its Jews were as inadequate as the Zionist litany of horrors in characterizing the conditions of Jewish life in Egypt after 1948.

In effect, the Jews of Egypt were held hostage pending the outcome of the Arab-Israeli conflict. Both the Egyptian and the Israeli governments collaborated in this hostage taking, which served their disparate interests. While minorities within the Jewish community embraced the official perspectives of the Egyptian or the Israeli government on the Arab-Zionist conflict and its implications for them, most struggled to preserve a social space that would allow them to maintain both their emotional, political, and economic attachments to Egypt and their Jewish identities, even as that space was radically constricted by the course of the Arab-Israeli conflict and the process of decolonization in Egypt.

THE ARAB-ISRAELI CONFLICT AND THE JEWS OF EGYPT

Before the 1936–39 Arab Revolt in Palestine, the dominant current among literate Egyptians regarded Egyptian Jews as full members of the nation.[6] Secularist political commentary carefully distinguished between Judaism and Zionism. The sharp Arab-Jewish clash over the Wailing Wall/*Haram al-Sharif* in Jerusalem in 1929 seemed to legitimize the representation of the Arab-Zionist conflict as a Muslim-Jewish religious dispute and to undermine secularist conceptions of the Egyptian polity. In response to Egyptians who began to portray the conflict in religious terms and who indiscriminately associated the Jews of Egypt with the Zionists in Palestine, *al-Ahram* editorially reaffirmed the secular basis of Egyptian nationalism by evoking the slogan of the 1919 nationalist uprising— "Egyptians above All: Religion is for God and the Homeland is for All."[7]

The Society of Muslim Brothers promoted the Palestinian cause during the Arab Revolt and thereby established itself as a major force in the Egyptian political arena. The Society organized volunteers and material aid to support the armed struggle and conducted a propaganda campaign embracing Palestine as a Muslim and Arab cause. As a means of exerting pressure on Zionist policy in Palestine, the Muslim Brothers called for a boycott of Egyptian Jewish merchants, most of whom were not Zionists—an expression of the organization's unwillingness to distinguish Jews from Zionists.

During the Arab Revolt, the Islamist, pan-Arab, and national chauvinist press in Egypt began publishing attacks on Jews, not only Zionists, repeating some of the same anti-Semitic stereotypes then circulating in Europe. The pan-Arab journal *al-Rabita al-'Arabiyya* (most of whose contributors were not Egyptians) complained about Jewish economic domination of Egypt, as did the press of the fascist-style Young Egypt organization. In declaring a boycott of Jewish stores as part of its "buy Egyptian" campaign, Young Egypt affirmed that it did not regard Jews as "real Egyptians." Supporters of Young Egypt were also arrested for engaging in anti-Jewish propaganda and attempting to bomb Jewish neighborhoods. From 1936 until the end of the monarchy, it was primarily the Islamist, national chauvinist, and pan-Arab political currents opposed to both the Wafdist and the Sa'dist governments that ruled from 1936 to 1937 and 1942 to 1952 that emphasized the Palestine question as an issue in Egyptian politics.

The first indication that there might be a popular base in Egypt for militant anti-Zionism spilling over into anti-Semitism was the anti-Jewish rioting of November 2–3, 1945. In mid-October the Front of Arab and Islamic Associations, including Young Egypt, the Muslim Brothers, and the Young Men's Muslim Association, called for demonstrations and a general strike on the anniversary of the issuance of the Balfour Declaration, a traditional Arab day of protest against Zionism.[8] On November 2, thousands of people marched to 'Abdin Square in Cairo, where they were addressed by the supreme guide of the Muslim Bothers, Hasan al-Banna. Following the rally, some demonstrators entered the Jewish quarter and attacked bystanders, shops, and synagogues. The rioting continued the next day and spread to the modern European sections of Cairo and to Alexandria, where its main victims were non-Jews. Six people were killed, several hundred were injured, and dozens of Jewish-, Coptic-, and Muslim-owned stores were looted. The most serious incident was the burning of the Ashkenazi synagogue in Cairo's Muski quarter. If we believe that there is a logic to the collective action of crowds, the selection of this target suggests that the most vulnerable Jews were those most closely identified with Europe. This conclusion is strengthened by the prominence of Greek casualties in Alexandria.

Prime Minister al-Nuqrashi, King Faruq, and the secretary general of the newly formed League of Arab States, 'Abd al-Rahman 'Azzam Pasha,

all denounced the violence against Egyptian Jews. The king invited Chief
Rabbi Haim Nahum for an audience, and the prime minister visited some
of the riot sites. Most of the Egyptian press also condemned the riots.
Egypt's leading political figures opposed the assaults on Jews largely out
of fear that such attacks might destabilize the regime and strengthen their
political opponents. Such self-interested motives are often more reliable
in political life than pious statements of principle. But political self-
interest is also subject to recalculation in changing circumstances.

The riots of November 2–3, 1945, highlighted the vulnerability of the
Jewish community to the consequences of the conflict over Palestine. The
riots represented the first occasion in modern Egyptian history that Jews
were collectively threatened by physical violence and marked the growing strength of political forces unwilling to regard Jews as full members
of the Egyptian nation under any circumstances. However, the riots did
not initiate a period of unremitting, escalating hostility toward Jews in
Egypt. Moreover, even at this bleak moment, there were Muslims and
Copts who acted collectively and risked their own safety to defend Jews
and uphold the principle of a secular national polity. According to Rif'at
al-Sa'id, all the members of the Democratic Movement for National Liberation (HADETU) in his hometown of Mansura stood guard in front
of a Jewish-owned store to protect it from harm by local demonstrators.[9]
This quasi-legal Marxist organization so strongly insisted on the principle of maintaining a sharp distinction between Jews and Zionists and
between citizen and noncitizen Jews that HADETU members in Mansura
were willing to compromise their own personal security by participating in a public demonstration that allowed the police to inventory the
entire local membership.

After the riots of November 2–3, 1945, Chief Rabbi Nahum wrote to
Prime Minister al-Nuqrashi on behalf of both Zionist and non-Zionist
Jewish leaders protesting the violence against the Jewish community. His
letter complained about the desecration of the Ashkenazi synagogue with
special vehemence. But even as Rabbi Nahum articulated the grievances
of the Jewish community and requested protection by the state authorities, he validated the official Egyptian discourse on Egyptian-Jewish relations by affirming that the Jewish community had been enjoying equal
rights and asserting (incorrectly) that there had not been a synagogue
desecration in Egypt since the advent of Islam.[10]

Many Egyptian Jews believed that because they had been enjoying
high status, substantial economic power, and full religious freedom, they
could serve as mediators in the Arab-Zionist conflict. Responding to a

lecture on Arab-Jewish relations delivered at the Alexandria Jewish
Community Center by Taha Husayn in November 1943, Maurice Fargeon, an acknowledged Zionist, wrote,

> We have always hoped that a movement of Jewish-Arab rapprochement
> would be initiated by the Jews of Egypt. By their geographical position, the
> Jews of this country are particularly well-placed to serve as a connecting link
> between these two vital branches of the human family tree, Islam and Ju-
> daism. Jews and Arabs are brothers not only historically, but demographi-
> cally. In fact, the Jews are Arabs.[11]

After the UN partition plan was adopted and Arab-Jewish fighting
broke out in Palestine, a delegation of Egyptian Jews travelled to the
United States on a reconciliation mission to promote an Arab-Jewish
compromise.[12] According to Maurice Mizrahi, this mission was blessed
by Prime Minister al-Nuqrashi.[13] Believing that such efforts would only
serve Arab objectives, American Zionist leaders repudiated this initiative. The details of this affair are unclear. It is unlikely that al-Nuqrashi
was seriously committed to this mission and even less likely that Zionist leaders in Palestine would have been prepared to compromise their
objective of immediately establishing a Jewish state in order not to endanger the Jews of Egypt. Some Zionist leaders insinuated that this intervention by Egyptian Jewish leaders was motivated by their selfish desire to preserve their status and privileges. Another way of expressing
the same point would be that many Egyptian Jews did not believe that
establishing a Jewish state in Palestine was in their interest if it entailed
an all-out conflict with the entire Arab world.

THE 1948 ARAB-ISRAELI WAR

On May 15, 1948, the British departed Palestine, and Egypt invaded the
country along with four other Arab armies in an effort to thwart the
UN partition plan. Prime Minster al-Nuqrashi seized the opportunity to
repress his internal opposition by imposing martial law. Zionism became illegal, and all the Zionist emissaries from Palestine left Egypt.
The organizations they led disbanded or went underground. The Jewish
community was pressured by the government and public opinion to
distance itself from Zionism. Several individuals made public statements denouncing Zionism, and it seems reasonable to presume that in
at least some cases they were subjected to direct or indirect coercion.[14]
    War with Israel made the status of Egyptian Jews an urgent public
question. The resolution of this question proposed by secular-liberal po-

litical theory was overwhelmed by perceived security considerations and the cessation of open, reasoned debate so commonly associated with war. The al-Nuqrashi government lacked the courage, vision, and popular mandate that would have been required to articulate a bold and principled stand. Lacking firm guidance, state officials reflexively tended to protect themselves from responsibility by adopting the most conservative, heavy-handed, and security-minded approach.

Egyptian Jews were also confused. The combination of martial law, fear, and the loss of most of the community's public organs make it difficult to trace the currents of Jewish opinion. But considerable evidence challenges the common assumption in Zionist and some Egyptian nationalist and Islamist historiography that following the outbreak of the Arab-Israeli War, the main subject of discussion among the Jews of Egypt was how and when to leave for Israel.

Within days after the outbreak of war, some 1,300 political opponents of the government from across the political spectrum were rounded up and sent to internment camps. They included 300 Zionist Jews and a roughly equal number of Jewish communists. There are many discrepancies in the reports of the total number of Jews detained, and accounts do not always distinguish between Zionists and communists. The maximum number of Jewish detainees at any one time was probably about 700–800.[15] The British ambassador reported that 554 Jews were interned at the end of June 1948, when some of the original prisoners had already been released.[16] Hostilities ceased in January 1949, but in July, 250 Zionists and 60 Jewish communists remained interned in Huckstep (160), Abu Qir (110), and al-Tur (40).[17]

To establish a sense of proportion without in any way justifying the practice of detaining people without trial, the internment of about 1 percent of the Jewish community by the Egyptian government during its war with Israel can be compared to the practice of the U.S. government a few years earlier. In 1942, the Western Defense Command ordered the internment of all of the 110,000 Japanese Americans residing on the West Coast. Even the families of those who served in the U.S armed forces remained interned for the duration of the war.

A martial law decree issued in late May 1948 authorized Egyptian state authorities to place under "administration" the property of anyone interned or under security surveillance. By January 1949, the property of about seventy Jewish individuals and firms was under state supervision.[18] Included were many of the Jewish-owned department stores in downtown Cairo and Alexandria (Adès, Chemla, and Gattegno) and

other well-known businesses with a high public profile (La Société
d'Avances Commerciales, J. H. Perez & Co., Peltours, S.A.E.). Many of
the businessmen whose assets were seized had been active Zionists and
could perhaps legitimately be considered security risks (Aharon Kras-
novsky, Emilio Levy, Marcel Messiqua, Roger Oppenheim). However,
the Egyptian state apparatus failed to make certain distinctions critical
to secular-liberal norms. For example, the members of the Perez family
were not political Zionists, but the assets of J. H. Perez & Co. were
nonetheless placed under administration, perhaps because they were major investors in Palestine Hotels Ltd., whose holdings included the King
David Hotel in Jerusalem.[19] A substantial quantity of property was
placed under administration, though this was very far from a wholesale
seizure of Jewish assets. The largest Jewish banks, insurance companies,
stock brokerages, and cotton export firms were not affected because
most of the wealthiest Jewish business families kept their distance from
Zionism.

During the summer and fall of 1948, Jews and their property were attacked repeatedly. On June 20, 1948, a bomb exploded in the Karaite
quarter of Cairo, killing twenty-two Jews and wounding forty-one. Several buildings were severely damaged.[20] The Egyptian authorities un-
convincingly blamed the explosion on fireworks stored in Jewish homes
and antagonism between Karaite and Rabbanite Jews. *Al-Ahram* reported that the police and firemen reacted to the fire quickly and effectively. But Jewish witnesses on the scene testified that the response of the
authorities was sluggish and negligent.[21] Reports and commentary on
the incident in *al-Kalim* were heavily censored. The editors left blank
spaces in articles in several issues following the bombing to protest the
government's handling of the incident and the censorship.[22]

On July 15, Israeli planes bombed a residential neighborhood near
the Qubba Palace in Cairo, killing many civilians and destroying many
homes. The attack took place during the Ramadan *iftar* (break-fast
meal), which undoubtedly amplified the anger of the victims, who began an angry march on the Jewish quarter.[23] On July 17, the Egyptian
authorities reported a second Israeli bombing attack. But there was no
actual attack. Volleys of antiaircraft fire were discharged, perhaps to
compensate for the army's failure to mount a defense against the previous bombing raid. In the tense atmosphere following one actual and a
second alleged Israeli bombing raid on Cairo, the Cicurel and Oreco department stores located on the fashionable Fu'ad al-Awwal (now 26th
of July) Street were bombed on July 19. This was followed by bombings

of the Adès and Gattegno department stores on July 28 and August 1. On September 22, an explosion in the Rabbanite Jewish quarter in Cairo killed nineteen and wounded sixty-two victims. The last of the attacks against the Jews of Cairo was the destruction of the premises of the Société Orientale de Publicité, a large publishing and advertising firm that continued to operate during the war, by a bomb on November 12.[24]

The government's response to these bombing attacks was inept and disingenuous, not because the authorities actually encouraged assaults on Jews, but because they were frightened by the apparent strength of the Society of Muslim Brothers. In mid-1948, the government became convinced that the Brothers were preparing an armed insurrection, and many members of the society were interned after the proclamation of martial law in May. On December 8, 1948, Prime Minister al-Nuqrashi officially dissolved the Society, and the state sequestered its considerable assets. In a 1950 trial, members of the Society were charged with carrying out all the bombings against the Jews of Cairo from June to November 1948. The prosecution argued that the bombings were part of a strategy to exploit the issue of Palestine to destabilize and undermine the regime.[25]

Vigorously defending the Jewish community of Cairo against the attacks of the Muslim Brothers during a war with Israel would have risked increasing the unpopularity of a government that was already illegitimate because the 1944 elections had been rigged to exclude the Wafd from power. For Prime Minister al-Nuqrashi, sacrificing the security of the Jewish community was a small consideration compared to maintaining power. Moreover, because of the strength of the Muslim Brothers, the government may not have had the capacity to deter these attacks. In retaliation against the government's dissolution of the society, a member of the Muslim Brothers assassinated al-Nuqrashi on December 28. Unsure of its ability to obtain a speedy legal resolution that would deter the Brothers from further violence, the government arranged the assassination of Hasan al-Banna.[26] The Egyptian government correctly assessed the seriousness of the challenge posed by the Muslim Brothers and lacked confidence in its capacity to counter it. The Jewish community found itself positioned between two contending forces, neither one of which regarded its interests or its security as a priority.

The government claimed to be acting only against Zionists, but the import of its actions was complicated by the fact that the Egyptian communist organizations had endorsed the partition of Palestine into an Arab and a Jewish state. On several occasions Prime Minister al-Nuqrashi lectured the British ambassador, Sir Ronald Campbell, and other British officials on his belief that all "Jews were potential Zionists, but that anyhow all Zionists were communists, and he looked at the matter as much from the point of view of communism as from the point of view of Zionism."[27]

Al-Nuqrashi apparently believed this nonsense. His personal anti-Semitism and political ineptitude may be a good part of the explanation for the government's disingenuous proclamations, inconsistent and excessive security measures, and failure to physically protect the Jews of Egypt in 1948. Other factors would include the government's poor intelligence, political confusion, and weak executive capacity. The cosmopolitan style of al-Nuqrashi's successor, Ibrahim 'Abd al-Hadi, reassured the Jewish community, and there were no violent incidents directed at Jews for several years after he assumed office.[28]

The detentions and property sequestrations of 1948 were erratic. Some notable Zionist leaders, like Léon Castro, were not arrested. Others were interned months after the war began. The wealthy fruit and vegetable exporter, Isaac Vaena, was interned though he was not a Zionist.[29] The inconsistency of the Egyptian government's actions encouraged multiple interpretations of their import. The detentions and sequestrations were a substantial threat to the security of the Jewish community. But their relatively modest scale and the fact that a few Zionists escaped them altogether encouraged some Jews to believe that their future in Egypt might resemble the comfortable and privileged lives many of them had led for the past several generations.

EMIGRATION/'ALIYAH

The 1948 Arab-Israeli War and its consequences made emigration to Israel a popular option in the Egyptian Jewish community for the first time. According to the Jewish Agency, 16,514 Jews left Egypt for Israel between 1948 and 1951.[30] The overwhelming majority of the departures were concentrated in 1949 and 1950. In addition, some 6,000 Jews emigrated to destinations other than Israel during these years. Among those were Jewish communists who were expelled from Egypt or voluntarily emigrated to France (small numbers went to Italy and England as well).

Emigration declined after the Wafd returned to power in January 1950 because many Egyptians, not only Jews, regarded rule by the only party with a substantial popular base as a sign of normalcy. From 1952 to 1956, 4,918 Jews left Egypt for Israel, while perhaps 5,000 others embarked for destinations in Europe, North America, and South America.[31] Approximately 50,000 Jews remained in Egypt on the eve of the 1956 Suez/Sinai War.[32]

Sephardim tended to remain in Egypt for longer than Ashkenazim. According to research carried out by the World Jewish Congress, there were 68,000 Jews in Egypt in 1950—65,000 Sephardim and 3,000 Ashkenazim. By 1954, the World Jewish Congress counted 45,000 Jews—44,900 Sephardim and 100 Ashkenazim.[33] Perhaps the Ashkenazim took the sacking of their synagogue in 1948 as a sign of imminent danger. Ashkenazim were also more likely to have connections in Israel or outside the Middle East. Alsatians who came to Egypt when their homeland was annexed to Germany or Russians who fled pogroms commonly had relatives in Western Europe or North America. Sephardim, especially the largely Sephardi business elite, were typically more rooted in Egypt and were more reluctant to leave. The World Jewish Congress study does not include the Karaites, whose numbers should be added to its estimate of the total number of Jews in Egypt in the early 1950s. There are no reliable statistics for the Karaites, but my estimate is that at least 60 percent of the roughly 5,000-member community remained in Egypt until 1956, and over 20 percent remained until the early 1960s. These figures suggest that Jews who were more assimilated to Arabo-Egyptian culture tended to remain in Egypt longer.

There are no accurate figures indicating how many Jews emigrated to destinations other than Israel or their social characteristics. In general, except for the minority of committed Zionists, poorer families tended to go to Israel and wealthier families tended to go elsewhere. Youth were more inclined to emigrate than the older members of the community.

From the point of view of Zionist historiography, the most important theme of the period 1948–56 is the heroism of the local Zionist activists and the Israeli agents in organizing 'aliyah from Egypt.[34] The central debates revolve around the relations among rival factions of the Zionist movement, whether the local activists or the emissaries from Israel deserve the most credit for organizing the 'aliyah, and whether or not there could have been a greater number of 'olim (immigrants) if the Zionist authorities had acted more wisely. Such accounts typically feature the daring exploits of individual Zionist leaders and the ineptitude, corruption, or indifference of Egyptian officials who contributed to the success of the 'aliyah effort. Some Egyptian Zionist activists claim that the quotas imposed on Jewish immigration from Egypt by the Jewish

Agency in Jerusalem in June 1950 hindered their efforts and radically reduced the number of 'olim, and they hint that these quotas were imposed for racist reasons.[35]

Zionist discourse presumed that Jewish life in Egypt was over and that Jews who did not understand this were victims of false consciousness or otherwise misguided. One Jewish Agency official responsible for supervising 'aliyah organizing in Egypt explained that Jews were "afraid to take the opportunity for 'aliyah" despite all that had happened in 1948.[36] But most of the Jews who remained in Egypt after 1950 were not sitting on their suitcases waiting for an opportunity to leave. Rather, they were struggling to maintain their multiple identities and to resist the monism of the increasingly obdurate Zionist and Egyptian nationalist discourses even as the social space in which it was possible to do so was gradually constricting.

STATUS AMBIGUITIES

This constriction of social space was most evident in the formal and public articulation of the relationship between the Egyptian state and Jewish residents. In November 1949, an article in al-Kalim, the only Jewish communal periodical still publishing, protested that Jews born in Egypt, even some whose families had resided continually in the country for 500 years, had difficulty establishing their citizenship and obtaining passports.[37] Similar grievances had been voiced in the Jewish community since the late 1930s, and they seem credible.

Nonetheless, the Karaite community continued to take every opportunity to demonstrate loyalty to Egypt and its political order. Much of the issue of al-Kalim for May 16, 1951, was devoted to celebrating the wedding of King Faruq and Narriman Sadiq. The Egyptian public was by then disgusted by Faruq's dissolute public behavior and looked askance at his second marriage because his first wife, Queen Farida, had been quite popular. Al-Kalim avoided any hint of these unpleasant topics and printed a qasida by Murad Farag and colloquial azgal by two other poets composed for the occasion. This demonstrative celebration of the royal wedding may have been a reflexive and preemptive gesture to stave off accusations of disloyalty or an expression of the traditionally warm relationship between the royal palace and elite Jews. But the ability of the small Karaite community to produce individuals capable of composing publishable poetry in both standard and colloquial Arabic was, in and of itself, an expression of cultural affinity with Egypt.

Functionaries of the state apparatus routinely abused citizens and extorted bribes for rendering ordinary services. Some Jews believed that their ambiguous status exposed them to more frequent victimization than non-Jews. Reports of Jews obtaining official documents or transacting business with the state apparatus by paying bribes are common.

To the extent that the state apparatus did discriminate against Jews in these ways, the practice was regarded critically in at least some influential non-Jewish circles. In 1951, an officer of the political police (*al-qalam al-siyasi*) stopped Césare Slamun, a wealthy businessman, on a main street in downtown Cairo, intending to arrest him. Slamun tried to convince the officer to release him by arguing that "It was true that he was a Jew, but he was an Egyptian above all and his arrest would harm him and his business."[38] After paying a bribe of £ E 200, a huge sum at that time, Slamun was released. When even a wealthy Jew who considered himself "an Egyptian above all" was exposed to arbitrary harassment and extortion, the weekly *al-Musawwar* critically reported this incident, along with several other short items satirizing the political police. *Al-Musawwar*'s editor, Fikri Abaza, was a wealthy, cosmopolitan Muslim into whose family at least one Jew had married.

Césare Slamun asserted that his status as an individual Egyptian citizen of substantial wealth who was contributing to the development of the national economy ought to protect him from arbitrary treatment by the police—a valid argument according to the prevailing understanding of secular-liberal nationalism. But the 1948 war accelerated the decline of secular-liberalism in Egypt and enhanced the tendency to regard Jews as a corporate group of suspect status collectively responsible for their good behavior. Simultaneously, Egyptian state officials, conscious of international criticism of the treatment of Jews in the Arab world, sought to project themselves as responsible and mature—in Euro-American terms—and capable of protecting the welfare of the Jewish community.

Both the Jewish community and Egyptian state officials sometimes represented their relationship as one that might be termed neo-*dhimma*—a concept that emphasized mutual obligation and equity, as opposed to civic rights and responsibilities. It drew on elements of the Islamic cultural repertoire for validation: the Qur'anic definition of Jews as *dhimmis* and the institutionalized form of Muslim-Jewish relations in the late Ottoman Empire, the millet system. This legacy provided Egyptians and Jews with a culturally authorized alternative to a discourse of rights and citizenship.

Of course, I do not mean to suggest that Muslim-Jewish relations in post-1948 Egypt simply reproduced a timeless Islamic model. The textually based classical model was always already inflected by local histories and particular circumstances that gave it a dynamic social history. Moreover, the discourse of neo-*dhimma* was intermittently deployed concurrently with the secular-liberal discourse of rights and citizenship, sometimes by the same people on different occasions. This generated hybrid practices that were easily destabilized by the state of war between Egypt and Israel and the consolidation of an authoritarian nationalist security state in Egypt after 1954.

Even in public discussion of relatively minor issues, the discourse of neo-*dhimma* suggested significant changes in the social position of Jews after 1948. For example, an article in *al-Ahram* criticized the Karaite neighborhood in Cairo for being unkempt and dirty, noting that this site was visited by tourists wishing to see the old Torah scroll in the Dar Simha synagogue. The author called on the authorities to clean up the Karaite quarter to preserve the honor of the Egyptian state.[39] *Harat al-yahud al-qara'in* was adjacent to the Muslim quarters of the Muski, the Khan al-Khalili, and Bayn al-Qasrayn, which were also in disrepair and even more frequently visited by tourists. *Al-Ahram*'s reporter apparently did not consider their condition dishonorable to the Egyptian state. The problem seems to have been that the state's honor could be impugned by failure to exercise good stewardship over a dependent population.

A very different tone informs articles in *al-Kalim* written by Karaites about their neighborhood before the 1948 war.[40] They proposed that the Karaite communal council approach the public works department and request paving of the streets, installation of street lights, and other improvements, or they suggested that the Karaite residents themselves carry out these improvements. The language of *al-Kalim* seems appropriate to citizens with a secure sense of rights, whereas the language of *al-Ahram* implies that the Karaite neighborhood and its residents were wards of the state, which should maintain proper appearances lest it be criticized by foreigners.

In the nineteenth and early twentieth centuries, the reputed inability of the Egyptian state to safeguard the welfare of non-Muslims was frequently adduced by European powers as an excuse for intervening in Egypt. Protection of minorities was one of the four points on which Great Britain reserved the right to intervene after declaring Egyptian independence in 1922. In this historical context, *al-Ahram*'s concern for the Karaite quarter might have been motivated primarily by a desire to avoid its condition becoming an excuse for foreign interference in Egypt's affairs.

Days after the Free Officers coup of July 23, 1952, in accord with the Talmudic precept that "The law of the kingdom is the law," Chief Rabbi Nahum sent a telegram to General Muhammad Naguib, the titular head of the new regime, affirming that "The Chief Rabbi and the Jewish communities in Egypt supported the revolution and asked God for its success."[41] Whatever Rabbi Nahum's political views, this statement was a pro forma, but nonetheless expected, gesture establishing correct relations between the Jewish community and the new regime. In offering it, Rabbi Nahum conducted himself exactly as the head of an Ottoman millet would have acted in delivering the allegiance of his community to a newly installed sultan. Because he had served as chief rabbi of Istanbul before coming to Egypt in 1924, this was certainly a familiar role for Nahum.[42]

A few days later, General Naguib responded in kind by issuing a statement on the importance of maintaining good relations with *ahl al-dhimma*.[43] Naguib's resort to the classical Islamic terminology suggests an attitude of benevolent paternalism toward the Jewish community and implies that he did not regard Jews as full and equal members of the Egyptian national polity. But Naguib extended himself far beyond formulaic statements in seeking to establish good relations with the Jewish community and unequivocally invoked the secular-liberal discourse of citizenship and rights. On Yom Kipur of 1952, Naguib visited the main synagogue of Cairo on 'Adli Street and met with Rabbi Nahum, the first and only courtesy visit by a head of state to a chief rabbi in modern Egyptian history.[44] Several days later, Karaite Chief Rabbi Babovitch and two leading members of the Karaite community, Lieto Barukh Mas'uda and Murad al-Qudsi (Mourad El-Kodsi), called on General Naguib in his office. Mas'uda affirmed the Karaites' Egyptian identity, and after a friendly discussion Naguib agreed to pay a return visit to the Karaite community.[45] On October 25, Naguib visited the Karaite synagogue in 'Abbasiyya and signed the guest register with a salutation declaring, "There is no difference between Jews, Muslims, or Christians. Religion is for God. The nation is for all." Murad Farag composed a poem to mark the occasion of the official visit.[46]

Naguib may not have noticed the contradiction between his reference to non-Muslims as *ahl al-dhimma* and his use of the secularist slogan of the 1919 revolution. As a Muslim Egyptian, he could easily commingle the terminology of different discourses because in either case his own status as an authentic Egyptian was secure. The Karaite community may also not have noticed the incongruence of the two references because, as noted in Chapter 2, its own self-conception was articulated through a hybrid discourse invoking both citizenship in the Egyptian nation and the older norms of the Ottoman millet system.

Despite their republican rhetoric, the Free Officers commonly continued to treat Jews as a corporate group and to consider the state responsible for maintaining the customary rights of the Jewish community. Individual Jews and the official leadership of the community acted within the boundaries defined by these expectations. For example, a March 1953 fire in the kosher oven in *harat al-yahud* operated by the Cairo Sephardi Jewish community destroyed most of the matzahs prepared for the upcoming Passover holiday. Chief Rabbi Nahum wrote to the minister of supply requesting special permission to import 20,000 kilograms of Australian or Canadian flour so that new matzahs could be baked. After some negotiation over the precise quantity of flour to be imported, the government allocated enough flour to remake the matzahs.[47] Even though the Egyptian state was formally defined in secular terms, the obligation of Muslim rulers to respect Christianity and Judaism as religious cultures was so deeply ingrained in Egyptian society that it would have been perceived as an illegitimate act to obstruct *dhimmis* from performing their religious duties. Because food imports were regulated by the Egyptian state, Rabbi Nahum had to petition the authorities for an exception to the regulations to allow the Jewish community to practice its religious obligations. In so doing, he reinforced the relationship of neo-*dhimma*.

If a similar incident had occurred in the United States or France, Jews would never have involved these secular states in facilitating the observance of their religious obligations. The Jewish community would have relied on itself and launched a fund-raising campaign to make up the losses. The issue of receiving permission to import flour would not have been a factor because metropolitan capitalist economies typically operated under more liberal trade regimes than countries pursuing state-led development strategies.

Expressing a similar conception of the appropriate obligations of public authorities toward recognized religious communities, the presidents of the Cairo and Alexandria Jewish communities, Salvator Cicurel and Edwin Goar, wrote to the governor of the National Bank of Egypt reminding him that the religious festivals of the Christian and Jewish communities had traditionally been observed as bank holidays.[48] The observance of Jewish holidays had been discontinued during the 1948 Arab-Israeli War. After the war, several banks informally permitted Jewish employees to take these days off. Cicurel and Goar appealed to the head of the leading bank in the county, which employed a significant number of Jews, including some in senior positions, to take the initiative in reinstituting the practice of closing the bank on the Jewish high holidays, as was the practice on Eastern and Western Christmas.

This request was informed by the structure of the political economy of Egypt during the colonial era and the blend of cosmopolitan, nationalist, and Islamist discourses of the period. Jews, other *mutamassir* minorities, and foreigners established most of Egypt's modern banking, insurance, stock brokerage, and mortgage companies and remained disproportionately prominent in the financial sector of the economy until the 1956 war. Some nationalists regarded this as an expression of the continuing domination of Egypt by European capital. Others regarded the economic activities of the Jews as a contribution to the development of the national economy. Public observance of Jewish holidays in an overwhelmingly Muslim country was a manifestation of colonial privilege. But it could also be justified as a beneficent accommodation of the religious needs of *dhimmis* by a Muslim society, an explanation that avoided confronting any discomfort some Egyptian Muslims might have felt as a consequence of adopting non-Muslim customs.

Similarly, on the eve of the 1953 high holidays, Chief Rabbi Nahum wrote to the commander of the Cairo police force and to the director-general of the Ministry of War informing them of the dates of the high holidays and asking them to give all the Jews in the police and the armed forces vacations on Rosh ha-Shanah and Yom Kipur. A similar letter was sent to the director-general of the prison administration requesting that Jewish prisoners be freed from labor on the holidays.[49] In fact, the overwhelming majority of Jews in prison were nonobservant communists. No Jews served in the police force and the armed services—a social distinction that distanced the Jewish community from the Egyptian state and the new conception of political community promoted by the Free Officers. But Rabbi Nahum, who was certainly aware of these circumstances, seems to have felt that it was important to preserve the principle that the state was obliged to respect the practices of recognized religious minorities.

Although the Islamic concept of *dhimma* acknowledged an obligation to treat Jews equitably, there was always a possibility that militant, revivalist interpretations of Islam could be used to attack Jews as

nonbelievers, betrayers of the prophet Muhammad, usurers, and so
forth. In February 1953, the minister of pious endowments (*awqaf*),
Shaykh Ahmad Hasan al-Baquri, gave a talk on the state radio, subsequently reported in the press, on "The Influence of Religion in the Formation of a Proper Citizen." The shaykh acknowledged that Judaism
was a valid religion, but went on to say that today Judaism was no longer
a religion and had become a racist ideology like Nazism, which should
be destroyed by the free peoples of the world. He referred to Jews as
swine, a particularly egregious insult in both Muslim and Jewish terms.[50]

Rabbi Nahum wrote to General Naguib and pointed out that the minister's words contradicted Naguib's own policy statements on the status
of Jews in Egypt. Nahum reaffirmed that the Jews of Egypt were faithful to their religion and loyal citizens of the state. He asked Naguib, as
president of the republic, to reassure the Jewish community.[51] In response, Naguib demanded that Shaykh al-Baquri make a formal apology to Rabbi Nahum. When al-Baquri proposed to express his regrets
by telephone, Naguib insisted that al-Baquri visit Rabbi Nahum at his
home and deliver a proper face-to-face apology.[52] General Naguib, whatever his motives and his conceptual framework, seems to have been committed to preserving correct relations between the Jewish community and
the Egyptian state.

In March 1954, supporters of Naguib and Abdel Nasser clashed over
the question of restoring democracy or maintaining military rule. Abdel
Nasser won a convincing victory, and the army remained in power.
Naguib and the political groups supporting him—the Wafd, the Muslim
Brothers, and the communists—were suppressed and removed from the
political arena. After a member of the Society of Muslim Brothers
attempted to assassinate Abdel Nasser in October 1954, the regime intensified its repression of the organized opposition forces. By late 1954,
the regime was beginning to embrace pan-Arab nationalism, which was
associated with a more hostile stand toward Israel and Zionism and, potentially, toward the Jews of Egypt.

Just as the power struggle between Naguib and Abdel Nasser was un-
folding, Shaykh Ahmad Tahir, speaking on a religious program on the
state radio, gravely insulted the Jews of Egypt, claiming that all Jews
were middlemen and usurers without honor or morality. Albert Mizrahi
reported this affront in his newspaper, *al-Tas'ira* (The price list), and argued that such "nonsense" would be used against Egypt by its enemies
and was inconsistent with the government's objectives. He noted that
one of the Jewish families directly offended by Shaykh Tahir had historic

roots in Egypt no less substantial than the shaykh's. Mizrahi demanded that Salah Salim, as the minister of national guidance and the authority ultimately responsible for the state radio, rebuke the shaykh, invoking the slogan, "Religion is for God and the nation is for all."[53]

Interest in this incident was apparently overwhelmed by the struggle between Naguib and Abdel Nasser, which reached its climax several days after Mizrahi's intervention. Although the state apparently did not intervene in this case, as Naguib had earlier in the incident of Shaykh al-Baquri's broadcast slur against the Jews, it is still remarkable that a Jewish newspaper editor identified with the Wafd, which was an opponent of the Free Officers' regime, was willing to demand publicly that a government minister intervene to protect the reputation and status of Egyptian Jews. Albert Mizrahi seemed confident that he was acting within his rights and that his demand was legitimate according to prevailing norms.

Jewish confidence in the government's interest in preserving Jewish rights seems to have diminished after Abdel Nasser established his unchallenged supremacy and Naguib was removed from power. Nonetheless, the state continued to affirm that it recognized the Jews as a legitimate religious community, and it acknowledged its obligation to facilitate their observance of their religious obligations. On Yom Kipur 1955, the state radio went so far as to broadcast the Kol Nidrei service.[54]

THE JEWISH PRESENCE

After May 15, 1948, the public Jewish presence in Egypt diminished, even in matters unconnected to Zionism and Israel. All the Jewish community newspapers except the Karaites' *al-Kalim* ceased publication; the royal court refrained from acknowledging its many connections with elite Jews; and the annual public celebration of Purim in Cairo's Ezbekiyya Gardens ceased.[55] Nonetheless, by the end of 1949, all but one of the Jewish detainees (the communist leader, Henri Curiel) had been released. The return of the Wafd to power in January 1950 suggested the resurgence of democracy, secular-liberalism, and cosmopolitanism; and many Jews began to think they might resume life as it had been before the war.

In many arenas, there was no diminution of the Jewish presence. In the early 1950s, Jews freely practiced professions with high public visibility—journalism, law, medicine, and finance. The Maccabi basketball team and other Jewish sports teams continued to compete, and Jewish athletes were members of teams representing Egypt in international competition. The hospital, schools, and other Jewish community institutions continued to function. In 1951, the London *Jewish Chronicle* reported that "there remained . . . a fairly self-sufficient community and there seemed to be no move toward mass emigration."[56] This perception of a "return to normalcy" persisted from late 1949 until the announcement of the apprehension of the Operation Susannah conspirators in October 1954.

Because Jews had a higher rate of literacy than Muslims or Copts, they were disproportionately represented in the fields of publishing, printing, and journalism. In September 1950, a new pro-Wafd political weekly, *al-Saraha* (Frankness), edited by Albert Mizrahi, a Jewish journalist of some repute, was established with the patronage of Fu'ad Sirag al-Din, minister of interior in the last Wafd government to rule Egypt. Mizrahi also owned and edited *al-Tas'ira,* a commercial weekly established in 1944 to record the official prices of commodities subject to government price controls, which continued to appear during and after the 1948 war. *Al-Tas'ira* and *al-Saraha* ceased publication in May 1954, probably because of Mizrahi's identification with the Wafd. During its first month of publication, *al-Saraha* carried several articles about the Jewish community and the Arab-Israeli conflict that suggested a distinctive Jewish viewpoint, but they did not speak for or exclusively to the Jewish community. Mizrahi's principal collaborators in *al-Saraha* were a Muslim and a Copt, a symbolic expression of the coexistence of the three religious faiths in the Egyptian national community evoking Nagib al-Rihani's popular play, *Hasan, Murqus, and Cohen,* which was made into a film in 1954. Nonetheless, Mizrahi's status was not entirely secure. Late in 1952, he was arrested and briefly detained. Mizrahi had sufficient confidence in his rights as a citizen to criticize the government editorially for detaining him without charge.[57] It is likely that Mizrahi's Wafdist sympathies, not his Jewish identity, were the cause of his difficulties.

One Jewish-owned publishing house, Dar al-Katib al-Misri (The Egyptian scribe), was temporarily closed in 1948. It soon reopened, and many Jews continued to work in publishing, as they had before the war.[58] The Société Orientale de Publicité, whose premises had been bombed by the Muslim Brothers during the 1948 war, continued to publish *Le Progrès Egyptien, La Bourse Egyptien, The Egyptian Mail,* and *The Egyptian Gazette.* Until 1954, the editor of *Le Progrès Egyptien* was a Jew. Salvator Adjiman, a member of the Cairo Jewish Community Council, directed the advertising department of *al-Ahram* from

1932 until mid-1954, when he was arrested and charged with illegally transferring capital out of the country.[59] E. J. Blattner continued to publish and edit the annual *Le Mondain égyptien: L'Annuaire de l'élite d'Egypte (The Egyptian Who's Who)* through the 1950s. The Weinstein stationery and printing firm continued to operate in Cairo under Jewish ownership as of the mid-1990s.

Jews had historically been quite popular with the Egyptian royal family. King Fu'ad bestowed Egyptian citizenship on Chief Rabbi Nahum shortly after his arrival in the country and appointed him as a founding member of the Arab Language Academy in Cairo in 1932. Both Fu'ad and Faruq had warm and respectful relations with Rabbi Nahum. Throughout his career, Nahum advocated cultural integration and loyal patriotism as the only strategy that would ensure the survival of a Jewish community in Egypt. On the night of the military coup that ended the monarchy, Rabbi Nahum's son, JoJo, attended a picnic hosted by Princess Fa'iza at White Sands in the Alexandria harbor.[60] Madame Qattawi Pasha (née Alice Suarès) was first lady-in-waiting to Queens Nazli and Farida. The Cicurel department store, the Perlo pharmacy, and the Weinberg photography studio were all purveyors to the palace. The Cicurel store was not placed under administration in 1948, and it was quickly rebuilt after being burned in the Cairo fire of January 26, 1952, with the support of the palace. Emmanuel Mizrahy Pasha was legal counsel to the palace and the ministry of pious endowments.[61] One of the better known of Faruq's many mistresses was the actress, Camelia (Liliane Cohen).[62] Their liaison began after 1948.

Karim Thabit, a Lebanese journalist in King Faruq's entourage, is commonly considered responsible for persuading the king to declare war on Israel in 1948. His articles in *al-Muqattam* during the war were full of incitement against Jews. Faruq's failure to reprimand or restrain his courtier seems to have been motivated by political expediency or lack of attention rather than anti-Semitism because after a hiatus during the war, the palace resumed its association with elite Jews. In June 1951, the king bestowed royal decorations on Jews for the first time since the outbreak of the Arab-Israeli War, a public indication that they were once again in royal favor.[63]

Egyptian Jews including Zaki Murad, Ibrahim Sahlun, and Zaki Surur were prominent among the revivers of Arabic music in the early twentieth century. The most famous of the Jewish musical figures is the Karaite composer Da'ud Husni (1870–1937). He was associated with the first generation of Egyptian nationalist composers including Sayyid

Darwish and Kamil al-Khula'i. Husni composed the first Egyptian opera, "Samson and Dalilah"; Husayn Fawzi, a well-known nationalist intellectual, wrote the libretto for another of Husni's operas, "Cleopatra's Night"; and Husni collaborated with Sayyid Darwish, the leading figure in the revival of Arabic music in Egypt, on "Hoda"—an operetta that remained unfinished because of Darwish's death.

The editor of *al-Kalim* was Da'ud Husni's son, so it is not surprising that the newspaper devoted an article to his life and work every December on the anniversary of his death. The anniversary of Husni's death was also regularly observed by performances of his work and musicological conferences by non-Jewish Egyptian aficionados of Arabic music during the last years of the monarchy and the first years of the republic. In December 1949, *al-Misri, al-Balagh,* and *al-Zaman,* dailies covering a considerable range of the political spectrum, all carried articles commemorating Husni's musical achievements.[64] A 1951 article in *Akhir Sa'a* noted the nationalist spirit of Husni's music.[65] On January 10, 1953, the Institute of Arabic Music in Cairo celebrated the bronze anniversary of Husni's death.[66] Until at least 1955, the state radio aired a special program of Husni's music annually on his memorial date.[67]

Husni's music is revered to this day in Egypt, though public acknowledgment of his Jewish origins seems to have diminished after 1948. This was not entirely due to reluctance to acknowledge a problematic fact in the context of the continuing Arab-Israeli conflict. Husni converted to Islam, and his second wife was a Muslim. This would ordinarily have excluded him from recognition as a Jew, yet the Karaite community proudly claimed him as one of their own and embraced his musical accomplishments as evidence of their own Arab and Egyptian cultural identity. Husni's non-Jewish Egyptian aficionados were content to overlook his Jewish origins if they might pose a barrier to enjoying his music; the Karaite community was willing to overlook Husni's conversion if it enhanced their claim to be authentic Egyptians. Thus, avoiding a sharp determination of Husni's ethnoreligious identity served multiple purposes and enhanced his appeal.

The contested character of Jewish identity and its national legitimacy in Egypt were apparent in a dispute that arose in 1955 when Israeli authorities sought to purchase the manuscripts of the nineteenth-century Egyptian nationalist Ya'qub Sannu' from his daughter Layla Sannu', who then resided in France. She refused to sell her father's papers to an Israeli archive and told the weekly *al-Musawwar,* "My father was not a Jew. He was Egyptian. His legacy is the property of Egypt." *Al-Musawwar* went on to explain that after four stillbirths, Ya'qub Sannu''s mother had consulted a Muslim saint and promised to raise her child as a Muslim if she were blessed with a live birth. *Al-Musawwar* noted that Sannu' participated in the culture of all three of Egypt's faiths, not unlike many Egyptians, I might add.[68]

Linking Jewish involvement in the publishing and music industries, the publishing house of Albert Mizrahi held an exclusive contract from the state radio to print the programs for Umm Kulthum's monthly concerts.[69] During 1953, when *al-Saraha* and *al-Tas'ira* began to appear erratically, their pages were filled with Umm Kulthum's songs. Her popular nationalist anthem "Sawt al-watan" (Voice of the homeland) was reprinted repeatedly.

Jews were also prominent among the pioneers of Egyptian cinema, especially before the establishment of Studio Misr in 1935. The films of producer, director, scriptwriter, and actor Togo Mizrahi—*Cocaine* (1930) and *The Children of Egypt* (1933)—are widely acknowledged as classics.[70] Studio Misr encouraged more Muslims to enter the industry, and the Jewish presence became less dominant. But Jews remained disproportionately overrepresented in the film and entertainment industry through the 1950s. Among the Jewish actresses who regularly played opposite the leading Muslim actors and singers of Egypt were Victoria Cohen, Nigma Ibrahim, Layla Murad, and King Faruq's mistress, Liliane Cohen.

LAYLA MURAD: POPULAR CULTURE AND THE POLITICS OF ETHNORELIGIOUS IDENTITY

From the mid-1930s to the mid-1950s, Layla Murad (1918–95), daughter of the composer Zaki Murad, was the leading Jewish performance artist.[71] Dubbed the "Cinderella of the Egyptian screen," Murad was considered by many Egypt's second diva after the inimitable Umm Kulthum. Murad first sang on stage in 1930, and she appeared in her first film in 1935. Muhammad 'Abd al-Wahhab, a pioneer of the musical film genre and the leading male vocalist of the interwar period, was an associate of Zaki Murad and recognized Layla Murad's vocal talent. In 1938, he chose her to play the female lead opposite him in *Yahya al-hubb* (Long live love). Murad was an instant success as a singer. Under the tutelage of Togo Mizrahi, her acting skills developed quickly. Her career and performing persona were firmly established by her leading roles in five musical romances directed and produced by Mizrahi from 1939 to 1944 that featured her name in the titles. Murad's liaison with the debonair young actor-director-producer, Anwar Wagdi, launched a new phase of her career in 1945. Their courtship captivated the public, and they turned it into an artistic and commercial event by celebrating their marriage in the final scene of *Layla bint al-fuqara'* (Layla, daughter of the poor). Murad and Wagdi costarred in six more films before their divorce in 1950. During the final phase of her career, Murad played leading roles in films directed by Henri Barakat, Husayn Sidqi, and Yusuf Shahin. After appearing in twenty-eight films and recording hundreds of songs, in 1955 Murad abruptly and without explanation retired. Thereafter, she appeared in public only on rare occasions, though she continued to live in Cairo until her death.

Among the likely factors contributing to Layla Murad's unexpected withdrawal from public performance at the height of her artistic power and popular acclaim was a report that circulated in the Arab and Egyptian press in September 1952 accusing her of visiting Israel and contributing the huge sum of £E50,000 to the Israeli government earlier that summer.[72] Murad was especially distressed by the charges because she had publicly announced her voluntary conversion to Islam in 1946, a year after marrying Anwar Wagdi. "I am an Egyptian Muslim," she declared, strenuously denying that she had any connection to Israel.[73] Murad produced bank statements and other documents to prove her innocence, including a letter from Anwar Wagdi (the two had become close again since their divorce and there were rumors that they would remarry) affirming that Layla Murad was a "genuine (*samim*) Arab Muslim beloved by all the Arabs whom she loves in return." Religious or political differences played no role in their divorce, wrote Wagdi.[74] The Egyptian authorities concluded that the charges against Layla Murad were without foundation. Nonetheless, the Syrian government persisted in enforcing a total ban on her films and songs.

Despite this incident, Layla Murad remained popular in Egypt. She starred in a film every year from 1953 until 1955. *Ruz al-Yusuf* reported regularly on her career, openly discussing her Jewish origins. In November 1954, a poll of directors and producers voted her rendition of "Is'al 'alayya" (Ask about me) the best song of the year, and, in December 1954, she performed in concert before an enthusiastic audience of 4,000.[75] During the negotiations for the establishment of the United Arab Republic in 1958, President Gamal Abdel Nasser personally insisted that Syria abandon the boycott of Layla Murad's songs and films. The Syrians complied, and Layla Murad's work once again became available in Syria.[76] Despite this unequivocal recognition of her stature and acceptance. Layla Murad could not be induced to end her self-imposed retirement and seclusion. Whether or not the unfounded rumor about her collaboration with Israel was the immediate cause of her withdrawal from the public, she seems to have felt that the milieu in which she flourished could no longer be sustained.

Religious conversions by performing artists like Layla Murad and Da'ud Husni were not unusual, but neither did they erase the Jewish identity of the converts. In February 1955, *Ruz al-Yusuf* related that Omar Sharif converted to Islam (according to some accounts, he was born Jewish) to marry Fatin Hamama and that Nigma Ibrahim converted from Judaism to Islam when she married 'Abbas Yunis.[77] There was (and continues to be) a substantial commercial market in Egypt for star-gazing gossip of this sort, and the Jewish origins of several of the stars did not diminish the public's interest in them. Aside from its commercial appeal, the main point of *Ruz al-Yusuf*'s reporting on the religious identities of Egypt's leading actors and actresses seems to be that conversion was common among movie stars, who generally did not appear to take their religious faith very seriously. Despite apparently having been motivated by convenience rather than conviction, these conversions were reported without any pejorative tone. This suspension of moral judgment was undoubtedly facilitated because all the conversions were to Islam, and apostasy from the true faith was not an issue. The easy acknowledgment of the Jewish presence in Egyptian popular culture by a magazine with strong Arab nationalist sympathies suggests that despite the significant changes in political culture that were already apparent, important sectors of the Egyptian movie- and concert-going public continued to embrace and enjoy a cultural cosmopolitanism akin to the Levantinism or Mediterraneanism of Jacqueline Kahanoff and Yitzhaq Gormezano-Goren.

DENOUEMENT

There were good reasons for Jews to be alarmed when a group of unknown army officers overthrew the monarchy and seized power on July 23, 1952. The army had no social or political links to the Jewish community. Several of the Free Officers had backgrounds in the Society of Muslim Brothers or Young Egypt, organizations that did not view Jews as authentic Egyptians. Political training in those milieux would not have included sensitivity to the rights of Egyptian Jews. Moreover, the event that precipitated the organization of the Free Officers was Egypt's ignominious defeat in Palestine in 1948, an experience likely to have bred a certain hostility toward Jews.

As previously noted, General Naguib, in his capacity as prime minister, exerted unusual efforts to maintain good relations with the Jewish community and to uphold the principle that Jews were full members of the national polity. Naguib's demise in March 1954, followed quickly by several events that exacerbated the Arab-Israeli conflict, undermined the self-confidence of the regime and virtually eliminated any possibility that the government would accept Jews as Egyptians. In August, Egypt and Britain initialed an agreement to effect the evacuation of all British troops by June 1956. The communists and the Muslim Brothers denounced this agreement as a betrayal of the nationalist cause because it stipulated conditions under which British troops could be invited to return to Egypt. In October 1954, a member of the Society of Muslim Brothers attempted to assassinate Abdel Nasser in Alexandria. Thousands of Brothers were arrested and held in detention camps for up to ten years. Six members of the organization were convicted and executed for their role in the assassination attempt. The next month the Israeli ship *Bat Galim* tried to break the Egyptian ban on Israeli traffic in the Suez Canal by provocatively sailing into the waterway. The ship was stopped, and the crew was detained for several months until their release was negotiated.

The most fateful development for the Jewish community was the government's announcement on October 5 that it had apprehended an underground network of Egyptian Jews who had engaged in spying and sabotage on behalf of Israel. This announcement and the subsequent trial provided an excuse to treat the entire Jewish community as potential subversives. Even at its best, the Revolutionary Command Council was overly security conscious and did not have great respect for civil rights and due process. Its popularity and authority had just been sharply challenged by an assassination attempt on the prime minister. In these circumstances, the discovery of the Operation Susannah conspiracy was more than enough to undermine official insistence on strict preservation of the formal rights of the Jewish community. The Israeli attack on Gaza on February 28, 1955, which many Egyptians understood as a retaliation for the execution of two of the Operation Susannah conspirators, began a countdown toward war between Egypt and Israel. Between October 1954 and October 1956, Egyptian Jews were caught between the two states moving toward an armed clash. Their circumstances became increasingly difficult, though not yet impossible.

Jewish British Labor MP Maurice Orbach visited Cairo soon after the trial of the Operation Susannah conspirators. He found that Jews were no longer employed in the civil service and that it was difficult for Jews to obtain Egyptian citizenship. They continued to work in the banking and finance sectors. The Jewish community was highly respected for its "correct business methods and its ethical and moral standing." In Cairo's *harat al-yahud,* the medical clinic, soup kitchen for the poor, and old-age home continued to function. Hebrew was taught and religious services were held regularly. Orbach concluded,

> I found no antagonism between Muslim, Copt, and Jew. Merchants, shop-keepers, and professionals were in friendly association, although there is grave anxiety among the Jewish community today.
>
> The unspoken heartfelt wish of every Jew in the Delta is that there should be peace between Egypt and Israel. Without that there can be no feeling of security.[78]

The security of the Egyptian Jewish community was irretrievably damaged by the outbreak of the Suez/Sinai War. In response to the British-French-Israeli attack on Egypt on October 29, 1956, Egypt took harsh measures against its Jewish community.[79] About 1,000 Jews were detained, more than half of them Egyptian citizens.[80] Thirteen thousand French and British citizens were expelled from Egypt in retaliation for the tripartite attack, among them many Jews. In addition, 500 Jews not holding French or British citizenship were expelled. Some 460 Jewish-owned businesses were sequestered. Many Jews lost their jobs. The government nationalized the assets of all British and French citizens, and Jews holding those nationalities were affected in that capacity. In November 1956, a presidential decree amended the Egyptian nationality law by imposing more stringent residence requirements and depriving Zionists of the right to claim citizenship. When the hostilities were over, Jews were subjected to unofficial pressures to leave Egypt and renounce their citizenship. According to the World Jewish Congress, between November 22, 1956, and March 15, 1957, 14,102 Jews left Egypt, just under one-third of those residing in the country on the eve of the Suez/Sinai War.[81] Most of them abandoned the great bulk of their assets in Egypt and came to Israel as impoverished refugees.

The military proclamation seizing Jewish property was rescinded on April 27, 1957, and the property of Jews who were not British or French citizens was returned. By then, the Jewish community was crippled beyond restoration. The chief rabbi of Alexandria, Aharon Angel, and the president of the Cairo Jewish community, Salvator Cicurel, were among those who left in the post-1956 wave of immigration. Karaite Chief Rabbi Babovitch had died several months before the Suez/Sinai War. Chief Rabbi Nahum was chronically ill and died in 1960. These key personnel losses combined with continuing political uncertainty meant that Jewish communal life could no longer be viably sustained in Egypt.

After the immediate crisis of the Suez/Sinai War subsided, Jewish emigration continued at a slower pace. From mid-1957 to mid-1967, about 17,000–19,000 departed, leaving about 7,000 Jews in Egypt on the eve of the third Arab-Israeli War. Most of the immigrants in this wave were economically better off than those who left immediately after the 1956 war and sought destinations other than Israel.[82] Among them were those who formed the core of the Karaite community in the San Francisco Bay Area (see Chapter 7). By the end of the mass emigration, between one-third and one-half of the Egyptian Jewish community had relocated in Israel. Brazil, France, the United States, Argentina, England, and Canada were the most popular destinations after Israel.[83]

The mass emigration of Egyptian Jewry in the years after the 1956 war, despite the coercion, humiliation, and pain it involved in many cases, did not erase all sense of affinity to Egypt. Dina Monet, a reporter for the *Jerusalem Post,* interviewed poor Arabic-speaking Jews housed in transit camps (*ma'abarot*) after their arrival in Israel in December 1956. Interviewing new immigrants was common in the Israeli press because it was a convenient vehicle for public reaffirmation of the validity of the Zionist project. Immigrants were typically invited to compare the discrimination, economic deprivation, and culturally impoverished character of Jewish life in the diaspora with their hopes and expectations of freedom in Israel. If the immigrants were housed in *ma'abarot,* they were assured that this was a temporary circumstance due to their massive numbers and Israel's limited economic capacity to absorb them. Reporters cataloged the exotic customs of new immigrant groups (especially those of Middle Eastern origins) and reassured a nervous public that such peculiarities would be submerged in the process of commingling the exiles (*mizug galuyot*) and the forging of the new Jew.

Occasionally, new immigrants inadvertently disrupted these expectations. One of the Egyptian Jews interviewed by Monet innocently explained, "Egypt is our country, we have no other, and our fathers were here [i.e., in Egypt] as long as any Moslems."[84] This spontaneous deviation from the scripted text constitutes a minor disruption of the Zionist discourse by both Dina Monet and her interviewee. It expresses the unpreparedness of many Egyptian Jews to adopt roles assigned to them by the Zionist project upon their arrival in Israel. They or their children were soon disciplined by service in the army and other socialization measures. By the 1967 Arab-Israeli War, very few Egyptian Jews in Israel would say of themselves, as Maurice Fargeon had in 1943, "In fact, the Jews are Arabs."

CHAPTER 4

Nazis and Spies

The Discourse of Operation Susannah

The Nazi mass murder of European Jews established the standard vocabulary, rhetorical frame, and social experience for assessing all subsequent threats, potential or actual, to any Jewish community, including the Jews of Egypt. In the second half of the twentieth century, there have been no instances of anti-Semitic oppression that can reasonably be compared to the distinctively modern, European practice of scientifically elaborated racism, mass-marketed propaganda, industrialized genocide, and global conquest of Nazi Germany. Nonetheless, concern to maintain a high level of vigilance against anti-Semitism, deep guilt throughout the Western world over the failure to adequately confront (in some cases, over actual complicity with) the Nazi genocide, lack of an adequate alternative lexicon, and a certain amount of cynical manipulation by Zionist publicists have installed Nazi-style anti-Semitism as a recurrent trope in discussions of the post–World War II Jewish condition.[1] Yet, in their worst moments, Jews in modern Egypt were very far from experiencing such intense, unremitting, and ideologically committed persecution.

The arrest, conviction, and execution of a network of Egyptian Jews charged with committing acts of espionage and sabotage on behalf of Israel in 1954–55—an intrigue code-named "Operation Susannah"— were critical moments in the elaboration of a discourse that cast the Egyptian regime, and ultimately all Arabs, as neo-Nazis. Here I want to consider how this discourse developed between 1948 and 1977 by comparing competing representations of Operation Susannah. During those

years, the imposition of a particular interpretation of the recent experience of European Jewry on events in Egypt and the insistence that this
necessarily informed the meaning of the lives of all Jews everywhere censored the voices of Egyptian Jews and blocked their ability to narrate
their own history.

THE 1948 ARAB-ISRAELI WAR AND THE "DISCOVERY" OF EGYPTIAN NAZISM

As noted in Chapter 3, the outbreak of hostilities between Egypt and the
newly established state of Israel on May 15, 1948, resulted in the internment of several hundred Zionists and communists, the sequestration
of Jewish assets, bombings in *harat al-yahud* and of Jewish stores in
downtown Cairo, and random attacks on Jews during the summer and
fall. There were crude anti-Semitic attacks on Jews in the Egyptian press
during the 1948 Arab-Israeli War. Consequently, Jews had reason to feel
apprehensive about their status in Egypt. These fears were relieved somewhat after the assassination of Prime Minister al-Nuqrashi, the official
dissolution of the Society of Muslim Brothers in December, and assumption of the premiership by Ibrahim ʿAbd al-Hadi, a cosmopolitan
who enjoyed good relations with elite Jews.

   The government of Israel forcefully described the developments in
Egypt as Nazi-like persecution. Its public statement on "The Position of
Jews in Egypt" cataloged the actions taken against Egyptian Jews with
only passing reference to the state of war between Egypt and Israel and
proclaimed that "the stringent measures taken against the Jewish population are reminiscent of the early days of the Hitler regime."[2] This characterization was uncritically reported in the *Palestine Post* (subsequently
the *Jerusalem Post*), a daily close to the government that served as a vehicle for disseminating its views to the diplomatic community and to
Jews outside Israel.[3]

   The notion that Egyptian Jews were suffering from Nazi-style anti-
Semitism began to crystallize in American Jewish circles as early as October 1948. Using terms similar to those of the Israeli government a few
weeks later, confidential reports began circulating among officials of the
American Jewish Committee asserting that "The situation of the 75,000
Jews in Egypt is in broad terms similar to that of the Jews in Germany
in the period beginning about 1936."[4] Other accounts circulating among
the American Jewish Committee leaders suggested that because of Oriental indiscipline, the situation of Jews in Egypt in 1948 was even worse

than that of Jews in Nazi Germany in the 1930s. One such report asserted, "The Egyptian press, written in Arabic, is more violent in their open attacks against Jews than any former Nazi paper would have dared to be."[5] Nessim Z. Moreno, who had lived in Egypt for many years before settling in the United States, was despatched by the American Jewish Committee to investigate conditions in Egypt. He reported, "Having lived in Germany in Hitler's time, I have seen terrible persecution of Jews first hand, but from the stories I heard of what went on in Egypt in the period from May 15, 1948, until the assassination of Nokrachi Pacha [i.e., Nuqrashi Pasha, December 28, 1948], the condition of the Jews in Egypt was in some respects worse than the condition of the Jews in Germany during the late thirties." According to Moreno, this was because in Germany "there was generally discipline in the carrying out of anti-semitic measures," whereas in Egypt "there were many recurrences of uncontrolled mob rule."[6]

Then, as now, Islamic radicalism was seen as particularly threatening by many in the West. A report to the Wiener Library in London that circulated among committee leaders described an encounter with the leader of the Society of Muslim Brothers:

> Hasan El Benna is a short, squat, ratty little man with puffed eyes, puffed cheeks, fleshy nose. His beard, running from ear to ear, crawls up then down his upper lip in an ugly black hirsute vine. Hasan El Benna's manner is mousy and furtive. . . .
>   I interviewed this religious fuhrer and was a trusted visitor at Ikhwan headquarters in Cairo and other cities.[7]

The undisguised racism and exoticist voyeurism of this description enhanced the author's conclusion that a "pogrom of Jews" was "an actual reality" in Egypt. "The pattern is the Hitler pattern—on a small scale."[8]

The American Jewish Committee drew on all these sources to compile its comprehensive *Report on the Jewish Situation in Egypt,* which was confidentially presented to U.S. government officials in November 1948 before being released to the public early the next year. According to the committee, the world knew so little about "Egypt's recent venture into Hitlerian brutality on a national scale" because of the press censorship in force since May 15, 1948.[9]

The credibility of assertions as ridiculous as those just quoted depended on Orientalist preconceptions, substantial ignorance, and the uncritical transfer of European terms of reference to Egypt. The hyperbole of the American Jewish Committee was probably motivated by the re-

cent memory of the passivity of the international community during the
Nazi era. But relying on this memory to assess conditions in Egypt is
analogous to generals preparing to fight the last war. Moreover, to reach
the conclusion that the government of Egypt was conducting Nazi-style
persecution of Jews, the American Jewish Committee had to ignore the
firsthand evidence it received from an unimpeachable source—the president of Cairo's Sephardi Jewish community, Salvator Cicurel.

Cicurel met with representatives of the committee in New York at the
end of October 1948. His assessment of the situation was informed by
the historically specific appreciation that "the recent anti-Jewish out-
breaks . . . [were] connected with the existence of Israel and the defeats
of the Egyptian Army there."[10] Cicurel specified that the army and the
Society of Muslim Brothers harbored anti-Jewish sentiments. He tried to
persuade the American Jewish Committee leaders to appeal to the U.S.
government to intervene to block the enforcement of the Egyptian Company Law of 1947. Such action, if successful, would have allowed Cicurel to continue to employ an overwhelmingly Jewish staff in his large
and fashionable Cairo department store. The Cicurel store had been
damaged by a bomb in July 1948, widely suspected to be the work of
the Muslim Brothers, who tried to foment anti-Jewish sentiment during
the Arab-Israeli War as part of their overall assault on the Egyptian
regime. But Cicurel enjoyed the personal favor of King Faruq and soon
reopened his store with the support and encouragement of the king. A
scant three years after World War II, he could hardly have thought that
he and his Jewish staff were in danger of Nazi-like persecution if he
planned to continue his business operations in Egypt.

In 1950, a comprehensive report prepared by S. Landshut for the
American Jewish Committee and the Anglo-Jewish Association criticized
the committee's 1949 report for its claim that Egypt was suffused with
"systematic thorough-going anti-Semitism . . . too firmly rooted to be
expected to disappear." Landshut, like many contemporary Western observers oblivious to the local experience of imperial rule, regarded any
anti-Western sentiment as xenophobia and was unable to accept the legitimacy of Egyptian nationalism. Still, he concluded that "it is wrong
to speak of any deeply-rooted anti-Jewish—as distinct from generally
anti-Western—feeling were it not that the Palestine question had temporarily crystallized Egyptian xenophobia into anti-Semitism."[11]

The efforts of well-informed individuals like Cicurel and Landshut
to describe the condition of the Jewish community in a judicious and

restrained manner were insufficient to overcome the emotional power
of the trope of Nazi anti-Semitism. Understanding and sympathy for
Egypt and the rest of the Arab world were minimal in the West, and
competition among Jewish organizations seems to have encouraged
their publicists and supporters to draw the most extreme conclusions on
the basis of limited or unreliable evidence. Many American Jews, shaken
by the realization that their response to the Nazi genocide had been inadequate, resolved not to underestimate any future threats to Jewish
communities abroad. This well-intentioned impulse generated a pre-
dictably regular misrepresentation of the situation in Egypt. Once the
theme of Nazi-like persecution was established in Jewish circles, it began to proliferate promiscuously. Fabrications and exaggerations were
repeated as truth and rarely subjected to rigorous investigation. Therefore, in 1954, when Egyptian authorities announced that they had apprehended the perpetrators of Operation Susannah and intended to
bring them to trial, this news was easily inserted into a well-defined discursive structure that had previously been established as appropriate for
understanding the situation of Egyptian Jews.

THE ISRAELI AND ANGLO-AMERICAN JEWISH DISCOURSE

The Israeli press first reported that Egyptian Jews were to be tried on
charges of espionage and sabotage on behalf of Israel in mid-October
1954. Days after the story broke, the *Jerusalem Post, Davar* (Word, the
Histadrut daily controlled by MAPAI), and *Herut* (Freedom, the daily
of Menahem Begin's party of the same name) began to compare the situation in Egypt with events in Nazi Germany. Because of its access to a
foreign audience, the coverage of the *Jerusalem Post* was particularly significant in establishing a common discursive frame regulating understanding of the events for both the vast majority of Israelis and a large
sector of the North American and Western European public.

The *Post*'s first account of the affair conveyed the contents of an article in the London *Jewish Observer,* a common technique to avoid Israeli
censorship restrictions.[12] A substantive original account appeared two
days later under the large headline "Egypt's Jews Said Panic-Stricken by
Persecution and Mass Arrests." Relying on information reaching
Geneva, the *Post* reported that 150 Jews had been arrested and interrogated with methods that "stagger the imagination." The article charged
the Egyptian police with beating Armand Karmona to death on August
7 (Egyptian authorities claimed he committed suicide, and the exact

circumstances of his death remain uncertain) and discussed extensively Marcelle Ninio's torture and attempted suicide. The *Post* concluded,

> The sole responsibility for this wave of terror, the reports said, rests with the newly formed National Egyptian Militia which is described as a para-military organization trained by former German Army officers on the storm trooper model. . . . Jewish leaders here were shocked when shown the reports. "If true," a Jewish official declared, "they are reminiscent of the days of Hitler."[13]

Every significant assertion in this report was totally fictitious or highly questionable. I have found no other reference to the National Egyptian Militia in any English or Arabic book or article on Egypt during this period. Apparently, it never existed or was utterly inconsequential. There were many recurrent reports of former Nazis living and working in Egypt in the 1950s and 1960s. But hard data supporting such allegations are illusive, and there is no credible evidence that former Nazis exercised a policy-making role in Egypt.[14] The arrest, trial, and sentencing of the Operation Susannah conspirators were carried out by the Egyptian police, internal security apparatus, and judiciary in response to actual bombings carried out by Egyptian Jews acting as agents of Israel. The arrests and investigations of Jews by security authorities after the discovery of Operation Susannah did not directly disrupt the lives of the vast majority of the approximately 50,000 Jews living in Egypt at the time.

Despite the spuriousness of the *Jerusalem Post*'s report, it was never retracted; and it established the terms for understanding the events in Israel and in Jewish circles abroad. There was simply no public consideration of the possibility that those arrested were actually guilty. This was partly due to the unprofessional character of the operation. The traditionally pro-Zionist *Manchester Guardian* editorially explained that the charges against the Operation Susannah conspirators must be fabricated because "any Jewish underground would presumably act with some sanity."[15] The ultimately anti-Semitic presumption of superior Jewish intelligence led to the conclusion that the accused were innocent victims of anti-Semitic persecution.

Because its format and style were designed to present Israel's case to an international audience, the coverage of the *Jerusalem Post* was more sensational than some of the Hebrew press. However, *Herut* presented the most incendiary reporting of the affair. Its editorial on the opening day of the Cairo trial explained that the defendants "are not only accused of spying. They have hung on their heads all manner of crimes that the Levantine imagination can invent for this purpose." The editorialist linked the Cairo defendants to a long list of victims of anti-Semitism beginning with Mendel Beilis (the victim of a 1911–13 blood libel in Russia) and explained that "in exile . . . Jews suffered because they were Jews. . . . Here they are suffering because of the existence of the state of Israel." Of course, *Herut* did not draw the obvious conclusion that the existence of the state of Israel apparently did not prevent the persecution of Jews and had perhaps even increased it. Instead, the newspaper resolved that the Israeli government was obliged to abandon self-restraint and intervene to protect the accused.[16]

Herut's coverage reached a peak of frenzy in reporting the suicide of Max Binnet. A front-page article carried his picture with a black border, and the editorial proclaimed, "The clique of Nazi-Levantine hangmen has claimed the life of one of the martyrs of the Egyptian blood libel." Max Binnet's blood "cries out to us from the earth and demands: revenge!"[17] Binnet was a major in the Israel Defense Forces who was already known and wanted in Iraq for previous espionage activity there. His mission in Egypt appears to have been far more substantial than Operation Susannah, with which he had no direct connection. He may have decided to take his own life to avoid being tortured and possibly revealing important state secrets. But like many other pieces of this story, this is impossible to determine with any certainty.

Herut's crude racism and its fascist-style land and blood imagery might easily be dismissed as the expressions of a marginal minority of fanatic militarists (Ben-Gurion and MAPAI considered Begin and his followers to be beyond the pale of respectable politics). But the newspaper closest to the government, *Davar,* just as insistently deployed the trope of Nazi-like anti-Semitism in Egypt, linking it to the entire history of Jewish persecution in Europe. Its editorial on the opening day of the Cairo trial claimed,

> The similarity is great between this trial and the trials of anti-Semitic hatred that were staged in the past by reactionary rulers in Europe. . . . The Cairo spy trial is an expressly anti-Jewish trial and constitutes a climax in the campaign of persecutions against the Jews of Egypt. . . . According to all the signs this Egyptian dictator [Nasser] is influenced by the spirit of the Nazis . . . also in his attitude to the Jews.[18]

A few days later, the headline of what purported to be a more considered analysis based on the information obtained from a foreign diplomat who had recently left Cairo proclaimed, "German Nazis are at the head of a 'Jewish Department' in the Egyptian government. They have staged the trial of the 13 and are preparing additional trials."[19] Although never supported by material evidence, the accusation of Nazi orchestration of Egyptian anti-Semitism was deeply engraved in the consciousness of a substantial portion of the public in Israel and abroad.

On the day of the execution of Shmu'el Azar and Moshe Marzuq, *Davar*'s editorial, just like that of *Herut* several weeks earlier, connected their fates to the history of anti-Semitic persecution of Jews in Europe, appropriating the language and imagery of religious martyrology for the national cause:

> The blood of these two Jewish martyrs flows into the river of blood of millions of our people, who were slaughtered and burned for the sanctification of the Name and the nation in our generation and in previous generations. But in the era of the state of Israel Jewish blood will not be cheap anywhere [*dam yehudi lo yihye hefker*]. . . .
> The state of Israel, in which capital punishment has been abolished, has the unassailable moral right to accuse Egypt before the entire world of miscarriage of justice and political murder.[20]

La-Merhav (To the region), the daily of Le-Ahdut ha-'Avodah, which had recently split from MAPAM, began to appear on December 6, 1954, and did not have the opportunity to write about Operation Susannah as fully as the other Israeli papers. Reflecting the activist military-political outlook of its party, *La-Merhav* was just as bloodthirsty as *Herut* in demanding Israeli retaliation against Egypt, though it did not invoke the entire history of anti-Semitism in Europe in the fashion of *Herut, Davar,* and the *Jerusalem Post* to justify it. Only MAPAM's *'Al ha-Mishmar* (The guardian) and the independent *ha-Aretz* (The land) covered the Cairo trial with relatively little inflammatory hyperbole.

Just as in 1948, American Jewish organizations took up the cause of Egyptian Jews and described their circumstances in exaggerated terms drawing on the lexicon of the Holocaust. The report of Nehemiah Robinson, director of the Institute of Jewish Affairs, the research branch of the World Jewish Congress, on "Persecution in Egypt" appeared first in the *Congress Weekly* and was widely reprinted. As evidence that the Jewish community was suffering from grave persecution, he cited the arrest of some Jews for participating in Zionist activities. He reported that "a process of expulsion was set in motion" during the 1948 war and that "the Jewish position is, if such a thing is still possible, aggravated by the ever-growing prominence of the 'National Militia' composed of uniformed armed youths on the Nazi storm trooper pattern, trained by Germans"[21]—the same dubious entity previously mentioned in the *Jerusalem Post*.

The official response of the Israeli government to the arrest of the Egyptian Jewish espionage and sabotage ring, although not as frenzied as the coverage of the press and the reports of international Jewish organizations, was equally adamant in insisting that the Cairo trial was an anti-Semitic hoax with no basis in reality. In his statement to the Knesset, Prime Minister Moshe Sharett proclaimed,

> The Government of Israel rejects most emphatically the fantastic libels that appear in the charges made by the Egyptian prosecution, which accuse the Israeli authorities of outrages and infernal plots against Egypt's international relations. . . . If their sin is their Zionism and their devotion to the state of Israel, then many Jews throughout the world are partners in this sin.[22]

Although the Israeli government was already informed that a military intelligence unit was involved in the bombings in Egypt, Sharett may not yet have known the full extent of the responsibility of Israeli military authorities. The Olshan-Dori Committee he established to investigate the affair delivered its report on January 12, 1955. Sharett may have believed (or hoped) he was being truthful; however, his statement was, in fact, entirely false. Whether it was a conscious or an unconscious misrepresentation, this is a striking expression of the powerful discursive order in which it was imbedded: Any accusation that Jews were guilty of espionage and terrorism in Egypt could only be due to the most heinous anti-Semitism.

The Israeli government and its U.S. supporters were well aware of the propaganda value of describing the Egyptian case against the Operation Susannah conspirators as a Nazi-style, anti-Semitic show trial. The day after the executions of Azar and Marzuq, Israeli Ambassador Abba Eban delivered an off-the-record talk in which he asserted,

> The Government of Israel . . . [knows] the complete falsity of the fabricated absurdities to the effect that these people, completely helpless and in the full control of the Egyptian state, were conducting in Egypt activities for the undermining of Egyptian security at the behest of the Government of Israel.[23]

One American Jewish Committee leader who attended expressed his satisfaction that "Eban's 'Background Talk' effectively exploits the trial as an occasion for condemning Western admiration for the Nasser dictatorship."[24]

The executions also provided a pretext for Israel to cease attending meetings of the Mixed Armistice Commission established by the United Nations after the 1948 Arab-Israeli War to supervise Egyptian-Israeli military relations in lieu of a peace treaty.[25] The commission had, from time to time, reported that Israel initiated violations of its common border with Egypt. Consequently, it was regarded with suspicion by Israeli military authorities, who objected to any restrictions on the timing and scale of the reprisal raids they conducted into the Gaza Strip in response to violations of the Egyptian-Israeli border by Palestinian refugees and others.

Suspension of Israeli participation in the Mixed Armistice Commission meetings meant there was no local forum for discussing its massive raid on Gaza on February 28, 1955. This operation was widely regarded as a retaliation for Egypt's execution of Azar and Marzuq and as a punishment for Egypt's opposition to Arab participation in the Baghdad Pact. It began a cycle of escalation of border violence that culminated in the 1956 Anglo-French-Israeli invasion of Egypt.

THE OFFICIAL EGYPTIAN STORY

Egyptian government officials were astounded by the reactions to the prosecution of the Operation Susannah conspirators. For them, this was a clear case of espionage and sabotage with both confessions and material evidence to support the prosecution's charges. They claimed they were reacting to the discovery of the conspiracy just as any European state threatened with subversion would. Government spokespersons and reports in the press repeatedly stressed that the accused were not on trial as Jews and that the Jewish community per se was not being subjected to any persecution. These claims were not entirely accurate. Jews faced continuing difficulties in establishing Egyptian citizenship (see Chapter 2), and many felt uneasy about their future after 1948. Though the Egyptian government's case against the conspirators was well supported by the evidence, there were aspects of its presentation and surrounding circumstances that made it difficult for a Western audience to accept the official Egyptian version of the story.

In the aftermath of the contest between Naguib and Abdel Nasser in March 1954, which definitively established the latter as the leader of the new regime, the government stepped up its anticommunist campaign in the press. A prominent feature of this effort was to accuse the communists of being Zionists. A month before the arrest of the Operation

Susannah conspirators was announced, lead articles in the major Egyptian dailies explained that the Egyptian communist movement was controlled by a Zionist Jew, Henri Curiel, who resided in Paris.[26] The campaign continued throughout the fall, concurrent with major trials of
communists, including several Jews. A photo essay in *al-Musawwar* asserted that the communists were Zionists, atheists, and sexually promiscuous. It featured a picture of Curiel in short pants, which made him appear totally alien and ridiculous by Egyptian cultural standards.[27]

The equation of Zionism and communism was common among conservative Arab leaders, including the Egyptian prime minister in 1948,
Mahmud Fahmi al-Nuqrashi, and King ʿAbd al-ʿAziz Al Saʿud of Saudi
Arabia. This notion was not an expression of primordial Arab or Muslim anti-Jewish sentiment. Its categories are too modern for that and obviously inflected with European anti-Semitic ideas, such as those in *The
Protocols of the Elders of Zion*. Developed as an instrument in the
struggle against Zionism, it offered a facile explanation for certain su-
perficially consistent facts—the disproportionately large number of Jewish communists, the strength of socialist Zionism in Israel, and the support for the partition of Palestine and the creation of a Jewish state by
the Soviet Union and the international communist movement. It may
also have been an effort to adapt to the Manichaean discourse of the
cold war in the United States during the McCarthy-Dulles era. That certain Egyptians and Arabs believed such claims to be effective arguments
against Zionism attests to the great gap between their conceptual universe and Euro-American political discourse. Especially after World War
II, these charges resonated with Nazi efforts to portray Jews as the animators of the international communist movement and could not but
arouse suspicion in Western Europe and North America.

Equally suspicious was the shift in the public representation of the seriousness of the conspiracy. After the announcement of the discovery of
the plot, the Egyptian police appeared to minimize the whole affair, calling it "child's play."[28] Perhaps this was because the authorities were embarrassed by failing to discover the operation before several bombings
had been successfully executed. Indeed, Operation Susannah caused no
personal injuries or deaths and resulted in relatively minor damage to
property. On the opening day of the trial, the headline of *al-Ahram*, like
all its previous headlines reporting the story, did not mention the bombings and referred only to "The Big Zionist Spy Trial before the Supreme
Military Court."[29] It was only two days after the trial began that the pa-

per's headlines acknowledged that the accused were charged with committing acts of violence.[30] If their crimes were insubstantial, as the Egyptian authorities first claimed, it did not seem reasonable to impose the death penalty or life imprisonment on the perpetrators. Foreign observers generally viewed the shift in the severity of the characterization of the actions of Operation Susannah in the Egyptian press as motivated by the concurrent trial and execution of the Muslim Brothers who had attempted to assassinate Gamal Abdel Nasser in Alexandria on October 26, 1954. These political circumstances aroused suspicion about the legitimacy of the charges and the fairness of the judicial procedures.

The cosmopolitan cultural qualities of the Operation Susannah conspirators and the political considerations that motivated them were discordant with Egyptian norms. However, they were easily recognizable in Western Europe and North America, which further enhanced Westerners' propensities to believe the worst about the Egyptian charges. The cultural and social differences between the Operation Susannah conspirators and the standards of urban middle-class Egypt were strikingly expressed in the representation of the gender relations among the conspirators. The prosecution portrayed Ninio as a beautiful and seductive Mata Hari who acted as chief liaison between the Cairo and Alexandria branches of the spy ring, charges reinforced and embellished by the Egyptian press.

Marcelle Ninio received the most extensive and graphic coverage of all the accused, including regular and detailed commentary on her physical appearance and dress. *Al-Ahram* featured her picture on its front page three times during the first week of the trial and described her as "a young Jewish woman with a great deal of intelligence, shrewdness, and spirit of self-sacrifice."[31] *Al-Musawwar*'s coverage was the most imaginative and developed the gender dynamics of the plot in greatest detail: Ninio "used her femininity to influence and control her abettors. She was the brains of the ring, which operated under her direction and instructions."[32] The young men, who had gone to Israel secretly and illegally to receive instruction in intelligence operations, "were trained by Israeli young women."[33] Under the subheading "Always . . . Money and Women," a subsequent article in *al-Musawwar* explained how the young male minors were seduced by money and pretty girls in Paris (where they stopped on their way to Israel), Israel, and Alexandria. The furnished flat in Alexandria, which was the operations center of the network there, was portrayed as a place for youthful foolishness full of girls, drink,

music, and wanton entertainment.[34] *Al-Musawwar* noted Marcelle
Ninio's admission that she had frequented the Alexandria flat and occasionally spent weekends there, a sure indication of debauchery by prevailing Egyptian standards. According to *al-Musawwar,* the young men
were simply enjoying themselves when an Israeli devil came and ordered
them to burn and destroy U.S. establishments and threatened to reveal
that they had been to Israel if they refused.

The Israeli and Western press also devoted disproportionate attention
to Marcelle Ninio's dress, physical appearance, and role in the trial. In
Egypt, the image of manipulative and uncontrolled female sexuality enhanced the prosecution's claim that the defendants' behavior was beyond
the norms of civilized behavior. But in Israel and the West, focusing on
Marcelle Ninio feminized all the defendants and made them appear less
threatening to Egypt and more vulnerable as victims. The differing effects of comparable representations of gender were one more reason for
Westerners to distrust the Egyptian account of the affair.

The Egyptian press repeatedly stressed that proper judicial procedures
were being followed in the trial. The Qur'an, the Hebrew Bible, and the
New Testament were all available in the courtroom for witnesses to
swear on.[35] To counter widespread reports that the accused had been
tortured to obtain their confessions, *al-Musawwar* published photos and
interviews of the defendants in jail, claiming they were properly treated
and well fed by prison authorities.[36] Because Marcelle Ninio had attempted to commit suicide, the authorities were especially anxious to
demonstrate how well she fared. Her prison diet was said to include
string beans, meat, cheese, winter cress, and tangerines—fare more
ample and varied than that enjoyed by most Egyptians. Her only com-
plaint about prison life was that she wanted to write a story about how
generous her jailers were to her, but she was not allowed to have a pen
and paper. No one familiar with prison conditions in Egypt could possibly believe such a description, and the interviews and photos of the defendants surrounding it were obviously staged. The defendants probably cooperated in this propaganda effort, hoping to improve their
situations. But it was unconvincing and could only arouse suspicion that
something was not right.

THE INTERNATIONAL CAMPAIGN FOR THE DEFENDANTS

International opinion in Great Britain and North America was generally
inclined to accept the Israeli version of events, and the trial coverage of

the major newspapers mirrored the Israeli press. Leading figures in the Jewish community and the government of Israel pressured the U.S. and British governments to intervene in the Cairo proceedings. Nonetheless, both governments were disinclined to make public statements because they were attempting to maintain good relations with the Egyptian government and because they had doubts about the Israeli version of the case.

In December 1954, the government of Israel officially asked the British Foreign Office to intervene on behalf of the Operation Susannah conspirators. This request was reinforced by a delegation of leading representatives of the World Sephardi Federation and the Anglo-Jewish Association.[37] The leader of the delegation consulted with the Israeli Embassy in London before the visit to the Foreign Office and reported its results to the embassy afterwards.[38] The British government avoided making any specific commitments. The permanent secretary of the foreign office, Anthony Nutting, advised A. L. Easterman, head of the political department of the World Jewish Congress, not to visit Egypt to observe the trial. Israeli officials claimed that Chief Rabbi Haim Nahum's statement of November 10, 1954, that Jews were not subject to systematic persecution in Egypt was issued under duress and had no value, but the British did not accept this argument. The Foreign Office regarded the trial as fair and unofficially determined that the defendants were not being mistreated. It discouraged the delegation from approaching the U.S. government. In opposition to the policies of the Conservative government, Labour MP Maurice Orbach, who was also a leader of the World Jewish Congress, visited Cairo from December 6 to 16 in an effort to convince the Egyptian government to be lenient with the accused.

On several occasions before the discovery of Operation Susannah, Egyptian Jews had been arrested on unrelated charges of membership in communist or Zionist organizations. American Jewish leaders met several times with State Department officials in Washington and requested inquiries into these arrests under the presumption that they must be part of an anti-Semitic campaign of the government. Jefferson Caffery, the U.S. ambassador in Cairo, was repeatedly directed to investigate and closely monitor the situation of Jews. Caffery consistently reported that there was no significant official anti-Semitism in Egypt. Only months before the apprehension of the Operation Susannah conspirators he wrote,

> There probably have been and still are instances of molestations, of discrimination against, individual Jews by various government departments and officials. There does not appear, however, to be any organized campaign by the

present regime against the Jewish community as a whole. On the contrary, Jews in Egypt are probably better treated than those in other Arab states.[39]

Caffery was close to Gamal Abdel Nasser and was not overly concerned about the welfare of Jews. He seems to have taken the many official statements about the equality of all Egyptian citizens and the formal gestures of cordiality to Jews by high government officials at face value. Nonetheless, because of the constant pressure on him from Washington on this matter, he probably would have reported anything of a substantial nature.

We do not know if the U.S. Embassy in Cairo considered the Operation Susannah defendants guilty. The available declassified embassy records contain no reference to an investigation indicating who, in its opinion, was responsible for the firebombings in Cairo and Alexandria and what the objectives of the perpetrators might have been.[40] This is a very suspicious omission because the library of the United States Information Service in Cairo was among the targets. It is difficult to believe that no inquiry into this matter was undertaken; very likely Caffery knew that the Operation Susannah conspirators had attacked U.S. government property in Egypt.

When the case came to trial, the government of Israel and a large number of American Jewish organizations pressed the State Department to intervene in favor of the defendants. The department resisted making a formal protest to the Egyptian government, probably because it knew that the charges were well founded and because it was still seeking good relations with Egypt. After the trial was concluded, Caffery visited Egyptian Foreign Minister Husayn Fawzi on at least two occasions to urge him not to permit any executions in the case.[41] The message from John Foster Dulles delivered by Caffery made no mention of the defendants' innocence or guilt. It referred only to the likelihood that executing any of the convicted prisoners would disrupt the possibility of progress in reducing tensions in the Middle East—a reference to ongoing secret talks between Egypt and Israel. These talks were indeed disrupted by the execution of Shmu'el Azar and Moshe Marzuq on January 31, 1955, and Israel's February 28 assault on Gaza.

Shortly after the Cairo trial began, representatives of Israel asked the American Jewish Committee to send their honorary president, Jacob Blaustein, to observe the proceedings. He was unable to make the trip, so the committee arranged for Roger Baldwin, U.S. chairman of the International League for the Rights of Man, who had a reputation of being sympathetic to the Arabs, to attend. Baldwin arrived in Cairo on January 8, 1955, after the trial was concluded, and left on January 27, before the verdicts were announced. This brief stay while the trial was not actually in session did not provide Baldwin the firmest basis for judgment. However, his reports did undermine many of the assertions circulating in Israel and the West. His most significant conclusion was, "There seems to be no doubt of some guilt of all the defendants." He was also quite clear that "By accepted western standards the trial was not fair," though in Egyptian terms proper procedures were followed.[42] Based on assurances that he and the U.S. Embassy had received from the Egyptian authorities, Baldwin reported to the American Jewish Committee leadership that he did not believe that death sentences would be imposed. When the sentences were announced and two of the accused were condemned to death, he termed this "shocking," "savage," and "vindictive" because

> [t]he conspiracy did not involve any serious acts of espionage or sabotage. It was, as the defense said, a childish and irrational affair of young people acting on instructions of two agents [Dar and Seidenwerg, alias Paul Frank] who escaped and were not condemned. . . . The explanation for such severity is to be found not in the trial record, but politics.[43]

When the sentences were announced, their severity became the focal point of Western attention. Many of the major U.S. and British papers editorialized against the trial or the sentences, including the *London Observer*,[44] the *New York Times*,[45] the *New York Herald Tribune*,[46] and the *Manchester Guardian*.[47] A *Washington Post* editorial termed the trial a "show trial . . . of 13 Jews . . . under trumped-up charges" and was so strong that the American Jewish Committee considered using it in its publicity work.[48] A *Washington Star* editorial called the sentences a "judicial lynching."[49] This barrage of criticism against the procedures and sentences of the trial inevitably drew attention away from Roger Baldwin's correct conclusion that the defendants were guilty.

AFTER THE EXECUTIONS

The Egyptian government's most comprehensive effort to convince a foreign audience of its case against the conspirators was presented in a pamphlet titled *The Story of Zionist Espionage in Egypt*. The central claims of the text were well supported by the evidence presented in court. However, some of its assertions were blatantly false, for example, the assertion that "during the Palestine War the Jews of Egypt were not interned."[50] The effort to link Operation Susannah to a history of "Zionist atrocities"—the assassination of Lord Moyne in Cairo in 1944, the assassination of Count Bernadotte in 1948, and violation of Muslim and Christian religious holy places by Israeli military forces during the 1948 war—was unconvincing because the first two actions were carried out by dissident Zionists opposed to the Jewish Agency and the Israeli government, and the last occurred during a war in which both sides attacked civilian populations. The rhetorical pretense that espionage and sabotage were not normal activities between states (especially those formally at war with each other, as were Egypt and Israel) was not credible. But for a Western audience, the part of the pamphlet that most damaged the credibility of the Egyptian government's claims was the section arguing that Zionism and communism share "one political objective— world domination. Both powers co-operate secretly and in public without friction since the power in the end will eventually go to Zionism."[51]

This superfluous contention reproduced elements of Nazi propaganda and discredited the entire Egyptian case in the eyes of many foreign observers. The American Jewish Committee distributed this text along with another Egyptian government pamphlet criticizing Israel's February 28 raid on Gaza, claiming these tracts demonstrated that the Egyptian Embassy in Washington was spreading anti-Semitic propaganda. Drawing attention to the anti-Semitism in the one pamphlet allowed the committee to obscure the Israeli aggression described in the second.[52]

The U.S. Embassy in Cairo complained to the Egyptian government about *The Story of Zionist Espionage in Egypt* and reported that Foreign Minister Fawzi was "embarrassed at having it brought to their attention and avoided any discussion of its contents."[53] The senior foreign ministry official was apparently familiar enough with Western political discourse to know the pamphlet's rhetorical strategy was self-defeating. The reports of the General Security Services (*al-mabahith al-ʿamma*) conveying the results of its investigation of Operation Susannah to the assistant permanent secretary for general security and police affairs of the Ministry of Interior do not mention communism. They are dry and factual accounts of the conspirators' trips to Israel, contacts with Israeli agents, and possession of wireless transmitters and encryption codes.[54] The police and general security investigators do not seem to have believed Philip Natanson's and Victor Levy's initial statements during their interrogations that they had acted on behalf of a communist organization. At the trial, the prosecution did not mention any links between communism and Zionism. Consequently, the source of the anti-Semitic content of the pamphlet appears to be the midlevel officials responsible for producing the tract in the Ministry of Information. They were probably unaware of the damage to Egypt's image that might be caused by equating Zionism and communism, and they may even have believed this absurd notion.

Despite such occasional expressions of official anti-Semitism, in late 1954 and early 1955, when the U.S. government had a favorable view of Gamal Abdel Nasser, informed observers like Ambassador Caffery resisted the charge that the Egyptian regime was practicing Nazi-style anti-Semitism. Such accusations became more common in some political circles and in the American media after Egypt purchased arms from Czechoslovakia in September 1955. According to the conceptually limited global map promoted by the brothers Allen and John Foster Dulles, Egypt could now be accused of being an enemy of the "Free World." The *New York Times,* reflecting the views of a good portion of its readership, began referring to Abdel Nasser as "Hitler on the Nile."[55]

Egyptian Jews again found themselves under pressure as a result of the Anglo-French-Israeli invasion of Egypt in October 1956. Many were arrested; their property was sequestered and confiscated; and, in contrast to the situation during the first Arab-Israeli War, the Egyptian government pressured them—or if they were foreign nationals, compelled them—to leave the country. As it had in 1948, the government of Israel took the lead in promoting the notion that the Jews of Egypt were being subjected to Nazi-like persecution. Prime Minister David Ben-Gurion reported to the Knesset after the war on Egypt's treatment of its Jews, "These acts remind us of those committed by Hitler before the world war." He went on to describe the Nazi character of the Egyptian regime in more general terms:

> Today we must remind the world of the fact that many people did not believe our warnings in the case of Hitler's *Mein Kampf* which many treated as nonsense and believed that no one would act according to the directions it gave. . . .
>
> I must remind members of this House that during the Israeli army's Sinai operation many of the Egyptian officers' vehicles were decorated with the swastika and that many of these officers had copies of *Mein Kampf* in an Arabic translation with them.[56]

Israel never presented any verifiable evidence regarding swastikas on Egyptian military vehicles and the like, but Ben-Gurion's allegations were uncritically reported in Israel and the United States. They confirmed what many people already "knew." The increased tensions between Egypt and the U.S. government as a result of the promulgation of the Eisenhower Doctrine in January 1957 encouraged American Jewish organizations to be more assertive in promoting their views about the Middle East because Egypt and by extension "the Arabs" now constituted a common enemy for both Israel and the United States.

After the war, French Jewish groups initiated an international conference of representatives of Jewish organizations to discuss the situation of Egyptian Jews. This undertaking may well be related to the French government's extreme agitation over the nationalization of the Suez Canal Company, a corporation registered in France and headquartered in Paris. The American Jewish Committee, the American Jewish Congress, B'nai B'rith, and all the large American Zionist organizations participated and endorsed a statement asserting, "The Egyptian authorities acted with the advice of notorious Nazis and with the aid of techniques elaborated by the totalitarian regimes whose existence has darkened the human scene during the past generation . . . and if they have singled out the Jews it is only because they have chosen to begin with the most defenseless minority."[57] The statement failed to mention that Israel had recently invaded Egypt or even hint that this might have affected the condition of Egypt's Jews.

In January 1957, B'nai B'rith, the largest American Jewish organization, held a press conference to announce that "former officials of the Nazi regime in Germany are administering the Egyptian government's anti-Jewish 'terror' program."[58] In response to the B'nai B'rith press release, Zachariah Shuster, the European director of the American Jewish Committee, wrote to the New York office that "the release has much information which is patently false and much which is greatly—and usually luridly—exaggerated. . . . We are confident that most of it is pure invention and represents a concoction of imaginary horror stories without any basis in reality."[59] Nonetheless, an American Jewish Committee fact sheet on "The Plight of the Jews in Egypt" issued in early 1957, although less elaborate and sensational, adopted the same style. It charged that three former Nazis, including one identified as an SS general, occupied positions of high responsibility in Egypt.[60] Ten thousand copies of this fact sheet were printed, and Representative Abraham Multer (D, NY) inserted its entire text into the *Congressional Record*.[61]

In 1955 or 1956, Don Peretz began to work for the American Jewish Committee as a consultant on Middle East affairs. After a two-week visit to Egypt in June 1957, Peretz reported to the committee leadership that "the situation [of Egyptian Jews] in no way resembles that as portrayed by most of the American press or by the American Jewish Committee fact sheets," which he regarded as "very misleading and not very helpful."[62] Subsequently the committee commissioned an investigation, apparently undertaken by Don Peretz, to verify a report in the *Frankfurter Allgemeine Zeitung* about former SS leaders at the head of the Egyptian gestapo. The investigation concluded that none of the persons named by the German paper could be traced, and no evidence of the presence of former SS leaders in Egypt could be established. All such press reports were based on information coming from the World Jewish Congress in New York and the B'nai B'rith. The investigation further charged that many of the alleged "facts" about this matter in an article in B'nai B'rith's *National Jewish Monthly* were false. The report concluded, "None of the known German councillors who have been active for years in Egypt has ever been able to have immediate political or other influence."[63]

The American Jewish Committee never publicized Peretz's unequivocal statements. His most substantial piece of research for the committee—a comprehensive and judicious summary titled "Egyptian Jews Today"—was also never published.[64] Peretz's essay discussed both the material prosperity of Egypt's Jews and their precarious position as a result of the trajectory of Egyptian nationalism and the Arab-Zionist conflict. It documented anti-Semitic expressions in Egypt's mass media, explaining their historical and political context, and also drew attention to several very careful and correct statements on the status of Jews by Egyptian officials. Peretz did not mention that any Nazis held official positions of authority in Egypt.

Released in January 1956, Peretz's report should have prepared American Jewish Committee leaders to understand that although the situation of Egyptian Jews was difficult, many of the stories circulating after the October 1956 war were grossly exaggerated. But for the committee to publicly oppose the claim that Egypt was practicing Nazi-like anti-Semitism would have been organizational suicide. Institutional American Jewish life was quite factionalized, and there was competition among the various groups to adopt the most vigilant and militant stand against anti-Semitism. The memory of Nazi mass murder and the refusal of Western political leaders to recognize its dimensions and mount a concerted response weighed "like a nightmare on the brain of the living."[65] This consideration decisively influenced the American Jewish discourse on Operation Susannah and every other discussion of the status of Egyptian

Jews. Despite the lack of evidence, Israeli government officials and publicists encouraged the dissemination of exaggerations and fabrications
about the persecution suffered by Egyptian Jews.

MARGINALIZING THE "HEROES OF THE AFFAIR"

The trial of the Operation Susannah conspirators and the execution of
Shmu'el Azar and Moshe Marzuq aroused a storm of public and official
protest in Israel and among Jewish communities in Europe and North
America. Nonetheless, concern for the convicted who remained alive and
in Egyptian prisons soon disappeared from the public agenda in Israel.
Exposure of the details of this episode threatened to destroy the careers
of leading figures in the political and military establishment. In fact, the
end of Ben-Gurion's career as prime minister of Israel in 1963 was directly related to the factional contention in MAPAI that erupted when
Israeli aspects of the affair were exposed in 1960–61 (see below).
Nonetheless, the details of what happened in Egypt in 1954 remained
shrouded in a veil of official secrecy until 1975.

Even relatively peripheral and minor information was banned from
the press and radio by the official censor. Thus, in late 1955, the Israeli
media were preemptively prohibited from reporting the fact that members of the families of the accused in the Cairo trial were about to arrive
in Israel on the grounds that this might endanger their security or the security of those remaining in Egypt.[66] A public welcome might also have
confirmed the veracity of Egypt's charges against the convicted and
risked further exposure of the case and its principals.

Security considerations are a plausible explanation for such a high
level of secrecy until the 1956 Suez/Sinai War. However, if Israeli authorities were so concerned for the welfare of the members of the Operation Susannah network, why did they fail to request their release in the
course of the general prisoner exchange after the war? Egyptian officials
expected such a request and were prepared to grant it. Yet the Israelis
did not mention the matter in the negotiations over the return of prisoners of war.[67] Me'ir Meyuhas and Me'ir Za'fran served out their seven-
year terms. Robert Dassa, Victor Levy, Philip Natanson, and Marcelle
Ninio were finally released in the prisoner exchange following the 1967
war. These four have repeatedly charged that individuals in the highest
echelons of the Israeli military, including Moshe Dayan, minister of defense in 1967, were uninterested in seeing them released.[68]

The charge is credible in light of the major political scandal provoked by Operation Susannah. The Olshan-Dori Committee established by Prime Minister Sharett in January 1955 was charged with determining which Israeli official had authorized Operation Susannah, which had never been discussed or authorized by the cabinet. But Olshan and Dori failed to determine whether Minister of Defense Pinhas Lavon or Director of Military Intelligence Binyamin Gibli had given the order. Lavon was forced to resign and accept responsibility for the Cairo "mishap," though he insisted that he had not authorized it. The issue smoldered under the surface of Israeli political life for several years and exploded in 1960 as a result of evidence presented at the 1959 trial of Avri Seidenwerg (Paul Frank), who was convicted of being a double agent and betraying the Operation Susannah conspirators. Seidenwerg had given perjured testimony to the Olshan-Dori Committee. A subsequent ministerial investigation determined that the key document establishing Lavon's responsibility had been forged. The political upheaval fomented by these revelations became known as the "Lavon affair."

When he learned of the perjured testimony, Lavon demanded exculpation. Prime Minister Ben-Gurion refused to exonerate Lavon because he did not want to damage the reputations of the Israeli armed forces, destroy Gibli's career, and implicate his close political allies Shimon Peres and Moshe Dayan, director-general of the Ministry of Defense and chief of staff of the Israel Defense Forces, respectively, in 1954. Exonerating Lavon would imply that Ben-Gurion's proteges in the Israeli security establishment were responsible for Operation Susannah. Moreover, if military officers acted without requesting proper civilian authorization, not only those personally responsible would be discredited. The leaders of the entire security establishment, and ultimately Ben-Gurion himself, would stand accused of complicity or negligence, or at least of creating an atmosphere permitting such behavior.

The terms of the Lavon affair established by the Olshan-Dori Committee and all the subsequent official inquiries focused entirely on relations among leading personalities within MAPAI and the Israeli army. The sharpest expression of this discourse is the title of the published version of the investigation ordered by Prime Minister Ben-Gurion but released only in 1979: *Mi natan et ha-hora'ah?* (Who gave the order?).[69] The Egyptian Jews who had undertaken espionage and sabotage on behalf of Israel were excluded from the narrative. If the perpetrators of

Operation Susannah had been released after the 1956 war, they would
have come to Israel and stated, as they have consistently since 1975,
when they were first permitted to speak, that they acted only under orders. They would have denied Gibli's version of the story, according to
which the earliest bombings in Operation Susannah were unauthorized
by any Israeli authority. During the years when this was a live issue in
Israeli politics, they were either jailed in Egypt or living in Israel under
a gag order.

Even Israelis highly critical of Ben-Gurion accepted the discursive
terms of the political and military establishment. In 1961, when the battle
between Ben-Gurion and Lavon was a fiercely contested public specta-
cle, the journalists Eliyahu Hasin and Dan Hurvitz wrote a scathing book
defending Lavon and criticizing Ben-Gurion, Peres, Dayan, and Gibli.
The essence of the matter, according to Hasin and Hurvitz, was that Lavon
was accused of giving "an ill-considered and unwise order which he had
in fact not given; however, giving such an order was within his legal authority and had no stain of criminality."[70] Hasin and Hurvitz were ex-
traordinarily daring in the extent to which they were willing to expose
duplicitous and criminal behavior by military and civilian leaders responsible for Israel's security. By directing its fire at Ben-Gurion, Dayan,
and Peres, their book challenged the activist politico-military outlook
these three MAPAI leaders had developed (usually designated as "activism") and the related view that the military, as the central institution
of Israeli society, should be insulated from public scrutiny and criticism.

It is therefore all the more striking that Hasin and Hurvitz never
clearly stated *what* the order was. They mentioned Operation Susannah
and the Cairo trial briefly on two occasions: once as part of a summary
of the events of 1954 and the deterioration of relations with Egypt and
again when noting that as late as 1960 Moshe Sharett apparently believed that the 1954 bombings in Egypt were undertaken without orders
from Israel (which is most unlikely because the Olshan-Dori Committee
had concluded in January 1955 that either Lavon or Gibli had ordered
the bombings).[71] Censorship very likely prevented Hasin and Hurvitz
from specifying clearly that the order in question was for Egyptian Jews
to begin a campaign of bombing in Egypt.

Despite their scathing criticism of Ben-Gurion and the Israeli military
establishment, Hasin and Hurvitz reinforced the discourse of national
security in which Operation Susannah was framed because the issue
was narrowly posed as who did or did not give a particular order. They
did not discuss whether such an order should have been given or what

its consequences were. Just as in the official Israeli government version, the executors of Operation Susannah were marginal to their own story; the interests and the fate of the Jews of Egypt were beyond the range of the investigations of Hasin and Hurvitz. For both the defenders and the critics of Ben-Gurion in the 1960s, the Lavon affair concerned a conflict among the leaders of MAPAI or a question about the competence of Israeli military intelligence, not events in Egypt that affected the lives of Egyptian Jews and the course of Egyptian-Israeli relations.

On the tenth anniversary of the execution of Shmu'el Azar and Moshe Marzuq for their roles in Operation Susannah, Shlomo Kohen-Tzidon, a native of Alexandria who had emigrated to Israel and become a member of the Knesset, published a book memorializing Shmu'el Azar and the Jews of Alexandria. As far as I have been able to determine, it is the first book about the Jews of Egypt to appear in Israel. Kohen-Tzidon's text reinserted the history of his community and what he regarded as its most heroic members into the Israeli public debate on Operation Susannah and the Lavon affair. While expressing a certain resistance to the exclusion of Egyptian Jews from the official narrative, the book's cautious manner limited its impact and ultimately reproduced and reinforced many elements of the prevailing discourse.

Recounting the "foolish and childish" exploits of Operation Susannah, Kohen-Tzidon wrote that he did not know all the details of what Azar and the other members of the network did or why they did it. He did not think it was credible that Israel would have recruited Jews as spies because as a minority they were highly visible and had greater difficulty of access to public institutions and to the masses of Egyptians. Yet Kohen-Tzidon did "know" that the treatment of the Egyptian Jews after their arrests was reminiscent of cruelest tortures of the gestapo.[72] This argument was reinforced by including a reprint of a newspaper article by another Egyptian Jew, Felix Harari, who wrote in the daily Yed'iot Aharonot on the occasion of the tenth anniversary of the Cairo trial, "Today there is almost no doubt that the Egyptian version of the story is false. . . . Today . . . it is clear that Victorine [Marcelle Ninio] was entirely innocent."[73] This focus on Marcelle Ninio once again feminized the perpetrators of Operation Susannah and diminished the severity of their actions.

Kohen-Tzidon also argued that Operation Susannah was emblematic of the Egyptian Jewish community's support for the Zionist project, hence its political and cultural legitimacy in Israel. Consequently, sixty pages after declaring the innocence of the Operation Susannah conspirators, Kohen-Tzidon appeared to admit the possibility of their guilt: "To the extent that the youths did what was attributed to them in the court, or a little of what was attributed to them, they acted good heartedly as a result of misdirection according to ill-considered instructions."[74] The guilt of the conspirators enhanced the status of the entire Egyptian Jewish community in Zionist terms.

This rupture in the text has several possible explanations. The book was hastily prepared and issued by a minor publisher without much editorial care. Moreover, it was a public relations device for the only Egyptian Jewish member of the Knesset attempting to establish his claim to represent all Egyptian Jews in Israel. Precision of expression was not the point.

There were also political and administrative pressures on the text. As a loyal Zionist and member of the Israeli parliament, Kohen-Tzidon could not launch a major public attack on Israeli political and military authorities for authorizing imprudent actions that might have endangered the Jews of Egypt. This would have constituted a challenge to the Zionist maxim that the existence of Israel unconditionally guaranteed the security of all Jews throughout the world. Suggesting that this might not be so could have destroyed his personal credibility and threatened his political career.

Overt censorship also contributed to limiting Kohen-Tzidon's challenge to the official version of events and their import. Parts of his printed text are rendered unintelligible by defaced type. Much of the censored material is in the section of the book reprinting journalistic accounts of the Cairo trial. One of the censored items was an article by Ze'ev Schiff that first appeared in *ha-Aretz*. Uncommonly, Schiff did ask whether it was permissible to endanger the Jewish community of Egypt by recruiting its members as spies. Moreover, in the original newspaper version, Schiff quoted from an assessment of the affair in *The New Statesman and Nation*:

> There is no doubt that the saboteurs were naive and inexperienced. We must add that just as Colonel Nasser should have acted with mercy, it would be best for Mr. Sharett [prime minister at the time] on his part, to exercise strong supervision over the Israeli Ministry of Defense and its various secret operations.

This passage was excised from Kohen-Tzidon's book despite having already appeared in *ha-Aretz* in 1955 and again in 1964.[75] Apparently, quoting from a published foreign source forced the censor to allow a disposable newspaper to intimate the guilt of the Operation Susannah conspirators and the responsibility of the Israeli government. Ten years after the trial, it was still not permissible to say the same in a more permanent book. Awareness of the censorship imposed on him may have produced Kohen-Tzidon's ambivalence about the guilt of the perpetrators of Operation Susannah and the responsibility of the Israeli government for their actions.

To have his book published, Kohen-Tzidon had to adopt a certain naiveté about Operation Susannah that minimized the possibility that Shmu'el Azar and his colleagues were guilty of espionage and sabotage on behalf of Israel. Because he was not an investigative reporter, but a politician seeking to advance his career and legitimize his social base of support, Kohen-Tzidon was willing to restrain whatever doubts he may have had about the official story. The result was a sentimental, unpolished, and unconvincing narrative.

In any case, the opinions of the politically aware sector of the Israeli public about what constituted the important issues at stake were already framed by a discourse emphasizing national security and the rivalry among the leaders of MAPAI. The regnant Ashkenazi cultural ethos of the 1960s was uninterested in the culture and history of the Jews of the Middle East. Kohen-Tzidon's book, although it attempted to focus attention on Egyptian Jews, did so in a way that could have little impact on public debate in Israel. Moreover, it ultimately reproduced and reinforced the discourse structuring the official Israeli version of Operation Susannah.

In the 1960s, Hasin and Hurvitz and Kohen-Tzidon were able to write books whose ostensible subject was Operation Susannah while managing to avoid a substantive discussion of what happened in Egypt in 1954, who did it, and why it was done. Hasin and Hurvitz accomplished this by focusing on the limited question of "Who gave the order?" in Israel. Kohen-Tzidon's concern to eulogize and commemorate Shmu'el Azar and the Jewish community of Alexandria and his confidence in the good faith of Israel's leadership allowed him to assert firmly as fact propositions that were highly questionable, if not yet demonstrably false. The effect of these books and supporting minor texts was to write the Egyptian Jews who undertook Operation Susannah out of their own history. Both the national security discourse of Hasin and Hurvitz and the martyrology of Kohen-Tzidon replicated the effect of the promiscuous deployment of the trope of Nazi-like persecution of Egyptian Jews from 1948 on, especially during the 1954 Cairo trial and the aftermath of the 1956 war. The fate of Egyptian Jews was rendered incidental to the needs and interests of the state of Israel as defined by its political leaders. Their experiences and conditions were defined through the lens of European Jewish history and its continuation in Israel.

CAN THE PERPETRATORS
OF OPERATION SUSANNAH SPEAK?

Twenty years after the 1954 Cairo trial, the Israeli government finally admitted that the conspirators had acted on its behalf. Robert Dassa, Victor Levy, and Marcelle Ninio appeared on television in March 1975 and declared that they had acted on orders from Israel.[76] Instead of asking who gave the order, they posed two new questions for the audience: Why were they abandoned after the 1956 war, and who was responsible for the decision not to request their release? These questions did not radically challenge the prevailing national security discourse on the Lavon affair, but they did attempt to reframe the narrative so that the members of the Operation Susannah network could reclaim their roles as historical actors. Ninio pushed right against the limit marked by the censor's pen in asking why they had not been allowed to publish their book, suggesting that she and her colleagues had a coherent version of what happened to them that challenged the official story. Their book, *Operation Susannah,* a collective memoir as told to Aviezer Golan (Philip Natanson participated in preparing the book but not in the television interview) unequivocally confirmed that the accused in the Cairo trial had engaged in espionage and sabotage on behalf of Israel, although Golan strained to avoid characterizing these acts as punishable crimes in Egyptian terms.

Operation Susannah conspicuously deploys the trope of Nazi-like persecution as exculpatory evidence for the accused. The German nurse in al-Muwassat Hospital in Alexandria, where Marcelle Ninio was confined after her suicide attempt, is gratuitously described as a surly blonde "whose appearance and behavior made her resemble the SS women in the European extermination camps."[77] More significantly and ostentatiously, former Prime Minister Golda Meir shamelessly exploited the memory of the Nazi era in her preface to the book. She recalled that upon meeting Dassa, Levy, Natanson, and Ninio when they first arrived in Israel in 1968,

> I thought of the Jews throughout Jewish history who faced discrimination, torture, danger, broken in body but never in spirit. I thought of the six mil-

lion Jews during World War II in Nazi camps, buried alive, tortured, gassed. I thought of the Jews in the Warsaw Ghetto who fought the Nazi tanks.[78]

Meir felt guilty that the "heroes of the affair," as they were referred to in the television interview that prompted the publication of *Operation Susannah*, had not received the recognition they deserved in Israel. She had been the first government official to admit that Dassa, Levy, Natanson, and Ninio were in Israel when she announced, after a cabinet meeting in November 1971, that she would be attending Ninio's wedding. For Meir, the long years during which the Israeli government denied any responsibility for its agents jailed in Egypt could be redressed by publicly embracing them and associating their story with the history of Nazi anti-Semitism and the resistance to it. Europeanizing the story of these Egyptian Jews was Meir's ultimate expression of their acceptance and legitimacy. Thus, even as Israeli authorities finally admitted that its agents were not victims of a Nazi-style, anti-Semitic show trial, Golda Meir reinforced that imagery and with it the barriers to a critical examination of Operation Susannah.

Le Caire, Entrée

ل الموسكي

1. Entry to *harat al-yahud* (the Jewish quarter) in Cairo (courtesy of the Association pour la sauvegarde du patrimoine culturel des juifs d'Egypte and Editions du Scribe)

2. Haim Nahum Effendi, chief rabbi
of Egypt, 1924–60 (courtesy of the
Association pour la sauvegarde du
patrimoine culturel des juifs d'Egypte
and Editions du Scribe)

3. Yusuf ʿAslan Qattawi (Cattaui)
Pasha (1861–1942), two-time cabinet
minister (1924–25) and president of the
Sephardi Jewish community of Cairo
(1924–42) (courtesy of the Association
pour la sauvegarde du patrimoine
culturel des juifs d'Egypte and Editions
du Scribe)

4. Isaac G. Lévi, secretary-general of the Egyptian Federation of Industries (1922–56) and vice-president of the Sephardi Jewish community of Cairo (1943–56) (courtesy of the Association pour la sauvegarde du patrimoine culturel des juifs d'Egypte and Editions du Scribe)

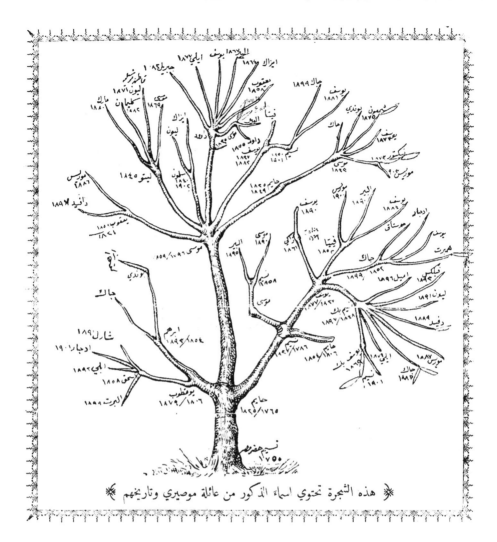

5. Genealogy of the male members of the Egyptian Jewish Mosseri family, 1750–1901 (courtesy of the Association pour la sauvegarde du patrimoine culturel des juifs d'Egypte and Editions du Scribe)

6. A Jewish boxer. Isaac Amiel and Salonichio were national boxing champions. From the 1920s to 1956, Jews represented Egypt in international competitions in several sports and won national championships in boxing, wrestling, fencing, tennis, and golf; the Maccabi team won several national basketball titles. (courtesy of the Association pour la sauvegarde du patrimoine culturel des juifs d'Egypte and Editions du Scribe)

7. Karaites at prayer in the 'Abbasiyya synagogue (courtesy of the Association pour la sauvegarde du patrimoine culturel des juifs d'Egypte and Editions du Scribe)

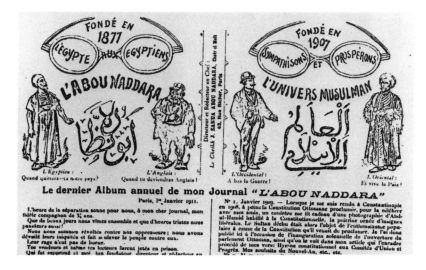

8. The last annual compilation of the colloquial Egyptian satirical journal *Abu Naddara*, founded in 1877 by Yaʿqub Sannuʿ (1839–1912). Sannuʿ was exiled from Egypt for his political and cultural activity and continued to publish *Abu Naddara* from Paris under several related names until 1910. He was the first to coin the nationalist slogan "Egypt for the Egyptians." (courtesy of the Association pour la sauvegarde du patimoine culturel des juifs d'Egypte and Editions du Scribe)

9. Cover page of the Karaite biweekly newspaper
al-Kalim, published by the Young Karaite Jewish
Association and edited by Yusuf Kamal from
1945 to 1956 (courtesy of the Association pour
la sauvegarde du patrimoine culturel des juifs
d'Egypte and Editions du Scribe)

10. Masthead of the French-language Jewish weekly *La Tribune Juive*, published from 1936 to 1948

11. Masthead of the first issue of the Arabic-language Jewish weekly, *al-Shams*, edited by Saʿd Malki from 1934 to 1948

Diasporas and the Reconstruction of Identity

CHAPTER 5

The Graduates of ha-Shomer ha-Tzaʿir in Israel

HA-SHOMER HA-TZAʿIR AND EGYPTIAN ZIONISM

Although organized Zionist activity began in Egypt at the turn of the century, the movement had a very limited social base until 1942–43. During the 1920s and 1930s, Egyptian Zionism was focused around philanthropic and cultural work, such as funding the Hebrew University of Jerusalem. Until the 1936–39 Arab Revolt in Palestine, such activity was not considered inconsistent with patriotic loyalty to Egypt. Zionist activism declined as the pan-Arab reverberations of the Palestinian resistance to Zionist settlement convinced many Jews and non-Jews that there might indeed be a contradiction between Zionism and loyalty to Egypt.

Because most Egyptian Jews were relatively secure and comfortable during the 1930s, few saw the point of risking their position by ostentatious support for Zionism. Moreover, before 1948, the small minority of Jews who identified themselves as political Zionists rarely expressed this in the form of immigration to Palestine. Between 1917 and 1947, only 4,020 Jews had left Egypt for Palestine, and a large proportion of them were Yemenis, Moroccans, or Ashkenazim who had resided only temporarily in Egypt.[1] The strength of Egyptian Zionism at the end of World War II may be measured by the fact that in preparation for the Twenty-Second Zionist Congress in 1946, 7,500 Jews—about 10 percent of the community—purchased *shekels*, the financial contribution bestowing the right to be represented at the congress.[2]

The concerted efforts of the Zionist emissaries from Palestine who arrived in 1943 and Zionist activists among the allied troops and the Palestinian Jewish Brigade stationed in Egypt gained Zionism a significant base of support in Egypt for the first time. They conveyed the news of the mass murder of European Jewry to Egypt and, by presenting this information in Zionist discursive terms, encouraged Egyptian Jews to draw conclusions about their future based on a particular understanding of the significance of the catastrophe in Europe. This message, especially in its labor Zionist from, appealed to French-educated youth influenced by internationalism and the united front against fascism in the 1930s and 1940s who might otherwise have joined one of the several communist groups.

The most dynamic elements of Zionism, in Egypt as elsewhere, were the youth movements, which advanced a radical vision of Jewish renewal through immigration to Palestine and physical labor in agricultural colonies on the frontier of Jewish settlement—immigration (*'aliyah*), settlement (*hityashvut*), pioneering (*halutziut*), and self-realization (*hagshamah atzmit*) in the labor Zionist lexicon. The largest labor Zionist youth movement in Egypt before 1947 was he-Halutz ha-Ahid (The unified pioneer): a new organization created by the Zionist Executive as a means to avoid exporting the factional tensions within MAPAI to the Middle Eastern diaspora.[3] Suppressing the vibrant political debate within the Zionist left preserved the overall dominance of MAPAI and was probably also linked to an assumption that Middle Eastern Jews were too backward politically to appreciate the nuances of such debate. The most disciplined and ideologically committed of the youth movements, and the largest after 1947, was ha-Shomer ha-Tza'ir (The young guard), which was affiliated with the Kibutz ha-Artzi federation and later with the Marxist-Zionist MAPAM after its establishment in 1948. The other youth movements active in Egypt were Bnai 'Akivah (Sons of Rabbi Akiva), affiliated with the labor wing of the National Religious Party, and Betar (Trumpeldor covenant), the youth movement of revisionist Zionism. Less ideologically committed members of the Maccabi and ha-Koah (Strength) sports clubs were also drawn into the network of Zionist activity.

Ha-Shomer ha-Tza'ir in Egypt was locally known until late 1947 as ha-'Ivri ha-Tza'ir (The young Hebrew). The movement was established in Cairo in the early 1930s. A small group of senior members left for Palestine and joined Kibutz 'Ein ha-Horesh in December 1934. For the next several years, like other Zionist activity in Egypt, ha-'Ivri ha-Tza'ir stagnated, and none of its graduates went to Palestine.

Ezra Zanona (Talmor) was the central figure in revitalizing ha'-Ivri ha-Tza'ir in the late 1930s.[4] He wrote to the leaders of ha-Shomer ha-Tza'ir in Palestine requesting that an emissary be sent to provide leadership for the Egyptian movement. In response, Sasha Korin of Kibutz Mesilot was despatched to Cairo in May 1938. Korin and Talmor reorganized ha-'Ivri ha-Tza'ir and opened a new branch (ken; pl. kinim) in the middle-class suburb of Heliopolis.[5] Relying on educational materials in English that Talmor requested from ha-Shomer ha-Tza'ir in New York, Talmor and Korin reinforced the ideological and organizational foundations of the movement—a combination of scouting, Marxism, and an intensely emotional collective life emphasizing immigration to Palestine and life in the kibutz. Between 1938 and 1944, five kinim of ha-'Ivri ha-Tza'ir were established: three in Cairo and two in Alexandria, with 700–800 members by the end of World War II.[6] The movement continued to use this local name until late 1947, when it went underground and adopted the name of the international movement: ha-Shomer ha-Tza'ir.

The Heliopolis ken, led by Ezra Talmor, became the largest and most developed in Egypt, with about 150 members by 1945. The ken met at the Abraham Btesh Jewish Community School. Most of the families of students at the Btesh school, like most other middle-class Egyptian Jewish families, were not religiously observant, but "traditional." They attended synagogue on major holidays, ate matzah at Passover, and observed the Jewish rites of passage. Although the curriculum at the Btesh school included Hebrew and other Jewish subjects, the primary language of instruction was French. Graduates of the school were not usually fluent in Hebrew. Perhaps even more so than other branches, the Heliopolis ken of ha-Shomer ha-Tza'ir was socially selective, even snobbish. At the older levels, only high school students were accepted for membership, a stringent requirement when secondary education was rare in Egypt. All kinim of the movement imposed strict rules of conduct on their members and expected that senior members would immigrate to Israel and settle on a kibutz.

In this milieu, Jewish culture had a cosmopolitan, radical, French inflection—an outlook that regarded Parisian intellectual and cultural life as the highest (perhaps the only true) form of civilization. The activities of the ken were conducted in French. Even today, many of the movement's graduates living in Israel speak French among themselves at social gatherings in their homes. Recommended reading for leaders of ha-Shomer ha-Tza'ir included Marx, Engels, Leontiev, Borokhov (the articulator of the Marxist-Zionist synthesis), the French communist daily, *L'Humanité,* and the classic literature of French, English, and Russian social realism. There was relatively little study of the history and politics of the Middle East or the Arab world.

Ezra Talmor personally exemplified this ambience. His parents had emigrated to Egypt from Aleppo. His grandparents spoke only Arabic, but his parents spoke both Arabic and French at home. The family was not religiously observant, and he received no Jewish education. Ezra's two older brothers studied at a French Catholic school, but Ezra attended the secular Collège Français du Caire. His brothers then transferred there because their parents feared they might be converted to Christianity. Ezra's older brother, Zaki, was not a Zionist. He worked for the National Bank of Egypt, rising through the ranks despite having finished only the eighth grade to become head of the foreign currency department before he left Egypt for Switzerland in 1956. Ezra knew Arabic well enough to read *al-Ahram* and pass the Arabic section of the Egyptian baccalaureate, but he was more comfortable in French, the main language of instruction during his schooling. Like many members of the Zionist youth movements, Ezra Talmor was attracted to ha-'Ivri ha-Tza'ir for social reasons before becoming fully committed to its ideology. While serving as the leader of the Heliopolis *ken* and secretary of the Egyptian movement and working part-time as a clerk in the Crédit Foncier Egyptien, he completed his O and A level exams in preparation for pursuing an external degree in philosophy at London University. He was attracted to European philosophy because he had learned that understanding Marxism required a study of Hegel and dialectics.

Because their social backgrounds and political positions had much in common, there were frequent ideological debates between members of ha-'Ivri ha-Tza'ir and the Jewish communists. One evening in 1938 two Marxist Jews—an English doctoral student in Orientalism, Bernard Lewis, and Henri Curiel, the future leader of the most influential of the Egyptian communist organizations, HADETU, visited the Heliopolis *ken.* There, Talmor, Lewis, and Curiel publicly argued in English and French over the relative merits of communism and socialist Zionism.[7] Such exchanges continued between left Zionists and communists in Egypt for the next ten years and more.

From 1942 until November 29, 1947, when the United Nations General Assembly voted to partition Palestine into a Jewish state and an Arab state, ha-Shomer ha-Tza'ir had a distinctive position within the Zionist movement opposing the establishment of an exclusively Jewish state in

Palestine. Instead, the movement favored a binational Arab-Jewish state—a position with some similarities, though based on different arguments, to the stand of the all-Jewish Communist Party of Palestine (Arab party members had left to form the National Liberation League) after 1946 and HADETU. In mid-1947, as the Soviet Union moved toward endorsing partitioning Palestine into two states, Lazare Guetta (Giv'ati), a leader of ha-'Ivri ha-Tza'ir in Alexandria, asked the movement headquarters in Palestine to despatch political materials in French and Arabic because they were "in deep discussions with Communist Jewish circles about Zionism, . . . Bi-nationalism, etc."[8] The pressure of constant debate with the communists led ha-'Ivri ha-Tza'ir to take its Marxism very seriously. In addition, Eli Peleg of Kibutz Gat, the movement's emissary from Palestine from 1946 until late May 1948, encouraged the older members of the movement to adopt a particularly militant version of the movement's ideology that attempted to fuse orthodox pro-Soviet Marxism-Leninism and Zionism.

In theory, ha-Shomer ha-Tza'ir and ha-Kibutz ha-Artzi struggled to uphold socialism and Zionism as coequal components of their ideology. In practice, a decisive majority of the movement always favored Zionism whenever there was a contradiction between Jewish national interests and socialist internationalism. The movement's conception of binationalism and Arab-Jewish coexistence in Palestine was naive and paternalistic, as is painfully evident from this excerpt from an essay on "colonization" in the internal bulletin of one of the Alexandria groups:

> Is that to say that our colonization in Palestine has harmed the Arabs and is to their detriment? No. Categorically not. Our colonization has been a balm for the backward eyes of our Arab cousins, and one may say that they have enjoyed a great benefit from it. With our colonization we hold out our hand to assist our cousins.[9]

The entire essay is framed by the same Eurocentric colonial outlook that informed the entire Zionist movement. Nonetheless, the Arab presence in Palestine and the surrounding countries was far more concrete for these Egyptians than it could be for European or American members of ha-Shomer ha-Tza'ir, who would probably not have referred to Arabs as their cousins. The fact that a pro-Soviet, Marxist-Zionist organization with the most conciliatory approach to the Palestinian Arabs in the entire Zionist movement became the largest and most active Zionist organization in Egypt is not accidental. Although movement members were themselves in the process of de-Arabizing their culture, they

retained a respect for and familiarity with Arab culture that influenced
their Zionist outlook in ways that tended to distinguish them from their
European and North American comrades.

When ha-Shomer ha-Tzaʿir and two other left Zionist currents—
Le-Ahdut ha-ʿAvodah and Left Poʿalei Tzion (Workers of Zion)—fused
to form MAPAM in January 1948, ha-Shomer ha-Tzaʿir abandoned bi-
nationalism and agreed to support the establishment of the state of Israel. Le-Ahdut ha-ʿAvodah and most of Left Poʿalei Tzion opposed the
creation of an Arab state in Palestine and did not accept the Palestinian
Arabs' right to self-determination. Although Le-Ahdut ha-ʿAvodah and
Left Poʿalei Tzion were a minority in the united party (a very large one
to be sure), their presence blocked MAPAM's adoption of a clear stand
on this and other vital issues.[10] The internal struggle among the component elements of MAPAM became an important influence on the fate of
many graduates of Egyptian ha-ʿIvri ha-Tzaʿir.

KIBUTZ NAHSHONIM

By the end of World War II, ha-ʿIvri ha-Tzaʿir was sufficiently developed
so that the senior members could entrust their younger disciples with
continuing the movement's educational work on their own. They formed
a *garʿin* (nucleus) and made plans to immigrate to Palestine and establish a new kibutz. Between 1945 and 1947, three contingents of about
30 members each left Egypt, leaving about 500 younger members of the
movement behind. The second contingent of the *garʿin* participated in
"Operation Passover" on April 11, 1946, which brought 65–100 immigrants to Palestine illegally.[11] This was the largest single group of
Egyptian Jews to reach Palestine before 1948—a good indication of the
scale of Zionist activity.

The first contingent of graduates of ha-ʿIvri ha-Tzaʿir arrived at Kibutz
ʿEin ha-Shofet in January 1945. ʿEin ha-Shofet was chosen to welcome
them in Palestine and provide agricultural training for the *garʿin* because
it was the first kibutz of ha-Shomer ha-Tzaʿir in North America, a branch
of the movement with which the Egyptians had been in contact. The second contingent of the Egyptian *garʿin* was received at Kfar Menahem, the
second kibutz of North American ha-Shomer ha-Tzaʿir. After completing
its agricultural training, in July 1946 the *garʿin* became independent and
moved to Ramat ha-Sharon, where it was joined by a group of French-
speaking graduates of ha-Shomer ha-Tzaʿir from Belgium, Switzerland,

and France. There the *garʿin* worked for wages while waiting for the Zionist authorities to allocate a plot of land for its future kibutz.

Members of the *garʿin* were recruited into the Palmah (the elite prestate Zionist military unit) on the eve of the UN partition decision. On November 14, 1947, they joined the Negev Brigade and took up a position at Hazali, a *heʾahzut* (militarily fortified agricultural settlement) about fifteen kilometers southeast of Beʾersheba. Hazali formed the southernmost triangle of Jewish settlement in the Negev together with Revivim and Halutza. It was besieged by the Egyptian army in the summer of 1948, but the *garʿin* held its position throughout the war. Members of the *garʿin* participated in all the major battles of the Negev against the Egyptian army, and four of them lost their lives in the fighting. The *garʿin* members were demobilized after the conclusion of hostilities in April 1949. On September 13, 1949, about fifty to sixty remaining members of the Egyptian *garʿin* and an Israeli *garʿin* established Kibutz Nahshonim at Migdal Tzedek, near Petah Tikva, on the border between Israel and Jordan.[12]

Ezra Talmor was one of the founders of Nahshonim, and he remained politically active during his first decade on the kibutz. From 1956 to 1959, he served as the representative of MAPAM in London. During this time, his wife, Sascha Talmor, obtained her Ph.D. in philosophy from the University of London. At the end of their stay, Ezra found enough time to study for an M.A. in philosophy from the same institution.

While the Talmors were in London, Fenner Brockway, a leader of the left in the Labour Party, reported that he had met with Michel Aflaq, a founder of the Syrian Baʿth Party. According to Brockway, Aflaq said that he was interested in meeting Israelis but could find no interlocutors. Ezra Talmor contacted Brockway and expressed his willingness to meet Aflaq. Consequently, he met several times with Syrian and Iraqi Baʿthist medical students in London. They drafted an outline of an Arab-Israeli peace agreement and sent a report of their meetings to Michel Aflaq, Meʾir Yaʿari, the leader of MAPAM, and Hugh Gaitskill, the leader of the British Labour Party. Talmor reported that Meʾir Yaʿari rebuked him for acting on his own initiative in this matter.

When he returned to Israel, Talmor wanted to be an activist in the Arab department of MAPAM because he "wanted peace between Jews and Arabs." He worked briefly with Simha Flapan and *New Outlook,* a nonparty monthly magazine devoted to promoting Arab-Israeli peace and heavily supported by MAPAM. Then he retired from political activity.

Talmor felt that he was excluded from a political career in MAPAM. "At first I thought it was simply racist. They could not accept that an Egyptian Jew would do something in political leadership," he said. Later he came to feel that his exclusion was due to the cliquishness of ha-Kibutz ha-Artzi and MAPAM and the fact that he did not belong to the inner circle of Me'ir Ya'ari composed of Eastern Europeans.

In the 1960s, Ezra Talmor obtained a doctorate in philosophy from the University of Paris. He and Sascha became professors at Haifa University in the Departments of Philosophy and English, respectively. In 1980, they founded and became editors of *History of European Ideas*— an interdisciplinary scholarly journal dedicated to studying the history of European cultural exchange and the emergence of the idea of Europe. This intellectual agenda is obviously in harmony with the political project of the European Union. The contents of the journal disclose that the Europe of the contributors and editors is almost exclusively England, France, Italy, and Germany—a traditionalist vision affirming the global centrality of the Western European Renaissance and Enlightenment. Today Ezra Talmor believes, "There is only one conceptual grid to grasp the world. It's a European conceptual grid."

Although we are all, even those who resist it, in some sense bound up in a European conceptual grid, Ezra Talmor's eager embrace of Europe can also be understood as a particular consequence of both the cosmopolitan, Francophone, left-wing political milieu of his youth in Egypt and in ha-Shomer ha-Tza'ir and the formative experiences of the founders of Kibutz Nahshonim that tended to make French culture a part of their identity as Egyptians. The Egyptian *gar'in* had to integrate with contingents of European French speakers and Ashkenazi Israelis. Their comrades fought and died in battle with the army of the land of their birth. They settled on rocky soil on the frontier with Jordan where hard physical labor was required to sustain themselves economically and it was tremendously difficult to remain politically informed and engaged. The social ideal of Israel in the 1950s and 1960s was the melting pot (*kibutz galuyot*). The members of Kibutz Nahshonim saw it as an important Zionist task to assimilate into Israeli Jewish culture, which was, in fact, heavily Eastern European in many respects. Consequently, although Nahshonim served as a gathering point for many French-speaking Jews, including those from Egypt and North Africa, it did not try to preserve the distinctive cultural characteristics of its founding members, nor was it able to make a distinctive political contribution drawing on the founders' origins in the Arab world.

In 1964, when Egyptian Jews still composed 40 percent of the membership of the kibutz, Ezra Talmor contributed an article titled "A Kibutz of Eastern Jews and Its Mission" to the weekly magazine of ha-Kibutz ha-Artzi to mark the fifteenth anniversary of the establishment of Nahshonim. He wrote,

> From the start, Kibutz Nahshonim was considered by its members and by ha-Kibutz ha-Artzi to have a special character and mission. Most of its members are from Eastern communities and hence it was clear that to their public mission a special feature was added. . . . [But we] have still not succeeded in realizing the dream of our youth: a kibutz that is active in the political arena mainly among Eastern Jews and Arabs. Nonetheless, our kibutz has still preserved its distinctiveness. Those who enter our homes will feel immediately the characteristic Eastern way of life. Here beats a wide and good Eastern heart which gives the settlement its special character.[13]

This assessment suggests that the kibutz had largely succeeded in adopting the political and cultural norms of Ashkenazi Israel. The only culturally distinctive attributes of Nahshonim Talmor could specify were the typically folkloric expressions of Middle Eastern lifestyle and hospitality. In 1993, I asked Ezra Talmor if he thought something distinguished Nahshonim from other kibutzim of ha-Shomer ha-Tza'ir as a consequence of the social origins of its founders. The only characteristic of the kibutz that came to his mind then was its food culture. "We know how to cook rice properly. We don't make hard white balls like the Poles. We have pride of rice."

Lazare Giv'ati, another founder of Kibutz Nahshonim and former head of the *ken* of ha-'Ivri ha-Tza'ir in the Ramle district of Alexandria, responding to the same question, replied, "Yes. Language and Western culture. We were different from the mainly Eastern European culture in Israel at the time. The entire country was Ashkenazi. We were less rigid and more compromising than the Poles."[14] Their former comrade, Sami Shemtov, a founder of Nahshonim who left the kibutz in 1961, agreed that the distinctive aspect of the kibutz was its Francophone cultural character.[15]

For these veterans of Nahshonim, being Egyptian meant being more Westernized than the majority of Israeli Jews. They were proud of their French education and culture, which they considered superior to the dominant Eastern European norms of Israel. Some felt that they had been discriminated against as Middle Eastern Jews, but they integrated into Israel when it was considered unpatriotic and culturally backward to identify this as an issue. Consequently, any feelings of pride they may have had as Egyptians were sublated to pride in their Francophone culture.

HA-SHOMER HA-TZA'IR
AND THE UNDERGROUND IN EGYPT

Unlike most other Egyptian Zionist groups, ha-Shomer ha-Tza'ir began to operate underground in late 1947 and early 1948. Consequently, only a handful of its senior leaders were apprehended in the roundup of Zionist activists at the start of the Arab-Israeli war in May 1948, and the movement maintained most of its strength. A *gar'in* was then preparing to immigrate to Israel to establish the second Egyptian kibutz of ha-Shomer ha-Tza'ir. Instead of leaving, the *gar'in* members remained underground in Egypt to organize Jewish immigration to Israel and to aid the other youth movements, which had been left without most of their leaders. From the end of May 1948 until April 1949, they acted without any direct assistance or guidance from the Zionist authorities in Israel. Ralph Hodara, Vita Castel, and David Harel (Wahba) led the underground work on behalf of the Jewish Agency and its 'Aliyah Organization (Mosad le-'Aliyah). They collaborated with Rudolf Pilpul, a lawyer who became the chief intelligence agent for the Israeli military in Egypt after Yolande Gabai Harmer, who had been collecting intelligence in Cairo for the Zionist authorities for the previous four years, was arrested in August 1948. In addition, Menasce Setton's travel agency in Cairo collaborated with the 'Aliyah Organization on a commercial basis. Benny Aharon and Victor Beressi took responsibility for the educational work of ha-Shomer ha-Tza'ir and the other youth movements. The youth leaders reported to Eli Peleg, the former emissary of ha-Kibutz ha-Artzi who became director of the Jewish Agency's Department for Middle East Jewry in Paris after he was forced to leave Egypt on May 25, 1948.

In the spring of 1949, Eliyahu Brakha and Haim Sha'ul were sent by the 'Aliyah Organization to assume responsibility for organizing immigration to Israel. Sha'ul was a graduate of ha-Shomer ha-Tza'ir in Cairo; Brakha had been a member of he-Halutz in Alexandria. As a member of MAPAI, the leading party of the Israeli government and the Jewish Agency, Brakha had the confidence of the official institutions of the state of Israel and the Zionist movement. The decision to send two emissaries may well have been motivated by the desire not to allow MAPAM to "control" Zionist activity in Egypt. Sha'ul recalled that his departure for Egypt was delayed until MAPAI could find an emissary to join him and that even though he had been waiting in Paris for months before Brakha arrived, Brakha was sent on to Cairo first.[16]

The arrival of the two emissaries transferred the internecine political rivalries of Israel, where Prime Minister David Ben-Gurion had excluded MAPAM from the government, to Egypt. Brakha was suspicious of ha-Shomer ha-Tzaʿir despite its considerable success under difficult conditions. Ha-Shomer ha-Tzaʿir's leaders complained repeatedly and bitterly that Brakha excluded them from the work and refused to hand over monies allocated to them.[17] Eli Peleg protested that MAPAI was conducting "unrestrained warfare" against MAPAM and that there was a "merciless battle" against his department, in which MAPAM members dominated, within the Jewish Agency.[18] As part of his effort to ensure the local dominance of MAPAI, Brakha split the he-Halutz movement by demanding that it abandon its officially nonpartisan status and transform itself into the new youth movement of MAPAI—ha-Bonim (The builders).[19] About half the members of he-Halutz refused and formed Dror—he-Halutz ha-Tzaʿir (Freedom—the young pioneer). Dror was the youth movement of the elements of the Kibutz ha-Meʾuhad federation affiliated with MAPAM from 1948 to 1954. It was politically situated between the social democratic MAPAI and ha-Shomer ha-Tzaʿir. However, for very local reasons, elements of Dror in Egypt developed a line that was to the left of ha-Shomer ha-Tzaʿir (see Chapter 2).

During 1949 and 1950, two contingents of the *garʿin* of senior members of ha-Shomer ha-Tzaʿir left Egypt. They made their way to Kibutz ʿEin-Shemer between the summer of 1949 and late 1951. The 80 members of the *garʿin* were augmented by perhaps 40 more Egyptians who had not been in ha-Shomer ha-Tzaʿir but were recruited to join the *garʿin*. They left some 350 members behind in Egypt, including 70 seniors.[20] In 1952, a small *garʿin* of Egyptian ha-Shomer ha-Tzaʿir arrived in Kibutz Mesilot, a veteran kibutz established in 1938. They joined the kibutz in September after living there for several months and studying Hebrew. Although ha-Shomer ha-Tzaʿir and the underground Zionist movement continued to exist until 1954, the wave of Jewish emigration ebbed after 1950, and no Israeli emissaries arrived after 1952.

THE EGYPTIAN *GARʿIN* AND KIBUTZ ʿEIN-SHEMER

The first contingent of the second Egyptian *garʿin* left Egypt in March 1949, shortly after the armistice between Egypt and Israel was signed. They first went to the Zionist training farm at La Roche in France because the authorities of ha-Kibutz ha-Artzi feared that if the *garʿin* arrived in Israel while the military situation was unsettled, the members would be immediately drafted into the army and that military service might undermine the social cohesiveness of the *garʿin* and disperse the members before they settled on a kibutz.[21] After three months at La Roche, in June–July 1949, the first members of the *garʿin* arrived at Kibutz ʿEin-Shemer, which had been founded in 1932 by members of ha-Shomer ha-Tzaʿir from Poland.

The *garʿin* planned to establish a new Egyptian kibutz, as their leaders had done at Nahshonim before them, after completing their agricultural training at ʿEin-Shemer. However, the leadership of ha-Kibutz ha-Artzi decided that the *garʿin* should remain at ʿEin-Shemer as a reinforcement (*hashlamah*) to augment the demographic composition of the veteran kibutz and provide an infusion of young labor power. Economically and socially, the Egyptian *garʿin* was a considerable asset to ʿEin-Shemer. The *garʿin* resisted settling at ʿEin-Shemer as a point of honor; they expected to do no less than their elders at Nahshonim. Movement discipline ultimately led them to accept the ruling of the leadership of ha-Kibutz ha-Artzi, but not without producing a certain tension between the *garʿin* and the veterans of ʿEin-Shemer.

Social friction between veterans and newcomers is a normal part of the process of absorbing (or not absorbing) a new *garʿin* in a kibutz. The strains that developed between the Egyptians and the kibutz veterans were not necessarily due to the ill will of individuals in either group. My main interest here is how the inevitable divergences between the veterans and the newcomers were constructed as cultural differences relating to the *garʿin*'s Egyptian identity despite the fact that both the veterans and the newcomers at ʿEin Shemer had experienced a very similar and ideologically intense education in ha-Shomer ha-Tzaʿir that created an initial presumption that there was a broad basis of agreement between the kibutz and the young *garʿin*.

Among the veterans of ʿEin-Shemer there were a few outstanding intellectuals and political figures—Yehiʾel Harari, Yisraʾel Hertz, and Yaʿakov Riftin—but most of them had not completed high school or attended college. Few spoke English, French, or Arabic. Most came from smaller towns outside Warsaw. Though they were fiercely loyal to the ideology of ha-Shomer ha-Tzaʿir, they tended toward an economist (*mishkist*) understanding of their political mission that regarded the prosperity of their own kibutz as the primary indicator of the success of the socialist revolution in Israel.

The Egyptians were all multilingual Cairenes or Alexandrians. Most were high school graduates, and some had studied at the university level as well. Some came from very comfortable homes and were unused to a rural life of physical labor, although by joining ha-Shomer ha-Tza'ir and settling on a kibutz, they had committed themselves to such a life as a matter of principle. The Egyptians had a sophisticated political education as a result of their backgrounds in ha-Shomer ha-Tza'ir and the intense political ferment of post–World War II Egypt. Many of them had read the classics of Marxism-Leninism in French. David Harel recalled that they were "intellectual youth of the diaspora for whom the importance of political organization took precedence over the kibutz idea. . . . We were more people of ideology . . . our leaders brought us to believe in pure Marxism-Leninism without compromises."[22]

Harel was referring to the particularly strong education in Marxism-Leninism of the Cairene contingent of the *gar'in* due to the influence of Eli Peleg. In addition, some senior members of ha-Shomer ha-Tza'ir in Cairo had participated in a forum where they met with members of the various underground communist groups and argued about ideological questions.[23] Several *gar'in* members agreed that the Marxist component of their education in Egypt was more prominent than the Zionist component.[24] However, there can be no doubt that they were Zionists because they did not join the Egyptian communist organizations but immigrated to Israel to live on a kibutz.

When the Egyptian *gar'in* arrived at 'Ein-Shemer, they were attracted to Ya'akov Riftin, a veteran of the kibutz who served as political secretary of MAPAM and one of its representatives in the Knesset. Riftin was also a leader of the left wing of MAPAM, along with 'Elazar Peri and Moshe Sneh. Their political orientation was to narrow the gap between MAPAM's socialist Zionism and orthodox Soviet-style Marxism-Leninism as much as possible. Many members of the Egyptian *gar'in* attended a study group on Marxism-Leninism organized by Riftin.

The left in MAPAM was impelled by an urgency born of the intensification of the cold war after the blockade of Berlin and the outbreak of the Korean War. Sneh and other leaders of the MAPAM left believed that the Red Army would soon enter the Middle East. The survival of the Jewish people would then depend on the existence of a Marxist Zionist leadership capable of marching in the direction of history. The leaders of the central current in MAPAM, Me'ir Ya'ari and Ya'akov Hazan, emphasized the primacy of the Zionist component of their ideological perspective. They were less insistently pro-Soviet than Sneh, Riftin, and Peri, but their political style was just as dogmatic. Even Hazan had stated in the Israeli Knesset that the Soviet Union was the "second homeland" of the Jewish people.

The Egyptians arrived with a highly idealized image of kibutz life as well as the inevitable social and cultural baggage of the urban, bourgeois, cosmopolitan culture they had grown up in. The *gar'in* was full of youthful audacity and rebelliousness, which were encouraged by ha-Shomer ha-Tza'ir but not well tolerated by the kibutz. David Harel, representing the memory of a minority of the *gar'in,* recalls that they were received excellently by the kibutz.[25] Most of the *gar'in* felt that the veterans of 'Ein-Shemer did not appreciate "who we were and where we came from."[26] Some spoke sharply about the veterans' perceptions that they must be "uneducated Arabs" because they came from Egypt.[27] When it became apparent that most of the Polish veterans were in fact less educated, less politically articulate, and less worldly than the Egyptians, the veterans experienced a severe case of cognitive dissonance. To alleviate their symptoms, some veterans argued that the Egyptians were bourgeois, scornful of physical labor, and too naive to appreciate the economic realities of the kibutz.

Some of the *gar'in* members' impressions about the veterans' negative views of them appear to have been validated in retrospect by Miyetek Zilbertal (Moshe Zertal), who served as secretary of the kibutz in the early 1950s. When interviewed by the daughter of a member of 'Ein-Shemer for a high school project, Zilbertal said, "Their problem was that they did not know Hebrew and the *gar'in* was very large. Their preparation in ha-Shomer ha-Tza'ir was not great. . . . The members of the *gar'in* were very new in the country . . . they had not acclimated themselves, but they had a leadership. They did not seek much connection to us. . . . It is possible that we did not pay sufficient attention to them."[28] In accord with the prevailing political culture in ha-Kibutz ha-Artzi, the socially and culturally conservative kibutz tended to define every expression of difference between the Egyptian newcomers and the veterans as a moral and political flaw on the part of the newcomers.

Despite the nominal commitment of the kibutz to egalitarian gender relations, women bore a disproportionate share of the burden of the social difference between urban bourgeois and kibutz life. Several of the Egyptian women brought elegant wardrobes suitable for urban Egyptian social life. Kibutzim of ha-Kibutz ha-Artzi then practiced a form of collectivism known as *komunah alef,* which required that individuals forgo personal ownership of clothing and draw what they required from a collective depository. Some of the Egyptian women were embarrassed by the comments of the veteran kibutz members about their stylish clothing and resented handing over their trousseaus to the kibutz.[29]

There were similar frictions over the fact that the Egyptians organized New Year's eve parties. In Egypt this was considered a fashionable, modern custom adopted by Europeanized Muslims, Jews, and Copts. Because it was not a traditional holiday on the Jewish calendar, veteran kibutz members regarded these celebrations as bourgeois and *goyish* (non-Jewish).[30]

The tensions between the Egyptian *garʿin* and the veterans of ʿEin-Shemer were exacerbated by the difficult economic circumstances of Israel in the early 1950s, the period of austerity (*tzenaʾ*)—high unemployment, black markets, and stringent food rationing. When Ninette Piciotto Braunstein arrived at ʿEin-Shemer in October 1951, she thought that she would be received as a heroine because she had spent a month imprisoned in the Cairo Citadel for her work in the Zionist underground. To her amazement, her comrades greeted her by telling her how lucky she had been to have remained in Egypt. "At least you ate," they said.[31] She found that the *garʿin* members had already begun calling the kibutz veterans "anti-Semites" and "racists" because of the way they were treated. "They received us with a great deal of contempt," Braunstein recalled.[32]

The kibutz wanted Braunstein to work as an English teacher in its school, but in keeping with the ideals of ha-Shomer ha-Tzaʿir, she agreed to become a teacher only if she could do physical work as well. She also asked to engage in some political activity, which she had been educated to regard as an essential part of life. The kibutz and the local MAPAM leaders assigned her to work in the labor office in the nearby town of Karkur. After several days of allocating work to unemployed new immigrants, she was called to a consultation with the kibutz leaders, who were upset with her performance. She had assigned work to applicants who were "not ours." That is, they were not members of MAPAM. At first she did not understand. "I am a Zionist. They are Jews. Don't they deserve to work too?" she replied.[33] For the kibutz veterans, such political naiveté was yet another expression of the Egyptians' lack of understanding of the realities of life in Israel.

Underprivileged children from poorer neighborhoods of Tel Aviv were brought to ʿEin-Shemer under the auspices of a shelter program (*korat gag*) to give them an opportunity to breathe fresh air and benefit from the healthy atmosphere of the kibutz. Members of the *garʿin* complained when they noticed that these children were fed less generously than the children of the kibutz veterans. "Don't they deserve to eat jam like your children?" they asked.[34]

Garʾin members also objected when they learned that the kibutz was selling some of its produce on the black market instead of through the marketing cooperative of the Histadrut. Selling on the black market brought higher prices and direct payment in cash, but the marketing cooperative took weeks or months to settle its accounts. The *garʾin* members criticized the kibutz for informally hiring new immigrants from the neighboring *maʿabarah* and paying them less than the official minimum wage required by the Histadrut.[35] Veteran kibutz members regarded protest against such practices as naive ignorance of the requirements of economic survival. They resented being criticized as politically deficient by inexperienced newcomers.

All these tensions exploded in the course of the "Sneh affair"—an internal ideological struggle within MAPAM and ha-Kibutz ha-Artzi set off by the arrest of Mordehai Oren, a member of Kibutz Mizraʿ who had travelled to Prague to represent MAPAM at a meeting of the World Federation of Trade Unions in November 1952.[36] The Czechoslovak communist authorities charged Oren with espionage in order to substantiate charges they had previously brought against Rudolf Slansky and other mostly Jewish party leaders who were accused of being bourgeois nationalists and Zionist agents. The Slansky and Oren trials were anti-Semitic frame-ups whose political objective was to smash any residual Titoist tendencies and impose the absolute authority of the Soviet Union over Eastern Europe.

Meʾir Yaʿari and Yaʿakov Hazan, the leaders of ha-Kibutz ha-Artzi and the centrist current in MAPAM, supported by the Le-Ahdut ha-ʿAvodah faction, demanded that MAPAM members unite behind a resolution denouncing the Prague trial. The left wing of MAPAM, led by Moshe Sneh, Yaʿakov Riftin, and ʿElazar Peri, refused to endorse a resolution that could be interpreted as anticommunist or anti-Soviet. Speaking at a meeting of the Political Committee of MAPAM on November 23, 1952, Riftin argued, "It is impossible to be an inseparable part [of the world of revolution—the slogan of the left in MAPAM] without being for Prague." Sneh presented the Prague trial as "a choice between national solidarity and international solidarity," and he believed that "in this matter there ought to have been international solidarity."[37]

After efforts to compromise failed, in January 1953 the left wingers announced they were forming a new independent faction in the party, the Left

Section. Although MAPAM was then organized on the basis of factions, party leaders demanded that this faction dissolve and that its leaders relinquish their public offices and party positions. When the Left Section refused this ultimatum, it was expelled from MAPAM. At the last minute, loyalty to ha-Shomer ha-Tzaʿir and to their kibutzim induced Riftin and Peri to accept the decisions of the leaders of ha-Kibutz ha-Artzi and MAPAM. They remained members of their kibutzim and the party, though they never again wielded any significant influence. Moshe Sneh, who was not a kibutz member, led several hundred activists out of MAPAM to form the Left Socialist Party. A year and a half later, Sneh and some 250 members of the Left Socialist Party joined the Communist Party of Israel.

Because ha-Kibutz ha-Artzi was affiliated with MAPAM and practiced a form of democratic centralism known as ideological collectivism, the split in the party had immediate and severe repercussions within its kibutzim, especially ʿEin-Shemer, where the left was very strong because of the presence of Yaʿakov Riftin and the Egyptian *garʿin*. On January 4, 1953, the Executive Committee of ha-Kibutz ha-Artzi decided that every kibutz should administer a three-part referendum/loyalty oath requiring each member to affirm the following: (1) The kibutz supports the resolution of the MAPAM Council denouncing the Prague trial. (2) The kibutz confirms the "absolute obligation" of all members of ha-Kibutz ha-Artzi to support the decisions of MAPAM and ha-Kibutz ha-Artzi on the basis of ideological collectivism. (3) The kibutz denounces factional activity in the kibutz and in ha-Kibutz ha-Artzi. Dissidents in the kibutzim were subjected to intense social, political, and economic pressures to conform. Consequently, the vote of 13.5 percent or 1,334 of the members of ha-Kibutz ha-Artzi against clause one of the referendum represented a substantial ideological crisis in the movement. The leaders considered this a statement of support for the line of Riftin and Peri, an undesirable, but legitimate opinion. A vote against clauses two and three was considered an expression of support for the line of Moshe Sneh and the Left Section. Those who persisted in these positions—between 160 and 220 kibutz members—were expelled from the kibutzim of ha-Kibutz ha-Artzi.[38]

A large majority of the Egyptian *garʿin* at ʿEin-Shemer, especially its leadership, identified with the political positions of Riftin or Sneh. During the factional struggle in MAPAM, members of the *garʿin* had attended meetings sponsored by the Left Section in Tel Aviv along with members of neighboring kibutzim. Veteran kibutz members regarded this as subversion and establishing an "underground" political opposition within the kibutz.[39]

One of the activities that most upset the veterans of 'Ein-Shemer and the leaders of ha-Kibutz ha-Artzi was the establishment of political ties by *gar'in* members with their Palestinian Arab neighbors in the villages of Wadi 'Ara. "They had already succeeded in acting in the Arab sector. It was not only an internal matter," explained Miyetek Zilbertal, the kibutz secretary.[40] The fear expressed in this comment reflects MAPAM's complex relationship of paternalism and alliance with the Arab citizens of Israel. The political activity of the Egyptians was a threat to the stability of this volatile mixture because the Arabic speakers among them had direct and unmediated access to Arabs and could form independent conclusions about prevailing opinions in the Arab community and the effectiveness of MAPAM's work there.

"I was in contact with the Arabs in 'Ar'ara, in Kafr Kar'a, and it is all lies," explained David Harel.

> I speak Arabic, and my comrades and I went several times to 'Ar'ara and Kafr Kar'a. . . . We went as ha-Shomer ha-Tza'ir. We invited them to 'Ein-Shemer. We sang and danced together, and I lectured in Arabic on socialism and American imperialism in the name of ha-Shomer ha-Tza'ir and MAPAM. All this was a year, maybe more, before the Slansky affair and the affair of Oren, Sneh, and Riftin. Before they ever dreamed of working with the Arabs. We believed in the brotherhood of nations [one of MAPAM's slogans], and in order to help them economically we helped them prepare chicken feed. I knew how because I worked in the chicken coop. . . . We were [politically] active in Egypt and we wanted to be active in Israel, and the area of activity was around 'Ein-Shemer as volunteers.[41]

Reports of David Harel's activities in Wadi 'Ara composed by more conservative members of MAPAM during the height of the internal struggle in the party contradict his memory of the significance of his contacts with the Arab neighbors of 'Ein-Shemer. Eli'ezer Be'eri, the head of MA-PAM's Arab Affairs Department, wrote to the leaders of 'Ein-Shemer that in January 1953 David Wahba (Harel) and Moshe Bilaysh, members of the Egyptian *gar'in*, had encouraged Arab members of MAPAM in 'Ar'ara to organize a demonstration of the unemployed without first requesting authorization from the institutions of the party. The MAPAM leaders subsequently agreed to the action, and the demonstration was held on January 25. Afterwards, Wahba and Bilaysh returned to 'Ar'ara to explain to MAPAM members there that the party was split and unable to help them. They advised them to contact Rustum Bastuni, a leading Arab party member who supported Sneh and the Left Section. Be'eri regarded this as factional organizing for the Left Section. Therefore, he planned not to deliver the entry permits to the villages of Wadi ʿAra that he had requested for the two Egyptians from the military government (all the Arab villages of Israel were then under military restrictions that required permits for anyone to enter and exit), although the permits had originally been requested on the basis of their tasks for MAPAM in the villages.[42]

ʿEin-Shemer held its referendum on March 14–17. By then, the secretariat of ha-Kibutz ha-Artzi had revised the wording of the text, making it even harsher. There seems to have been an understanding between the kibutz secretariat and the secretariat of ha-Kibutz ha-Artzi before the referendum was administered that members of ʿEin-Shemer who voted against any of the clauses would be expelled from the kibutz.[43] The kibutz veterans were probably exasperated by the oppositional activity of the Egyptian garʿin by then and anxious to cut their losses and return to normalcy. Twenty-three members of the Egyptian garʿin did vote against the referendum, and the following day the general meeting of the kibutz decided to remove their names from the work schedule, which was tantamount to expulsion.[44] In response, on March 28, the Egyptians declared a hunger strike. Embarrassed and confused about how to handle a situation that overtaxed the kibutz's repertoire of social remedies, ʿEin-Shemer sealed itself off from outside contact. In this superheated and isolated environment, the confrontation between the veterans and the Egyptians led to an exchange of blows. The hunger strike ended the next day. Twenty-two Egyptians signed an agreement to leave the kibutz after negotiating terms for financial compensation.[45]

Among the Egyptians expelled from ʿEin-Shemer were many former leading members of ha-Shomer ha-Tzaʿir, including several who have been previously mentioned in this chapter and whose activities in Egypt would be regarded as heroic in Zionist terms: Haim (Vita) Castel, Benny Aharon, David Wahba (Harel), Haim Aharon, ʿAda Yedid (Aharoni), Ninette Piciotto Braunstein, and Victor (David) Beressi. In the following weeks and months, most of the other members of the Egyptian garʿin left ʿEin-Shemer as well. When I interviewed members of ʿEin-Shemer in 1993, only ten members of the original Egyptian garʿin remained there.

A substantial number of Egyptians were also expelled from Kibutz Mesilot in the course of the Sneh affair. Months after the referendum was held, one of the members of the Egyptian garʿin at Mesilot participated in the founding congress of the Left Socialist Party. This was considered a violation of ideological collectivism, and the kibutz general meeting decided to expel him from the kibutz. Several members of the garʿin walked out of the general meeting in solidarity with their friend and comrade. Twenty-six of them signed a petition to the secretariat of the kibutz saying they viewed themselves as expelled from the kibutz for ideological reasons. On June 5, 1953, nineteen Egyptians held a hunger strike in the kibutz dining hall. That evening, the general meeting voted to expel them. Twenty-four Egyptians eventually left Mesilot over the Sneh affair. The kibutz secretariat's original official account of the Sneh affair at Mesilot minimized its significance. A more candid statement on the occasion of the thirtieth anniversary of Mesilot frankly admitted that most of the Egyptian *gar'in* was expelled.[46]

The social background and education in ha-Shomer ha-Tza'ir of the expelled members of Mesilot were similar to those of their older comrades at 'Ein-Shemer. Consequently, the expulsions of the Egyptians from 'Ein-Shemer cannot be explained solely as the result of the normal social frictions between the *gar'in* and the kibutz veterans, although such tensions probably did motivate the mass departure of the remainder of the Egyptians after the expulsion of the ideological leaders of the *gar'in*. The similarity between the events at 'Ein-Shemer and Mesilot suggests that the political and cultural formation of Egyptian ha-Shomer ha-Tza'ir was incompatible with the orientation of MAPAM and ha-Kibutz ha-Artzi once the synthesis of Zionism and socialism became strained by the intensifying cold war and the harsh actualities of intra-Jewish ethnic relations and Arab-Jewish relations in Israel.

The identification of Egyptians with "leftism" in the kibutzim was enhanced by the fact that at Kibutz Yir'on, an affiliate of ha-Kibutz ha-Me'uhad, a federation largely loyal to the le-Ahdut ha-'Avodah faction of MAPAM, a similar struggle broke out over the Prague trial and the Sneh affair. An Egyptian *gar'in* of about forty members arrived in Yir'on in 1950. They had been in he-Halutz in Egypt, and many of them had moved leftward after Eli Brakha arrived and split the movement. During the Sneh affair, ha-Kibutz ha-Me'uhad conducted a referendum among its members similar to the one organized in ha-Kibutz ha-Artzi. Seven of the Egyptians at Yir'on were expelled for holding positions sympathetic to Sneh.[47] They and twenty other Egyptians left Yir'on and joined Yad Hanah, the only kibutz in Israel that was prepared to welcome supporters of the Left Socialist Party and the Communist Party.

AUTOBIOGRAPHY AND ETHNOGRAPHY

I met several of the former members of the Egyptian *gar'in* at 'Ein-Shemer in Tel Aviv at Ninette Piciotto Braunstein's home in June 1993, where some spoke bitterly about their time on the kibutz.[48] My ten years as a member of ha-Shomer ha-Tza'ir and my familiarity with Egypt allowed me to feel like a full partner in the discussion. Their vocabulary and conceptual universe were intimately familiar to me from my own personal history. Their ordeal on 'Ein-Shemer was far more intense than my encounter with kibutz life and had been framed by the issues of Stalinism and the cold war that were no longer relevant when I lived in Israel. But their tribulations resonated eerily with my experiences on Kibutz Lahav. At Lahav, cultural and political clashes between my *gar'in* of North Americans and the *tzabar* founders of the kibutz led to the departure of virtually all the Americans within a few years of our arrival in 1970. I felt a deep emotional link with the Egyptians expelled from 'Ein-Shemer because we had shared similar ideals and disappointments in our teens and early twenties. We were now in different physical and political spaces, but sharing the same beginnings in life easily allowed us to make sense of each other's trajectories.

The conclusions drawn by those in the room since our departures from kibutzim were not politically uniform. Sitting in Ninette Braunstein's living room and enjoying her hospitality as we reminisced, this seemed less important than it undoubtedly would have been at other times and places. In any case, our views on politics in Israel were not incommensurable. Despite the undeniable ideological differences among us, which have constituted sharp lines of demarcation in Israeli politics in certain periods, we could, in a vague and general way, all be considered part of the same camp. I sensed that we all understood this and took pleasure in it.

CHAPTER 6

The Communist
Emigres
in France

In the late 1930s, Jews participated prominently in the revival and re-formation of the Egyptian communist movement.[1] They founded and led several of the most important rival organizations. Perhaps 1,000 or more Jews participated in the Egyptian communist movement from the 1930s to the 1950s. Thousands more were sympathetic to Marxist ideas in one form or another. The substantial Jewish presence among the members and supporters of the communist movement has encouraged the common misperception that Egyptian communism had no social base among Muslims. Though Jews were highly disproportionately represented in the movement, they were far from a majority of its adherents. Secularization of the prophetic message of social justice, the global challenge of fascism, and the urgent necessity of resisting Nazi anti-Semitism drew many Jews into the ambit of Marxist politics during the era of the united front against fascism. In Egypt, international developments as well as local conditions—the continuing British occupation, the limitations of a parliamentary democracy tightly supervised by the monarchy and the British Embassy, the intensification of the Palestinian-Zionist conflict, and the increasing numbers of unemployed high school and university graduates frustrated by the lack of appropriate opportunities—radicalized political life from the late 1930s on. Excluded by definition from both Islamist currents like the Muslim Brothers or the quasi-fascist Young Egypt, Jewish youth searching for political expression in the 1930s and 1940s (a minority of the community, to be sure) increasingly turned toward Marxism or Zionism or, as in the case of ha-Shomer ha-Tza'ir, a combination of the two.

The most outstanding Egyptian Jewish communist leader was the legendary and charismatic Henri Curiel (1914–78), the younger son of the Cairo banker, Daniel Curiel. The Curiel family held Italian citizenship, but upon reaching the age of majority in 1935, Henri Curiel became a citizen of Egypt. However, he had been educated in the Jesuit Collège des Frères in Cairo and never became fluent in Arabic, despite his deep attachment to Egypt. In the late 1930s and early 1940s, Curiel was active in several antifascist political formations based in the *mutamassir* communities before he formulated a strategy of Egyptianizing the communist movement by giving priority to the Egyptian national struggle against British imperialism: "the line of popular and democratic forces." In 1943, he founded the Egyptian Movement for National Liberation (HAMETU—*al-Haraka al-Misriyya li'l-Tahrir al-Watani*), which formed the core of what became Egypt's most influential communist organization for most of the next twenty years.

Another Francophone Jew, Hillel Schwartz, founded the Iskra (Spark) organization, named after Lenin's Bolshevik newspaper, in 1942. Iskra was the largest of the communist organizations in the mid-1940s, with a high proportion of middle- and upper-class intellectuals, Jews, and other *mutamassirun* among its members. Jewish students at elite French secondary schools recruited their Muslim and Coptic schoolmates into Iskra through a combination of political-intellectual and social activities that enabled young men and women to mix freely, openly defying prevailing social norms. There were many premarital sexual affairs and mixed couples (Jewish-Muslim or Coptic-Jewish) in the communist milieu, especially Iskra—a practice that anticommunists and communists critical of Jewish influence in the movement considered an expression of the culturally alien character of Marxism or the baleful effects of the prominence of foreigners in the movement. Curiel personally opposed Iskra's social style, but his critics nonetheless considered him, his organization, and sometimes Jews in general responsible for it.[2]

Early in 1947, Iskra absorbed People's Liberation (*Tahrir al-Sha'b*), an organization founded and led by Marcel Israel, a Jew of Italian citizenship. Then, in May, Curiel's HAMETU united with Iskra to form the Democratic Movement for National Liberation (HADETU—*al-Haraka al-Dimuqratiyya li'l-Tahrir al-Watani*). Three Jews—Curiel, Schwartz, and Aimée Setton—were among the fifteen members of the first

HADETU Central Committee.[3] Marcel Israel had been willing to assume leadership of a preparty Marxist formation, but refused to join the Central Committee of HADETU, which saw itself as the nucleus of the Egyptian communist party, even though, as Curiel himself admitted, Israel was "by far the most Egyptianized, the only one who knew Arabic perfectly" of the three Jewish communist leaders.[4] Nonetheless, Israel insisted, "We were foreigners. He [Curiel] couldn't accept that."[5]

A fourth communist tendency, grouped around the magazine *al-Fajr al-Jadid* (New dawn), was founded by three Jews—Yusuf Darwish, Ahmad Sadiq Sa'd, and Raymond Douek.[6] When the New Dawn group established a formal organization in 1946, it recognized the problematic status in the communist movement of Jews, Greeks, and other *mutamassirun* who were not educated in Arabo-Egyptian culture and resolved it by what they called "the corridor" (*al-mamarr*): Those who mastered Arabic and identified with Egypt passed through the corridor, were considered 100 percent Egyptian, and were admitted to the organization; those who did not were excluded.[7] The textile workers of the northern Cairo suburb of Shubra al-Khayma and many other labor activists were satisfied by this procedure. Their high regard for Yusuf Darwish, who served as legal counsel for several trade unions in the 1940s and 1950s, was undiminished by his Jewish origins. Intellectuals in the communist movement tended to be more concerned about the Jewish origins of Darwish, Sa'd, and Douek, even after they had all formally converted to Islam.

The smallest of the major communist tendencies in the late 1940s and early 1950s was the Communist Party of Egypt (al-Hizb al-Shuyu'i al-Misri), popularly known as al-Raya (The flag) after the name of its underground newspaper. Al-Raya was composed largely of intellectuals and a disproportionate number of Copts from middle Egypt, where the organization had some local strength. Its leaders, Fu'ad Mursi, Isma'il Sabri 'Abd Allah, and Sa'd Zahran, vehemently criticized Curiel and the role of Jews in the Egyptian communist movement. Mursi spoke of the "very bad experience with Jews in the Egyptian communist movement. It was a symbol of dissolution: sexual dissolution, moral dissolution."[8] Consequently, al-Raya, refused to admit Jews to its ranks.

Thus, in the period of the movement's reformation, there was considerable disagreement among Egyptian Jewish communists and their comrades about their identity and its political consequences. Marcel Israel believed that Jews (at least those with a European education like himself) were foreigners and therefore not eligible to lead the communist movement. The Jews of New Dawn believed that mastering Arabic and embracing the Egyptian national cause would eliminate any problematic consequences of the circumstances of their birth. They considered themselves Egyptians in all respects and were accepted as such by their organization. Schwartz and Curiel and those close to them rejected the view that foreigners were ineligible in principle to lead the Egyptian communist movement. They felt that their ethnonational identity, however defined, should not pose an impediment to their participation at all levels of the communist movement because Marxism-Leninism was an internationalist ideology. Hence, the ethnic identity of the Egyptian movement's leaders was merely a tactical question. It was politically desirable to promote indigenous Egyptian leaders, but this did not mean others should be systematically excluded. Curiel, in particular, had actively and with considerable success promoted the Egyptianization of the movement. He recruited many Egyptian workers and intellectuals to HAMETU and HADETU and influenced several of them enormously despite his broken Arabic.

THE PALESTINE QUESTION AND THE JEWISH COMMUNISTS

The 1948 Arab-Israeli War forced the Jewish communists to confront their identity status and its political consequences. According to Raymond Stambouli, a member of HADETU close to Curiel,

> The war in Palestine was a staggering blow to us. . . . It marked the end of a dream that had been coming true. We had thought of ourselves as Egyptians, even while admitting that Egyptians saw us as foreigners. Now it was all over. Now we weren't just foreigners, but Jews, therefore the enemy, a potential fifth column. Could any of us have foretold that?[9]

The unity of HADETU lasted less than a year and may very well have been undermined by disputes over the Palestine question, though this remains a hotly contested question closely linked to the identity status of the Jewish communists. Curiel's leadership of HADETU was challenged by Shuhdi 'Atiyya al-Shafi'i—the first Muslim intellectual to become a leader in Iskra and the editor of HADETU's weekly newspaper, *al-Jamahir* (The masses)—and Anouar Abdel-Malek—a Coptic intellectual who subsequently gained considerable recognition as the author of a critically supportive analysis of the Nasser regime, *Egypt: Military Society*, first published in France, where Abdel-Malek has lived since the mid-1950s. They formed a faction known as the Revolutionary Bloc (*al-Kutla al-Thawriyya*). The contending explanations for this split in HADETU, the first of several, imply different assessments of how great an impediment the Jewish identity of many HADETU members was to their political effectiveness.

HADETU, like almost all communist formations in the Arab world, followed the lead of the Soviet Union and endorsed the November 29, 1947, decision of the UN General Assembly to partition Palestine into separate Jewish and Arab states. The first challenge to Curiel's leadership occurred during the debate over the partition of Palestine. The struggle against the Jewish leadership was fused with opposition to the UN partition plan and the creation of the state of Israel. The obvious, but incorrect, conclusion of many of Curiel's rivals was that HADETU had endorsed the partition of Palestine *because* several of its leaders were Jewish and perhaps even secretly Zionists. Sa'd Zahran's history of Egyptian politics emphasized the extent to which the Jewish identity of Curiel and others in the HADETU leadership and the disagreement over the partition of Palestine were factors in the breakup of HADETU.[10] Mohamed Sid-Ahmed, a former communist who was never a follower of Curiel, remembered that al-Shafi'i and Abdel-Malek were so shocked that the government and others attacked communism as Zionism that they took an extreme anti-Jewish line that he thought some might consider "anti-Semitic a bit . . . a violent reaction against the feeling that the whole movement was held and perhaps manipulated by Jews and that their commitment to Marxism was colored by things that might be alien to an authentic Egyptian Marxism."[11] More recently, Sid-Ahmed noted with sadness, "There was an element of anti-Semitism in the Egyptian communist movement."[12]

Curiel and those close to him never agreed that the Palestine question was an issue in the split in HADETU because this would be tantamount to admitting that their Jewishness ultimately limited their roles in the Egyptian communist movement. They believed that they supported the partition of Palestine, as nearly all communists around the world did, for internationalist motives and out of loyalty to the Soviet Union. Indeed, there is no evidence that Curiel and his supporters had any secret Zionist sympathies, as many of their opponents in the Egyptian communist movement, including some Jews, implied in the polemical exchanges among the various organizations.[13] Curiel and his supporters, like all orthodox communists, first followed the lead of the Soviet Union and were subsequently motivated by the desire to find a peaceful solution to the Arab-Israeli conflict that would allow Egypt and its communist movement to advance beyond the stage of national liberation to addressing the social agenda.

Curiel characterized the struggle against his leadership as an expression of Egyptian national chauvinism with no particularly anti-Jewish element:

> Unity brought some very brilliant intellectuals [i.e., al-Shafi'i and Abdel-Malek from Iskra] into HADETU. They aspired to lead the party. On the one hand, as intellectuals they were a little chauvinist and saw no reason why Egyptianization should not be completed by the elimination of Yunis [Curiel's nom de guerre]. On the other hand, if the role of foreigners was to be reduced to zero, they had a tendency to underestimate the stage of proletarianization; for them the essential was to be Egyptian.[14]

In this passage from his unpublished autobiography, written in France in 1977, Curiel apparently accepted that he and other Jews like him in the movement were "foreigners." He did not here specify what attributes (or lack thereof) made them so, perhaps because he considered this both self-evident and unimportant. Curiel's argument against al-Shafi'i and Abdel-Malek relies simply on the communist movement's ideological commitment to proletarian internationalism and its ideological rejection of nationalism.

Upon invading Israel together with the other Arab states on May 15, 1948, the Egyptian government proclaimed martial law. *Al-Jamahir* was closed; hundreds of communists, including Curiel and other Jews, were arrested along with members of most other oppositional political tendencies. Roughly as many Jewish communists as Zionists were detained in the Huckstep, Abu Qir, and al-Tur internment camps during 1948 and 1949. Their fierce ideological debates continued in detention while the government saw them as members of the same political camp because both groups endorsed the UN partition plan for Palestine.

The political prisoners were all released by the time the Wafd returned to power in January 1950. Maneuvering among the contradictions within the Wafd and the new government, HADETU began to reorganize with considerable success. The Wafd's devotion to democracy was circumscribed by its commitment to preserve the monarchical regime, so in response to the resurgence of the communist movement, Henri Curiel was arrested again on July 25, 1950. Despite his having held Egyptian citizenship for fifteen years, the court ordered him deported "as a foreigner dangerous to public security."[15] On August 26, he was placed in a locked cabin on an Italian ship that eventually disgorged him in Genoa.

Curiel remained only briefly in Italy. Although he had no residence papers, he soon established himself in Paris, where he was joined by other Egyptian Jewish communists who were deported or left Egypt voluntarily between 1949 and 1956. Some of Curiel's political opponents in the Egyptian communist movement also settled in France in the 1950s and 1960s. Several, like Hillel Schwartz, abandoned political activity altogether. Others, like Raymond Aghion, joined the Communist Party of France. Curiel and former members of HADETU constituted the largest faction of Egyptian Jewish communists in France. They maintained a distinctive organizational identity as a branch of HADETU and its successor organizations for most of the 1950s.

EMIGRE POLITICS AND RETERRITORIALIZATION

The Egyptian Jewish communists who found themselves in France were compelled to redefine their identity and their relationship to the land of their birth under new and rapidly changing historical circumstances. As the only organized formation, Curiel and the HADETU members were the most persistent in articulating a coherent response to these questions. Curiel, although he briefly contacted the Communist Party of France when he first arrived in the country, refused to join it because to do so would be tantamount to accepting the judgment of the Egyptian government and his critics in the communist movement that he was a foreigner and should therefore abandon his activity in Egyptian politics.

The first member of HADETU to reach Paris was Yusuf (Joseph) Hazan, who was intensely loyal to Curiel.[16] Because he had a French passport, he had been sent there by the organization in 1949 to establish a safe haven in the event of necessity. Hazan settled himself in a successful printing business relatively soon after arriving in Paris and was therefore well positioned to serve as the treasurer of the group and the publisher of its printed materials. Eventually, some twenty to thirty Jewish members of HADETU gathered under Curiel's leadership in Paris. They adopted "the Rome Group" as their nom de guerre. Functioning as a branch of HADETU was a clear statement that they considered themselves Egyptians in exile. Curiel remained a member of the HADETU Central Committee, periodically sending back to Egypt reports on theoretical and strategic matters written in invisible ink. In addition to Henri Curiel and his wife Rosette, the Rome Group included Raymond Biriotti, Joyce Blau, Alfred Cohen, Ralph Costi, Jacques Hassoun, Yusuf Hazan, Didar Rossano-Fawzy, Armand Setton, and Raymond Stambouli.

The ideological formulations and political practices of the Rome Group were informed by the struggle for national independence and against neocolonialism in Asia, Africa, and Latin America as well as the local conditions in Egypt. As anti-Zionists, they rejected the Zionist solutions to their predicament: both Ben-Gurion's maximalist negation of the diaspora and milder forms of Zionism that merely saw Israel as the center of Jewish existence. They also rejected Bundism, the diasporic nationalism that had been popular in leftist Eastern European Jewish circles in the late nineteenth and early twentieth centuries. Lenin and the Bolsheviks had polemicized against the Russian Bund on the grounds that maintaining a separate Jewish organizational form was an expression of nationalist particularism that weakened the Russian revolutionary movement. A Bundist-inspired diasporic Jewish national identity was therefore unlikely to attract political activists who considered themselves orthodox communists. The members of the Rome Group were educated in French culture. They admired the rationalism, secularism, and democratic values of the French republican tradition. But Jews born in an Arab country were not readily accepted as "true Frenchmen" by many circles in France, especially in the era of Algeria's struggle for independence. In the 1950s, all communists, despite their ideological commitment to proletarian internationalism, acknowledged that they had to have an ethnonational identity. In the era of decolonization, the only legitimate form this could assume for communists in colonial or semicolonial countries was heroic nationalism. Lenin had theorized that the anti-imperialist national liberation movements in such countries were allies of the proletarian revolution. The Egyptian communists were, therefore, militant nationalists who believed that the Egyptian national movement was "objectively" part of the international proletarian revolution. Insisting on their Egyptianity was the form of identity most consistent with the political commitments of Curiel and his comrades.

Refusing to accept the determination of the government of Egypt and many of their own comrades that they were foreigners, the Rome Group maintained a high level of political activity entailing great personal risk, especially for those like Curiel, who did not hold French citizenship, and substantial financial sacrifices.[17] They seemed to believe that demonstrating their political commitment and willingness to sacrifice for the cause would secure their right to be Egyptians. The more political developments appeared to lead to the conclusion that they could not be accepted as Egyptians or participate fully in Egyptian politics, the more they insisted on asserting their commitment to Egypt.

At least until after the 1956 Suez/Sinai War, Curiel steadfastly believed that he would return to Egypt and to a leadership position in the communist movement. According to Gilles Perrault's biography, an authorized narrative based largely on information supplied by Curiel's friends, Curiel felt himself more Egyptian in Paris than he had in Cairo: "Perceived in Cairo as a foreigner and accepting it, Henri Curiel discovered in his physical uprooting the impossibility of being anything else but Egyptian. Exile Egyptianized him."[18]

Curiel was not the only one among his comrades to discover a more intense feeling of Egyptian identity as a response to repression and exile. Joyce Blau, who became Curiel's loyal and devoted lieutenant, served as a courier between Curiel and the HADETU leaders in Egypt until she was arrested in 1954. Her prison experience strengthened her feelings for Egypt:

> It was in prison . . . that I was first introduced to Egypt. I didn't speak Arabic and I didn't know any Muslims. I discovered what misery really was when I spoke to the "common law," non-political prisoners. It was incredible. . . . The warden couldn't have been nicer to me. When I had jaundice, he came and sat with me in the infirmary. The doctor was wonderful. I felt surrounded by respect and affection.[19]

These comments suggest that as an extension of the Rome Group's decision to continue operating as a branch of HADETU, its members began to recreate their identity and their relationship with Egypt. When they lived permanently in Egypt, their connection to the country was undeniable, even if some Egyptians considered them to be outside the boundaries of the national community. In Paris, where the "naturalness" of their bond to Egypt was exposed to question, they had to be more assertive about their right to a place in the Egyptian national topos. The Rome Group underwent what Deleuze and Guattari have called, in postmodern language, a "reterritorialization": a reconfiguration of the Egyptian national space and their location in it that enabled them to persist in their political commitments. However, the group's militant engagement in the modernist project of liberating the Egyptian nation-state from semicolonial domination meant that they could not conceivably adopt the "rhizomorphous" conception of identity or the "nomad thought" advocated by Deleuze and Guattari even if their subsequent political practices suggest that they might be considered its avatars.

If, as Deleuze and Guattari asserted, "anything can serve as a reterritorialization, in other words, 'stand for' the lost territory,"[20] in this case the group itself fulfilled this role. In addition to its activities as a politi-

cal organization, the Rome Group functioned as a family—Perrault repeatedly called them a "clan"—a personality cult, and an immigrant support group much like the *landsmanshaften* (home town societies) that
united Yiddish-speaking Jewish immigrants to Paris in the pre–World
War II era on the basis of their former residences in various localities in
Eastern Europe.[21] Curiel's eccentric personal and political style, the stric-
tures of revolutionary emigre politics, and the closing down of social
horizons common in organizations subject to Marxist-Leninist discipline
in the era of high Stalinism all contributed to the Rome Group's capacity to serve as a replacement for the national territory of Egypt.

The peculiarities of Curiel and the Rome Group made it difficult for
the Communist Party of France and other orthodox communists to accept them as genuine and politically reliable. Anticommunists as well
have entertained a variety of conspiracy theories to account for their activities. In my opinion, despite whatever criticisms may be directed at
their tactics or their ideology, there is no evidence to support doubts
about their sincerity.

EXILE AND COMMUNIST POLITICS

In February 1951, the Rome Group began to publish two informational
bulletins about Egypt and the Sudan: *Paix et independance,* a short-lived
united front–type publication to promote and publicize the work of the
Egyptian Partisans of Peace in the campaign for world peace launched
by Frédéric Joliot-Curie's Stockholm appeal, and *Bulletin d'information
sur l'Egypte et le Soudan* (with many subsequent changes in name and
varying frequency), "edited under the supervision of the Democratic
Movement for National Liberation and the Sudanese Movement for National Liberation" (the precursor of the Communist Party of the Sudan).
These publications contained news of Egypt and the Sudan, translations
of HADETU publications, reports of the activities of HADETU and its
mass organizations, especially the Partisans of Peace, and analysis of the
situation in Egypt and the Sudan in accord with the HADETU line.

The Free Officers' military coup of July 23, 1952, created dramatically
new political conditions that Curiel's comrades in Egypt felt he could not
properly appreciate from abroad. Curiel's advice, indeed his existence,
was increasingly ignored, especially after HADETU underwent another
split in mid-1953 over the organization's attitude toward the new military regime. In addition, communication with Curiel was impaired because HADETU was organizationally weakened by the arrest of many

members during the anticommunist campaign unleashed by the new regime with the encouragement of the U.S. Embassy in Cairo.

All the Egyptian communist tendencies except HADETU, in concert with the line of the Soviet Union and the Communist Party of France, opposed the Free Officers' regime on the grounds that it was an undemocratic military dictatorship, some of whose leaders had close ties to the U.S. Embassy and the CIA, and because it had brutally suppressed a major strike of textile workers in the town of Kafr al-Dawwar only weeks after coming to power. HADETU, inspired by Curiel's strategic conception that gave priority to the struggle against British imperialism, supported the coup d'état of the Free Officers and the Revolutionary Command Council they established as an expression of the "national democratic movement."[22] This did not exempt HADETU members from arrest and torture in Gamal Abdel Nasser's prisons for much of the next twelve years.

Curiel's status in HADETU was further complicated in November 1952 when the Communist Party of France impugned his faithfulness and reliability by implicating him in the Marty affair—a late Stalinist intrigue aimed at eliminating "rightists" (i.e., those who continued to advocate a popular front despite the intensifying cold war) from the leadership of the French and other communist parties. The case against Curiel was based on circumstantial evidence and innuendo. The French party's decision to attack him by insinuation may have been due to the influence of Curiel's opponents among Egyptian emigres who did join the Communist Party of France, its distaste for his unorthodox ways, or its disapproval of HADETU's and Curiel's support for the Free Officers in opposition to the line of the Soviet Union. Under the prevailing norms of Stalinist orthodoxy, the veiled criticism of Curiel by the Communist Party of France rendered him a political pariah. The suspicions of his longtime critics appeared to be vindicated, and even some who knew him well and had followed his leadership now distanced themselves from him. Those who opposed Curiel no longer needed to argue that the problem with him and the Rome Group was that they were Jews who had supported the partition of Palestine with more enthusiasm than any Arab intellectual could muster—an argument that might open its proponents to charges of anti-Semitism or lack of commitment to internationalism. Now it was sufficient and compelling to say that the international communist movement regarded Curiel as a questionable element and that he should be avoided for that reason.

Despite the cloud over Curiel, the Rome Group remained convinced of his innocence and continued to function under his leadership. Members of the group other than Curiel represented HADETU at meetings of the various popular front organizations of the international communist movement such as the International Association of Democratic Jurists, the World Federation of Democratic Women, the World Federation of Democratic Youth, and the World Peace Council. When HADETU changed its line in late 1953 and attacked the Free Officers' regime, the Rome Group complied, despite Curiel's personal disagreement with the new policy, and distributed pamphlets signed by the Egyptian National Democratic Front (in which HADETU participated) attacking the Egyptian government at the meeting of the Congress of Asian Jurists and at the Bandung Conference of Asian and African States in 1955.[23] HADETU members living in Egypt could not attend these meetings without being arrested on their return home; and there was no objection to the Rome Group's representing the organization in this way.

HADETU members in Egypt did object when the Rome Group used these meetings to make contact with the Communist Party of Israel and to promote dialogues aimed at resolving the Arab-Israeli conflict. These efforts were always in accord with the generally accepted communist line, which affirmed the validity of the November 1947 UN General Assembly resolution partitioning Palestine into an Arab state and a Jewish state and recognized the right to national self-determination of both the Jewish and Arab communities of mandate Palestine. But communists living in Egypt did not feel the need to seek direct contact with Israelis, even communist Israelis with whom there was basic agreement on many matters. As the conflict with Israel sharpened, promoting Arab-Israeli peace became less important and less possible for them.

From late 1954 on, the Nasser regime became increasingly committed to pan-Arab nationalism. The international communist movement at first regarded pan-Arabism as a British-sponsored scheme to maintain an imperial presence in the Arab world. But by 1954, Arab and Egyptian communists began to embrace this orientation as an expression of anti-imperialism. By late 1955, due to Nasser's endorsement of "positive neutralism" at the Bandung Conference, the close relations Nasser established with the leaders of China, India, and Yugoslavia, and the announcement that Egypt would purchase arms from Czechoslovakia, the communist movement reconsidered its opposition to the regime. The rapprochement between the communists and the regime was based primarily on support for Nasser's anti-imperialist foreign policy, which was, in Nasserist political discourse, nearly synonymous with pan-Arab nationalism. Understanding the popularity and power of this idiom, the communists embraced it with only faintly articulated reservations about the continuing undemocratic character of the Nasser regime, its prohibition of strikes, its efforts to control the leadership of the trade union movement, and its refusal to allow overt communist political activity. These were considered secondary problems because, according to the prevailing Marxist orthodoxy, anything that contributed to the struggle against imperialism was regarded as contributing to the victory of the international proletariat.

In the 1940s, Jews had been accepted in the communist movement on the basis of a shared commitment to local Egyptian patriotism. It was problematic, but not unreasonable, to consider Jews as Egyptians. Even before 1948, the designation "Arab Jew" was uncommon; after the establishment of the state of Israel, it became unthinkable to regard Jews as Arabs. When the focal point of political loyalty for Egyptians shifted toward the Arab world, and Arabism came to be perceived as embodying an anti-imperialist essence, the tension between Arabism and its other—Israel—made it increasingly difficult for Jews and non-Jews to coexist in the same political movement or, indeed, in the same country. The Rome Group failed to respond adequately to this development and continued to function as before.

The rapprochement between the various communist tendencies and the Egyptian regime encouraged a parallel movement toward unity within the highly factionalized communist movement. In February 1955, HADETU and six organizations that had previously split from it fused to form the Unified Egyptian Communist Party (UECP—al-Hizb al-Shuyu'i al-Misri al-Muwahhad). The Jewish emigres were so out of touch with their comrades in Egypt by this time that they learned of this development from friends in the Communist Party of Sudan. They supported the move toward communist unity, but their enthusiasm was dampened because, as a condition of unity, HADETU's partners had insisted that Curiel's membership in the UECP be suspended in light of the suspicions that had been raised about him in the Marty affair. Four members of the UECP living in Egypt who were known to have close relations with Curiel were also suspended.

Even though it regarded the UECP's actions as "submission to bourgeois nationalism," the Rome Group continued to function as a branch of the party, redoubling its efforts to promote the new party's views by publishing a French translation of the UECP's underground Arabic newspaper, *Kifah al-sha'b*, (People's struggle) and a monthly Arabic bulletin, *Kifah shu'ub al-sharq al-awsat* (Struggle of the peoples of the Middle East), "issued by the Unified Egyptian Communist Party," while continuing its monthly French bulletin, *Nouvelles d'Egypte*, now "published by the Unified Egyptian Communist Party." In July 1956, the party memberships of Curiel and the four others suspended with him were restored. Curiel regained his seat on the Central Committee after the 1956 war.

The Jewish emigre group felt that the UECP had unfairly taken sanctions against their leader because he was Jewish or because he was considered a foreigner. Though they maintained their confidence in Curiel, they did not violate the Leninist rules of discipline and continued to uphold the line of the party while voicing their disagreements through internal channels. Apparently, they believed that the best way to convince their comrades of Curiel's loyalty (and their own) was to remain faithful and to identify even more closely with Egypt and with the UECP. The years 1955–56 were the high point in the Rome Group's political activity, and the initiation of an Arabic publication, though it was short-lived, suggests that the group made an effort to accommodate itself to the rising tide of Arabism.

The Bandung Conference of Asian and African States in 1955 adopted a resolution calling for a peaceful settlement of the Arab-Israeli conflict on the basis of Arab recognition of Israel in exchange for an Israeli retreat to the borders allotted to the Jewish state by the 1947 UN partition plan. This resolution was endorsed by Egypt and the other Arab states participating in the Bandung Conference; according to some accounts, it was initiated by Abdel Nasser himself. Yusuf Hilmi, a Muslim Egyptian lawyer and secretary-general of the Egyptian Partisans of Peace, saw this as an opportune moment to press for a resolution of the Arab-Israeli conflict.[24] He adopted the strategy of calling on Abdel Nasser to pursue the commitment he had made at Bandung with an appropriate diplomatic initiative. Simultaneously, Hilmi addressed the Israeli people and called on them to make a positive response to the Bandung resolution, which he considered a manifestation of Arab willingness to coexist with Israel.

The Rome Group enthusiastically promoted Hilmi's efforts and identified with them wholeheartedly. Though Hilmi was not a party member when he began this initiative, the content of his proposals was consistent with the line of the UECP. However, his rhetoric was much more conciliatory to Israel than that of the party. Some UECP members living in Egypt were uncomfortable with the Rome Group's support for Yusuf Hilmi and demanded that the group be expelled from the party for that reason. Although no steps in this direction were taken, once again some Egyptian communists suspected that their Jewish comrades might be more sympathetic to Israel than they felt was proper, especially in the context of the general rapprochement between the communists and the regime of Abdel Nasser, who, though he did engage in indirect, secret diplomatic contacts with Israel before and after the Bandung Conference, was unwilling to undertake a public initiative to follow up the Bandung resolution on the Arab-Israeli conflict.

THE SUEZ CRISIS AND AFTERMATH

When Nasser announced the nationalization of the Suez Canal on July 26, 1956, the Rome Group responded with intense patriotic fervor. The group defended the legality of the Egyptian government's action and used its European contacts to try to persuade French and British leaders to resolve their dispute with Egypt peacefully. When the die was cast, Curiel sided with Egypt against France. Twenty days before the Anglo-French-Israeli invasion of Egypt on October 29, 1956, he obtained a copy of the plan of attack and forwarded it to 'Abd al-Rahman Sadiq, the Egyptian press attaché in Paris. Abdel Nasser saw the plan but thought the idea was too outlandish to consider seriously. After the Suez/Sinai War, Curiel worked hard to repair the damaged relations between Egypt and France. Sarwat 'Ukasha, the Egyptian military attaché in Paris, was aware of Curiel's efforts and asked Abdel Nasser to restore his Egyptian citizenship in recognition of his patriotic activity, but he was rebuffed.[25]

Despite Egypt's military defeat, Nasser emerged from the Suez crisis as the heroic leader of anti-imperialist pan-Arabism. All the Egyptian communists now supported the regime's foreign policy wholeheartedly, and moving closer to the regime encouraged the factionalized movement to unite its own ranks. The first stage of unification was the fusion of al-Raya with the UECP (composed largely of the former HADETU) to form the United Egyptian Communist Party (al-Hizb al-Shuyu'i al-Misri al-Muttahid) in July 1957. As a condition of unity, al-Raya insisted that Jews be excluded from the leadership of the new party and that the Rome Group be dissolved.

The exclusion of Jews from the leadership had no practical significance in Egypt because, except for Curiel, there were no longer any Jewish leaders of the UECP; and there had never been any Jews at all in al-Raya. The Jewish members of the UECP in Egypt quietly became rank-and-file members of the United Egyptian Communist Party. The dissolution of the Rome Group was a more substantial matter, but in response to al-Raya's posing this demand, some members of the UECP (especially those who had not previously known Curiel personally as members of HADETU) breathed a sigh of relief. Even Curiel's disciples in Egypt understood that he and the other Jewish emigres in Paris were an easy target for the government and others who attacked the Egyptian communists as Zionists and agents of Israel. Therefore, as the Egyptian historian and HADETU partisan Rif'at al-Sa'id put it, some members of the UECP "were also pleased with this decision [to expel Curiel and the Rome Group], even though they did not wish to undertake it."[26]

Those who sought to sever the Egyptian communist movement's ties with Curiel and all that he was assumed to represent had substantial international support for doing so. Because of their French educations, the Communist Party of France had great authority for many Egyptian communists. None of them were closer to the French party than the leaders of al-Raya, Fu'ad Mursi and Isma'il Sabri 'Abd Allah, who had been members of the Communist Party of France and its "group of Egyptians in Paris" when they were students in the late 1940s and early 1950s. Al-Raya's conditions for unity thus carried considerable ideological weight, despite the fact that it was the smallest of the tendencies engaged in the unity discussions. In October 1957, the Political Bureau of the United Egyptian Communist Party informed the Rome Group that it was dissolved.

Meanwhile, unity discussions continued with the third, and by now the largest communist group, the Workers' and Peasants' Communist Party (WPCP—*Hizb al-'Ummal wa'l-Fallahin al-Shuyu'i*), whose nucleus was the former New Dawn group. Yusuf Darwish and Ahmad Sadiq Sa'd were members of the Central Committee of WPCP. Accepting the demand to bar Jews from the leadership would mean their exclusion from the new united party's Central Committee, of which they would otherwise undoubtedly have been members. Over the protests of many of its own members, the WPCP leaders reluctantly accepted the conditions for unity. Thus, when the united Communist Party of Egypt (CPE) was established on January 8, 1958, the Central Committee included no Jews, though several Jews remained rank-and-file party members. The Jewish emigres in Paris were excluded from membership in the new party at the same time that they were informed that their financial contributions to it would still be welcome.

There was little objection to this measure in Egypt. The Jewish former WPCP members Ahmad Sadiq Saʿd, Yusuf Darwish, and Raymond
Douek detested Curiel, in part because they considered him too sympathetic to Zionism. They were glad to see him and the Rome Group excluded from the new party. None of the other Jews who joined CPE was
influential enough to register a serious protest. The common commitment to the priority of the anti-imperialist national liberation project dis-
abled critical judgments that might have emerged about the meaning and
consequences of this course of action.

The Rome Group regarded these decisions as submission to racism.
A detailed letter from the group to the Political Bureau indicates that objections to its activities promoting Arab-Israeli peace by communists residing in Egypt had been one of the factors prompting the demand for
its dissolution.[27] Thus, at the very end of their career in the Egyptian
communist movement, the Jewish emigres in Paris hinted that there was
a political difference between them and the other Egyptian communists
on the question of the Arab-Israeli conflict: Most non-Jewish communists were much less concerned about resolving the Arab-Israeli conflict
than Curiel and the Rome Group were, in part because demanding that
the Egyptian government take bold initiatives in this regard would risk
a break with Abdel Nasser and the pan-Arab nationalist movement that
looked to him for leadership. Admitting this political difference would
have placed a question mark over the Rome Group's identity as Egyptians because this difference could easily be dismissed as a function of
ethnic origin and lack of enthusiasm for pan-Arab nationalism, hence
conciliation with Zionism and imperialism. The Rome Group's claim
that the decision to exclude Jews from the party constituted racism was
valid according to the norms of the international communist movement.
But the issue was much more complex than this, and the Rome Group
had neither the political standing nor the analytical tools to launch a full-
scale political debate on the matter.

The Rome Group's claims to be a legitimate part of Egypt were contested not only by the regime they opposed but also by their closest political allies. This was a consequence of the rapprochement between the
communist movement and the regime and the communists' acceptance
of the ethos of pan-Arabism. As it was transmitted to the Rome Group,
this meant that Jews cannot be Arabs. The form of Egyptian national
identity adopted by the Nasserist anti-imperialist project situated the
Egyptian Jewish communists in the location defined by Edward Said as
"just beyond the perimeter of what nationalism constructs as the nation,

at the frontier separating 'us' from what is alien" in "the perilous territory of not-belonging."[28]

Less than a year after the Rome Group was expelled from the Egyptian
communist movement and its major tendencies fused, the Communist
Party of Egypt split into two factions: CPE and CPE-HADETU. The reappearance of the HADETU faction without any Jews in the leadership suggests that the Jewishness of Curiel and other historic HADETU leaders
was not primarily responsible for the persistent factionalism in the
Egyptian communist movement, as some of its opponents charged. Only
months later, on the eve of January 1, 1959, the Nasser regime launched
a campaign of mass arrests that culminated in the imprisonment of almost
all the active communists and many others. Intense ideological debates in
jail brought most of the communists to support the Arab socialist policies
adopted by Nasser in the early 1960s. The narrowing of the differences
with the regime and the deepening relationship between Egypt and the Soviet Union led to the release of the communists from jail in 1964. A year
later, both of the main communist parties were dissolved.

POLITICAL NOMADISM

The demise of communism as an organized political force in Egypt impelled the members of the former Rome Group to reorient their political commitments and identities. Despite the cavalier treatment they received from their comrades in Egypt, the members of the former Rome
Group loyally contributed large sums of money to support the families
of jailed party members and conducted propaganda work in Europe to
bring public attention to their plight.[29] However, these acts of solidarity
and compassion, though impressive in their own terms, were not an
adequate long-term substitute for the high level of political commitment
and engagement the members of the Rome Group had experienced as
disciplined cadres in the Egyptian communist movement. They also
postponed addressing the question of the ethnic identity of those who
undertook them. Having invested great efforts in demonstrating their
Egyptianity, the Rome Group members could not instantly become
French. Having insisted that their Jewishness was of little significance,
they could not easily become Jews. The members of the group, along
with several other former Egyptian Jewish communists in France, were
thus compelled to invent new political and cultural personalities from
the now permanently dislocated fragments of their Egyptian, Jewish,
and French identities.

Henri Curiel took the first step in this direction in November 1957 when he and some members of the Rome Group—primarily Rosette Curiel, Joyce Blau, and Didar Rossano-Fawzy—began to work with a French network of support for the Algerian revolution led by Francis Jeanson. Behind-the-scenes support was provided by the printing enterprise of Yusuf Hazan. "We were mad with joy," said Rosette Curiel, "because we were once again useful."[30]

By 1960, Curiel supplanted Jeanson as the leader of the National Liberation Front (FLN) support network. Because of his work in support of the Algerian revolution, Curiel was arrested by the French security services on October 21, 1960. He remained incarcerated until after the signing of the Evian accords on Algerian independence in 1962. The dedication and self-sacrifice of Curiel and his associates forged intimate relations between the small group of Francophone Egyptian Jews around Curiel and the Francophone Muslim Algerian leaders of FLN. As an expression of that relationship, after Algerian independence, Didar Rossano-Fawzy took up residence in Algiers and remained there until the military coup that deposed Ahmad Ben Bella and brought Houari Boumedienne to power in June 1965.[31] In addition, Henri Curiel donated his family's mansion, located on Brazil Street in the fashionable Zamalek district of Cairo, to the government of independent Algeria for use as its embassy in Egypt. The building still serves that function today.

While a subset of its members began to work in solidarity with the Algerian FLN in 1957, the Rome Group as a whole continued to consider Egypt as its field of action. Their illusions were definitively shattered in January 1959 when Didar Rossano-Fawzy came back to Paris from Egypt, where she had been active in the women's movement since the end of the Suez/Sinai War, and reported that Curiel's supporters wanted him to return. With most of the party leaders in jail, they were perhaps prepared to reconsider the value of Curiel's contribution to the Egyptian communist movement. By then, Curiel had concluded that his role in Egypt was over. Other members of the Rome Group had come to that conclusion when they were officially expelled from the Communist Party of Egypt the previous year. Although Curiel went through the initial motions, he did not aggressively pursue this opportunity to return to Egypt, which he would have eagerly seized upon a few years earlier.[32] As Gilles Perrault reported, "He had understood. Marginality was his lot. . . . Expelled from Egypt and Italy, clandestine in France, then a conditional, temporary resident. . . . Marginality was his political destiny."[33]

After Algeria gained its independence, Curiel expanded his work in support of FLN into broad solidarity work for anticolonialist revolutionary movements in Asia, Africa, and Latin America. Several members of the former Rome Group had reservations about extending their political activities to the entire world. There was a certain logic and continuity to working for Algerian independence, but a global anticolonialist support movement seemed too diffuse and politically adventurist.[34] Only Curiel's closest comrades from the Rome Group—Joyce Blau, Rosette Curiel, and Didar Rossano-Fawzy—joined him on this new political journey far beyond the boundaries of Egypt and the Middle East. Their former comrades supported their efforts in exceptional circumstances. At the first annual congress of Solidarité (Solidarity) on December 1–2, 1962, about thirty socially and politically diverse individuals—Catholic and Protestant clergymen, pro-Soviet communists, and political adventurers, many of them veterans of the FLN support network—gathered around Curiel's leadership.

Solidarity provided lodging and safe houses, communications and courier services, forged travel documents, medical assistance, and intelligence and military training to many anticolonialist and oppositional revolutionary movements in Asia, Africa, and Latin America. Among the beneficiaries of Solidarity's services were the MPLA of Angola, FRELIMO of Mozambique, ANC of South Africa, ZAPU of Zimbabwe, FAR of Argentina, VRP of Brazil, MIR of Chile, FAR of Guatemala, PDK of Kurdistan, and the communist parties of Haiti, Iraq, Israel (MAKI and RAKAH), Morocco, Sudan, and Réunion.

Though Solidarity devoted most of its efforts to causes outside the Middle East, Curiel justified his activism in terms of Egypt: "Me, I began in Egypt. You can't know how hard it is to start from zero, to have to learn everything. One loses time. One makes mistakes. Why not let others profit from the experience acquired? You see that you can teach them a lot."[35] Solidarity maintained another vital Middle Eastern connection: from Algerian independence until the coup d'état of Houari Boumedienne in June 1965. It was financed by the government of Algeria.[36]

Solidarity's social and political diversity, its mixture of conspiratorial professionalism and amateurism, the intense but naive political devotion of its activists, and Curiel's complex political baggage and personal peculiarities led many to suspect that Solidarity was not what it claimed to be. The Egyptian government and some of Curiel's former comrades in Egypt had long thought he was a Zionist agent. The Communist Party of France refused to have anything to do with him. The Communist Party of Israel, an exceptionally dogmatic party, also kept its distance from Curiel, despite the fact that Curiel had repeatedly tried to introduce Arab and Israeli communists to each other, a project that the Israeli party in principle supported wholeheartedly.

Curiel's uncommon political career was brought to the attention of the French public in 1976 when the news weekly *Le Point* featured a cover story, "The Boss of the Terrorist Aid Networks," by Georges Suffert. This sensationalist exposé included a capsule political biography of Curiel that was wrong in nearly every detail.[37] Suffert's sources in the French intelligence community believed Curiel was "in constant contact with the KGB."[38] They hypothesized that the Soviet Union, because it opposed the use of terrorism by left-wing groups, deployed Curiel to gather information and to monitor and restrain them.

Most Americans who know the name of Henri Curiel probably encountered it for the first time in Claire Sterling's *The Terror Network: The Secret War of International Terrorism,* a key text in the articulation of the discourse on terrorism, which became a major justification for U.S. foreign policy in the Reagan-Bush era. Terrorism conveniently linked the two Easts—Islam and communism—and provided a unifying theme for a foreign policy of global rollback from Iran to Nicaragua during the second cold war. Sterling drew much of her information on Curiel from Suffert's *Le Point* article, including all its incorrect biographical details. She agreed with Suffert's suggestion that Curiel was a KGB agent. But the main thesis of Sterling's book was that there was a vast conspiracy of international terrorism directed by the Soviet Union against the West: the polar opposite of Suffert's explanation of the KGB's motive for using Curiel. This inconsistency did not diminish *The Terror Network*'s influence as a rationale for Reagan era foreign policy. Believers in the existence of an "evil empire" were temperamentally unsuited to examining Sterling's propositions critically.

Suffert, Sterling, and other conspiracy theorists purporting to explain the activities of Curiel, Solidarity, and its successor organization of the mid-1970s, Aide et Amitié (Aid and friendship), have never provided evidence that could be independently checked and verified to support their assertions. Therefore, it is worth considering the possibility that the motivations and objectives of Curiel and his comrades were more or less what they proclaimed them to be. "Never forget that it was the misery of the Egyptian people that led him [Curiel] to politics," explained Yusuf Hazan.[39] Perhaps the unusual combination of Curiel's political dedication, his exile and expulsion from the national community he most wanted to be part of, and his repeated efforts to recreate an authentic political and personal identity removed from the native space that he came to understand he would never possess formed Curiel's persona as an eccentric. Reflecting on his own experience as a Palestinian exile, Edward Said observed, "Exiles are always eccentrics who *feel* their difference (even as they frequently exploit it). . . . This usually translates into an intransigence that is not easily ignored."[40]

EGYPTIAN JEWS AS INTERMEDIARIES IN THE ARAB-ISRAELI CONFLICT

This chapter could end at this point, and the dramatic tension of the narrative might be enhanced if it did. But this would unduly emphasize the persona of Henri Curiel and suggest that he succeeded in transforming his social marginality into a lever of historical agency through conscious, self-actualizing, heroic-eccentric, political action. Curiel's personal qualities of determination and dedication certainly contributed to making him a singular (even if perhaps, ultimately, not an especially effective) historical subject. But the political action of Curiel and the Rome Group also forms part of a larger story in which many left-wing Egyptian Jews acted as intermediaries between Arabs and Israelis.

The cultural and political formation of Jews born in Egypt, educated in French, and politicized in the era of the united front against fascism entailed a proclivity to temper intransigent nationalisms intolerant of ambiguous and hybrid cultural identities. Some individuals did act heroically in this context, but their actions were enabled by their historically formed political, cultural, and geographic positions. A significant number of such Egyptian Jews embraced the opportunities, challenges, and responsibilities presented to them as a result of the historically structured experiences that configured their personal and political identities to engage in some form of public efforts to mediate the Arab-Israeli conflict.

The remaining sections of this chapter examine some of these activities. Much of the narrative has the character of a conventional diplomatic history. The events are significant, interesting, and widely misrepresented enough to justify such a conventional approach, but this risks reemphasizing the heroic-eccentric historical agency of singular individuals. Therefore, I reiterate that my argument is that subjects with the potential to act as they did were formed by historically structured circumstances. Moreover, many other unrecorded, private forms of mediation also occurred. Though I have been unable to recover their traces, their significance may nonetheless have been considerable.

EGYPTIAN JEWS IN PARIS AND THE ARAB-ISRAELI CONFLICT AFTER THE 1967 WAR

The 1967 war reconfigured the significance of the Arab-Israeli conflict in world affairs and restored the question of Palestine to the international agenda after a long absence. In these more urgent circumstances, left-wing Egyptian Jews living in Paris found that their fragmented social and cultural formations, their commitment to political internationalism, and their strategic location at a cosmopolitan European crossroads enabled them to serve as political and cultural intermediaries. Arabs and Israelis seeking to step beyond the boundaries of their respective national consensuses to explore the possibility of reaching resolutions to their conflict based on mutual recognition and coexistence found a common language with left-wing Egyptian Jewish emigres in Paris who were able to function comfortably in all of the dialects that different parties brought to this encounter.

Raymond Aghion (b. 1921) was one of the first Egyptian Jews to undertake a project of political and cultural mediation after the 1967 war.[41] Aghion, Henri Curiel's cousin and a member of a wealthy Alexandrian family of Italian citizenship, pursued a political career parallel, though sometimes antagonistic, to his better-known cousin. He was educated at the Lycée de l'Union Juive pour l'Enseignment of Alexandria and began his political career by purchasing *al-Majalla al-Jadida* (The new magazine) so that it could be used as a forum for leftist opinions. During World War II, Aghion and Curiel established L'Amitié Française to support the French resistance against the Nazi occupation. Rosette Curiel was then an employee of the French legation in Cairo. Through her efforts, L'Amitié Française received official diplomatic support and political cover for conducting Marxist education in the guise of promoting the progressive face of French culture.

Despite this early collaboration, Aghion was never an adherent of Curiel; their future political careers were formed in divergent currents of the same broad stream. Aghion left Egypt in 1945 and took up residence in Paris, where he resided continually except for four years in Italy from 1952 to 1956. He returned to visit Egypt only once, in 1970, and maintained no organizational ties with the Egyptian communist movement after leaving the country. Instead, Aghion joined the Communist Party of France and its "group of Egyptians in Paris" along with Fu'ad Mursi and Isma'il Sabri 'Abd Allah, the future leaders of al-Raya.

In the early 1950s, Aghion and 'Abd Allah collaborated with Maxime Rodinson in the publication of a nonparty journal, *Moyen-Orient* (Middle East), one of the first publications based on the collaboration of Arabs and Jews. *Moyen-Orient* was almost unique in the West after the 1948 Arab-Israeli War because it spoke of the Palestinians as a national community, not simply as refugees in need of humanitarian assistance. The journal also advocated Arab neutrality in the cold war, a position that anticipated the positive neutralism developed by Abdel Nasser, Nehru, and Tito after the Bandung Conference. This collaboration ended in 1951 when Isma'il Sabri 'Abd Allah returned to Egypt, where he rejoined Fu'ad Mursi, who had already established al-Raya after completing his studies in Paris. Aghion remained active in the Communist Party of France during the 1950s and 1960s and did not again undertake any particular responsibility for political action in the Arab-Israeli arena until after the 1967 war.

In April 1968, former Prime Minister Pierre Mendès-France published an article in *Le Nouvel Observateur* calling for an Arab-Israeli peace settlement on the basis of UN Security Council Resolution 242, the intentionally vague diplomatic formula adopted at the conclusion of the 1967 Arab-Israeli hostilities.[42] Though Mendès-France rarely identified himself publicly as a Jew, he was married to the niece of Salvator Cicurel, the last president of the Sephardi Jewish community of Cairo, so he had a personal as well as a political stake in the resolution of the Arab-Israeli conflict. At the urging of several Arab friends, on April 27, 1968, Aghion wrote to Mendès-France (using the pseudonym Francis Lagache) explaining that the Arab states bordering Israel had already agreed to implement UN Security Council Resolution 242, whereas Israel did not accept the principle of evacuating all the Arab territories it occupied in 1967 in exchange for a contractual peace with the Arab states. Mendès-France's reply to Aghion was lukewarm and noncommittal, and the events of May 1968 soon overwhelmed whatever potential this exchange might have had.[43]

Some of Henri Curiel's almost incidental activities of the mid-1950s assumed a new significance in the post-1967 circumstances. Soon after Curiel began working in support of the Algerian revolution, Amos Kenan, an Israeli journalist who had been a minor party in Arab-Israeli discussions in Paris generated by Yusuf Hilmi's 1955 peace initiative, introduced him to Uri Avnery, the editor of the iconoclastic Israeli weekly *ha-'Olam ha-Zeh* (This world). Curiel explained to Avnery that if Israelis actively supported the inevitable victory of the Algerian FLN, then Algeria would become Israel's first friend in the Arab world and be able to mediate between Israel and Egypt. Following Curiel's advice, Avnery, Kenan, and their comrades—Natan Yalin-Mor, Maxime Ghilan, and Shalom Cohen—established the Israeli Committee for a Free Algeria.[44]

The historic political roots of this circle were on the margins of Israeli society and politics—ETZEL (the Irgun, or National Military Organization) and LEHI (the Stern Gang, or Fighters for the Freedom of Israel), as opposed to the hegemonic labor Zionist movement. Even in those dissident circles, their trajectory was distinctive because they did not join the Herut Party or its successor, the Likud, as the leaders of ETZEL and LEHI, Menahem Begin and Yitzhak Shamir, and many of their followers did. In the 1950s, they were the animators of Semitic Action, a political expression of the Canaanite movement, which advocated that Hebrew-speaking Israelis cut their ties with the Jewish diaspora and integrate into the Middle East as natives of the region on the basis of an anticolonialist alliance with its indigenous Arab inhabitants. Avnery's magazine was popular among devotees of soft-core pornography, muckraking investigative journalism, and avant garde culturopolitical ideas. But in the heyday of MAPAI rule and Ben-Gurionist statism, initiatives emanating from a current so far beyond the labor Zionist mainstream of Israeli politics and culture could have no immediate practical consequences. Only developments after the overpowering Israeli victory in the 1967 Arab-Israeli War and the inconclusive standoff at the end of the 1973 war invested these contacts between Israeli Jews and the Algerian FLN mediated by Henri Curiel with historical status as a new beginning of the dialogue, largely suspended outside the ranks of the Communist Party of Israel since 1948, between Arabs and Jews seeking coexistence on the basis of equality in the Middle East.

In 1969, Curiel received from several former comrades in Egypt a letter asking him to define his position on the Arab-Israeli conflict. Curiel sent a lengthy response articulating the principles that guided his efforts to serve as an intermediary between the parties to the conflict during the 1970s. The starting point of Curiel's analysis was that the Jews of Israel constituted a national community with the right of self-determination, even if Israel were regarded as a colonial fact, "because many national states have their origins in colonial facts, a truth well-verified in Africa and the Middle East."[45] This was the same argument that the Soviet Union and the international communist movement had deployed to justify the UN partition plan for Palestine in 1947. The Egyptian and other Arab communists modified this line in response to exacerbation of the Arab-Israeli conflict and the unequivocal alignment of Israel with Anglo-French neocolonialism in 1956.[46] Curiel steadfastly upheld the formulations of 1947–48, and this was one of the reasons some of his former comrades came to suspect and distrust him. Curiel maintained that armed conflict, which had begun to escalate in 1969 with the outbreak of the war of attrition between Egypt and Israel across the Suez Canal, served the interests of imperialism and reactionary forces in the Arab world and in Israel. He regarded the slogan of "War until Victory" as an ultraleft illusion that caused great Arab suffering in the name of defending the interests of the Arab nation by rejecting any political solution to the conflict with Israel. He opposed this slogan, just as the Egyptian communists had opposed the Arab declarations of war on Israel in 1948.

Curiel believed that the Arab-Israeli conflict constituted a barrier to pursuing a progressive social agenda in both Israel and the Arab states. Therefore it should be settled as soon as possible. To break the deadlock, it was necessary to appeal to the masses of Israelis over the heads of their militarist leaders and to convince them that they could achieve peace and security by evacuating the Arab territories occupied in 1967 and recognizing the establishment of a Palestinian state. According to this analysis, the weakness of the Israeli peace forces was a consequence of their isolation from progressive Arabs. A regional political realignment was possible if the progressive forces in the Arab world recognized, supported, and defended the Israeli peace camp, just as the Vietnamese National Liberation Front had established links with the U.S. antiwar movement.

Colonel Ahmad Hamrush, a former member of HADETU and a former Free Officer who had served as a liaison between HADETU and Abdel Nasser in the early 1950s, travelled to Paris in 1968 and decided on his own initiative to renew his contact with Curiel. He was impressed with Curiel's insistence that there were Israelis who favored an Arab-Israeli peace based on Israeli withdrawal from the Arab lands occupied in 1967 and reported their conversation to Abdel Nasser, who instructed Hamrush to pursue this contact. As a result, Curiel arranged informal meetings between Hamrush and Amos Kenan and Natan Yalin-Mor, who had been members of the Israeli Committee for a Free Algeria, as well as Labor Party Knesset member Lova Eliav and journalist Amnon

Kapeliuk, who were new to this circle. Sa'd Kamil, secretary of the Egyptian Partisans of Peace, participated in some of the meetings. Eventually, Abdel Nasser agreed to convene a meeting of Egyptian and Israeli delegates in Paris, under the auspices of a French government minister, but Golda Meir, then prime minister of Israel, rejected this proposal.[47]

Striving to maintain the momentum, Yugoslavian President Josip Tito and the French journalist Eric Rouleau helped to arrange a meeting between Nahum Goldmann and Gamal Abdel Nasser in April 1970. Henri Curiel may have played a role in this endeavor as well. Both parties were willing to meet on the condition that the Israeli government be informed of their encounter at some later date. Neither Goldmann nor Abdel Nasser requested that the Israeli government approve their meeting in advance or grant it an official status. However, Golda Meir thwarted their initiative by asking the Israeli cabinet to approve the Nasser-Goldmann rendezvous. Some ministers informally supported such an encounter as a way to test whether Egypt had any serious intention of seeking a diplomatic resolution of the Arab-Israeli conflict. Meir undermined these expressions of interest in a negotiated settlement by requesting a vote of approval for the proposed meeting by the cabinet. The Israeli government could not be a party to undermining its own sovereignty and Zionist ideology by appearing to delegate a noncitizen, diaspora Jew to negotiate on its behalf. Consequently, the cabinet voted not to authorize the meeting. After the proposed Nasser-Goldmann meeting fell through, Eric Rouleau tried to maintain the momentum by arranging a meeting between Goldmann and Ahmad Hamrush at his home in Paris.[48]

The proposed Goldmann-Nasser meeting and Israel's role in blocking it were widely reported in the international press.[49] Many Israelis, anxious to end the war of attrition with Egypt, break the Arab-Israeli impasse, and test Arab intentions, supported this modest undertaking. Hundreds of students at the Hebrew University disrupted traffic for hours on one of the main boulevards of Jerusalem to protest Golda Meir's intransigence and obstruction of an opportunity to pursue peace. This demonstration, one of the first acts of mass civil disobedience against the annexationist policies of the Israeli government, seemed to confirm the validity of Curiel's strategy.

Eric Rouleau, whose intermediary efforts were spurned by Golda Meir, is widely recognized as an exceptionally well informed and well connected journalist. He covered the Middle East for *Le Monde* for many years and subsequently served as French ambassador to Tunisia and Turkey during the presidency of François Mitterand. Serving as an intermediary in arranging an Arab-Jewish meeting was a new field of endeavor for him. But Rouleau's entire journalistic oeuvre, particularly his reporting on Egypt during the regime of Gamal Abdel Nasser, can be regarded as a project of cultural and political translation between his early life experiences as an Egyptian-born Jew and his adult professional world of French journalism, when he became especially close to the Egyptian president. Rouleau grew up in the Cairo suburb of Heliopolis and had an intense interest in international affairs. After World War II he joined the Iskra communist group. When HADETU split into several fragments in 1948, Rouleau joined one of the most dogmatic splinters—the Egyptian Communist Organization (al-Munazzama al-Shuyu'iyya al-Misriyya). He left Egypt for France and a career in journalism in 1950.

It is more than an ironic accident that the Egyptian ruler most excoriated by Israel and the West often selected an Arabic-speaking Jew as his favored journalistic conduit to the West. The symbolic significance of their connection could not have escaped either of the parties. Whether or not Rouleau or Abdel Nasser ever consciously thought of their relationship in these terms, the high level of rapport and understanding they developed over many years suggested the possibility of a different model for Arab-Jewish relations. Because Rouleau was neither a sycophant nor an uncritical supporter of Abdel Nasser, his judgment that the Egyptian president was not an anti-Semite is worth recording.[50]

After Egyptian President Anwar al-Sadat's trip to Jerusalem in 1977, Abu 'Iyad (Salah Khalaf), a founder and leader of al-Fatah, the principal group in the PLO, asked Eric Rouleau to help him write his political autobiography. The exceptional circumstances of al-Sadat's peace initiative and the possibility that it would culminate in a separate Egyptian-Israeli peace probably impelled the PLO leadership to approve this effort to present the Palestinian cause in human terms that might receive a sympathetic hearing in the West. The leading members of the PLO rarely assigned much importance to this task.

The resulting text was the first extensive account of the life and political outlook of a historic leader of the PLO in a Western language—a tremendous professional scoop for Rouleau.[51] Although he clearly stated his disagreement with some of Abu 'Iyad's positions, especially on the legitimacy of attacks on unarmed civilians, such as the kidnapping of the members of the Israeli team at the Munich Olympics in September 1972, Rouleau was impressed by Abu 'Iyad's skills as a negotiator. He also noted that Abu 'Iyad was the first PLO leader who publicly advocated creating a Palestinian state alongside Israel. Rouleau's ability to perceive

flexibility in the position of the PLO leader most closely identified with
Black September and his empathic presentation of Abu 'Iyad's personal
history undoubtedly owes something to the commingling of Egyptian,
Jewish, and French influences in his life. His familiarity with the Arab
milieu and prestige as a leading French journalist positioned him well to
serve as the transmitter of Abu 'Iyad's narrative.

The meetings between Ahmad Hamrush and Israeli peace activists in
Paris convinced Henri Curiel that there was a political basis for con-
vening a nongovernmental Arab-Israeli peace conference that would
bring together progressive Arabs, Israelis, and interested third parties.
After receiving a green light from Gamal Abdel Nasser, Curiel and several former members of the Rome Group began to organize such a meeting in collaboration with Hamrush.[52] As part of the preparatory arrangements, Khalid Muhyi al-Din travelled to Paris to meet Israelis who had
been recommended to him by Hamrush. The preparations were inter-
rupted by Abdel Nasser's death and Anwar al-Sadat's assumption of the
presidency of Egypt. Because Khalid Muhyi al-Din had been close to
HADETU and was identified with the left, the new regime ordered him
placed under house arrest.

However, Anwar al-Sadat did not oppose extending peace feelers to
Israel. In February 1971, in response to questions submitted to Israel and
the belligerent Arab states by UN envoy Gunar Jaring, Egypt stated it
was willing to sign a contractual peace agreement with Israel in exchange
for Israeli withdrawal from all the Arab territories occupied in the 1967
war. The Israeli government failed to respond in a similar spirit to Jaring's questions, indicating it insisted on annexing at least some Arab territories. Because official channels were closed by Israel's intransigence,
Anwar al-Sadat eventually authorized Khalid Muhyi al-Din to proceed
with preparations for a nongovernmental international peace conference. Curiel and a few of his former Rome Group comrades now made
the Middle East their personal priority and intensified their organizational work to prepare the peace conference.[53]

The International Conference for Peace and Justice in the Middle East
convened at Bologna, Italy, on May 11, 1973, under the auspices of the
communist-led city council. It was the first public meeting of Arab and
Israeli peace activists since the end of the Palestine mandate. The Israeli
attendees included Yossi Amitai, Amos Kenan, Uri Avnery, Natan Yalin-
Mor, and members of the Communist Party of Israel (RAKAH). Khalid
Muhyi al-Din represented Egypt. Ahmad Hamrush was to have attended
but did not because of the rupture in his relations with Anwar al-Sadat.[54]

Several of the Israeli participants had previously been introduced to Hamrush or Muhyi al-Din in Paris by Henri Curiel. Curiel himself did not attend the Bologna conference. His point of view was represented by Joyce Blau and Raymond Stambouli, former comrades in the Rome Group who were among the active organizers of the meeting.[55]

No one was more aware of the limitations of the Bologna conference than Curiel himself. He noted the absence of Palestinian, Lebanese, and Algerian delegations; weak representation from Israel; lack of U.S. participation; significant absences of other non–Middle Eastern delegations; and a flawed final document.[56] Nonetheless, Curiel insisted that this unprecedented encounter had rendered the hypothesis that there was a basis for understanding among progressive Arabs and Israelis credible. Consequently, he proposed that a second and much larger international conference be convened to continue the work begun at Bologna. However, the near victory of the Arabs in the 1973 war and Anwar al-Sadat's willingness to abandon his Russian patrons for the United States reconfigured the balance of forces in the Middle East and opened other, more daring possibilities.

The outcome of the 1973 war also convinced two young Egyptian Marxists, ʿAdil Rifʿat and Bahgat al-Nadi, who wrote under the pseudonym Mahmoud Hussein, that an Arab-Israeli dialogue was now possible and desirable.[57] They sought out Israelis who supported the concept of Israeli evacuation of the Arab territories occupied in 1967, recognition of a Palestinian state, and peaceful coexistence with the Arab world. With the assistance of Jean Lacouture, they chose as their interlocutor a liberal historian, Saul Friedländer. Their colloquy was published as a book titled *Arabs & Israelis: A Dialogue*.[58]

It is both unexpected and manifestly sensible that in one of the first published political exchanges between Israelis and Arabs, one of the two Arabs was also a Jew. ʿAdil Rifʿat is the nephew of Hillel Schwartz, the founder of Iskra. He had a stormy relationship with his parents and, after a teenage love affair with a young Muslim woman, converted to Islam and became estranged from his family.

ʿAdil Rifʿat and Bahgat al-Nadi had belonged to one of the few communist tendencies that did not join the united Communist Party of Egypt in 1958: Wahdat al-Shuyuʿiyyin (Communist unity). Its leader, Ibrahim Fathi, was the most vitriolic of Henri Curiel's critics in the Egyptian communist movement.[59] Rifʿat and al-Nadi were arrested and jailed with the other communist prisoners from 1959 to 1964. In prison, they developed a Maoist orientation. Consequently, they opposed the dissolution

of the Egyptian communist parties in 1965. Their efforts to continue oppositional political activity led them to a clash with the regime at a time
when most of the other communists and former communists were actively allying themselves with the Arab socialist phase of Nasserism. In
1966, they left Egypt for Paris. *The Class Struggle in Egypt, 1945–1970*
presents Mahmoud Hussein's comprehensive understanding of Egypt in
Maoist terms, combining historical and sociopolitical analysis and a critique of the theory and practice of the Egyptian left.[60] Their Maoist orientation allowed Mahmoud Hussein to develop close ties to the Palestinian armed resistance movement in the early 1970s, when the Soviet
Union still kept its distance from the PLO because it disapproved of the
PLO's military tactics and its goal of replacing Israel with a secular democratic Palestinian state. Mahmoud Hussein's relationship with the
Palestinian resistance made them ideal interlocutors for an Israeli look-
ing for a dialogue with Arabs at a time when the PLO was still reluctant
to speak with Israelis and most Israelis regarded contacts with the "terrorist" PLO as treason.

In historical perspective, the contents of the discussion between Mahmoud Hussein and Saul Friedländer are less important than the fact that
it took place. The flawed political assessments and fallacious historical
arguments of both parties map the substantial perceptual gap between
them. This dialogue derived its significance from the common belief of
both parties that the requisites of a peaceful resolution of the Arab-Israeli
conflict were an Israeli evacuation of all (or almost all) the territories occupied in 1967, at least partial Arab sovereignty in Jerusalem, and Palestinian national self-determination. However, in July 1974, when Mahmoud Hussein and Saul Friedländer met, Henry Kissinger had already
begun to pursue an Arab-Israeli accommodation structured by a Pax
Americana in the Middle East in which common understandings reached
by individuals and groups concerned about achieving a just and peaceful resolution of the conflict were irrelevant.

Shortly after the publication of the dialogue between Mahmoud Hussein and Saul Friedländer in French, *After the Guns Fall Silent: Peace or
Armageddon in the Middle East* by Mohamed Sid-Ahmed appeared in
Arabic.[61] Sid-Ahmed had been a member of the Political Bureau of the
Communist Party of Egypt. After the dissolution of the communist parties, he became a prominent journalist. When Anwar al-Sadat legalized
political parties, Sid-Ahmed became a leading member of the National
Progressive Unionist Party (Tagammu'), the left pole in the limited and
strictly supervised multiparty system. Because it was published in Ara-

bic by a journalist of repute identified with a current in Egyptian politics highly regarded elsewhere in the Arab world, *After the Guns Fall Silent* was a more consequential intervention in Arab politics than Mahmoud Hussein's discussion with Saul Friedländer. The book provoked a lively debate in the Arab world, where few political thinkers had previously raised the question of what kind of peace with Israel was possible or desirable. Sid-Ahmed and Mahmoud Hussein agreed that the consequences of the 1973 war made an Arab-Israeli accommodation possible for the first time. Sid-Ahmed implied that he agreed with Curiel and with Mahmoud Hussein that continuation of the Arab-Israeli conflict was a barrier to social progress in the Arab world and that a diplomatic resolution of the conflict was therefore desirable in principle, even if it would not provide absolute justice for the Arab side. Perhaps the elements of commonality between the analyses of Mahmoud Hussein and Mohamed Sid-Ahmed owe something to the three years 'Adil Rif'at and Mohamed Sid-Ahmed shared a cell in the Wahat prison camp, where they were interned as communists from 1959 to 1964.

Arriving in France, 'Adil Rif'at was reunited with part of his family: his mother and half-brother, Benny Lévy, who had settled in Paris after the 1956 war. In the late 1960s and early 1970s, Lévy emerged as the leader of one of the boldest of the groups to the left of the Communist Party of France, La Gauche Proletarienne (Proletarian left).[62] Lévy and his Maoist group won a significant popular base with tactics like stealing 50,000 Paris Metro tickets and redistributing them free of charge to passengers and kidnapping the manager of a Renault auto assembly plant. La Gauche Proletarienne also cultivated good relations with al-Fatah, the leading tendency in the PLO. Several of its members visited Palestinian refugee camps and commando bases in Jordan. Members of al-Fatah residing in France and La Gauche Proletarienne collaborated in organizing Arab workers in the Mouvement des Travailleurs Arabes (Arab workers' movement). There were also contacts between the underground section of La Gauche Proletarienne and armed elements of al-Fatah, although the French organization dissented from al-Fatah's attacks on unarmed civilians.

During the early 1970s, 'Adil Rif'at was primarily engaged in Egyptian emigre politics, while Benny Lévy's domain of struggle was France. In both arenas, the Palestinian resistance movement was a strategic ally. For Lévy, embracing the PLO opened a door to organizing the large immigrant Arab working class in France. Benny Lévy's origins as an Egyptian Jew prepared him to attach importance to the Arab immigrants, in contrast to the policy of the Communist Party of France, which discouraged its members from devoting significant efforts to organizing noncitizens with no right to vote. For Rif'at, the PLO was the main force that continued to represent a revolutionary alternative in the Arab world after the defeat of 1967.

'Adil Rif'at may have been unconscious of any concern about his Jewish origins when he decided that the consequences of the 1973 Arab-Israeli War established a basis for an Arab-Israeli peace dialogue. Nonetheless, his outlook after 1973 situated him, along with Mohamed Sid-Ahmed, in the current of opinion within Egyptian Marxism that regarded the Arab-Israeli conflict as a barrier to social progress that should be resolved rather than an existential battle of national destiny. This commitment brought Rif'at into contact with Israeli Jews like Saul Friedländer and, though there was never any organized collaboration among them, joined his efforts to those of other Egyptian Jews like Raymond Aghion, Henri Curiel, and Eric Rouleau.

HENRI CURIEL, THE PLO, AND THE ISRAELI COUNCIL FOR ISRAELI-PALESTINIAN PEACE

The 1973 Arab-Israeli War also prompted political rethinking among the ranks of the PLO. Elements of a new approach to the conflict with Israel were expressed in articles in *The Times* after the 1973 war by Sa'id Hammami, the PLO's representative in London,[63] and in an interview Na'if Hawatma, the leader of the Democratic Front for the Liberation of Palestine, granted to the mass circulation Israeli daily *Yedi'ot Aharonot,* on March 22, 1974. Although the Palestinian formulations were cautious and tentative, they hinted that a peaceful settlement of the dispute with Israel was possible on the basis of what came to be known as the "two-state solution"—Israeli evacuation from all the Arab territories occupied in 1967 and the establishment of a Palestinian state in the West Bank and the Gaza Strip alongside the state of Israel in its June 4, 1967, borders. In response to the circulation of such ideas among Palestinian political thinkers, the twelfth Palestine National Council meeting in June–July 1974 adopted a resolution in favor of establishing "the people's national, independent, and fighting authority on every part of Palestinian land to be liberated."[64] This formulation was an ambiguous compromise that attempted to maintain unity within the PLO between proponents of the new thinking and adherents of the slogan "Revolution until Victory." These trial balloons were ignored by the

Israeli government. In the mid-1970s, only a small number of Jewish Israelis believed that an Israeli agreement with the PLO was an indis-
pensable ingredient of a comprehensive Arab-Israeli peace. Most of them
were in the orbit of the Communist Party (RAKAH), which represented
the majority of Israel's Arab citizens, but only a few hundred Jews. As a
largely Arab and non-Zionist political formation, RAKAH was outside
the boundaries of Jewish politics in Israel. One of the few noncommu-
nists who actively sought out the PLO was Uri Avnery.

Sa'id Hammami's search for unofficial Israeli interlocutors after the
Israeli government ignored his initiatives led him to meet with Uri
Avnery in London in January 1975. Hammami hoped that if he identified representative Israelis who would engage in a dialogue with the PLO
on the basis of the two-state solution to the Palestinian-Israeli conflict,
it would be easier to win support for this approach within the PLO. As
he had hinted to Avnery, on March 20, 1975, Hammami delivered a public speech in London titled "A Palestinian Strategy for Peaceful Coexistence: On the Future of Palestine" calling for the establishment of a Palestinian state alongside Israel, mutual recognition, and a peace agreement
between the two states. This was a major breakthrough in the evolution
of Palestinian political thinking. Although Hammami did not abandon
the ultimate ideal of a "democratic secular state," in retrospect it is clear
that his willingness to defer this goal to the indefinite future was the first
step toward abandoning it altogether. Because there was no positive Israeli response to Hammami's signal of PLO moderation, few Arabs felt
compelled to volunteer the concession of abandoning the vision of a democratic secular state until the PLO took this step in 1988.

Uri Avnery expected that such a significant public declaration by an
authorized Palestinian spokesperson would compel a positive response
from the Israeli government. But the government of Prime Minister
Yitzhak Rabin utterly ignored and the mass media devoted little attention to Hammami's speech.[65] Consequently, Avnery resolved to gather a
small group of individuals who would be prepared to identify themselves as Zionists, unlike the communists whom Avnery detested and
regarded as hopelessly unrepresentative, to promote a resolution to the
conflict along the lines suggested by Hammami. Avnery believed that
the PLO's commitment to the two-state solution would be deepened if a
group of Zionist Israelis publicly supported it as well. Avnery and Yossi
Amitai, a former Arab affairs activist in MAPAM who left the party
when it established the electoral alignment with the Labor Party in
1969, drafted the founding manifesto of what came to be the Israeli

Council for Israeli-Palestinian Peace (ICIPP). Amos Kenan was abroad and had given Avnery a proxy to use his name for political purposes, so Kenan's name was added to the published statement without his having seen it. In February 1976, the ICIPP was expanded by the addition of Matti Peled, Me'ir Pa'il, Lova Eliav, Ya'akov Arnon, Eliyahu Eliashar, and David Shaham—prominent personalities formerly identified with the Labor Party. Pa'il and Peled had served on the general staff of the Israel Defense Forces, the ultimate legitimation in Israeli politics. The reconstituted council published a new and somewhat watered-down manifesto endorsed by one hundred signatories. Hammami had promised Avnery that the PLO would begin a dialogue with a broad-based Israeli body that advocated establishing a Palestinian state in the West Bank and the Gaza Strip. The addition of defectors from the labor Zionist mainstream to the ICIPP—no prominent figures in the Labor Party were then willing to speak publicly with the PLO under any circumstances—meant that this dialogue could begin.[66]

In May 1976, Rif'at al-Sa'id, a member of the recently reconstituted Communist Party of Egypt too young to have known Curiel in Egypt but closely identified with Curiel's most devoted followers within the communist movement, met with Yusuf Hazan and a Palestinian representative in Athens to discuss opening a PLO-Israeli dialogue. Yusuf Hazan was chosen to represent the Curielists because he was a relative of the wife of Abu Khalil, the PLO's representative in Dakar. In June, Henri Curiel called Daniel Amit, a professor of physics at the Hebrew University of Jerusalem and a peace activist associated with the Israeli New Left (SIAH) to a meeting in Yusuf Hazan's office attended by Curiel, Hazan, Joyce Blau, Raymond Stambouli, and Dr. 'Isam Sartawi, a member of the Executive Committee of the PLO. Sartawi asked to meet with representatives of the ICIPP, and Amit transmitted his request to Uri Avnery and Matti Peled.

On July 21, Matti Peled, Lova Eliav, Ya'akov Arnon, and Yossi Amitai flew to Paris and met with 'Isam Sartawi under the aegis of Henri Curiel and his friends. Curiel also arranged a meeting among Sartawi, the Israelis, and Pierre Mendès-France.[67] Subsequently, Uri Avnery, Me'ir Pa'il, and the other members of the ICIPP Executive Committee also met with 'Isam Sartawi and other PLO officials, including Abu Mazin, Abu Faysal, and Sabri Jiryis.

The Israelis involved in these encounters reported on them to Israeli Prime Minister Yitzhak Rabin, elevating them to the status of indirect talks between the PLO and Israel.[68] Nonetheless, Rabin continued to insist publicly that the PLO was not a partner for negotiations with Israel because negotiating with any Palestinian element would establish "a basis for the possibility of creating a third state between Israel and Jordan," which Israel "firmly, clearly, categorically" opposed.[69] The resignation of the Rabin government under a cloud of financial scandal on December 19, 1976, eliminated any possibility of an official Israeli response to the PLO's feelers.

Consequently, from December 1976 to May 1977, Henri Curiel and his friends organized a new round of meetings between representatives of the ICIPP and the PLO designed to enhance the prestige of the ICIPP.[70] This objective required that the dialogue be made public, so on January 1, 1977, Curiel organized a press conference for Matti Peled and 'Isam Sartawi in Paris, where the ongoing meetings of the two parties were acknowledged for the first time.[71]

Sartawi's encounters with Zionist Israelis were sharply attacked by the hard-liners at the thirteenth session of the Palestine National Council in March 1977, where Yasir 'Arafat publicly defended Sartawi, calling him "a great Palestinian patriot."[72] However, the PNC's resolution on contacts with Israeli peace activists was vague. It affirmed "the significance of establishing relations and coordinating with the progressive and democratic Jewish forces inside and outside the occupied homeland, since those force are struggling against Zionism as a doctrine and practice."[73]

This formulation seemed to disavow the talks between 'Isam Sartawi and the members of the ICIPP organized by Henri Curiel because it suggested that contacts should be maintained only with non-Zionist Israelis. Although the relationship of some of its members to Zionism was rather attenuated, the ICIPP defined itself as a Zionist body. Uri Avnery and the members of the ICIPP were deeply offended by the rebuff. In contrast, Henri Curiel decided that the Palestine National Council resolution actually endorsed his efforts because, "through a remarkable piece of exegesis, Israelis who accepted Israeli withdrawal from the occupied territories and the establishment of a Palestinian state in these territories . . . were not to be considered Zionists."[74] Curiel's analysis was overly optimistic but characteristic of the political acrobatics that enabled him to persist in the face of apparent failure.

The clear preference of the PLO for contacts with non-Zionist Israelis led to breaking off the official contacts between members of the ICIPP and the PLO. Any chance that they might be resumed was destroyed when the Likud came to power in the Israeli elections of May 17, 1977. Faced with an ideologically intransigent Israeli government, the PLO seemed to have little to gain from continuing contacts with Israelis if this only sharpened the differences within the PLO. On the Israeli side, Anwar al-Sadat's trip to Jerusalem in November 1977 diminished the importance of contacts with the PLO. As Egyptian-Israeli negotiations became the main act in the protracted and convoluted diplomatic performance designated as "the peace process," the PLO focused its attention on trying to block the conclusion of a separate Egyptian-Israeli agreement that did not address the question of Palestine. As it turned out, this was exactly the character of the Egyptian-Israeli treaty signed in 1979.

Henri Curiel was assassinated in Paris on May 4, 1978, by unknown assailants. Suspicions focused on the Palestinian extremist Abu Nidal and right wingers in the camp of the former Algerian colons. But the French authorities never resolved the case. Sa'id Hammami had been assassinated exactly four months earlier, possibly also by agents of Abu Nidal. Curiel's demise and the start of direct negotiations between Egypt and Israel brought an end to the role of Egyptian Jews as mediators in the Arab-Israeli conflict. The efforts of Curiel and others were not a great success. A failed Israeli occupation of Lebanon in 1982, the Palestinian intifada of 1987–91, and the devastation of Kuwait and Iraq in the Gulf War, which left the administration of President George Bush heavily indebted to several Arab states, were required to bring about the start of direct Israeli-Palestinian talks in 1991 under far worse circumstances and with less likelihood of reaching a just and lasting peace than might have prevailed over a decade earlier. Nonetheless, Didar Rossano-Fawzy took great pleasure in noting that the handshake seen around the world between Yitzhak Rabin and Yasir 'Arafat on September 13, 1993, took place on the birthday of Henri Curiel.[75]

CHAPTER 7

The Karaites of the San Francisco Bay Area

The Karaite community of San Francisco was already well established when I began teaching at Stanford University in 1983, but I was completely unaware of it. The local Karaite Jewish community was not widely known or discussed. The fact that Karaites still existed at all was a bit of exotic specialized knowledge shared by a few individuals with an esoteric interest in their history and religious traditions. It was not integrated into the canons of modern Egyptian or modern Jewish history. I was circuitously introduced to the community in San Francisco through my friendship with one of the few remaining Karaites in Cairo, and my interest in them was shaped by this connection.

While conducting research for my Ph.D. thesis in Cairo in 1980, I met Nawla Darwish and spent time in her house reading the papers of her father, Yusuf Darwish. In 1986, I was again living in Cairo when Yusuf Darwish and his wife, Iqbal, returned to Egypt after living abroad as political refugees and representatives of the Communist Party of Egypt. Yusuf Darwish had been involved in the reorganization of the Communist Party, which publicly resumed its existence in 1975 after a ten-year hiatus. When he learned that the police were aware of his political activities, the Darwishes left Egypt shortly after the 1973 Arab-Israeli War. Yusuf had already spent three terms in prison in Egypt and did not wish to risk a fourth.

Yusuf Darwish was born into the Karaite community; Iqbal was a Rabbanite Jew. In Egypt, as in Israel, civil law incorporates religious law to adjudicate matters of personal status. Marriage and similar issues were determined by the religious laws of each confessional community (administered by communal religious courts until 1955) supervised by the civil courts. Hence, Yusuf and Iqbal could not be married as Jews unless Yusuf converted to Rabbanite Judaism, a long and difficult process in which, as a communist, he had no interest. It was much easier for Yusuf to undergo the relatively quick and simple procedure of converting to Islam. This enabled him to marry Iqbal in 1949 because Muslim men may marry Jewish and Christian women. Neither Yusuf nor Iqbal was observant, so the conversion was a formality for both of them. Nonetheless, when the three principal tendencies in the communist movement united to form the Communist Party of Egypt in 1958 and resolved that Jews could not be members of the Central Committee, Yusuf Darwish was excluded from the leadership of the party on the grounds that he was a Jew.[1] Their daughter, Nawla, is Jewish according to Rabbinic *halakhah* (religious law) and Muslim according to the *shari'a*. She prefers to define herself as Egyptian.

Although I had spent many hours formally and informally interviewing Yusuf Darwish about his life history and political experiences, I did not know that he had family in the United States until the fall of 1990, when he wrote me to announce that he was coming to visit his sister, Nelly Masliah, in San Francisco and invited me to call her so that we could all get together. This served as the occasion for my introduction to the Karaite Jewish community of San Francisco.

Jacob and Nelly Masliah invited my family to dinner with Yusuf at their home. They prepared a copious Egyptian meal and welcomed us warmly. Yusuf would normally have spoken to his family in French. But because I am more comfortable in Arabic than French, and Yusuf's English is weak, the easiest common language was Arabic. The cuisine, the social ambience, and the Arabic conversation recalled our best moments in Cairo. Yusuf also visited a second sister in the Boston area while I was in town for a meeting of the Middle East Studies Association. There I met Yvonne Masliah and her family and enjoyed another fine Egyptian dinner with Arabic conversation. Afterwards I arranged to have the video cassettes of recent Egyptian films that Yusuf had brought as presents for his family converted from PAL to NTSC format. They seemed eager to view these films, which suggested that they remained curious about Egypt and still felt a positive connection to its culture.

Thus, Boston and San Francisco were added to Cairo and Paris on the list of locales where my common language with other Jews was Arabic. This would have been normal in the Mediterranean basin in the medieval era, but in the late twentieth century it felt subversive. The American Karaites certainly do not see themselves in political terms, and they are generally uninvolved in the debates over the cultural politics of ethnic identity in the American Jewish community. Nonetheless, it seemed to me the practices of the Karaites of San Francisco resisted incorporation into many prevailing assumptions about Jewish identity and Arab-Jewish relations. This attracted me to take an interest in their community even before I began to think systematically about the subject of this book. Therefore, when I resolved to write about Egyptian Jews, I was in a position to discuss them in more detail than others who have previously written about Jews in modern Egypt.[2] My argument for the validity of doing so is presented in Chapter 2. Because I could not eliminate from my consciousness the personal relationships I had formed, the bits of information I had already learned, and the contacts that were available to me as a consequence, my roles as friend, historian, and ethnographer were woven in a fabric that could not be usefully unraveled.

THE KARAITE EMIGRATION FROM EGYPT

According to an informal Jewish Agency census, nineteen Karaites resided in Jerusalem in 1939.[3] But by 1948, only one Karaite (of undetermined origins) remained there to preserve the Karaite community's claim to their property: the most ancient standing synagogue in the old city. After the first Arab-Israeli war, a small number of Karaites began to leave Egypt and establish themselves in Israel. The first to leave were the poorest members of the community or exceptional families of means who could transfer their assets out of Egypt.[4] Business and property owners tended to remain in Egypt longer. The Karaites were not keen to transform themselves from urban merchants and craftsmen to rural farmers and physical laborers, the ideal of labor Zionism and the likely fate of new immigrants to Israel. They were also fearful of the difficult economic and political circumstances of Israel during the early 1950s.

According to the records of the Karaite *bet din* (religious court) in Cairo, fewer than 100 Karaites left Egypt before 1956.[5] This is probably an underestimate. Families who departed for Israel may not have reported their departure to the court for fear of implicating the community in their actions. Moreover, members of the community who did not attend synagogue regularly might not have been in close contact with the communal authorities. Maurice Shammas estimated that by the time he arrived in Israel in 1950, 500 Karaites already resided there.[6] The daughter of the first Karaite chief rabbi of Israel, who arrived in Israel in 1949 at the age of nine, thought that there were 200–300 Karaite families in the country by the 1956 Suez/Sinai War.[7]

The policy of the Jewish Agency and Israeli government was to concentrate Middle Eastern Jews in new *moshavim* (agricultural cooperative villages) or development towns in remote parts of the country. The Karaite immigrants were settled in the *moshavim* of Matzliah and Ranen, established in 1950 and 1951, respectively. Karaites also settled in the town of Ramlah, their historic center in the tenth and eleventh centuries. The central synagogue of the community, which is now the Karaite World Center, opened there in 1961. When the Karaite population in Israel increased in the late 1950s and 1960s, urban concentrations were established at Ashdod, Be'ersheba, and Ofakim. Karaites also live in the greater Tel Aviv area (especially Bat Yam), Yavneh, Kiryat Gat, Kiryat Malakhi, Acre, Bet Shemesh, and Jerusalem, where a Karaite *bet midrash* (religious seminary) has recently been established. The number of Karaites in Israel has always been sharply disputed and cannot be established with certainty because the official Israeli census does not list Karaites as a category and the community abides by the traditional Jewish prohibition on conducting a direct census. Figures range from 15,000 to 30,000.[8]

Upon arriving in Israel, the Egyptian Karaites were surprised to find that the Orthodox Rabbinic establishment there was suspicious about their identity as Jews. Until 1977, the pragmatic alliance between MAPAI and the Orthodox Zionist Mizrahi Party (today the National Religious Party), allowed MAPAI to run the Israeli government in exchange for adopting the status quo as it had crystallized during the Mandate and Ottoman eras on religious matters. Consequently, in Israel matters of personal status are, with some exceptions, adjudicated according to the *halakhah*. The state has declared what defines who is a Jew, but the Orthodox rabbinate has the sole legal authority to determine who may be married as a Jew, buried in a Jewish cemetery, and so forth. The rulings of Orthodox Rabbinic religious courts (*batei din*) are the normal forum for adjudicating such matters, although civil courts have some authority to intervene. These courts regard the Karaites as under suspicion of being bastards (*safek mamzerim*). Hence, they are not eligible marriage partners for Jews, even Jews who are unconcerned with the status of Karaites according to *halakhah,* because the only legal way to be married as a Jew in Israel is for an Orthodox rabbi to perform the ceremony.

The Karaites have their own *bet din*. However, the authorities of the state and the Orthodox rabbinate do not recognize its rulings or jurisdiction. It has only de facto authority among members of the Karaite community who voluntarily accept its rulings.

Prodded by the personal interest of its second president, Yitzhak Ben-Tzvi, the state of Israel decided to treat the Karaites as Jews and subjected them to compulsory military service, the most significant marker of Jewish identity in Israel. However, in matters over which the state has ceded its authority to the Orthodox rabbinate, the validity of the Karaites as a Jewish religious community is constantly subjected to question. This embarrasses many secular Zionists. But they have not mounted a sustained campaign to rectify this anomaly because it would require a direct challenge to the secular authority of the Orthodox rabbinate in Israel and provoke a Jewish *kulturkampf* for which Zionism does not have a resolution consistent with the political discourse of secular nationalism, citizenship, and equal rights.

Sumi Colligan's perceptive doctoral thesis succinctly summarizes the transformation of Karaite Jewish identity that accompanied the transition from Egypt to Israel:

> In Egypt, the Karaites were recognized as a Jewish minority and lived as other minorities in the Middle East, endogamously and self-governing. The general societal ideology which structured their identity was religious communalism and hence, the expression of the content of their Jewishness was not obstructed or questioned. Both the Karaites and the other members of Egyptian society shared the same set of concepts and symbols regarding the structuring of social identity. In Israel, however, other ideologies of "Jewishness" have challenged the grounds on which the Karaites make claims to Jewish identity, and for the majority of Israelis, Karaite is the form, the social category, by which the group is designated. That is to say, many Israelis have a tendency to think of Karaites less as a type of Jew than as a separate social group altogether.[9]

This perception is shaped by nationalist practices that legitimize the particularist prejudices of the Orthodox rabbinate, which went so far as to attempt to keep the Karaites out of Israel altogether. In 1949, the 'Aliyah Department of the Jewish Agency acceded to pressure from representatives of Mizrahi in the Jewish Agency Executive and asked its agents in Egypt to halt the immigration of Karaites to Israel. The local Egyptian 'aliyah activists rejected this demand. Egyptian members of Bnai 'Akivah, the Orthodox Zionist youth movement, appealed to the Mizrahi Women's Organization in the United States to persuade their

Israeli compatriots to relent. The Egyptian Zionists declared that they would not allow a single Jew to leave for Israel if this decision were not reversed. In fact, immigration was actually stopped for a month in 1950 until instructions were received permitting Karaites to come to Israel.[10]

Because the Orthodox rabbinate never fully accepted the state's determination that the Karaites were Jews eligible for 'aliyah, members of the community continued to suffer considerable difficulties after arriving in Israel. One of the most publicized examples concerned Yosef Marzuq, the brother of Moshe Marzuq, who was executed for his role in Operation Susannah. In 1961, Yosef Marzuq wanted to marry a Rabbanite woman. The rabbinate of Tel Aviv refused to approve this union. Yitzhak Ben-Tzvi intervened on Marzuq's behalf, both because of Marzuq's brother's services to the state of Israel and because of his long-standing support for the Karaites. As a result, the case was transferred to the more lenient Haifa rabbinate, which issued Marzuq a bachelor's certificate, the requisite document to permit his marriage. But the Rabbinic court made it clear that this would not be a precedent for future Karaite-Rabbanite mixed marriages.[11] Secularist Zionists considered it a great scandal that the brother of someone who gave his life for the Jewish state had difficulty being married as a Jew in Israel.

The Karaite chief rabbi, Tuvia Babovitch, did not encourage Karaite immigration to Israel because of the unsettled political conditions and problematic status of Karaites there. Of course, as a matter of religious conviction, Babovitch, like all observant Jews, believed that Jews had a special attachment to the holy land, especially to Jerusalem. But like many Orthodox rabbis in the first half of the twentieth century, Babovitch did not endorse political Zionism. His attitude undoubtedly influenced many Karaites to remain in Egypt after 1948 and to carry on their communal life as normally as possible. Rabbi Babovitch died in August 1956 and was not replaced. There was no Egyptian Karaite sufficiently learned in the religious tradition to undertake this duty.

This cannot be attributed to the maltreatment of Jews in Egypt in the 1940s and 1950s. Babovitch himself was brought from the Crimea to assume the position of Karaite chief rabbi in 1934. Already at that time, when there was little mistreatment of Jews in Egypt, most members of the Karaite community who had the intellectual talent and interest to pursue advanced studies sought secular rather than religious careers. This was no different from the prevalent pattern among Rabbanite Jews. But the small Karaite community apparently failed to produce a sufficient number of piously minded exceptions to sustain and reproduce their religious institutions.

With the outbreak of the 1956 Suez/Sinai War, the principal of the Karaite elementary schools, Mourad El-Kodsi, was interned. Thereafter, the government gradually diminished the Karaite community's control over its schools until they were nationalized in 1962.[12] The community's Arabic newspaper, *al-Kalim,* also closed after the 1956 war. The death of its chief rabbi and the demise of the community institutions as a result of the 1956 war precipitated the rapid decline of the Karaite community. Its collapse was more dramatic than the similar and parallel process in the Rabbanite community because before the 1956 war, a larger proportion of Karaites than Rabbanites remained in Egypt despite the difficult circumstances.

Between October 1956 and March 1957, some 40 percent of the Karaites (and a similar proportion of Rabbanites) left Egypt, mostly for Israel. Still, some 2,000 Karaites remained in Cairo when Mourad El-Kodsi left in 1959. The nationalization of large sectors of the economy during 1960–62 impelled a third wave of immigration, though 1,000 Karaites remained in Egypt until October 1966, the date of the last communal elections. By 1970, only 200 Karaites remained in Egypt, a number too small to maintain a communal structure.[13]

THE KARAITE JEWS OF EGYPT IN BAGHDAD BY THE BAY

Most of the Karaites who emigrated from Egypt during the 1960s did not go to Israel. Between 1964 and 1970, a substantial segment of the community settled in the San Francisco Bay Area, where there are now some 130 Karaite families and a total population of over 400. In addition, 300 Karaite families live elsewhere in the United States, with small concentrations in the New York, Baltimore, Boston, Chicago, Los Angeles, and San Diego metropolitan areas. The Karaites of the San Francisco Bay Area have made substantial efforts to reestablish their community. This has entailed preserving and modifying both the Jewish and Egyptian elements of the practices and self-presentation of the Karaite community of Cairo.

Coming to the United States, like coming to Israel, was a great psychological upheaval for the Karaites. In America, "We were no longer privileged *khawagat* (foreigners). I had never worked for anyone else before. Now we were at the bottom of the social pyramid and rejected as

Jews," said the community's acting rabbi, Joe Pessah.[14] The Karaite immigrants to the San Francisco Bay Area belong to several generations; some arrived in their early teens, and others were in their early fifties. Many of them had belonged to the urban middle strata in Cairo, working as merchants in gold or other goods, jewelers, and professionals. Only four of thirty respondents to a questionnaire administered by Jehoash Hirshberg to the San Francisco Karaites in 1986 had lived in the traditional Karaite quarter, *harat al-yahud al-qara'in*, in Cairo. Only one of them, Joe Pessah, had attended daily prayers at the Dar Simha synagogue there.[15] Fifteen respondents had lived in the middle-class neighborhood of 'Abbasiyya; Jacob Masliah was one of only a dozen people who had participated in daily prayers at the Moshe al-Darʿi synagogue there. Most of the other congregants of the 'Abbasiyya synagogue had attended services only on Friday night and holidays. Upon arriving in the United States, a high proportion of the Karaites entered technical professions, especially the computer industry. Most of the Karaite immigrants have maintained the economic status they enjoyed in Egypt or improved their conditions in the United States.

I compiled the following vignettes through formal interviews and informal participant observation at various events of the Karaite community. They demonstrate a range of ways in which the San Francisco Karaites both maintained their Egyptian communitarian identity, which was (always) already being reshaped, and began the process of adapting to America and the norms of its Jewish community.

Jacob Masliah (Yaʿqub Farag Salih, b. 1913) has been a leading member of the San Francisco Karaite community.[16] His identity has been shaped by a rich fabric of social experience in Egypt and the United States refracted through deep religious commitment and substantial learning in the Karaite tradition and draws on both the millet-communitarian and the Egyptian national elements of the Karaites' self-conception in Egypt. In some important respects, his background differs from the majority of the Egyptian Karaites because the Masliahs were relatively new to Egypt, having emigrated from Tunis in the nineteenth century. Moreover, Jacob Masliah was not employed in the Karaite ethnic economy, although he did use his family connections to enhance his career. He was one of some 150 Karaites who worked in the free professions in the 1940s.[17] Hence, his family enjoyed a comfortable upper-middle-class life.

In other respects, the Masliah family was similar to other Karaites. Jacob Masliah knew Arabic well and felt culturally, socially, and economically secure in Egypt at the same time that he remained fully conscious of his status as a member of an ethnoreligious minority. He graduated first in his class with a degree in architecture from the Royal Engineering College in Cairo in 1936. He was very proud of this achievement and the opportunity it afforded him to be photographed with King Fu'ad. Shortly after graduating, Masliah submitted a request for a certificate of citizenship so that he could work for the government. The request remained pending when he left Egypt in 1964.

Masliah worked designing air raid shelters and other military structures in the Alexandria area during World War II. Then he established a partnership with Nasim Yahya, a member of one of the leading Muslim business families of Alexandria. The legal aspects of the partnership were arranged by his brother-in-law, Yusuf Darwish, a founding member of the New Dawn communist group and a prominent Cairo area labor lawyer.

Among Masliah's design projects was the shrimp processing factory in Port Said established by another brother-in-law, Leon Darwish. This was a new area of economic endeavor for the Karaite community because shrimp is not a kosher food in the Jewish tradition. The factory was quite successful and built up a substantial export trade. During the wave of nationalizations in 1961, Leon Darwish was forced to hire a Muslim to manage the factory. Consequently, he left Egypt in 1962.

Jacob and Nelly Masliah made their home in the fashionable suburb of Heliopolis, far from the center of the community in *harat al-yahud al-qara'in*. They belonged to the Heliopolis Sporting Club, where Nelly taught exercise classes for women. The wife of 'Abd al-Latif Baghdadi, one of the original members of the Revolutionary Command Council that governed Egypt after the coup of July 23, 1952, was a student in one of Nelly's classes. Jacob joined a Masonic lodge and rose to the status of third degree freemason. Seventy percent of the members of his lodge were Jews. But the lodge was affiliated with the Masonic federation of the Arab countries and considered itself Egyptian.

Nadia Hartmann, one of Jacob and Nelly's two daughters, was a member of the Egyptian national water ballet team in high school. I met her at her parents' home and asked her about her memories of Egypt. One of her strongest and most detailed recollections was of her trip to Syria in 1961 with the water ballet team to participate in a pan-Arab swimming competition. Before the trip, Nadia's schoolteacher called to assure the Masliah family that they should have no fears about Nadia travelling to Syria to represent Egypt because the school considered her to be an Egyptian like any other student. In recalling her trip to Syria,

Nadia's face lit up with excitement. She emphasized that she still remembered the trip "like it happened yesterday."[18] Preservation of this memory with warm intensity seemed to be a way for Nadia to preserve a positive connection with Egypt.

At the Heliopolis Sporting Club, Nadia became friendly with Shuhdan al-Shazli, the daughter of Sa'd al-Din al-Shazli, who later became a general and one of the Egyptian heroes of the 1973 Arab-Israeli War. In the late 1970s, the al-Shazlis were forced to leave Egypt because of General al-Shazli's criticism of Anwar al-Sadat. Shuhdan al-Shazli eventually made a new home for herself in Sacramento, California. Nadia Hartmann and Shuhdan al-Shazli renewed their friendship when they met in California as exiles from Egypt.

Until the early 1960s, the Masliahs did not feel discriminated against as Jews in Egypt because "the Karaite Jews of Egypt have a special character that is different from other Jews," as Jacob Masliah explained. He felt that the Karaites' Arabic cultural orientation made them a more integral part of Egypt than other Jews. Then, in 1962, they were asked to stop coming to the Heliopolis Sporting Club. The women in Nelly Masliah's exercise class very much regretted her leaving the club and came to the Masliahs' home in Heliopolis to carry on with their class. But in November 1964, the Masliah family left Egypt because the Karaite community was dwindling in size and they did not want their daughters to marry non-Jews.

Although economic conditions in Israel were considerably improved in the mid-1960s, the Masliahs did not want to live in Israel because they considered the situation there too unstable. They visited Israel for three days on their way to the United States. They chose San Francisco because some of their friends had already settled in the area and because of the city's reputation for good weather. By 1968, Jacob Masliah was working in his profession for the Pacific Gas and Electric Company. Ten years later, he retired at the age of sixty-five, though he continued to work for ten more years in the business of a friend. Economically, they have adjusted well and prospered in the United States. They eventually bought a home in San Francisco's Sunset district, a comfortable, middle-class neighborhood within walking distance of the Pacific Ocean.

The social and economic status of the family of Henry Mourad (b. 1945) in Egypt was similar to that of the Masliahs. The Mourads lived in the heavily Rabbanite neighborhood of Dahir, where Henry attended the Ecole du Commaunauté Israelite du Caire. As a young man,

Henry was fluent in Arabic and felt he could easily pass for a Muslim. The Mourads were Egyptian citizens and quite comfortable economically. Henry's grandfather owned a jewelry company, one of the traditional economic pursuits of the community. The Mourad family business was sequestered during the 1956 war and nationalized in 1961. Forced to abandon most of their property and assets, the family left Egypt for the United States in 1964. Henry still remembers with bitterness the personal humiliation and degradation they suffered at the time of their departure.

Henry Mourad's social interactions with non-Jewish Egyptians became strained because the Arab-Israeli conflict emerged as a prominent political issue during his years in high school and university. After being harassed and taunted as a Jew while studying engineering at Cairo University, he pretended to be a Muslim.[19] He remembers feeling proud about Moshe Marzuq's spying and sabotage on behalf of Israel, although he understood that he had to denounce these activities in public.

When I asked Henry Mourad if he felt Egyptian, he was ambivalent. He remembered liking Egypt and feeling comfortable in Arabic, but he resented the abuse and discrimination he suffered. "You can't be Egyptian if you are not accepted," he said.

Henry's wife, Doris (b. 1948), responded much more definitively that she never felt Egyptian. Her family held Tunisian citizenship and lived in the elite neighborhood of Zamalek, far from either of the two Karaite synagogues in Cairo. Her father did not participate in activities of the Karaite community. Doris attended the Lycée Française of Zamalek, where she refused to learn Arabic because she felt it was unnecessary. For this, she was left back a year in school. She felt isolated both from the Karaite community and from other Egyptians. Her family emigrated to the United States in 1962, when she was fourteen.

Doris Mourad's unequivocal rejection of any sentiments of identity as an Egyptian may be due to her family's distance from the Karaite community in Egypt and her isolation as a child. Moreover, she arrived in the United States as a young teenager, an age when social pressure to conform is extremely intense. Her lack of identification with Egypt is rare among Karaites I have met.

The Mourads live in the suburban midpeninsula area, an hour away from San Francisco. They joined a Reform Jewish temple, and their daughters attended its religious school and participated in its youth activities. They continue to identify as Karaites and take an interest in the cultural heritage of their community. But they do not think their Karaite identity should constitute a barrier to their participation in and identification with their local Jewish community.

ASSIMILATION AND ESTRANGEMENT FROM THE JEWISH COMMUNITY

As a minority within a minority, Karaites in the United States faced powerful assimilationist pressures. Even deeply religious individuals, like Jacob Masliah and Joe Pessah, acknowledged that they were too constrained by the economic burdens of settling their families in a new country, establishing careers, and educating their children and the cultural burdens of mastering English and learning to feel comfortable in the United States to devote much attention to the affairs of the Karaite community during the 1960s and 1970s. They continued to pray and observe other rituals in their homes, but organized gatherings of the community were limited to high holidays, marriages, and the like.

The American Jewish community's ignorance of the existence of the Karaites was another factor constraining their collective assertion of identity of the San Francisco area Karaites. Some were concerned that they might be ostracized by the organized American Jewish community. Some joined Reform or Conservative congregations. The Reform and Conservative rites are not as hostile to the Karaites as the Orthodox rabbinate. Nonetheless, Henry and Doris Mourad recall that the rabbi of their Reform congregation said that the Karaites were extinct. They felt negated by this uninformed assertion.[20]

Even Joseph (Joe) and Raymonde (Remy) Pessah, who became the most energetic and capable organizers of the community in the 1980s, felt unable to claim their identity as Karaites when they first arrived in the United States.[21] Joe Pessah (b. 1945) grew up in an Arabic-speaking home in *harat al-yahud al-qara'in*. He studied engineering at Cairo University. As a boy, he knew Moshe Marzuq and recalls taking pride in Marzuq's status as a doctor when seeing him in the synagogue. After Marzuq was arrested, Pessah thought that he also wanted to be a spy. When Marzuq and Azar were executed, Pessah thought only of Marzuq, not of Azar. Pessah's identification with Marzuq seems to have been primarily personal rather than ideological. Marzuq was someone he knew—a Karaite who had done well and become prominent. Pessah recognized that the Karaites belonged to a broader Jewish community and fondly remembered the good relations between the Karaites and the

Rabbanites in Egypt, but he believed that the Karaites had something special because they treated their children "like jewels." He considered that the Karaites of Egypt had a religious attachment to Jerusalem and believed that going to live in Israel would hasten the coming of the messiah. But this was not a commitment requiring secular political action.

Joe Pessah was among the Jewish men detained in prison camps during and after the 1967 Arab-Israeli War. He had already met and become engaged to Raymonde Gazzar, a chemistry major at the American University in Cairo. They were married in an Egyptian jail while Joe was still interned on May 31, 1970. Less than a month later, on June 21, 1970, Joe was released. Before the end of the year, Joe and Remy Pessah immigrated to the United States with the assistance of the Hebrew Immigrant Aid Society.

Two months after arriving in the San Francisco area, they were remarried in a Jewish ceremony performed by Rabbi Herbert Morris of Congregation Beth Israel-Judea, a Conservative-Reform synagogue. A front page story including a picture of the happy couple in the weekly newspaper of the San Francisco Jewish community celebrated their marriage as a symbol of Jewish perseverance and the heroic struggle of Israel against Arab aggression.[22] However, the article did not mention that they were Karaites and members of a community with several hundred adherents in the Bay Area, some of whom presumably attended the wedding. The Pessahs did not inform Rabbi Morris that they were Karaites because they felt he would not understand who they were. Only after Joe Pessah became successfully established in his own business as a computer consultant did he begin to devote substantial time and energy to organizing the community.

ORGANIZING THE KARAITE JEWS OF AMERICA

During the 1960s and 1970s, the cohesion of the San Francisco area Karaite community was maintained by sporadic observance of religious rituals, regular social contact, and the collective memories of Egypt shared by the older generations. Jacques Mangubi, the former president of the Karaite community in Cairo, organized a Karaite association in Chicago in the mid-1970s. He died in 1977 and others could not sustain his initiative. In San Francisco, at the initiative of Jacob Masliah and Elie Nounou, some twenty-five members of the community met in private homes to conduct high holiday services. In addition, several families gathered regularly on Saturday nights to socialize and play poker. Doris

Mourad recalled the ambience of this scene with insightful irony, noting that while the adults played cards, the teenagers, who were less interested in the forms of sociability and other cultural practices their parents brought with them from Cairo, cruised around San Francisco learning how to become Americans.[23]

Many of the first-generation children succeeded in assimilating American culture and even married non-Jews. Several of Joe Pessah's siblings, for example, married Christians. The prospect of disappearance through gradual assimilation encouraged urgent and self-conscious reflection about action to preserve the Karaite community and its complex identity. The task was especially difficult because many of the middle-class Karaites who came to the United States had not been strictly religiously observant in Egypt and did not have a deep knowledge of the religious tradition of the community. Jacob Masliah and Joe Pessah were exceptional in this respect. Moreover, in all of the United States, there was no ordained Karaite rabbi to provide traditionally sanctioned leadership and guidance.

By the 1980s, the San Francisco Bay Area Karaites were established well enough to consider reorganizing their communal affairs. The community collected $112,000 to finance its activities between 1983 and 1985. Jehoash Hirshberg's 1986 survey of ninety-three community members revealed that half of the respondents were then willing to devote time to community activities.[24] When the Bay Area Karaites began to discuss what kind of institutions would best preserve their community and its identity, two opposing views surfaced. More pious and observant families, like the Pessahs and the Masliahs, favored establishing a traditional synagogue similar to those the community had maintained in Cairo. More assimilated and Americanized families, like the Mourads, favored an educational center that would preserve and transmit the historical heritage of Karaite culture but would not obstruct the Karaites' integration into the broader American Jewish community.

The proponents of establishing a religious center began to organize and in 1982 elected Jacob Masliah as president of their association. In May 1983, Fred Lichaa (b. 1947), who arrived in the United States in 1968 and subsequently established himself as a computer programmer, arranged for the Karaite community to hold once-a-month Sabbath prayers at Temple Sinai, a Reform congregation in Foster City on the San Francisco Peninsula, where his family resided. On other Sabbaths, prayers were held in individual homes. This initiative provided a focal point for members of the community who identified themselves as Karaites primarily on the basis of religious commitment.

In July 1983, the Karaite Jews of America (KJA) was formally established as a nonprofit organization.[25] The first board of directors was composed of: Jacob Masliah, president; Moussa El Kodsi, vice-president; Maurice Pessah, secretary; and Elie ʿOvadia, treasurer. Joe Pessah has served continually as the acting rabbi of the congregation. Since then, the activists of the community have energetically expanded their activities and programs.

In 1984, Joe and Remy Pessah began to publish the *KJA Bulletin*. It appears at Rosh ha-Shanah and Passover and contains news of the Karaite community, commemorations of births, deaths, weddings, high school and university graduations, and bar/bat mitzvahs, and articles about Karaite history, beliefs, and practice. The bulletin proudly reproduces the rare articles about their community in the mainstream Jewish press and respectfully but firmly explains the differences between Karaite and Rabbanite beliefs and practices while consistently upholding the Jewish identity of the Karaites. The Pessahs also maintain a computerized mailing list of all the Karaites in the United States, with some additional families in Canada, Europe, and Israel.

Every summer the Pessahs organize a Karaite summer camp at Lake Tahoe, California. Two-week sessions are held for seven- to eleven-year-olds, twelve- to fifteen-year-olds, sixteen- to twenty-one-year-olds, and those over twenty-one. The camp provides an opportunity to gather together Karaites from all over the United States. Educational programs for the children are designed to teach them their religious and cultural heritage and strengthen their feelings of connection to the community.

For young adults, the summer camps are an opportunity to meet potential marriage partners so that they will not be forced to marry outside the community. This is especially important because the Karaites do not accept converts. The rate of Karaite intermarriage in the United States is very high, so some members of the community advocate modifying the ban on conversion. Others adopt a wait-and-see attitude until they can have a sense of the level of knowledge and commitment of the children of Karaite-Rabbanite mixed marriages.

Another endeavor contributing to maintaining the communal cohesiveness of the Karaites begun in 1993 is the construction of a Karaite family tree undertaken by David Elichaa of Imperial Beach, California. In Cairo, all the Karaite families were related. This project is intended to enhance community cohesion by documenting the family connections.

The KJA also participated in subsidizing the publication of Mourad El-Kodsi's *The Karaite Jews of Egypt, 1882–1986*, the most easily

accessible modern history of the Karaites of Egypt in English. It serves
as a semiofficial text, though some members of the community have
reservations about it. The volume is rich with photographs, facsimiles
of the community's newspapers and other documents and memora-
bilia, mostly in Arabic, as well as extracts of prayers in Hebrew with
English commentaries.

The decision to document and transmit the Karaite heritage poses a
pressing question: What is essential? Many of the Karaites' practices in
Cairo cannot be reproduced in the San Francisco area because the community is geographically far more dispersed. Moreover, American-born
children already have absorbed some ideas about what it means to be
Jewish from their Rabbanite Jewish friends. Therefore, Karaite leaders
have had to make conscious decisions about what can and must be preserved and what accommodations can be made to their style of life in
the United States and to American Jewish culture.

THE SAN FRANCISCO AND DALY CITY SYNAGOGUES

By 1991, the KJA was institutionally stable and sufficiently solvent to
purchase a house in San Francisco's Sunset district to serve as a synagogue and community center. Joe Pessah led services there on Saturdays
and festivals. Prayers were not held on Friday evenings because many
congregants had to drive long distances to reach the synagogue. Travelling times on Friday evenings were unpredictable due to the start of the
weekend rush hour, so it was impossible to gather a substantial number
of congregants. In Cairo, those who attended synagogue only once a
week would typically come on Friday evening. In San Francisco, Saturday morning services became the primary weekly prayer gathering. The
annual Purim party is a particularly important occasion because it is an
attractive event for the children of the community. For the children, celebrating Purim is both fulfillment of a religious duty (commemorating
the deliverance of the Jews from Haman) and "fun" in secular American terms.

The purchase of a building was an important step forward in crys-
tallizing the Karaite community and regularizing its religious obser-
vances and social occasions. But the leaders of the synagogue were dis-
satisfied with the limitations of the building. The neighbors of the
synagogue, many of them Asian Americans, objected to the Karaites'
plans to expand their building to allow construction of a social hall. The
neighbors justified their opposition on the grounds that this would in-

crease the flow of traffic on weekends and holidays. But some Karaites regarded the neighbors' objections as anti-Semitism.

The Karaite synagogue coped with this situation without resolving it for several years. Then a rare opportunity presented itself when a synagogue in Daly City, a suburb of San Francisco, disbanded and put its building up for sale. In June 1994, the KJA purchased the premises of the former Congregation B'nai Israel; their offer was accepted even though it was not the highest bid because the leaders of Congregation B'nai Israel preferred to maintain the Jewish character of the building. Purchase of the new synagogue building necessitated a vigorous fundraising campaign. Karaites throughout the United States contributed or loaned over $100,000 to the KJA to finance the transaction, enabling the KJA to sell its San Francisco house and celebrate Rosh ha-Shanah of 5755 (1994) in its new quarters in Daly City.[26]

The formal organization of the Karaite community facilitated its recognition by other American Jewish rites. In 1984, the Conservative Rabbinical Assembly resolved that Karaites should be regarded as Jews as long as they did not reject Rabbanite tradition. The Reform rabbinate adopted a similar decision. In fact, there are sharp divergences in certain Karaite and Rabbanite customs, which this formulation avoids addressing. For example, Karaites do not celebrate Hanukah, a particularly prominent festival in American Jewish life, on the grounds that the holiday is not mentioned in the Torah. Its historical origins are in the postbiblical era. The Karaites also reject the calendrical reforms introduced by the rabbis in the ninth century, and their holidays may fall at slightly different times than the Rabbanite festivals. Hence, the decisions of the Reform and Conservative rabbis express a spirit of goodwill toward the Karaites without fully accepting the validity of their tradition. Even this somewhat conditional acceptance has allowed the Karaites to gain gradual recognition as part of the Jewish community of the San Francisco Bay Area. In 1995, the *Northern California Jewish Bulletin* began to include the KJA in its weekly list of Jewish congregations in the San Francisco Bay Area.

The character of Karaite Jewish identity remains religiously, politically, and culturally distinctive. For most American Jews, support for Israel is the most prominent expression of their Jewish identity. Visiting Israel for a summer has become an important rite of passage for Jewish teenagers of the San Francisco Bay Area. The Karaites certainly support the state of Israel. They visit and maintain close ties with their relatives and the official leadership of the Karaite communities there. But the core of their identity as Jews is their religious commitment and their cultural heritage. Their Jewishness is not dependent on their political relationship with Israel, certainly not with the leaders of the state. Few American Jews except the ultraorthodox are willing or able to preserve their identity in the same terms.

Jehoash Hirshberg has explained the central role of liturgy and paraliturgical songs in maintaining the continuity of Karaite tradition in the San Francisco Bay Area Karaite community since its buildings, institutions, and books were all left behind in Egypt.[27] Joe Pessah is primarily responsible for liturgical matters. He consciously strives to preserve the purity of the Karaite liturgy and other customs from outside influences because the Karaite tradition in the United States is a young and fragile transplant liable to be destroyed by the excessive integration of Rabbanite or other exogenous practices. Pessah makes a clear distinction between traditional Karaite tunes and Egyptian folk melodies, which the Karaites of Israel appear to have freely integrated into their paraliturgical songs. Nonetheless, Pessah and other community members encourage their children to listen to commercial recordings of Egyptian music so that American-born Karaites will be familiar with their cultural roots and be exposed to an alternative to contemporary Western music and what they regard as its associated negative influences. Joe and Remy Pessah also maintain close contact with Egypt through regular reading of popular Egyptian magazines like *Ruz al-Yusuf* and *Uktubir,* which they shared with me when I visited their home.

Such continuing attachments to Arabo-Egyptian culture are common among members of the community who grew up in Egypt. Jacob Masliah fondly recalled that his geometry teacher was the brother of renowned novelist Naguib Mahfouz and that the Mahfouz family lived near his childhood home in 'Abbasiyya. An older member of the community advised me that if I wished to improve my Arabic pronunciation, he would be glad to lend me his set of audiotapes of Qur'an chanting. Just as Muslims do, he considered the language of the Qur'an to be an ideal form of Arabic. He recalled that at school he had been the best student in his class in Arabic grammar and poetry, and he was proud that when he visited Muslim Egyptians, they were surprised by his retention of excellent Arabic despite having left Egypt thirty-six years ago. He brought to the synagogue a large pile of current Arabic dailies (*al-Ahram, al-Hayat, al-Sharq al-Awsat,* and *al-Watan*), whose contents he shared with other members of the congregation during the meal after the services. As I was preparing to leave the synagogue, he passed them on to me to help keep my knowledge of Egypt current.[28]

REFORM KARAITES

The organization of a synagogue and related projects gave the San Francisco Bay Area Karaite community a firm institutional structure that it had lacked during the first twenty years of the Karaite presence in the United States. The lapse of organized communal religious life for a generation and the rapid assimilation and Americanization of younger members of the community ensured that despite efforts to maintain and reproduce the historical practices of the community in Cairo, the new synagogue would incorporate substantial novel elements into its services. The ritual core of the synagogue service in San Francisco maintains continuity with the Cairo tradition. The traditional prayer book is used, and prayers are recited in Hebrew with only an occasional informal English commentary. No significant liturgical innovations were introduced, and Joe Pessah endeavored to maintain a unified singing style.

About thirty to forty people participated in regular weekly Saturday morning services in San Francisco when I attended periodically from 1991 to 1993. As in the Rabbanite tradition, the core of the service is the reading of the weekly Torah portion. Because no one in the community could chant the weekly portion reading from an unvoweled handwritten Torah scroll, Joe Pessah and others read from a voweled printed volume. Great attention was lavished on correct pronunciation and cantilation of the text.

The Karaite pronunciation of Hebrew is distinctive, more antique than modern Hebrew, and closer to the sound of Arabic. Karaites continue to pronounce the velarized s for the *tzadik,* the semigutteral h for *het,* and the j for a dotted *gimel.* Because the Karaites do not operate their own religious school, children who have studied Hebrew in the United States have learned the standard modern Israeli pronunciation of Hebrew at religious schools of various Reform or Conservative congregations. Knowledgeable and concerned parents and elders have tried to rectify the children's Hebrew pronunciation. But many children become confused during prayers in the synagogue. It is considered sinful to make an uncorrected error while publicly reading from the Torah, and some senior members of the congregation extend their concern over correct pronunciation to the recitation of prayers. Although I tried to use the

Karaite pronunciation of Hebrew when attending the San Francisco synagogue, my pronunciation was sometimes corrected and even preempted
lest I make a predictable error.

In Cairo, most women did not study Hebrew, receive formal religious
training, or attend synagogue regularly. When women did attend, the
separation of men and women in the synagogue was observed. In San
Francisco, some women continued to refrain from regular synagogue at-
tendance. Even though her husband was one of the most active members of the community, Nelly Masliah did not attend Sabbath services
unless there was a special occasion like a bar mitzvah.

The San Francisco synagogue gestured in the direction of traditional
gender separation, although the physical structure of the building imposed a degree of proximity that would have been unacceptable in Cairo.
The former living room of the home served as the main prayer hall. A
sign at the entry to the living room announced, "This is a kosher place
for prayer. Women enter through the kitchen." Observing this instruction allowed women to assume their places in the dining room of the
house, directly behind the living room and not physically separated from
it, without entering the living room. Nearly half those who attended services were women, some of whom recited their prayers in loud and energetic voices, a marked departure from the Cairo custom.

At the conclusion of the reading of the weekly Torah portion, there
was a break in the service. Every congregant then rose and shook the
hand of everyone else present and conveyed the traditional greeting, *sha-
bat shalom* (a peaceful Sabbath). Individuals who had entered the synagogue at different times and did not have an opportunity to speak before prayers briefly exchanged social news. During this time, men and
women spoke to each other, shook each other's hands, and crossed into
previously gender-segregated spaces. After the greetings were completed,
men and women withdrew to their segregated spaces, and the service
resumed. The positive value of strengthening the bonds of the community by the greeting ritual was apparently judged to supersede the importance of strictly maintaining the traditional gender segregation of
space in the synagogue.

After services, everyone went to the basement of the house and shared
a large meal featuring traditional Egyptian cuisine. There were often
comments about the excellence of particular dishes or the fact that only
certain individuals remembered how to make a special dish properly.
This is not necessarily an indication that people actually forgot what they
once knew. Even in Egypt, not every woman was equally proficient in

the kitchen, although the tone of voice with which such matters were discussed suggested the opposite. This feature of Karaite social life differs little from Rabbanite Jewish customs. Comparing culinary skill in preparing traditional dishes is a prominent component of community chitchat at nearly any Jewish social gathering where food is served. Conversations during the meal were held in Arabic, French, and English.

None of the children and teenagers speaks any Arabic, though several understand some of the spoken language. Some of the teenagers are highly Americanized. It is unclear whether enough of them have the knowledge and commitment to resist assimilationist pressures and maintain the distinctiveness of the Karaite tradition once the generation that remembers the life and customs of the community in Egypt departs.

On several occasions when I attended the synagogue, I used the meal and social time after prayers to make arrangements to meet and interview people in their homes. Writing is prohibited on the Sabbath, but I would always bring a pen and paper. I knew that I would be able to remember names, addresses, and dates for only a limited time. So I planned to write down my appointments and any other interesting information in my car after leaving the synagogue and before driving home. Because I did not want to take out a pen and paper in the synagogue building, I was embarrassed when the most devout leading members of the congregation asked me if I would like them to write down for me their addresses and directions to their homes. Although I am not religiously observant, I did not want to ask people to violate their religious beliefs on my behalf.

Joe Pessah explained to me that in the United States certain accommodations of this sort were necessary in order to preserve the community. In Cairo, everyone walked to the synagogue because riding in a vehicle is prohibited on the Sabbath. But some people drove as many as fifty miles to attend Sabbath services in San Francisco. He thought that it was much better to encourage such people to drive and attend synagogue because it was obviously impossible for them to do so if they did not drive.

Other ritual innovations practiced by the San Francisco Bay Area Karaites include the institution of bat mitzvah ceremonies. Joe Pessah's mother, Sarina Pessah, did learn Hebrew in Cairo but did not have a bat mitzvah because the community did not observe this rite of passage. She commemorated the opening of the new synagogue in Daly City and her seventieth birthday by celebrating her bat mitzvah.[29]

Some leading members of the community now celebrate Hanukah in their homes. "I never knew about Hanukah until we came here," said Fred Lichaa. "It was too much to compete with Hanukah and

Christmas. It was easier to say [to the children], 'You'll get your gift at Hanukah.'"[30]

The San Francisco Karaite community and its leaders are guided by an attitude of flexible pragmatism. Their supreme value is preserving the existence of the community, and they are prepared to compromise strict observance of rituals in order to promote this objective. Thus, the San Francisco community observes what might be regarded as "reform Karaism." No one has attempted to articulate the legitimacy of this practice in the same way that the Rabbanite Reform and Conservative rites have justified their departures from Orthodoxy. The Karaite community of San Francisco can live with this contradiction because, as in all Middle Eastern Jewish communities, membership is defined by acceptance of the authority of the acknowledged leadership and the belief that ethnoreligious identity is ascriptive and permanent. Piety and precision of observance are desirable, but not necessary for membership in the community. Some Karaite leaders aspire to preserve the traditions and customs of the community as they remember them being practiced in Cairo; others are aware that some changes are inevitable. The social adaptations necessary to maintain a community in the United States make it unlikely that the practices of the Cairo community will ever be fully reproduced, even if the Karaites succeed in passing their traditions on to the second American-born generation.

ON THE PERILS OF ETHNOGRAPHY

When I began to study the Karaite community of the San Francisco Bay Area systematically, they welcomed my interest because the personal relationships I had established led them to trust that I would represent the community sympathetically. And I had every intention of doing so. I understood that my interpretation of the significance of Karaite practices did not necessarily accord with the self-understanding of most Karaites. This difference did not seem likely to generate antagonism, especially because my attention was focused on the Karaites of San Francisco rather than broad political questions about the Middle East and the Arab-Israeli conflict. But after I met Karaites in Israel and began to learn about the issues affecting their community, some difficulties developed.

Between Passover and Rosh ha-Shanah 1993, the San Francisco community hosted an extended visit by the former Karaite chief rabbi of Israel, Haim Levy. I was in Israel conducting research for this book when he arrived, so I did not meet Rabbi Levy until the latter part of his stay in San Francisco. In Israel, I spent considerable time reading in the library of the World Karaite Center in Ramlah, where I was generously hosted by First Assistant Chief Rabbi Avraham Gabr. Because there was no heat in the library, Rabbi Gabr invited me to use his office as a reading room. This allowed me to observe the regular comings and goings of his daily business, and it allowed him to keep an eye on me.

Rabbi Gabr spoke to those who visited his office in Hebrew or Arabic, whichever was more comfortable for the visitor. I normally spoke Hebrew with Rabbi Gabr and his visitors, but from time to time people would take an interest in who I was, and to test my credentials or amuse themselves, they would speak to me in Arabic. I found conversing in Egyptian Arabic with Jews in the middle of Israel deliciously iconoclastic.

I felt a connection to these Karaites that had something to do with our common identification as Jews as well as the normal human contact we had established as a consequence of my regular visits to Ramlah. In addition, our relationship was sustained by shared knowledge outside the boundaries of normative discourse in Israel: my interest in modern Karaite history, my sympathy for the Karaites as a victimized minority in Israel, a network of common friends and acquaintances, an appreciation for Arabo-Egyptian culture, and fond memories of certain localities in Egypt. The Karaites of Ramlah preserved important elements of their Egyptian culture—language, food, music, religious rituals. Beyond these tangibles, the humane, face-to-face social style, an almost naive trust in the integrity of one's fellow human, an unpressured approach to accomplishing tasks that always allowed for the possibility of human frailty, and a deep preference for the needs of real people over abstract principle situated the World Karaite Center in Ramlah closer to Cairo than to Tel Aviv.

This was the dominant impression in my mind when I returned to the United States and met Rabbi Levy. I had a long discussion with him during which he repeatedly asserted that the Egyptian Karaites were active Zionists and had prepared to emigrate to Israel even before 1948.[31] He insisted that there were no significant differences between the Karaites and Rabbanites, both in Egypt or in Israel, and that the Karaites were not subjected to any significant discrimination in Israel. This was a rather different story from what I had heard from any other Karaites in San Francisco, Ramlah, or Cairo. Rabbi Gabr, for example, though hardly a political radical, resented the Israeli government's unwillingness to recognize the Karaite *bet din* and felt that "as long as we have no representation in the Knesset, we are treated unjustly (*mekupahim*)."[32] Rabbi Levy became hostile to me because he apparently decided that my

questions about these matters were motivated by the traditional antagonistic Rabbanite perspective that portrayed the Karaites as Arabizers
and adopters of Muslim customs.

Rabbi Levy was one of the first Karaites to arrive in Israel in 1949.
He served in the army and attended the Hebrew University. He was therefore far more Israeli in his outlook than most members of his community in Israel and San Francisco. He was a strict proponent of religious
orthodoxy and would not profane the Sabbath by writing. But he also
advocated a high degree of accommodation to Israeli norms, including
a revised vision of the history of the community in Cairo that transposed
religious attachment to the Holy Land into political Zionism. Rabbi Levy
was removed from his post as Karaite chief rabbi of Israel because some
leading members of the community felt that his policies diluted the community's distinctive identity and traditions. His visit to San Francisco
took place after his deposition and may have been an aspect of his strategy to recoup his standing in Israel.[33]

Rabbi Levy's clash with me was based on his correct perception that
I did not see his community as he did. He presumed that I was motivated
by anti-Karaite Rabbinate prejudices and the standard Zionist view that
immigrating to Israel was "good" and remaining in Egypt was "bad."
At first, I was extremely distressed that Rabbi Levy was suspicious of me
and my motives. In retrospect, I have come to think that it was his right
to suspect me. My presence and my research agenda accentuated the
Egyptian Arab face of the Karaites I met. If I had been a fluent speaker
of French and had spoken no Arabic, if I had been interested in Karaite
religious doctrine and its historical development, if I had not spent considerable time in Egypt myself, a rather different interpretation of the
meaning of Karaite experience and identity would have been available
to me. Rabbi Levy regarded the representation of the Karaites implicit
in the questions I put to him as a threat to the well-being of his community in Israel because he understood that I was interested in the cultural differences between Karaites and Rabbanites. In terms of the prevailing norms during the period of his socialization in Israel, when even
the assertion of Middle Eastern Rabbanite identity was unacceptable, he
was correct.

However, the majority of the Karaites I have met were not embarrassed or reluctant to share the Egyptian Arab face of their identity with
me. I am convinced that this component of their identity is as "real" as
the face that they may present to the official Jewish communities in the
United States and Israel. Because the norms of Jewish life in Israel and

the United States assign a negative value to it, some Karaites unself-consciously and reflexively mask this face. Rabbi Levy is one of the few who consciously deny it. Others display it proudly to those who can appreciate it and affectionately recall many aspects of their life in Egypt even as they recognize that continuing that life was impossible and that it is unlikely that any Egyptian Jewish community will be reestablished in the foreseeable future.

One Sabbath I attended services in San Francisco when Rabbi Levy delivered a sermon—in Arabic, the only common language between him and the majority of the congregation because they do not understand modern spoken Hebrew and he is not fluent in English. During the sermon, he paused and asked me to translate a phrase for him from Hebrew to Arabic. I was flustered because I did not expect such a request, which blurred the boundary between my status as an ethnographic observer and my identity as a Jew participating in a religious service. Ultimately, I was pleased and flattered to be asked to serve as translator. In the course of writing this book, I have come to accept the inevitable perils of those who live on cultural boundary lines and serve as translators.

PART THREE

Egyptian-Israeli Peace and Egyptian Jewish Histories

CHAPTER 8

The Recovery of
Egyptian Jewish Identity

Among the Mizrahi communities in Israel, Egyptian Jews were often particularly invisible. They shared many of the obvious characteristics associated with this group: They came from the Middle East; the religious traditions of the majority were Sephardi; and they spoke Arabic or French, or both. However, the exceptional internal diversity of the Egyptians and their particular history distinguished them from other Mizrahi communities. The Egyptians included a small minority of Ashkenazim. The Karaites were a distinctively Egyptian group (except for a minuscule number of Karaite immigrants from Turkey and elsewhere) with a highly Arabized culture, like the Iraqi or Yemeni Jews. Although French served as a lingua franca for all Middle Eastern Jews, many Egyptians also spoke Italian, Greek, or English. Unlike Algerian Jews, who were all French citizens, Egyptian Jews possessed a plethora of passports and European cultural orientations, yet the majority of those who arrived in Israel were *apatrides*—residents of Egypt with no legal nationality. The religious, linguistic, social, and cultural diversity of the Jews of Egypt diminished their salience as a distinctive group after their arrival in Israel.

In Egypt, Jews had been overwhelmingly urban, multilingual, middle-class merchants and professionals. They had acclimated rapidly and flourished in its cosmopolitan urban milieus. Most were not strictly religiously observant and did not live as a community apart. They used those same skills of cultural accommodation to assimilate successfully into relatively anonymous roles in urban Israeli life, where they commonly found work in banking and insurance (sectors in which they had been prominent in Egypt) or the police force (where knowledge of Arabic was an asset). Geographically, they were dispersed from Be'er-sheba to Haifa, though a concentration of Egyptian Jews developed in the southern Tel Aviv suburbs of Holon and Bat Yam.

Another factor that inhibited the formation of a distinctive Egyptian Jewish identity in Israel was the relatively small size of the community compared to the much larger immigrant groups from Morocco (to which Algerians, Tunisians, and Libyans were often agglomerated), Iraq, and Yemen. In 1961, when most of the Egyptian Jews who eventually resettled in Israel had already arrived, the census enumerated 35,580 Jews born in Egypt and Sudan.[1] The great majority of them pursued urban, middle-class lives that did not fulfill the ideals of labor Zionism: settlement of the frontier, physical labor in agriculture, and active participation in the military struggle to establish the Jewish state. Most of them arrived after the Suez/Sinai War, and it was the public articulation of the meaning of their experiences during and immediately after that conflict that became the basis for establishing the collective identity of Egyptian Jews in Israel.

The earliest efforts of Egyptian Jews to assert their distinctive collective identity and presence in Israel emphasized two themes: They had been Zionists in Egypt; and they had been victims of anti-Semitic persecution. Emphasizing these aspects of their experience created points of contact between Egyptian Jews and the recent experience of European Jews. For Jews and non-Jews in Europe and North America, the memory of the mass murder of European Jewry provided the overwhelming moral justification for creating the state of Israel, and the Zionist interpretation of its significance became a central factor shaping Israeli values and norms. Establishing a claim to recognition in these terms encouraged Egyptian Jews to pass their history and experience through the sieve of Ashkenazi Zionist discourse, leaving incompatible memories and understandings behind in Egypt.

Shlomo Kohen-Tzidon's memorial volume for Shmu'el Azar, *Dramah be-aleksandriah ve-shnei harugei malkhut* (Drama in Alexandria and two martyrs), discussed in Chapter 4, was the first literary expression of the existence of a distinct Egyptian Jewish community in Israel. Publishing this book enabled Kohen-Tzidon to establish the Zionist credentials of his community by calling attention to the ultimate sacrifices for the cause of Shmu'el Azar and Moshe Marzuq in Operation Susannah. By defending the Zionist pedigree of his community, Kohen-Tzidon asserted his status as its leading spokesperson. Azar and Marzuq were the emblematic Zionist heroes of their community and, as most Israelis saw matters, its most prominent victims. Subsequently, Kohen-Tzidon extended the image of victimhood to the entire Egyptian Jewish community. In an article on the Jewish community of Cairo in the monthly magazine of the chief rabbinate of the Israeli army shortly before the 1967 Arab-Israeli War, he asserted that after the establishment of the state of Israel, hundreds of Jews were transferred to "concentration camps" (*mahanot rikuz*).[2] The Holocaust imagery invoked by this term drew strength from the established representation of Gamal Abdel Nasser and the Egyptian leadership as Nazis (see Chapter 4). In addition, Kohen-Tzidon claimed that after 1948, "the Jews of Egypt were defined as enemy subjects and Israelis in all respects."[3]

As we have seen in Chapter 3, there certainly were detentions, sequestrations of property, physical attacks on Jews and their property, and a constriction of Jewish communal life. But the majority of the Jewish community remained in Egypt after 1948, and many Jews hoped that the patterns of their lives would be restored. The Egyptian government made a point of distinguishing between Jews and Zionists in principle, if not always in practice. Kohen-Tzidon's exaggerations could be printed as unquestionable truth in a semiofficial publication because few Israelis knew or cared about the details of Jewish life in Egypt. The general terms of Kohen-Tzidon's presentation confirmed what was already known: Jews were victims everywhere in the world of the *goyim* (non-Jews). Good Jews drew the proper lesson from their experience and became Zionists. Consequently, Kohen-Tzidon was not compelled to explain how and why the majority of the Jews could remain in Egypt until 1956 under such circumstances.

Kohen-Tzidon was willing to exploit vocabulary linking the Egyptian government to the Nazis to validate the history of his community and to make it understandable in Ashkenazi terms. But he also acknowledged that his implied analogy was imperfect by going on to explain that mob action against Jews in Egypt "never reached the pathological proportions of hatred of Jews by the Christians in 'civilized' central Europe (Poland and Germany) or the satanic and murderous 'organization' of the Nazis."[4] This disclaimer preserved Kohen-Tzidon's pride in his identity as an Egyptian Jew raised in a civilized and relatively tolerant country.

His identification with Egypt was also expressed through a distinctive approach to the Arab-Israeli conflict, arguing that "the source of the tension between Israel and Egypt was the sad and tragic misunderstanding between two national liberation movements." He believed that "understanding between these two movements was possible." This allowed him to assert the incoherent and implausible proposition that Azar and Marzuq had betrayed neither Egypt nor the Jewish people.[5] Because Kohen-Tzidon was a Knesset member who endeavored to represent the Egyptian Jewish community in terms consistent with prevailing Ashkenazi Zionist norms, the inconsistencies in his texts were overlooked by the public and did not become an issue. These logical ruptures in minor texts by a political figure of secondary importance assume significance only through the process of recovering the severed threads of Egyptian Jewish identity, which can not be rewoven into a single coherent fabric.

Kohen-Tzidon was the legal counsel for the Organization of the Victims of Anti-Jewish Persecution in Egypt founded by Sami (Shmu'el) 'Atiyah. 'Atiyah, a native of Alexandria, owned a successful shirt making factory and managed the cooperative that supplied raw materials to all the shirt makers of Alexandria.[6] He used his business and governmental connections to participate in organizing Jewish immigration to Israel after 1948, although he was not a member of any Zionist party, and he himself chose to remain in Egypt. As a successful businessman and a friend of the brother of Gamal Abdel Nasser, 'Atiyah was able to maintain good relations with the Free Officers' regime. On November 1, 1956, following the Anglo-French-Israeli attack on Egypt, 'Atiyah was arrested and his property was confiscated. Like most holders of foreign passports (his passport was Moroccan, but this meant a connection to France), he was expelled from Egypt; he reached Israel in 1957 and settled in Holon.

In 1958, 'Atiyah initiated the Organization of the Victims of Anti-Jewish Persecution in Egypt with the approval of Minister of Finance Levi Eshkol. The primary objective of the organization was to register and document the claims of Jews who lost property in Egypt, whether abandoned, confiscated, or sold under compulsion at below market prices, so that the claimants could somehow recover moral and material damages for their losses. By 1978, 4,000 files had been opened (including about 1,000 from claimants living outside Israel), registering private assets with an estimated value of $197 million (in 1950s dollars).[7] Jewish communal property abandoned in Egypt was not included in this accounting.

Another focal point of the organization was to request that members who had been interned in Egypt be granted the status of "prisoner of Zion" (*asir tziyon*). This is a vague designation commonly used to refer to Soviet Jews or others who had expressed a desire to emigrate to Israel and were prevented from doing so. The title conferred no formal, legal rights in Israel. It is not entirely appropriate for Egyptian Jews because both before and after the 1948 war those who wanted to leave were able to do so. Raising this demand was a way to insist that Egyptian Jews be admitted to a status already established by the categories of Ashkenazi history so that their experiences could be acknowledged in the only terms recognized by Israeli public culture.

The Organization of the Victims of Anti-Jewish Persecution in Egypt sought to represent Egyptian Jews as having undergone experiences parallel to those of European Jewry. Even as this representation was rhetorically accepted by the Israeli public and political leadership, it did not win the Egyptian Jewish community the recognition that Shlomo Kohen-Tzidon and Sami ʿAtiyah sought. They and their organization were associated with the Liberal Party (a component of what eventually became the Likud). The MAPAI/Labor governments were uninterested in a cause identified with their political opponents.

Even after the Egyptian-Israeli peace, the Israeli government refrained from pursuing its claims for strategic and diplomatic reasons. Dr. Maurice Sachs, president of the council of the Organization of the Victims of Anti-Jewish Persecution in Egypt complained,

> In the [Israeli] Ministry of Justice and the Ministry of Foreign Affairs they would invent different excuses for not dealing with our affairs. Before the signing of the peace treaty [with Egypt] they would say there is no one to speak to. Afterwards, they said it was necessary to wait to establish the joint committee for mutual claims. In the end, they said that at the time the property was taken from us we were not citizens of Israel, and therefore the state can not represent us. If my memory is not mistaken, the Jews of Europe who received compensation as a result of the agreement with Germany were not exactly citizens of Israel at the time of the Holocaust. Why for them yes and for us no?[8]

Sachs's sarcastic tone expresses his exasperation that even though he and his organization accepted the Ashkenazi Zionist framework for interpreting the historical experience of the Jews of Egypt, their claims were not accorded the same importance given to Ashkenazi claims. Professor Yaʿakov Meron, who was responsible for the Egyptian Jewish claims in the Ministry of Justice, suggested that the Israeli government declined to press them because it feared that if it did so, the Egyptian government would make a counterclaim for compensation for the value of the petroleum that Israel illegally lifted from the Abu Rudeis oil fields during its occupation of the Sinai Peninsula from 1967 to 1982.[9] Just as in the case of Operation Susannah, authorities of the state of Israel apparently determined that the interests of Egyptian Jews were subordinate to the broader interests of the Jewish state.

REWRITING THE HISTORY OF ZIONISM

After its electoral victory in 1977, the Likud encouraged its supporters to rewrite the history of Zionism to accord more substantial weight to the revisionist Zionist movement and to its heavily Mizrahi electorate. This was not a particularly coherent project because Vladimir Jabotinsky and the revisionists had been almost as insistently Eurocentric as the labor Zionists. Support for the Likud developed among Mizrahim primarily as a response to feelings of neglect by MAPAI/Labor governments *after* they arrived in Israel.

In response to the Likud initiatives, supporters of the Labor Party and MAPAM began to document the history of their activists in Middle Eastern countries. One such project was a series of public roundtables on "Jewish Defense in the Lands of the East" organized by the Institute for Research on the Zionist and Pioneering Movement in the Lands of the East at Yad Tabenkin, the research and study center of ha-Kibutz ha-Me'uhad (now part of TAKAM, the United Kibutz Movement), a federation historically affiliated with the Le-Ahdut ha-'Avodah Party. Yad Tabenkin also initiated a new journal devoted to the history of Zionism in the Middle East: *Shorashim ba-Mizrah* (Roots in the East). "Illegal Immigration (*ha'apalah*) and Defense in Egypt" was the title of one of these colloquies at which the oral testimony of Egyptian Zionist activists and the emissaries dispatched from Palestine and Israel to lead them was featured.[10]

This event was organized by Shlomo Barad, a Tunisian-born veteran of ha-Shomer ha-Tza'ir and member of Kibutz Karmiah. He had no direct tie to Egypt, but as a Mizrahi member of the Zionist organization that had been most active in Egypt in the late 1940s, he felt an obligation to set the record straight.[11] Relying on the oral testimony of the participants in the roundtable and other sources, he published the first comprehensive history of Zionist activity in Egypt.[12] Barad affirmed and elaborated on the perspective of the Egyptian Zionist activists:

> After the arrest of most of the leaders of the Zionist organizations, adult and youth, [in May 1948] a new leadership for the confused Jewish masses emerged outside the internment camps in the form of the youth of the Zionist underground. . . . The news was whispered in every Jewish home that an organiza-

tion existed which encouraged *'aliyah* to Israel, and that it was the only means of exodus from exile to deliverance (*ha-yetzi'ah min ha-golah le-ge'ulah*).[13]

Like most Zionist ideologues, Barad sees *'aliyah* as the inevitable, re-demptive telos of Jewish existence, which is not indefinitely sustainable in "exile." He unquestioningly imputes this consciousness to the inhab-itants of "every Jewish home" in Egypt, affirming their full participation in Jewish national history and the labor Zionist movement before the es-tablishment of the state of Israel. No one at the roundtable addressed the questions about identity, dispersion, and retrieval of identity that have been the central concerns of this volume.

The speakers at the Yad Tabenkin symposium eagerly seized the op-portunity provided by the occasion to secure their places in Zionist and Israeli history. Ada Aharoni confirmed the official Zionist paradigm of Jewish history even as she disputed its Eurocentric version by insisting, "Zionism was not imported into Egypt [by emissaries from Palestine]. It was there." This conclusion, she asserted, emerged from the research she had done for her novel, *The Second Exodus,* a romance set in the milieu of the Zionist youth movements of Egypt (see below).[14]

David Harel spoke at the Yad Tabenkin symposium, recounting his exploits as one of the underground youth leaders of ha-Shomer ha-Tza'ir referred to by Shlomo Barad in the previous quote.[15] Harel has consis-tently affirmed the Zionist potential of the Egyptian Jewish community. Several years later he told a reporter for a Passover edition of the *Jerusalem Post,* "Already by the time I was 10 or 11 I didn't identify my-self as an Egyptian. . . . I felt we were strangers in Egypt. I started to think about how I would get to Israel."[16]

David Harel and Ada Aharoni were members of the *gar'in* of ha-Shomer ha-Tza'ir members who settled in Kibutz 'Ein-Shemer. Their Zionist and socialist commitments encouraged them to imagine the land of Israel as an ideal space—a national homeland to be rebuilt and the site of the Jewish contribution to the worldwide proletarian revolution. Like many adherents of revolutionary ideologies in the twentieth cen-tury, they were frustrated by the social materialities they encountered on the road to realizing their vision. In Chapter 5, I argued that their ex-pulsion from the kibutz suggests that they could not easily shed aspects of the cultural and political identities they brought with them to Israel despite their strong Zionist commitments. But this was not a subject for discussion at the Yad Tabenkin roundtable or in the Passover supple-ment of the *Jerusalem Post.* Instead, the memories they evoked on these occasions of public commemoration expanded on the image of Egyptian Jewry previously established by Sami 'Atiyah and his organization. Not only were Egyptian Jews persecuted like European Jews and alienated from the lands of their birth; they independently realized that Zionism and immigration to Israel offered the solution to their predicament. The history, culture, and Israeli social status of the Jews of Egypt was valorized by presenting them in a form that conformed to the norms of Zionist discourse. Because the testimonies offered at the Yad Tabenkin roundtable and many similar occasions confirmed the Israeli national narrative, most of the public has not been anxious to cross-examine them too closely.

THE ASSERTION OF EGYPTIAN JEWISH IDENTITY

The convoluted military positions of Egypt and Israel at the end of the 1973 Arab-Israeli War forced the parties to negotiate a disengagement of forces. Between January 1974 and September 1975, indirect talks between Egypt and Israel orchestrated by U.S. Secretary of State Henry Kissinger resulted in two Sinai interim agreements and a partial withdrawal of Israeli forces from Egyptian territory occupied since 1967. Anwar al-Sadat abandoned Gamal Abdel Nasser's program of positive neutralism, pan-Arab nationalism, and Arab socialism. He announced a new open door economic policy, sought ties with the United States, and negotiated the first agreements between Israel and an Arab state since 1949.

The prospect of a negotiated peace between Egypt and Israel reconfigured the political context and offered Egyptian Jews in Israel an opportunity to construct a new social role for themselves. Daily norms of life in Israel were deeply shaped by a powerful consensus on Arab-Jewish relations, past and present, that led most Israelis to regard almost everything Arab as frightening, sinister, and utterly alien. Immigrants from Arab countries were under constant and massive social and cultural pressure to align their memories with these public norms. Egypt was especially vilified and feared because it had led the Arab camp against Israel. Consequently, most Egyptian Jews minimized or avoided mentioning their former lives in the land of Israel's most formidable military adversary. In Chapter 2, I argued that Rahel Maccabi's *Mitzrayim sheli* (My Egypt), published at the height of Egyptian-Israeli conflict in 1968, can be understood as a text confirming the prevailing negative images of Egypt in post-1967 Israel. Once peace with Egypt became a possibility, evoking and celebrating previously long suppressed positive memories of Jewish life in Egypt could be understood, not as sympathy for the enemy, but as a contribution to constructing a human bridge for peace. Having lived in Egypt and known its people and culture well, Egyptian Jews considered themselves uniquely positioned to serve as intermediaries between the land of their birth and their new home. Situating themselves as promoters of peace and mutual understanding permitted and even required them to reassert the Arabo-Egyptian elements of their own identity because they were now important credentials qualifying them for this role.

Even before President Anwar al-Sadat's dramatic visit to Jerusalem in November 1977, Sami 'Atiyah offered his services to Defense Minister Moshe Dayan to serve as an intermediary in conveying peace offers from the Israeli government to Egypt. 'Atiyah recommended that Egyptian Jews renounce their claims to financial compensation for their property losses if this would promote peace talks between Egypt and Israel.[17] In effect, 'Atiyah was prepared to relinquish his status as a victim of anti-Jewish persecution in Egypt in exchange for peace, a very substantial gesture because the assertion of victimhood and the demand for restitution had been the central purposes of his organization's activities and the basis on which they asserted Egyptian Jews' claim to status in Israel. When al-Sadat did visit Jerusalem, 'Atiyah and Maurice Sachs sent him telegrams of welcome, praising his courage and declaring, "we are with you in your struggle for peace, and God is the grantor of success" (*allah wali al-tawfiq*).[18] Invoking this traditional Islamic formula demonstrated that the senders of the telegram were familiar with Arabo-Egyptian culture and knew how to behave appropriately according to its canons. The senders identified themselves as heads of the organization of Egyptian Jews in Israel, apparently hoping that acknowledging their link to Egypt would benefit the cause of Egyptian-Israeli peace.

The signing of the Egyptian-Israeli peace treaty in April 1979 and its implementation by Israel's evacuation of the Sinai Peninsula in 1982 (except for Taba) unleashed a flurry of activities by Egyptian Jews in Israel and around the world. Projects officially sponsored by the state of Israel or Zionist institutions, privately initiated associations devoted to documenting and memorializing the cultural heritage of the Egyptian Jewish community, publications sponsored by associations of Egyptian Jews, and writings by individuals acting on their own all expressed a reassertion of the distinctive collective history and identity of Egyptian Jews. Each of these initiatives was rooted in its own particular local circumstances, and the politics of these projects were rarely explicit; they were commonly founded on the assumption that remembering and recording what had been was an unqualified good in itself. Consequently, there was great variety and eclecticism in what was selected for remembrance and the purposes these memories served.

Soon after the Egyptian-Israeli peace treaty, Egyptian Jews in Israel established the Association for Israeli-Egyptian Friendship. Levana Zamir, the president of the association, was born in Cairo in 1938 and emigrated to Israel in 1950. In 1980, she organized an Egyptian culinary competition in Tel Aviv under the patronage of Sa'd Murtada, Egypt's first ambassador to Israel. The event was a success, and Zamir pursued her promotion of Egyptian food by publishing a book of Egyptian recipes. Her introduction to the volume acknowledged that "Israeli-Egyptian peace aroused in me a pent up nostalgia for the land in which I was born and for all the happy smells of childhood."[19]

Some Egyptian foods are familiar to Israelis because many Middle Eastern dishes have been assimilated to Israeli cuisine. Nonetheless, the cover blurb of Zamir's cookbook promoted it as a compendium of "exotic" cuisine. The recipes are framed in a typically Orientalist style: All the illustrations in the text are images of ancient Egypt. Besides the recipes themselves, the only evocation of modern Egypt is Ambassador Murtada's preface. Levana Zamir and her publisher seem to have agreed that ancient Egypt was more appealing and less threatening for a middle-class and disproportionately Ashkenazi Israeli book-buying audience. As a marketing and a political strategy, this allowed them to avoid any contemporary references that might disrupt the benign image of Egypt they sought to convey.

The warm and positive associations of food are an ideal medium for nostalgia. Cuisine crosses ethnoreligious boundaries easily. There are some distinctively Egyptian Jewish dishes, but Jews generally ate the same foods as other Egyptians of their social class. Focusing on culinary culture allowed Levana Zamir to claim a depoliticized connection with her past that posed no threat to either the Israeli or the Egyptian government. Nonetheless, promoting Egyptian food in Israel appeared to have weighty import. The preface contributed by Ambassador Murtada hailed the book as an initiative that would "broaden the familiarity, the rapprochement, and the understanding between the Egyptian and Israeli peoples."[20]

In January 1984, a nucleus of families convened in Haifa to revive the activities of the long moribund Union of Egyptian Jews (Hitahdut Yotzei Mitzrayim). They began to meet regularly and to publish a mimeographed bulletin, *Goshen: alon moreshet yahadut mitzrayim* (Goshen:

Bulletin of the heritage of Egyptian Jewry).[21] The Haifa group sponsored regular lectures on all aspects of Egyptian Jewish life, hosted social events for Passover, Purim, and Hanukah, and promoted the publication of literature by and about Egyptian Jews. *Goshen* published articles in French and Hebrew, with an occasional contribution in English, including memoirs of life in Egypt, summaries of lectures delivered at meetings of the group, notices of books and articles published about the Egyptian Jewish community, and reports of the association's social activities. Less active branches of the union were revived or established in Tel-Aviv, Bat Yam, Acre, and Or Yehudah.

The organization of Egyptian Jewish collective memory was not restricted to or centered in Israel. The most active and successful initiative was based in France. In December 1978, the topic of Egyptian Jews was introduced to a public meeting of about 400 people at the Centre Rachi in Paris, an enormous crowd in light of the strong disinclination of mainstream French culture and politics to recognize ethnically or religiously based minorities.[22] This event inspired the formation of the Association pour la sauvegarde du patrimoine culturel des juifs d'Egypte (ASPCJE—Association to safeguard the cultural patrimony of the Jews of Egypt) in September 1979. During the early 1980s, the ASPCJE held monthly events in Paris; and from 1980 to 1986, it published twenty-five issues of a quarterly journal, *Nahar Misraïm* (The Nile River). Its leaders sought out contacts with Egyptian Jews in Israel and the United States, some of whom contributed to *Nahar Misraïm*. The ASPCJE was in some way connected with nearly every organized activity of Egyptian Jews and every publication about them during the 1980s.

Inspired by the activity of the ASPCJE, Paula Jacques (Abadi), a radio journalist born in Egypt in 1949, revisited her birthplace in 1981 for the first time since leaving after the Suez/Sinai War. On her return, she reported on her trip on the prestigious *France Culture* radio program.[23] The previous year she had published her first novel, *Lumière de l'oeil,* set in Cairo in 1952. Since then she has written three more novels whose principal characters are Egyptian Jews.[24] Her work has been praised by the French literary public, and her fourth novel, *Déborah et les anges dissipés,* won the Prix Femina in 1991. Egyptian Jews familiar with her work have been disappointed and upset that she has filled her novels with what they consider unflattering characters—beggars, orphans, swindlers, and the like—who do not represent a "true" image of their life in Egypt.

The principal animators of the ASPCJE included several former communists who had worked with Henri Curiel and the Rome Group: Jacques

Hassoun, Raymond Stambouli, and Ibram Gabbai. They were joined by representatives of several other sectors of Egyptian Jews in and around Paris. However, the tone of ASPCJE publications and its network of contacts reflected the leftist (but no longer communist) outlook of the nucleus of former communists as well as younger left activists like Eglal Errera. Hassoun's three trips to Egypt in 1977 and 1978, his first return since he was expelled as a communist in 1954, prepared the way for the organization of the ASPCJE.[25] Hassoun also served as editor of *Juifs du Nil,* a history of the Jews of Egypt from antiquity to the modern era published by a press associated with Egyptian communist exiles.[26] Alfred Morabia, a major contributor to that volume and an ASPCJE Executive Committee member, had belonged to the Egyptian Communist Organization, one of the short-lived splinter groups of the communist movement. Jacques Stambouli, the son of Raymond Stambouli, was the editor and publisher of a lavish photo essay, *Juifs d'Egypte: Images et textes,* one of the most substantial projects of the ASPCJE. He and Hassoun had met as members of the Trotskyist Revolutionary Communist League in the 1970s.[27]

Because of the prominence of leftists in the ASPCJE, its dominant, though unofficial, outlook was neo-Bundism—diasporic Jewish nationalism—the same orientation militantly rejected by the Rome Group in the 1950s (see Chapter 5). The leading figures of the ASPCJE were not Zionists, but neither were they hostile to the existence of the state of Israel. Several had public records of supporting the national rights of Palestinian Arabs as an essential element of a peace based on the coexistence of Israel and a Palestinian state. The demise of the leftist internationalist project that had attracted them from the 1950s to the 1970s in Egypt and France left them with only one arena for political activism: their own community. They did not abandon their progressive commitments but adjusted them to the task of retrieving and preserving their heritage with great determination, connecting themselves to every form of activity relating to Egyptian Jews they could identify.

People who began their political lives as Marxists probably never imagined they would be involved in a struggle to preserve the remnants of the Jewish cemetery at Basatin, a suburb of Cairo on the road to Ma'adi, a project with religious overtones and no apparent "practical" value. But the ASPCJE contributed hundreds of thousands of francs to finance the efforts of Carmen Weinstein, one of the few remaining active Jews living in Cairo in the 1990s, to construct a wall around the cemetery and engage a guard to protect it from squatters.[28] I met Carmen Weinstein in Jacques Hassoun's home in Paris in 1994. Though both are secular Jews with little attachment to orthodox religious observance, they were united by a fierce determination to preserve the cemetery as material evidence that a Jewish community had lived and flourished in Egypt.

Egyptian Jews in the United States also began to organize themselves in the late 1970s and early 1980s. I discussed the organization of the Karaite Jews of America in San Francisco in Chapter 7. A Rabbanite Egyptian Jewish community settled in Brooklyn, New York, following the 1956 Suez/Sinai War. Some of its members, especially those of families who came to Egypt from Aleppo in the nineteenth century, assimilated to the larger and previously established Syrian Jewish immigrant community. In the late 1970s, Egyptian Jews in Brooklyn established the Ahaba ve-Ahva synagogue, which practiced the Egyptian liturgical tradition.

In October 1995, a group of Egyptian Jews gathered at the Ahaba ve-Ahva synagogue to initiate the formation of the Historical Society of Jews from Egypt. Their objective was to record and preserve their cultural heritage, the same purpose that motivated the formation of the French ASPCJE. Among the leading activists in this initiative with some previous public exposure were Victor Sanua, a research psychologist who has gone beyond the boundaries of his field to publish historical articles about Egyptian Jews, and Mary Halawani, an independent film maker whose short documentary, *I Miss the Sun,* records her grandmother's fond memories of Egypt.[29] The society began publishing a newsletter, *Second Exodus,* and organized a series of lectures in private homes. This form of ethnic organizing has been quite common and acceptable in the United States, so it is remarkable that it has begun so recently. The leading individuals had been in contact with Jacques Hassoun and the ASPCJE and were obviously inspired by that example; but the New York group was organized several years after the demise of the French association, and its leading members did not share the same political commitments.

These associations have had modest and limited success as institutions; a certain kind of failure is inherent in the nature of such activity. The Jewish community of Egypt is nearly extinct, and there is little prospect for its revival in the foreseeable future. Those who remember their lives in Egypt are gradually passing away. Most of their children, even those who maintain some level of curiosity and engagement with their parents' heritage, have become assimilated to the dominant cultures of Israel, France, and the United States.

Therefore, examining the revival of Egyptian Jewish identity associated with these institutions cannot be an effort to map out a coherent cultural or political alternative. Rather, it is an excursion into memories and current sensibilities that have not found adequate space for expression in the brave new world of national states in which Egyptian Jews have found themselves after their dispersion. I have argued that the Egyptian-Israeli peace agreement altered the insistently negative images associated with Egypt sufficiently to allow Egyptian Jews to begin the process of recalling and reconstructing their past and representing it to themselves, their children, and the public. In the remainder of this chapter, I elaborate this argument, focusing on the post-1977 literary production of Egyptian Jews living in Israel.

PEACE AND VICTIMHOOD

Ada Aharoni (b. Andrée Yadid, 1933) was a pioneer in reviving and reconfiguring Egyptian Jewish memories of Egypt in light of the Egyptian-Israeli peace process. She was born in Cairo and educated at the Alvernia English School for Girls in the elite neighborhood of Zamalek, where she began to write poetry in English. Her family spoke French at home and held French citizenship. They left Egypt for France in 1949, after her father's business license was revoked. In 1950, Aharoni left her family in France, went to Israel, and joined the *gar'in* of ha-Shomer ha-Tza'ir at Kibutz 'Ein-Shemer. She and her husband, Haim Aharoni, were among the twenty-two Egyptians expelled from the kibbutz in 1953 as a result of their political stand in the Sneh affair (see Chapter 5). Eventually, Ada Aharoni pursued her childhood interest in English literature at the Hebrew University and at London University, obtaining a doctorate in English literature from the Hebrew University in 1975. She writes in English and Hebrew. Her early poems and other writings were composed in English and translated into Hebrew by others. More recently, she has translated her own poems and a novel into Hebrew, revising them in the process.

Aharoni began writing poetry on the theme of war and peace during the 1973 Arab-Israeli War. Since then, her career has been closely identified with promoting Arab-Israeli peace. She represented Israel at the 1975 Middle East Peace Poetry Forum in Boston. The same year she founded The Bridge: Jewish and Arab Women for Peace in the Middle East, a nonpolitical association of Jewish and Palestinian Arab Israeli citizens. In 1992, she presided over the Thirteenth World Congress of Poets in Haifa, whose theme was "Creating a World beyond War through Poetry." On that occasion, she received the Shin Shalom Peace Poetry Prize.[30]

Convinced that the Egyptian Jewish community in Israel could be a bridge to peace with Egypt and the rest of the Arab world, Aharoni designed a questionnaire to survey their opinions. The initial results suggested that in April 1993 (before the Israeli-PLO Declaration of Principles was signed), 80 percent of Egyptian Jews in Israel were prepared to accept Israeli evacuation from substantial portions of the West Bank and the Gaza Strip and the establishment of either a Palestinian-Jordanian federation or a Palestinian state in those territories. Comparable opinion polls indicated that these solutions to the Palestinian-Israeli conflict were then acceptable to only 35 percent of all Jewish Israelis.[31] Hence, the survey research confirmed Aharoni's hypothesis that Egyptian Jews were more conciliatory toward the Palestinian Arabs than the general Israeli Jewish population.

In most of Aharoni's first published poems on the theme of war and peace, her Egyptian origins linger discreetly in the background. The Egyptian-Israeli negotiations and interim Sinai disengagement agreements following the 1973 war apparently encouraged her to advance beyond general calls for peace to articulate more specifically what peace meant to Aharoni through recollections of her previous life in Egypt. Since then, she has emerged as a prominent public advocate for Egyptian Jews in Israel.

As is apparent from her remarks to the Yad Tabenkin roundtable on "Illegal Immigration and Defense in Egypt" quoted earlier, Aharoni has fully associated herself with the dominant Zionist narrative of Egyptian Jewish history. Moreover, she has made herself more acceptable to the general Israeli Jewish public by leaving her political origins in MAPAM on the left edge of the labor Zionist movement and joining the Labor Party. However, like Shlomo Kohen-Tzidon, Aharoni believes in the distinct mission of the Jews of Egypt, who form "a unique type of Judeo-Mediterranean community bridging East and West." She acknowledges that the literary representatives of her community "cherish warm memories of the Egyptian people and of their own life in Egypt" and regards them as "messengers of goodwill built on understanding, realism, and a shared past."[32] Thus, Aharoni very self-consciously offers herself and her community in the service of Egyptian-Israeli peace.

"Ha-Shalom ve-ha-sfinks" (Peace and the Sphinx) seems to have been written in 1975 because its themes appear in other poems that can be dated to that year. It offers a precise and succinct definition of peace formed by Aharoni's memories of Cairo. She longs to resume her relationship with a schoolmate and friend and to revisit sites that marked her passage from childhood to adolescence.

Peace and the Sphinx

Peace for me is an eternal flowing golden river
It is to embrace Kadreya in Cairo
And the house where I was born in Freedom Square
To check if I am as tall as a Pyramid stone
And as wise as the Sphinx[33]

The English version of this poem, "What Is Peace to Me?" is longer and more elaborate. The main thematic innovation is the poet's reminder that she and her family were expelled from Egypt, a topic that recurs in several of Aharoni's other writings. Nonetheless, she continues to use Egyptian criteria to measure her maturation.

Peace for me
is to visit
Kadreya in Egypt, and
the spicy house in Midan Ismaileya in Cairo
now the Square of Freedom,
where I was born, and evicted.

To place again my open palm
on the Sphinx's paw,
and check if now I'm as tall
as a Pyramid stone.

Peace for me
is all this,
and so much more—[34]
. . . .

Although Hebrew is Aharoni's third language, the Hebrew version of the poem seems more lyrical. Writing in Hebrew has often been more critical of dominant norms in Israel than writing in English, a global language accessible to an international audience. The English poem seems to strike a measured political balance in its underlying message: Despite having been expelled, I long for peace and retain fond memories of Egypt and its people. This is congruent with the message that Israeli political leaders have always projected to the international community: Israel always sought peace with its unreasonably hostile Arab neighbors. Aharoni's innovation is to propose that her connection to Egypt makes this goal more achievable. But just as Israel's governments have been unwilling to examine critically the sources of the conflict, Aharoni does not ask why she was expelled from Egypt.

Kadreya appears once again as the addressee in "Letter to Kadreya: From Haifa to Cairo with Love," which Aharoni published in the Israeli daily *ha-Aretz*.[35] The letter is an autobiographical memoir recalling the friendship and intellectual adventures of the two girls as co-editors of their school literary magazine. It is also an ideological manifesto in response to Kadreya's question, "Why are you leaving Egypt? You were born here, this is your country!"

Aharoni's answer constitutes the central portion of the text and describes her experience as a "frail girl of six" (seven in the Hebrew version) when her family's maid, Muhsena, led her on a walk through the Bab al-Luq market several blocks from her home in downtown Cairo. Young Ada was repelled by the "sordid and unknown world" of Cairo's streets. She felt insulted when she was accosted as "*ifrangiyya*" (foreigner) and imagined that the people on the street were "hating her for no reason at all." She was alarmed that Muhsena "seemed different; from her usually cheerful submissive self she had become incommunicative, bent on her private pursuits." When they arrive at a confectionery shop, the proprietor, whose connection to Muhsena is unclear, explained to her that *ifrangiyya* is not an insult; it simply meant she was a European, "not an Arab like us." When she objected that she and her parents were born in Egypt, the shop owner conceded, "If you want to think you're not then you're not, but how will you convince the others?" Then he offered her a sugar doll, a sweet made for the occasion of *mawlid al-nabi* (the Prophet's birthday), suggesting that she take a white one, like the color of her own skin, rather than a brown one.

The memory of this experience constitutes a proof text legitimating Ada Aharoni's feeling that she did not belong in Egypt. Alienated from the land of her birth, she spent the rest of her years in Egypt trying to understand where she did belong. Arriving with her family in France, she learned that, despite her citizenship and knowledge of French, she did not feel welcome there either. Aharoni made her way to Israel, where she at last felt wanted and at home. Today she feels herself "an Israeli in the full sense of the word." Consequently, she explained to Kadreya, "Israel just had to exist for rootless people like me."

On the surface, the story is a morality tale affirming the central tenet of Zionism: Jews cannot live a secure and fulfilling life anyplace but Israel. The narrative is completely uncontextualized. It is difficult to fathom why all this is happening, and Aharoni does not expand on elements of the

narrative that might suggest alternative interpretations, or at least a critical understanding of its significance. The story raises many questions
that remain unanswered: What were the social and political implications
of attending an English language school while the British were still occupying Egypt? Why didn't she know enough Arabic to understand what
ifrangiyya meant? What was it about her appearance that caused her to
be noticed on the street? Why did she feel frightened walking in the streets
only a few minutes away from her home? What social relations produced
her discomfort that the family servant was not acting submissively? An-
swering these questions might suggest that Ada Aharoni's family was economically and socially privileged, identified with European culture,
looked down on indigenous Egyptians, and kept themselves remote from
the poverty, disease, and misery of the daily lives of those who lived on
the streets outside their European-style home. A young girl of seven might
not grasp that the family maid had "her private pursuits," but because
they seem to have motivated the entire episode, it seems like a disdainful
expression of class privilege for an adult not to attempt to understand
them. Thus, Ada Aharoni had more than enough reasons to feel alienated from Egypt, even if the Arab-Israeli conflict had not made her Jewish identity an especially difficult and painful issue to grapple with.

This experience, although undoubtedly traumatic for a sheltered
young girl unaccustomed to walking the crowded, noisy, chaotic streets
of Cairo, seems inadequate to bear the explanatory weight that Aharoni
assigns to it: a justification for the course of her life and for the establishment of the state of Israel presented to a Muslim Egyptian friend who
sincerely believed that Egypt was Ada Aharoni's country. Aharoni's own
assessment of the significance of this story seems somewhat contradictory. On the one hand, she explained that the memory "has left a sore
spot in my mind even after all this while." On the other hand, she feels
that it happened to a person "so remote from me today that I can only
recall her in the third person." Who or what is being protected by narrating the story in the third person? How could the memory of this experience be so powerful if the narrator can no longer identify herself as
the subject of the narrative?

This same scene is retold and embellished in Aharoni's first novel, *The
Second Exodus*, in a form that offers clues that may explain why this experience as a six- or seven-year-old left such a powerful and permanent
impression.[36] *The Second Exodus* is a historical fiction set in the milieu
of an Egyptian Zionist youth movement from 1946 until the heroes' emigration to Israel. The principal characters, Inbar Mosseri, the nineteen-

year-old daughter of a wealthy judge, and Raoul Lipsky, a survivor of
the mass murder of European Jewry who has sought refugee with his
aunt in Cairo after losing all the other members of his family, meet
through the activities of the Zionist youth movement. Raoul is attracted
by Inbar's romantic and innocent view of the world. Inbar, having lived
a sheltered life of privilege in Egypt, has difficulty understanding Raoul's
cynical world outlook. They fall in love. Raoul shares his memories with
Inbar. She decides that having heard the "horrible intimate details" of
Raoul's past, she should reveal to him a secret from her own childhood
so that "he will realize at least, that I, too am scarred."[37]

What follows is an expanded recounting of the scene in the "Letter
to Kadreya." The streets of Cairo are described in much more elaborate
and sordid detail. Inbar is accosted not only as a foreigner but also as a
Jew. The most striking difference between the two accounts is that the
confectionery shop owner, identified as 'Ali, the brother of the maid
Muhsena, in the novelized narrative, urged on by his mother, attempts
to rape Inbar and fails only because he ejaculates before penetrating her.
Inbar relates that she later learned that her older brother, Gaby, had previously had intercourse with Muhsena. Moreover, Muhsena's family had
requested Inbar's father, the judge, to intervene on behalf of 'Ali and
Muhsena's father when he was imprisoned for theft. Inbar's father refused, and 'Ali and Muhsena's father went to prison, where he died. Inbar concludes, "Through the attempted rape, ['Ali] was getting back not
only at my father and brother but at all the Jews."[38]

Raoul, the Ashkenazi Jew, provides the logic and moral force sus-
taining this interpretation of Inbar's experience. As might be expected
of a teenage young man hearing of an assault on his beloved, Raoul fo-
cuses exclusively on Inbar as an innocent victim. He minimizes the significance of Gaby's sexual offense in terms that express his feelings of
class and racial entitlement: "To sleep with the maid was a widespread
affair, even in Europe. They were paid well for it, too!" Moreover,
Raoul accepts Inbar's ordeal as comparable to his own survival, saying,
"So, you've had your share of the hell of this world, too, Inbar." Then,
deploying a world outlook shaped by his understanding of his own experiences in Europe previously resisted by Inbar as too pessimistic,
Raoul establishes an incontrovertible link between Inbar's rape and her
Jewish identity: "Isn't it clear to you now that he tried to rape you
mainly because you're Jewish [emphasis added]?" [39]

Because this second version of the narrative is fictionalized, we cannot simply assume that Ada Aharoni actually survived an attempted rape

as a young girl in Egypt, although that would explain why the memory of the experience she recounted to Kadreya remained with her so powerfully even as she tried to distance herself from it. It is possible that Aharoni did not want to admit publicly to having been attacked by a rapist because, as the novel explains, "if a girl is raped, she, as the victim, is usually considered the main culprit."[40]

If the novel does not necessarily constitute a fictionalized version of a personal truth Aharoni was reluctant to acknowledge, it does affirm a broader social truth. The definitive interpretation of young Inbar's experience has been provided by Raoul, whose understanding of the world and of the Jewish place in it has been formed by his agony in Europe. In the forward to the novel, Aharoni explains, "Inbar and Raoul represent two aspects of the Jewish people: the Oriental-Sephardi Jews from Arab countries—and the Ashkenazi Jews who experienced the Nazi Holocaust. Together they symbolize the unified Jewish people in Israel."[41] This unity is possible because Inbar does not openly contest the meaning of her experience provided by Raoul, although she does not necessarily embrace it either. But the unity of the Jewish people in Israel depends on accepting mass murder as the central experience of Jewish history. Aharoni therefore legitimated the distinctive voice of the Egyptian Jewish community by representing its history as a mirror image of the experience of Ashkenazim in Europe.

This correspondence is reinforced in the chapter following the recounting of the sexual assault on Inbar. In early 1948, the members of Inbar's Zionist youth organization gather at their meeting hall and discover that it has been closed by the Egyptian authorities (all the Zionist organizations were indeed banned at this time). Inbar immediately thinks of the Spanish Inquisition and Nazi Germany and concludes, "We're being pushed out again!"[42] Once more, European Jewish experiences are immediately available to define the meaning of events in Egypt. The group activity was to have been a lecture on the history of the Jews of Egypt prepared by Inbar. They reconvene to hear it in the nearby home of one of the members, and the closure of the meeting hall, represented as comparable to the worst persecutions of Jews in Europe, frames Inbar's presentation.

When the Egyptian-Israeli peace negotiations opened, Ada Aharoni took the opportunity to reconnect herself to Egypt by sending her "Letter to Kadreya" and a poem titled "From Haifa to Near Faraway Cairo" to Jihan al-Sadat "to extend a hand in Salam-Shalom to you, Kadreya, and the women of Egypt whom I remember with warmth."[43] Aharoni's writings and cultural-political activity express a sensibility that undeniably reflects her Egyptian origins, while she has consistently represented her personal history and that of her community in the terms of the Euro-Zionist interpretation of Jewish history. This has given her a relatively broad audience in Israel, especially for someone who writes primarily in English. Other audiences may regard her exclusive focus on Jewish victimhood, central in her work as it is in general Israeli political culture, as a barrier to peace and reconciliation.

The Second Exodus was the subject of a lengthy and hostile review by 'Ali Shalash that appeared in seven installments in the weekly *al-Majalla* and was republished as the first section of his book, *al-Yahud wa'l-masun fi misr* (The Jews and the Masons in Egypt).[44] Shalash's essay constructs a counternarrative, correctly pointing out many flaws in Aharoni's version of Egyptian Jewish history. He emphasizes Egypt's tolerant welcome of the Jews, while the Jews sought connections with foreign capital, preferred foreign citizenship, and subverted Egypt by spreading Zionism and communism. Some of the errors in Shalash's historical account mirror those in Aharoni's novel, and it would be tedious and pointless to explicate them in any detail. The anti-Semitic character of Shalash's riposte is advertised in the title and the theme of the book—the Jews and the Masons as social minorities who are, by implication, not "real Egyptians."

One can perhaps draw some hope from the fact that Aharoni and Shalash are engaged in a direct dialogue that would probably not have taken place before the Israeli-Egyptian peace treaty. The dialogue is severely constrained by each participant's insistence that only one of the parties to the conflict has a legitimate national grievance. The painful limits of this dialogue suggest that the diplomatic maneuvers commonly designated as the Arab-Israeli "peace process" have left unaddressed complex sentiments of victimhood that will have to be attenuated if a stable peace is to be established.

A NATIVE DAUGHTER

The Egyptian-Israeli peace treaty included provisions establishing travel and tourist links between the two countries. Security restrictions and more than the usual degree of bureaucratic red tape deterred all but the most determined nonofficial Egyptians from visiting Israel. Anyone who requested a visa for Israel was subjected to an extensive investigation. By contrast, the Israeli government regarded tourism as an important symbolic and material expression of peace. It encouraged touristic visits to Egypt, and hundreds of thousands of Israelis seized the opportunity to travel to the only contiguous country open to them since the 1948 Arab-Israeli War. The first wave of Israeli tourists included many Egyptian Jews.

Among them was Anda Harel-Dagan (b. Andrée Wahba, 1934), the younger sister of David Harel (Wahba). Like her older brother, Andrée was a member of ha-Shomer ha-Tzaʿir. To allow David to continue his illegal work in the underground Zionist ʿAliyah Organization after 1948 and relieve him of concern for the security and welfare of his family, the Zionist authorities arranged for Andrée and her mother to be brought to Israel in early 1949. They came via Marseilles, where an Israeli emissary changed Andrée's name to Anda because he felt she should have a real Israeli name. When I met her in 1993, Harel-Dagan noted sarcastically that Anda is, in fact, a Polish name. She was resentful that the emissary regarded Anda as genuinely Israeli, whereas her French-Egyptian name was unacceptably foreign to him.[45] The entire family relinquished the Arabic name of Wahba, common to Muslims, Christians, and Jews in Egypt, in favor of Harel, the very modern Israeli name of one of the brigades of the Palmah. Young Anda was placed in a Youth ʿAliyah program in Kibutz Mishmar ha-ʿEmek, where she graduated high school. After her army service, she joined Kibutz Nirim. Since 1965, she has made her home in Kibutz Hatzor.

Harel-Dagan published two volumes of poetry in the early 1970s. The only explicit reference to Egypt in these early poems is in "Avi haya" (My father was), the first poem in her second book, *Avraham haya* (Abraham was), a memorial to her father, who died in Cairo in 1944. The verse describes her father's hand as "wide as a mosque on a holiday" or a cart "on which virgins dance to Allah, the only one." The poet remembers herself and her siblings walking with their father "in a sea of sugar dolls"—the confection associated with the feast of the Prophet's birthday that Ada Aharoni recalled in her tale of horror.[46] Harel-Dagan strove to speak and write Hebrew like a native Israeli, so she distanced herself from the experiences and images of her childhood in Cairo. But she felt that a volume dedicated to her father, Ibrahim Wahba, a native speaker of Arabic to whom she had spoken Arabic at home, should include some reference to his cultural milieu.[47]

After a thirty-one-year absence, Harel-Dagan returned to Egypt in 1980. Like many others who took the opportunity to revisit the land of their birth, she arranged to leave her organized tour group to search out her family's former home in the ʿAbbasiyya district of Cairo. Egyptian-Israeli peace and physical reconnection to the place of her birth inspired a volume of poetic memories, *Po'ema kahirit* (A Cairo poem), which features descriptions of Cairo streets, recollections of her grandfather and father, and portraits of a schoolmate, her concierge, and a minibus driver. "Avi haya" reappears in this volume, richly recontextualized by poems and photographs of Cairo. *Po'ema kahirit* uses a disarmingly simple, even naive, style to establish an unpretentious ambience in which innocent childhood memories can be fondly invoked. But the poems also disrupt the reader's expectations with unanticipated language, images, and associations.

Harel-Dagan discovered that she still spoke colloquial Egyptian Arabic well enough to be considered a native (*bint al-balad*) by those she spoke with. She proudly embraced this identity in the final lines of "Jum'a the Minibus Driver" in which Jum'a gives her three strands of jasmine flowers and "murmurs Allah akbar, inti bint al-balad/ inti bint bladna" (God is great, you are a native daughter/ you are a daughter of our country).

The poet unambiguously asserted her Egyptian identity by inscribing both her names—Anda Harel-Dagan and Andrée Wahba—in Arabic on the verso of the title page of *Po'ema kahirit*. However, because she did not learn how to read and write Arabic well, as her older brother and sister did, the Arabic calligraphy was done by another member of her kibutz. For Israelis who do not read Arabic, she included her French-Egyptian name in Latin letters on the title page.

The trip to Egypt not only enabled Harel-Dagan to reclaim elements of her former identity; it allowed her to express a new poetic voice that had been repressed during the years of her building a new life in Israel. "I could not publish these poems until there was peace and I could return and verify if things were the way I remembered or not," she said.[48] In contrast to her earlier poems, in which she strove to emulate a *tzabar* style, the language of *Po'ema kahirit* is hybrid, consciously mixing Hebrew and Egyptian elements. *Po'ema* is, of course, not a purely Hebrew word, but a Hebraization of the English. Its use in the title of the volume (rather than the more usual *shir* or *shirah*) suggests a Levantine cultural mélange, which is amplified by the colloquial Arabic expressions that punctuate several of the poems.

"Dahir Street" recalls a street in the heart of the middle-class Jewish neighborhood of Cairo and welcomes the Egyptian-Israeli peace by commingling the words of the messianic vision of the prophet Amos, an Arabic phrase, and an allusion to a popular Israeli song, with its pomegranate tree transposed to a guava tree in Cairo.[49]

. . . .
Behold, the days are coming
Clear days
Sane days
Behold, women with covered faces
Pronounce a blessing
In shah Allah [God willing]
In Dahir street
In the synagogue courtyard
The guava tree gives forth its fragrance—

Two of the poems—"Saʿid al-bawwab" (Saʿid the concierge) and "Ji-hantab ʿAbd Allah"—recall an incident of mob violence against Jews (perhaps during the anti-Zionist demonstrations of November 2, 1945, but the reference is not specific). However, this image, predictable within the Zionist discourse, is complicated because the subjects of both poems are individual Muslim Egyptians with whom the poet has a deep personal and emotional connection. Saʿid lifted her onto his shoulders to rescue her from the crowd shouting "nitbakh al-yahud" (let's slaughter the Jews) while murmuring the *basmallah* (in the name of God the merciful, the compassionate). The poem concludes with an unequivocal statement of identification with Cairo and its people. The soothing "Do not fear" (*al tira*) is conveyed in biblical language, the same words with which God reassured Abraham, Isaac, and Jacob.[50]

. . . .
In Misr-Cairo my city
Do not fear when it is black as night
Saʿid al-bawwab is my brother.

Similarly, the poet identifies with Jihantab ʿAbd Allah, a Muslim classmate who gave her comfort when Jews were detained and crowds shouted "Zionists out" and "Let's slaughter the Jews."

Jihantab ʿAbd Allah

No, I haven't forgot her,
Shy girl
Yes, she sat next to me at the Lycée Française du Caire.
Her face is my face and
My laughter is her laughter.
My sister;
Jihantab ʿAbd Allah

ya ukhti, ya ʿalbi [My sister, my heart]
Jihantab Nefertiti
. . . .

Growing up in ha-Shomer ha-Tzaʿir and living on a kibutz affiliated
with MAPAM's ha-Kibutz ha-Artzi federation situated Anda Harel-
Dagan politically in the camp that enthusiastically welcomed the peace
with Egypt. Nonetheless, she felt that her poems on Egypt were not well
received in ha-Kibutz ha-Artzi. She was disappointed that the public response to Po'ema kahirit was greater outside her kibutz movement than
among those she considered closest to her. MAPAM's publishing house,
Sifriat ha-Poʿalim, normally the publisher of choice for members of
kibutzim of ha-Kibutz ha-Artzi, was not interested in publishing Po'ema
kahirit, even though it had previously published Harel-Dagan's first
book. She felt that the problem was not that the book was about Egypt,
but that its style was alien to the narrow tzabar sensibility of the kibutz-
born generation of writers in the leadership of the writers' organization
of ha-Kibutz ha-Artzi.⁵¹ Sifriat ha-Poʿalim did publish the Egyptian
memoir of another member of Kibutz Hatzor, Rahel Maccabi's
Mitzrayim sheli. So writing about Egypt was clearly not a barrier; the
question was how to write about Egypt and be published by a press
highly self-conscious of its ideological mission.

Anda Harel-Dagan was pleased to present herself as a native daughter of Cairo and to celebrate that long-suppressed element of her identity through the publication of Po'ema kahirit. The construction of a
self-consciously hybrid identity can leave imperfections and gaps because the disparate components do not fit together seamlessly. Hence,
some of the Arabic phrases in Po'ema kahirit are not quite right; and
the use of the J rather than the G in names like Jumʿa and Jihantab is
not Cairene pronunciation. These are not malicious lapses. They suggest that the poet was stretching with exertion across years of Hebrew
acculturation to retrieve the Arabic sounds of her childhood. Perhaps
she purposely transformed her Cairene Arabic into the Palestinian dialect that would be more recognizable to Israeli readers.

HARAT AL-YAHUD (THE JEWISH QUARTER): AN ARAB JEWISH NEIGHBORHOOD

No such exertion was necessary for Maurice Shammas, an Arabic-
speaking Karaite born in Cairo's harat al-yahud in 1930. Shammas wrote
for the Arabic Jewish weekly, al-Shams, and the Karaite biweekly,

al-Kalim, and worked in Arabic theaters in Cairo before emigrating to Israel in 1951. He now lives in Jerusalem and is not very involved in the Karaite community. Nonetheless, he has remained actively engaged with Arabic culture throughout his life in Israel by working for the Arabic department of the Israel Broadcasting Authority writing plays, producing programs, and eventually becoming director of musical programs.

To mark the signing of the Egyptian-Israeli peace treaty, Shammas published his first and only book, *Shaykh shabtay wa-hikayat min harat al-yahud* (Shaykh Shabtay and stories from the Jewish quarter), a collection of Arabic short stories portraying his memories of life in *harat al-yahud.* Shammas regarded the peace treaty as imposing on him an obligation to present these memories of Jews who "lived among the Egyptian people, as part of that ancient people." For Shammas, the Jews of *harat al-yahud* were authentic Egyptians—"carbon copies of *ibn al-balad* (a native son)." After leaving Egypt, he preserved his memories of his childhood in *harat al-yahud* "like a whiff of pure perfume."[52]

Shammas intends his portrayal of *harat al-yahud* to apply to both Rabbanites and Karaites because he never mentions the existence of the two sects or specifies that any of his characters belong to one or the other. This is consistent with his current belief that Karaites should not emphasize their distinctive identity in Israel because this would separate them from other Jews.[53] Most of the characters in the stories are Jews and have distinctively Jewish names. There are occasional references to Jewish customs, such as the dowry (instead of the Muslim *mahr,* or bridal gift), kosher food, and a bar mitzvah. Otherwise, there is no reason why most of the stories could not be about Muslims or Christians in any Cairene popular neighborhood.

In contrast to both Ada Aharoni and Anda Harel-Dagan, Shammas relates only positive memories of relations between Jews and Muslims. "Al-ʿAmm Mahmud" (Uncle Mahmud) tells the story of a poor Muslim man who lived in *harat al-yahud* happily and amicably for several years with no difficulties. After becoming an "inseparable part of its human and social reality," he suddenly disappears from the quarter.[54] Some time later he returns to introduce his son, who has just graduated from the University of London medical school, to the "good people with whom I lived one of the happiest periods of my life."[55] The young doctor then opens a clinic in the *hara.*

In "Cafe Lanciano," patrons are gathered around the journalist Albert Mizrahi, discussing the veracity of a rumor that Layla Murad has converted to Islam (see Chapter 3). Some of the patrons become angry when they learn that the rumor is true. Lanciano, the proprietor, is the most upset. He turns off the radio when the announcer introduces a song by Layla Murad and orders her picture removed from the cafe wall. Others are not dismayed. For Sa'adya, it is a simple matter: "I don't understand. Why are you angry? Is she your relative? Your sister? Someone falls in love and wants to marry the one she loves. What's wrong with that?"[56] The debate remains unresolved. The next morning the quarter is buzzing with the story that Layla Murad secretly visited the Maimonides synagogue in the *hara* at midnight and asked the sexton to pray for the soul of her father, Zaki Murad. Everyone is relieved. At the cafe, Lanciano selects a Layla Murad record to play and orders her picture restored to the wall. Having honored her father appropriately, Layla Murad regains the esteem of the Jews of the *hara*. Her formal religious affiliation no longer constitutes a barrier to her acceptance by the Jewish community, just as her Jewish origins did not obstruct her popularity with her broader Egyptian audiences.

THE AMBIGUOUS LEGACY OF LEVANTINE CULTURE

In Chapter 2, I introduced Jacqueline Kahanoff and her book of essays, *Mi-mizrah shemesh* (From the east the sun), and argued that she advocated a creative Levantine cultural synthesis combining the progressive ideas of post-Enlightenment Europe with the refined civilization of Egypt. Kahanoff *was* a Levantine by cultural and social formation, as were many Mizrahim. But all the parties in the Zionist movement vehemently rejected Levantinism as an element of the modern, Hebrew culture they sought to create. *Tzabar* culture absorbed many material influences from its Middle Eastern environment—food, music, dance, language, architectural elements, and so forth. But its dominant exponents militantly insisted that the Arabs had no worthwhile ideas or social practices (except perhaps their customs of hospitality) to offer.

Mi-mizrah shemesh was published after Anwar al-Sadat's visit to Jerusalem and the start of the Egyptian-Israeli peace negotiations, and it is a component part of the literary movement asserting Egyptian Jewish identity in Israel that I have been describing. But only a few readers and reviewers were able to accept its positive portrayal of Levantinism. Yitzhaq Gormezano-Goren's *Kayitz Aleksandroni* (Alexandrian summer), also discussed in Chapter 2, was a part of this literary movement as well. His "Mediterraneanism" was also rejected by most Israeli reviewers. These works were the first major literary efforts to present a new and more positive view of Egypt to an Israeli audience through the opening created by the peace negotiations. But the reconsideration of cultural orientation they explicitly proposed could not yet be seriously contemplated by most Israelis. These Egyptian-born authors wrote of and from their own memories. Most critics could easily discount their sensibilities as a backward-looking nostalgia for an exilic past that Zionism sought to negate and transcend.

Nearly two decades later, Ronit Matalon, the daughter of Egyptian Jewish parents born in Israel, dramatically revalorized Levantinism in her intricate saga of a Jewish family's past in Egypt and their imperfectly reconstructed lives in Cameroon, Israel, and New York—*Zeh 'im ha-panim eleynu* (The one facing us).[57] Matalon reproduced verbatim two of Kahanoff's most distinctive essays, "Childhood in Egypt" and "Europe from Afar" (including the passages I have quoted in Chapter 2) as chapters in her novel. This demonstrative invocation of Kahanoff's authority was aesthetically and politically effective because in the years since the publication of *Mi-mizrah shemesh,* Kahanoff's work and reputation have gained stature among Mizrahi intellectuals and others searching for ways to integrate Israel into its Middle Eastern location. The publication of *Mi-mizrah shemesh* marked the launching of a broad Mizrahi cultural movement that amplified the effects of the assertion of the Egyptian Jewish presence in Israel.[58] *Zeh 'im ha-panim eleynu,* a complex and highly original novel preoccupied with Levantinism, benefitted from these changes in cultural sensibility and was highly praised by critics in the daily press and literary scholars.[59]

Each chapter of the novel is built around an introductory photograph from the narrator's family album. Some are images of Matalon's actual family; some are random shots taken outside Egypt for which Matalon provides fictionalized captions situating them in Egypt; and some pictures are "missing." *Zeh 'im ha-panim eleynu* is therefore far more than a novel with substantial autobiographical elements. Matalon is aware that she cannot reproduce a complete and historically objective picture of her family's life in Egypt and beyond. Incorporating imperfection and contradiction in a nonlinear narrative style, she poignantly reconnects fragments of individual lives, family relationships, and social situations, evoking the flavor of Levantine culture by liberally sprinkling phrases in French, Arabic, and occasionally English over her highly refined and sophisticated Hebrew text. The family members have idiosyncratic and widely varying attitudes toward Egypt, which Matalon renders empathically without fully endorsing. She avoids the temptation to establish a comprehensive and definitive representation of Jewish life in Egypt, leaving open many possible understandings shaped by personal idiosyncrasies, individual responses to the accidents of history, and the vagaries of human memory.

The novel opens as the narrator, seventeen-year-old Esther, who has just finished eleventh grade in Israel, lands at the port of Douala in Cameroon, where her uncle Cicurel (Jako Cicurel) owns a fishing fleet. Jako and his wife, Marie-Ange, have lived in Brazzaville, Gabon, and Douala since leaving Cairo in the 1950s. "They are sending me there, to Africa, to the glorious uncle so that he might perhaps straighten out my head a little," she muses.[60] Esther's parents, born in Egypt and living in Israel, thus reverse the common pattern of middle-class American Jewish families who send their teenage children on trips to Israel to secure their Jewish identities and bond with the Jewish state. Most of the first third of the novel unfolds in Douala, giving the reader a diaspora-centered perspective on Esther's family history, despite the fact that most of the family resides in Israel.

Although the social and economic relations of postcolonial Douala continually recall the life of Esther's family in Cairo, she cannot "return" to Egypt. Matalon is quite clear that the colonial world in which Egyptian Jewish life was situated has ended and cannot be recreated. Uncle Cicurel has internalized the racialized hierarchies of the colonial order and lives a life of postcolonial privilege modulated by paternalistic concern for his African workers and sincere respect for their human dignity. But he is not fully European himself, so he resents and fears Europe and chooses to live in Africa. "Through this choice he found a twisted line of continuity of himself and of his world in which there was no real place allotted for national identity, but in which huge expanses were open to nourish any spark of individual human endeavor imaginable."[61] The dangers of this world are revealed when Uncle Cicurel is stabbed by one of his workers toward the end of the book. But he does not consider abandoning it, and it is clear that he will recover without permanent damage and remain in Douala.

Like Esther's maternal grandfather, Uncle Cicurel vehemently rejects Zionism as destructive of the spirit of the family. Guided by this spirit, he retains strong ties to his family in Israel, including his sister, Ines, and her husband, Robert—Esther's parents. But he and Marie-Ange have visited Israel only once for forty-eight hours in the late 1950s.

Esther's oldest uncle, Moise, introduced Zionism to the family: "ha-Shomer ha-Tza'ir, Le Mouvement, Marcelle Ninio, and all that," as

Esther dismissively refers to it.[62] Ninio was a member of or close to ha-Shomer ha-Tzaʿir before becoming a spy for Israel. Recalling this connection as Moise's Zionist commitments are related for the first time invokes the images of incompetence, scandal, and betrayal associated with Operation Susannah and the Lavon affair. Like many of the young Jews in the milieu described in Jacqueline Kahanoff's essays included in the novel, Moise believed that "the options before us are very clear . . . to be a Zionist or a communist."[63] He chose Zionism and left Egypt for Palestine in the late 1940s to join a kibutz.

Except for Uncle Cicurel and Esther's father, who died in Egypt, the rest of the family joined Moise some years later. Only Moise and Ines try to adapt to Israeli society, and they do not really succeed. Grandmother Fortuna even seeks to put Esther in a Catholic boarding school in Jaffa so that she will receive a proper education, but Ines will not hear of it. "La vraie Ines, I left her in Egypt," mumbles Fortuna.[64] She yearns for the refinement of the Arab and Francophone cultures of Egypt and disdains life in both Israel and Douala.

Esther's youngest uncle, Edouard, was raised on Moise's kibutz but leaves Israel to seek his fortune with his elder brother in Africa. Edouard beats the African workers Jako has charged him with supervising. His Israeli upbringing has taught Edouard a racism too crude for Jako to tolerate. Edouard returns to Israel and becomes head of the General Security Services investigation unit in the Gaza Strip. Eventually, he becomes "entirely Arab," speaks Arabic almost exclusively, and criticizes Moise and Ines for assimilating to Ashkenazi culture and for their moderate attitudes toward the Palestinian Arabs (a political stand commonly associated with Ashkenazim). Moise does not understand where Edouard's embrace of Arab culture comes from. "Where did he see these things at home, all this hoo-hah?" he asks. "Maybe they were there and we didn't know it," says Ines. "Maybe we didn't see."[65]

In the 1960s, Moise asked the kibutz to allow him to study drawing. His request was denied, and Moise abruptly left the kibutz, feeling that he was discriminated against because of his Mizrahi origins. Moise does not abandon his Zionist commitment and determines to retain "only the good in it."

Esther's father, Robert, mocks Moise: "Your enlightened ones there in the kibutz, the miserable racists who are settling on Arab land, are they good or bad?"[66] Robert supports pan-Arab nationalism and admires Gamal Abdel Nasser. He is emotionally devastated by Egypt's defeat in the Six Day War. "What did we win? You will eat this conquest until it comes out of your nose," he proclaims prophetically.[67] Coming to Israel, "a piece of land not worth a spit," was a nightmare for Robert.[68] He turns his anger over the treatment of Mizrahim in Israel into political activism and runs for a city council seat, raising the issues of "discrimination against Sephardim," "the permanent lie of security of the state," and "the hatred of the Orient of the ruling stratum."[69] He looses the election to a MAPAI nominee by two votes and, frustrated and depressed, abandons his home and family. Robert is an emotionally unstable character, and his preposterous political commitments (for a Jew living in Israel) ensure that readers will not regard his voice as definitive. But this enables Matalon to express, through Robert, fundamental criticisms of Israeli society with rare clarity.

Robert's sister Nadine lives in New York. He and Esther come to look for her when she becomes mentally ill and disappears. They engage a private investigator, Armando, who asks Robert when he last saw Nadine. Hearing that it was forty-one years ago, Armando mistakenly concludes that Robert is a Holocaust survivor. Robert tries to explain in broken English: "No Holocaust, no camp, mister Armando, understand? EGYPT, you know Egypt? Good life, good people, good country, no Holocaust."[70]

Nadine's very Americanized and stereotypically superficial daughter, Suzette (Zuza), comes to Israel to interview Ines for a book about her roots, the breakup of the family, and the breakup of the colonial world. Ines has a brief and simple story: "I can only say that we were very happy. We were all very happy in Egypt, much happier than here. We ate a lot, we played, we did silly things, we laughed at any silliness, Zuza, like children. That's what I can tell you about our lives."[71]

Suzette tries to extract more information. "Are you sorry that you left Egypt, tante?"

"Not sorry," replies Ines. "Longing for it, dying from longing, that yes, not sorry. Our lives there were over, Zuza."

"But your roots are there tante," protests Suzette.

Ines closes the conversation, "A person does not need roots, he needs a home."[72]

Ines offers a very limited justification for Israel, not as a revival of the ancient Jewish homeland or a site for the creation of the new Jew, but as a necessary refuge when it was no longer possible to continue life in Egypt. This pragmatic, Levantine outlook eschews ideological abstraction. Indeed, no one in Esther's family presents an ideologically coherent solution to his or her condition. Moise's abandonment of the kibutz expresses his disillusionment with the Zionist idealism of his youth, though he will not renounce it. Uncle Cicurel is wealthy and comfortable in Douala but knows he does not "belong" there. Ines is physically secure in Israel but impoverished and socially marginal. Robert is deeply unhappy and psychologically distressed. Edouard lives a schizophrenic existence, adopting Arab culture while working in the repressive apparatus of the Israeli occupation of the Gaza Strip. Nadine is either homeless or has flown into the sky at 6th Avenue and 59th Street in New York (but appears alive and well in the next chapter). Suzette is insubstantial, self-centered, and oblivious to the poverty of her aunt, Ines. Left to make sense of her family's history, Esther concludes only that she is her father's daughter, no matter what. No wonder she arrives in Douala in a state of confusion.

POST-ZIONISM

Zeh 'im ha-panim eleynu was published after the signing of the 1993 Israeli-Palestinian Declaration of Principles, which most of the liberal Israeli intelligentsia unproblematically regarded as heralding the end of the occupation of the West Bank and the Gaza Strip. Anticipation of this momentous political change and the accumulated weight of the critique of Zionist practice elaborated by the "new historians" and political opponents of the occupation since the late 1970s led some Israeli intellectuals to propose that Israel was entering a post-Zionist phase of development. Post-Zionism, as distinct from anti-Zionism, tends to avoid pursuing the morally difficult questions about Israel's formation and the historical practices of Zionism to the limits of political reasoning. Although its primary advocates have been Ashkenazi university professors, journalists, and authors, post-Zionism has a certain Levantine element. It accepts that the past cannot be undone and tries to make the best of the present and the future without pressing for a fully consistent critique of the Zionist project, which would undermine the viability and potential appeal of post-Zionism to Israeli Jews primarily motivated by a desire for "normalcy" rather than anguish over the fate of the Palestinian Arabs.

The deliberate ambiguity of post-Zionism is unsatisfying for a historian trained to search for causes and effects or for anyone who has tried to make moral sense out of the course of history. It is also inadequate for many Arabs, especially Palestinians, who will not find sufficient attention to their sense of grievance in post-Zionism. Nonetheless, it may turn out to be politically more effective than the absolutist nationalisms it seeks to supplant.

Ronit Matalon's sympathetic portrayal of the contradictory ideological positions of all the members Esther's family suggests a spirit of post-Zionist tolerance and an ability to appreciate the positive qualities of Arab and other neighboring cultures. In an interview in *Davar,* Matalon seemed to endorse a post-Zionist reading of her novel:

> As an Israeli who was born and educated here, I was very surprised by how preoccupied I was with cultural and political options that are not necessarily what Zionism proposes. Zionism and the cultural option it prefers are only one possibility, and not necessarily the most generous one. . . . As an Israeli, I was very, very attracted to the cultural and moral richness of the wandering Jew, who does not have one nationality or one country, has many languages, is open to everything human, and does not always close himself off from [foreign] influences. In this sense, the Levantine option of live and let live, which in my opinion is the opposite of Zionism, very much attracted me.[73]

Post-Zionism, despite its shortcomings as a historical perspective, offers a sufficiently clear break from nationalist discourse to allow for a critical reevaluation of the heritage of the Jews of Egypt within contemporary Israeli culture. In the early 1990s, the anthropologist Emanuel Marx served as the director of the Israeli Academic Center in Cairo, an institution commonly vilified by Egyptian nationalists as a center for espionage and subversion.[74] After leaving Cairo and returning to his teaching position at the University of Haifa, Marx proposed that if it were not for Operation Susannah, the Jewish community in Cairo would not have been destroyed: "Those responsible for the dirty business (*'esek ha-bish*) exploited Jews in Egypt for unimportant purposes. This caused the rupture."[75] He went on to suggest that it was possible to renew the existence of a Jewish community in Egypt and criticized the Israeli Embassy in Cairo for opposing this project

> because they are prisoners of Zionist ideas according to which all Jews must immigrate (*la-'alot*) to Israel. We live in a post-Zionist era. . . . Israel has become quite a large state, and it's time we stopped the idiotic activity of encouraging the dissolution of Jewish communities throughout the world.[76]

It is not necessary to share Marx's judgment about the consequences of Operation Susannah or his confidence about the possibility of restoring the Jewish community of Egypt to appreciate the novelty and expansiveness of his perspective in an intellectual environment dominated by Zionism and Israeli nationalism. Marx's ideas are particularly

remarkable coming from someone who recently completed a semiofficial mission in Egypt.

Post-Zionism abandons the conviction that Jews can live meaningful
lives only in Israel. It relinquishes the fearful conception that because of
the mass murder of European Jewry, Jews require an absolute guarantee of physical security that can be provided only by the armed forces of
Israel. It allows Jews to appreciate and participate in other cultures without feeling guilty for betraying their heritage and opens the possibility
that Israel can become integrated into the Middle East.

Zeh 'im ha-panim eleynu is a cultural and historical statement constructed on the terrain first valorized by Jacqueline Kahanoff and Yitzhaq
Gormezano-Goren. It also expands on the less fully articulated Levantinism and post-Zionist sensibilities implicit in Anda Harel-Dagan's
Po'ema qahirit and Maurice Shammas's embrace of Arabo-Egyptian culture expressed through *Shaykh shabtay wa-hikayat min harat al-yahud*.
Matalon proposes a tolerant and expansive vision of her family's past in
Egypt and, by extension, the modern history of Egyptian Jews. Her de-
liberately fragmented literary style is well suited to representing the disparate elements of the community's experiences and outlooks that could
easily be homogenized and churned into propaganda by a conventional
history. And it allows her to avoid making an unambiguous political
statement that might undermine the human dimension of her narrative
and its reception in Israel. The production and popular reception of *Zeh
'im ha-panim eleynu* suggest that the broad reassertion of Egyptian Jewish identity in post-1977 Israel may open important cultural possibilities that, in favorable political circumstances, could contribute to the
long and torturous process of constructing a viable vision for Israel's future relations with its Arab neighbors.

CHAPTER 9

Opposing Camp David and Remembering the Jews of Egypt

Trends in Recent Egyptian Historical Writing

By the time of Anwar al-Sadat's visit to Jerusalem in November 1977, an entire generation of Egyptians had matured having never personally seen or known a Jew. They often had great difficulty imagining Jews as members of the Egyptian national community. There were no more than several hundred Jews in Egypt in the late 1970s. Their existence and their history had rarely been mentioned in the Egyptian mass media or in scholarly writing since the 1956 Suez/Sinai War. Those determined to do so could still find public evidence of a substantial Jewish presence in Egypt's recent past in the names of department stores throughout the country (Cicurel, Benzion, etc.), shops in the Sagha, Muski, and Suq al-Hamzawi quarters of Cairo, and the synagogues and other communal buildings that remained standing in Cairo and Alexandria. But these names and sites meant little to most Egyptians or foreign visitors. The Egyptian-Israeli peace treaty of 1979 prompted nationalist Egyptian intellectuals to take an interest in the modern history of the Jews of Egypt for the first time in a generation. Because Egyptian writers have been motivated by opposition to the terms of the peace treaty, the representation of Egyptian Jews in their recent work is largely negative and even anti-Semitic.

Since the appearance of Yehoshafat Harkabi's *Arab Attitudes to Israel,* Israeli researchers have regularly compiled catalogs of instances of Egyptian and Arab anti-Semitism.[1] Rivka Yadlin has argued that anti-Semitic writings published in Egypt after the signing of the peace treaty with Israel expressed a "primordial, general animosity towards the Jewish-Zionist complex" conceptually equating Jews, Zionists, and

Israelis. This primordial animosity persisted and perhaps even increased despite the formal peace.[2] Such ahistorical essentialism cannot constitute an adequate explanation for any social phenomenon. The anti-Semitic elements in post-1979 Egyptian representations of Egyptian Jews examined in this chapter have been motivated not by racial or religious animosity, but by opposition to the peace agreement with Israel. The historical themes and concerns of the authors are shaped by contemporary political criticisms of the terms of the treaty, its limitations, and apprehensions about the consequences of its implementation. This contextualization does not excuse expressions of anti-Semitism; it merely historicizes them and differentiates them from ideologically or theologically based sentiments that have long histories in European culture.

The recent writings of nationalist intellectuals I survey in this chapter constitute a genre distinct from texts in the Islamic tradition. Although hatred of Jews does not have the same theological basis in Islam as in Christianity, there is an identifiable Islamic style of vilifying Jews (just as there are Islamic formulae for promoting Muslim-Christian-Jewish coexistence, though they have not been prominently disseminated recently). The public presence of this discourse has expanded dramatically as the Islamist movement has become the principal opposition to the government since the 1980s.[3] But I do not examine it here because its main themes are much more predictable and are fairly consistent with the representations of Jews promoted by the Muslim Brothers and Young Egypt since the late 1930s (see Chapter 3).

The Egyptian-Israeli peace treaty raised in Egypt at least as many fears as hopes about future relations between the two countries. The 1978 Camp David accords, the precursor to the treaty, separated the fundamental question of Palestine from the narrower issue of Egypt's recovery of its territory occupied by Israel in the 1967 war in exchange for the conclusion of a peace agreement and "normalization" of Egyptian-Israeli relations. The framework for resolving of the Palestinian-Israeli conflict negotiated at Camp David was unacceptable to the PLO and the vast majority of Palestinians because it did not recognize their right to national self-determination and did not require any Israeli withdrawal from the West Bank and the Gaza Strip. Moreover, because Israel would not then consider negotiating with the PLO, implementation of this framework was to be resolved through Egyptian-Israeli negotiations, which soon reached an impasse. Nonetheless, normalization of Egyptian-Israeli relations moved steadily forward despite the stalemate on the Palestinian-Israeli conflict.

For nationalist Egyptians, Israel's actions in the Arab world after al-Sadat's visit to Jerusalem—the invasions of Lebanon in 1978 and 1982, the bombing of the nuclear reactor in Baghdad in 1981, and the extended repression of the Palestinian intifada from 1987 on—seemed inconsistent with peace between Egypt and Israel. Even many who did not oppose the concept of peace with Israel in principle rejected the Camp David process because it did not adequately address the grievances of the Palestinian Arabs. Some feared that formally abandoning the Arab rhetorical consensus on Palestine would weaken Egypt's leading position in the Arab world. Intellectuals were particularly apprehensive that they might become isolated from their colleagues and broader Arab audiences. Symbolically and materially, the treaty expressed Anwar al-Sadat's abandonment of the Nasserist program of pan-Arab solidarity, Arab socialism, and positive neutralism in favor of local Egyptianism, opening the economy to foreign trade and capital, and alignment with the United States. Opposition to the Egyptian-Israeli peace treaty was therefore often an element of a broader program of resistance to al-Sadat's economic, political, and diplomatic reorientation.

As an expression of their opposition to the Egyptian-Israeli peace treaty, many Egyptian intellectuals declared a total boycott of Israel and all the consequences of the normalization of Egyptian-Israeli relations. They refused to meet official and unofficial Israeli visitors, even Palestinian Arab citizens of Israel. Protests and demonstrations against Israeli participation in the Cairo Book Fair constituted an annual rallying point for proponents of a cultural boycott of Israel in the early 1980s. The Committee to Defend the National Culture was organized in response to what some leftist intellectuals considered the subversion of Egypt's authentic national culture by Zionist influences. Universities, research centers, publishing houses, and cultural institutions refused all forms of contact and collaboration with their Israeli counterparts. Nonetheless, the new political circumstances impelled journalists and others to engage in public discussion of a wide range of topics related to Israel, Zionism, and Jews.

These conditions informed the emergence of the modern history of the Jews of Egypt as an object of systematic knowledge for Egyptian intellectuals. Before the treaty, only one Arabic book on this topic (as distinct from Israel and the Arab-Israeli conflict) had been published in Egypt.[4] From the early 1980s on, Egyptians opposed to the Egyptian-Israeli peace treaty produced a regular stream of texts on this theme. These historical works are often based on extensive research documented in academic style, creating the effect of constituting objective, scientific knowledge. However, the history of the Egyptian Jewish community is usually presented in an antagonistic and tendentious manner as little more than a prologue to the Arab-Israeli conflict. Political opposition to the Egyptian-Israeli treaty broadened the circle of Egyptians willing to indulge in anti-Semitic representations of Egyptian Jews beyond the Muslim Brothers and Young Egypt to intellectuals with a secular, nationalist orientation. Their writings are the principal concern of this chapter.

My discussion of these texts concentrates on two themes: the Egyptianity of Jews and their role in the Egyptian economy from the late nineteenth century until 1956. These topics have been particularly prominent in the writing of secular nationalist intellectuals because they enable the exclusion of Jews from the Egyptian national community in terms that can be made to appear consistent with modern European conceptions of the nation-state and the duties of its loyal citizens. The first of these questions has been a central concern of this book, and it seems appropriate to note how contemporary Egyptian intellectuals view the matter. Representing Jews as economic parasites, usurers, and rapacious capitalists has a long tradition in Europe and has now become quite common in Egypt. But it would be incorrect to argue that Egyptians have simply imported European anti-Semitic stereotypes. Many Jews did occupy a privileged position between European capital and Egypt, and it is necessary to consider carefully its development over time to understand it adequately. My response to these accounts of the Jewish role in the Egyptian economy allows me to suggest some general ideas about how to theorize the concept of imperialism and the role of *mutamassir* (resident ethnic minority) entrepreneurs in Egypt, including Jews, in light of recent research.

CAN JEWS BE EGYPTIANS?

The title of Siham Nassar's study of the Egyptian Jewish press, *al-Yahud al-misriyyun bayna al-misriyya wa'l-sahyuniyya* (The Egyptian Jews between Egyptianism and Zionism), succinctly poses the fundamental issue in most post-1979 Egyptian works on Egyptian Jewish history: Are Egyptian Jews *real* Egyptians? The intensification of the Arab-Israeli conflict after 1948 gradually diminished the numbers of Arab and Egyptian intellectuals and publicists willing to insist on differentiating between local Jewish communities and Zionism and the state of Israel. As noted in Chapter 4, the Egyptian government officially continued to maintain this distinction during the prosecution of the Operation Susannah network in 1954 and beyond, though during and after the 1956 war its practical significance diminished considerably. By minimizing the distinction between Jews and Zionists, Nassar effectively reverses the official position of the Egyptian government and the dominant political currents of the country in the first half of the twentieth century. According to Nassar, while Jews enjoyed all the civic rights guaranteed by the 1923 constitution, "most of the Jews, who found in Egypt every consideration, supported Zionism."[5]

'Awatif 'Abd al-Rahman's *al-Sahafa al-sahyuniyya fi misr, 1897–1954* (The Zionist press in Egypt) was issued by a publishing house associated with the Communist Party of Egypt. She uses many of the same primary sources as Siham Nassar and seems to have relied extensively on Nassar's unpublished M.A. thesis, which was readily available to her because 'Abd al-Rahman is on the faculty at Cairo University's College of Communications, where Nassar received her degree. 'Abd al-Rahman introduces some distinctively Marxist themes into the argument: Zionism flourished in Egypt as a consequence of a specific economic and social formation imposed by imperialism. Poorer Jews were more closely linked to Egyptian society and culture. The communists, including the Jewish Anti-Zionist League established by members of the Iskra organization, were sincere anti-Zionists.[6] These themes lead 'Abd al-Rahman to a less categorical condemnation of Egyptian Jews than Nassar. Nonetheless, the two books follow the same basic line of exposition, and 'Abd al-Rahman is complicit in delegitimizing Jews as Egyptians even though Marxist theory regarded Jews throughout the Arab world as properly citizens of their country of birth, just as in Europe and elsewhere.

The main source for the research of both Nassar and 'Abd al-Rahman is the Egyptian Jewish press in Arabic. This provides a substantial documentary basis for their work. But it also gives them great leeway to interpret texts without reference to their social context. They have little appreciation for nuances of opinion within the Jewish community, and their analysis is always open to attributing the worst of motives to Jews.

For example, Nassar acknowledges that encouraging the Egyptianization and Arabization of the Jewish community was one of the most important goals of the Arabic Jewish weekly, *al-Shams,* established in 1934. But she unreasonably complains that this did not extend to intermarriage with Muslims and Christians or cultural assimilation. Unsupported by any evidence, Nassar speculates that the Egyptianization campaign of *al-Shams* might have been an "application of a higher Zionist policy designed by the Jewish Agency." It was not a result of the editors' "belief that the Jews were a part of Egyptian society," but rather from their "belief in the necessity of being loyal to and being part of that society."[7] Like Nassar, 'Abd al-Rahman regards *al-Shams* simply as a Zionist publication.

The editor of *al-Shams,* Sa'd Malki, embraced both Egyptian nationalism and moderate Zionism, as many Egyptian Jews did in the 1920s. Malki's distinction was to maintain these dual commitments until May 1948, when *al-Shams* was closed by the government.[8] His outlook was internally inconsistent and ultimately untenable, but that does not necessarily make it insincere. Malki's emphasis on the Egyptian and Eastern character of Egyptian Jews was not particularly welcome in the Zionist movement and is unlikely to have been inspired by any official Zionist body. Rather, his contradictory political commitments express the hybrid identities and loyalties shared by many Egyptian Jews.

Similarly, based on *al-Kalim's* publication of a letter from an individual Karaite expressing his concern that there were not enough Karaites in Jerusalem to maintain their synagogue and proposing that young Karaites consider moving there to fulfill this religious duty, Nassar accused the Karaite newspaper of encouraging "the immigration of Egyptian Jews to Palestine."[9] Having established that the Karaites were Zionists on the basis of this evidence, she regards *al-Kalim's* criticism of the establishment of the state of Israel and its repeated assertions that the Karaites were integrated among the Egyptian people as a ruse.[10]

'Abd al-Rahman does not appear to regard *al-Kalim* as a Zionist organ because she does not discuss it at all. By failing to mention *al-Kalim,* she avoids a topic that would have allowed her to demonstrate the existence of a community of Arabized Jews who considered themselves Egyptians, participated in Arabo-Egyptian culture, and were not, as a community, political Zionists.

Both Nassar and 'Abd al Rahman acknowledge that Albert Mizrahi, the publisher of *al-Tas'ira, al-Misbah,* and *al-Saraha* (see Chapter 3 and also the discussion of Maurice Shammas's "Cafe Lanciano" in Chapter 8), was not a Zionist.[11] Nassar undermines Mizrahi's political stand by arguing that he was motivated solely by financial gain and promoted his newspapers by extortion and incitement. 'Abd al-Rahman is willing to regard Mizrahi's political stand as sincere. Nonetheless, like Nassar, she concludes that the Zionist press successfully recruited "the great majority of Egyptian Jews to serve its propaganda objectives."[12]

Both Nassar and 'Abd al-Rahman espouse an organicist conception of Egyptian national identity that allows religious and ethnic minorities little space for any expression of collective identity. This same conception has motivated recent expressions of hostility to defining Copts and Nubians as minorities in Egypt. Nonetheless, they regard Egyptian national sentiment as extremely fragile and easily undermined by the Zionist ideas promoted in the Jewish press. Thus, some of the leading political thinkers and authors of the twentieth century, such as Ahmad Lutfi al-Sayyid, Ahmad Shawqi, Muhammad Husayn Haykal, and Taha Husayn, were easily duped into collaborating with Zionism (a prominent example mentioned by Nassar and 'Abd al-Rahman is Taha Husayn's service as editor of *al-Katib al-Misri*, a literary journal owned by the Harari brothers).

Other recent modern histories of Egyptian Jews by 'Arfa 'Abduh 'Ali and Sa'ida Muhammad Husni follow Siham Nassar's and 'Awatif 'Abd al-Rahman's conception of the Jews as foreigners who overwhelmingly embraced Zionism.[13] Nabil 'Abd al-Hamid Sayyid Ahmad, a professor at Minya University who is not a propagandist for radical Islamist views, extends this perspective to its extreme limit by expressing a certain sympathy for the view of the Muslim Brothers, who rejected the proposition that one could and should distinguish between the Jews of Egypt and the Jews of Palestine (and later Israel).[14] Ultimately, he argues, "reality proved that it is difficult to distinguish between a Zionist Jew and one who is not."[15] Ahmad thus effectively obliterates the distinction between Jews and Zionists.

One of the few published opinions in the 1980s to insist on the importance of upholding this distinction is Shihata Harun's *Yahudi fi al-qahira* (A Jew in Cairo). Harun joined the Democratic Movement for National Liberation led by Henri Curiel in the 1940s and ultimately became a member of the Communist Party of Egypt. He is one of the handful of Jewish communists who continued to live in Egypt after the 1950s. His book is a collection of letters, interviews, and essays written from 1967 to 1985 in which he defines himself as an Egyptian Jew, an anti-Zionist, an Egyptian nationalist, a supporter of the national rights of the Palestinian people, and an opponent of the Camp David process. In a 1975 interview in *Ruz al-Yusuf,* Harun stated, "I am a Jew, yes, and a leftist, yes. But the most important characteristic is that I am an Egyptian. As far as I know, being an Egyptian is not conditional on changing either my religion or my political beliefs."[16]

The interviewer, Salah Hafiz, was a former communist who was prepared to offer Harun a forum for this argument. But many of Harun's
comrades were less bold. The name of the Marxist publishing house that
issued *Yahudi fi al-qahira* was slightly altered on the title page of the
book (Dar al-Thaqafa al-Haditha instead of Dar al-Thaqafa al-Jadida),
suggesting that the directors of the press were ambivalent about Harun's
position and unwilling to take full public responsibility for it even though
it was entirely consistent with orthodox Marxist doctrine.

During the 1970s and 1980s, Harun often expressed his views to the
Arab and international press and at international conferences. Nonetheless, he was arrested with all the other able-bodied Jewish males during
the 1967 war; and he was arrested as a communist in 1975 and again in
1979. Neither the government of Gamal Abdel Nasser nor that of Anwar al-Sadat was willing to accept the sincerity of his anti-Zionist and
Egyptian nationalist commitments or his Marxist convictions. By the
mid-1980s, very few Egyptians (mainly some of those who had been
strongly influenced by Marxism for a period of their lives) were willing
to insist publicly on making a principled political distinction between
Jews and Zionists.

JEWISH CAPITALISM IN EGYPT

One of the great apprehensions among Egyptian nationalist opponents
of peace with Israel was that normalizing economic relations would permit Israel's technologically more advanced and more highly capitalized
economy to undermine Egypt's national economy. Israel would then be
able to dominate Egypt economically, as they believed foreign capital
had done in the era of British supremacy. These concerns were enhanced
by the already visible negative effects of President Anwar al-Sadat's open
door economic policy introduced in 1974 and by his extravagant public statements about Egyptian-Israeli relations, such as his proposal to
divert part of the Nile River waters to irrigate the Israeli Negev. Al-
Sadat's policy of pursuing peace with Israel was linked to his drive to rein-
tegrate Egypt into the world capitalist market, so those who opposed his
economic policies tended to oppose his diplomatic reorientation toward
the West and toward peace with Israel and attempted to show the connection between the two.

One of the early and prominent expressions of this sentiment was a
series of articles by Anis Mustafa Kamil on the history of "Jewish capitalism in Egypt." These articles provided those who opposed al-Sadat's

economic and diplomatic policies with a historical argument characterizing the Egyptian Jewish business elite as compradors who made their
fortunes by collaborating with the economic domination of Egypt by European capital. They appeared in the respected *al-Ahram al-Iqtisadi*
(Ahram economist), a serious weekly representing the left wing of establishment opinion.[17] Despite Kamil's assertion that the object of his
study is "Jewish capitalism" and not the Jewish faith, he promotes a conspiratorial view that resonates with anti-Semitic stereotypes of Jewish financial power.

   Kamil's analysis is based on the assertion that "the Jewish groups that
undertook a capitalist role in Egyptian history were predominantly non-
Egyptian in origin"—a factor he regards as constant throughout the
Pharaonic, Ptolemaic, Fatimid, Ottoman, and modern eras.[18] In addition to this ahistorical conception of Jewish economic history, Kamil relies on absolutist economic and cultural categories. Thus, he classifies
any firm with significant Jewish participation as "Jewish," exaggerating
the influence of Jewish investors and corporate managers (which was
certainly substantial) and permitting their representation as a monolithic
bloc of Jewish capital that can easily be distinguished from other blocs
of capital and from the authentic Egyptian national economy, to which
it is alien.

   For Kamil, both Jews and capitalism are inherently external and antagonistic to the organic and authentic Egyptian political and economic
community, whose parameters he never specifies. His desire to identify
Jews with a capitalist ethos foreign to Egypt leads to some ludicrous mis-
understandings—for example, the notion that Karaite Jews originating in
North Africa were more entrepreneurial than the Rabbanite majority because they embraced a Weberian Protestant spirit.[19] Although some
Karaites did emigrate to Egypt from Tunisia in the nineteenth century, most
had resided in Egypt for many centuries, and they tended to be the most
culturally and economically assimilated Jews. For Kamil, the otherness
of the Jews explains the comprador character of their economic activity,
its nefarious effects on Egypt's national economy, and Jewish collaboration with French and British imperialism and Zionism in the nineteenth
and twentieth centuries. Thus, he concludes, "It is impossible to speak of
Jewish capitalism except as a branch of imperialist capitalism."[20]

   Nabil 'Abd al-Hamid Sayyid Ahmad develops Kamil's line of argument in three books, two of which are devoted exclusively to the recent
history of Egyptian Jews.[21] Ahmad received his doctorate from the
premier institution for the study of the modern history of Egypt, 'Ayn

Shams University, and he is a professor of modern and contemporary history at Minya University. His books are based on extensive research in the files of the Department of Corporations (Maslahat al-Sharikat) and other archival materials. The most recent of his three volumes includes a preface endorsed by the prestigious Center for the Documentation and History of Contemporary Egypt.[22] Both his first and third books were published by the state-owned General Egyptian Book Organization. Because Nabil 'Abd al-Hamid Sayyid Ahmad's scholarly formation and career profile are linked to major Egyptian institutions, his research method and intellectual outlook have great credibility.

Like most Egyptians who have written on Egyptian Jewish history, Ahmad reminds us that Jews enjoyed excellent economic conditions in Egypt and were subject to no discrimination or disability until 1948.[23] He joins 'Ali Shalash in refuting Ada Aharoni's contention that it was impossible for Jews to obtain Egyptian citizenship except through bribery (see Chapter 8). Why then didn't the wealthy family of Inbal Mosseri use their money to obtain citizenship, he asks.[24] This is a weak argument that hardly seems to engage the debate. It suggests that by 1991, when Ahmad's study of the economic and social life of the Jews in Egypt from 1947 to 1956 appeared, Jews had come to be considered so alien to Egypt that it was not necessary to offer significant evidence to demonstrate the point. Nonetheless, I offer this brief response.

Until the capitulations were cancelled by the 1937 Montreux Convention, there were few advantages to becoming an Egyptian citizen. This was a new political category that came into existence only in 1922, and those who had a choice were not eager to abandon foreign citizenship for it. A prominent minority of the Jewish business elite (like the Qattawis and the Cicurels) were Egyptian citizens, but most were not. Chief Rabbi Haim Nahum repeatedly urged Jews to become Egyptian citizens. However, by the late 1930s, when the advantages of Egyptian citizenship had become clear, the application of the 1929 citizenship law made it more difficult for Jews to claim Egyptian citizenship. Poor and middle-class autochthonous Jews found it difficult to prove that their families had resided continuously in Egypt since 1848, as the law required. They constituted the main group of Jews who were entitled to Egyptian citizenship, and they were often refused or subjected to lengthy bureaucratic delays when they officially applied for it.[25]

Like Kamil, Ahmad defines Jews by their business acumen and cultural otherness. For example, he attributes the success of the Tractor and

Engineering Company, in which the major investors were the Mosseri, Curiel, and Qattawi families, to "masterful Jewish thinking and proper planning."[26] This firm organized dances in its social club, which Ahmad notes led some to accuse the Jews, along with a minority of the non-Jewish elite, of responsibility for introducing customs inconsistent with the conservative nature of Egyptian society. Ahmad's account of this successful firm concludes with a reminder of the role of Egyptian Jews in the establishment of Israel and the dispossession of the Palestinians, though he offers no evidence of pro-Zionist activity or sympathy on the part of the Jewish directors of the firm, and the anti-Zionism of some of them is well known.[27] Like Kamil, Ahmad links Jewish capital with Zionism by his claim, unsupported by any evidence, that Jewish profits left Egypt "in intricate ways so that most of them contributed to building the state of Israel and thus harmed the national economy, security, and safety of Egypt."[28]

Anis Mustafa Kamil and Nabil 'Abd al-Hamid Sayyid Ahmad share the organicist and essentialist conception of Egyptian national identity advanced by Siham Nassar and 'Awatif 'Abd al-Rahman and recast it in a materialist form through their economic histories. The vehicle for accomplishing this is an idealized model of national economic development based on the notion that proper capitalist development can occur only under the aegis of a patriotic "national bourgeoisie." This category was originally developed by Marxists to designate the class that would carry out a bourgeois-democratic revolution against persisting feudal forms of land tenure and politics in Asia, Africa, and Latin America. Kamil, Ahmad, and historians of the Egyptian nationalist school—Marxists, Nasserists, and others—have argued that until 1952 Egypt was governed by an alliance of large landowners and foreign capital that opposed the development of a strong industrial economy in Egypt. Consequently, a national bourgeoisie would have to emerge to undertake this project and struggle to overcome foreign capital's domination of the country. Tal'at Harb and the founders of Bank Misr are usually designated as the leading aspirants for this role. Their failure to build an autochthonous, industrialized national economy before 1952 is explained as the result of the continued influence of foreign or *mutamassir* capital, including Jewish capital, or defects in the composition of the Egyptian bourgeoisie. Capitalism is therefore necessarily a structurally flawed, incomplete, and perhaps inherently alien project because Egypt's capitalist class was overwhelmingly composed of foreigners, compradors, and *mutamassir* minorities linked to European capital.

This representation and the absolute opposition it posits between compradors and foreigners, on the one hand, and a patriotic national bourgeoisie, on the other, undermine the Egyptian identity of Egyptian Jews by identifying the entire community with its most cosmopolitan elements, who are, moreover, conceived of as being engaged in activities inimical to the national economy. Although advanced by nationalist Egyptians, it is entirely compatible with a militant Zionist outlook, which is equally committed to asserting that Jews were always aliens in Egypt. Both nationalist historiographies rely on ahistorical and essentialist conceptions of the nation and its others. In what follows, I offer an alternative approach to conceptualizing the operations of imperialism and its local allies, including the Jewish business elite, in Egypt.

COLONIAL CAPITALISM

Although almost all Egyptian Jews were desperately poor in the nineteenth century, a small minority had access to and was experienced in the management of liquid capital. Jews migrating to Cairo and Alexandria from Salonika, Izmir, Aleppo, or other late Ottoman cities used their family connections throughout the Mediterranean basin as a business asset in setting up circuits of commerce and credit. The commercial skills of Jews were the result of the limits and opportunities created by their history as a diasporic people. Hence, capital was both an economic category and a marker of cultural difference. There is no doubt that the Jews' use of French in their community schools, their openness to European culture, the prominence of their business classes, and the high proportion of foreign citizens among them distinguished them from most Muslim Egyptians.

Many members of the Jewish community enjoyed an array of legal, fiscal, and social colonial privileges in Egypt. No adequate account of the community can fail to acknowledge this. But the operations of foreign capital in Egypt were more complex than the Egyptian nationalist version allows. Moreover, many Jews, like Muslim and Coptic elites, did not feel that their privileges made them any less Egyptian. The most prominent members of the Jewish bourgeoisie were also among the most vocal anti-Zionists in the community. Generally speaking, the popular base for Zionism was in the Europeanized lower-middle-class elements of the community, who attended the Jewish community schools, not the upper-middle-class and business elite, who were usually educated in secular and even clerical French schools.

As ʿAsim Disuqi and Eric Davis have convincingly argued, it makes little sense to conceive of the large landholders of Egypt in the nineteenth and twentieth centuries as feudalists.[29] Cotton cultivation was an integral part of the capitalist world economy. It was based on private ownership of the means of production, production of commodities for a market, commodification of labor, rational calculation of profits, a tendency toward capital accumulation, and the emergence of bureaucratically administered, large-scale enterprises. Large cotton growers sought to maximize their profits, though this was not incompatible with maintaining elements of precapitalist social relations in the countryside. Many of the first Muslim and Coptic industrialists, including the majority of the initial investors in Bank Misr, emerged from the ranks of the large cotton growers. There was never a fundamental clash of interests between the large cotton growers and industrialists. Therefore, I concur with Anouar Abdel Malek and Roger Owen in characterizing the social formation of Egypt from the mid-nineteenth century until 1956 as "colonial capitalism."[30]

Colonial capitalism was not a static social formation. Technological developments in agriculture and urban migration altered crop patterns, market relations, and the social character of village communities. The depression of the 1930s stimulated consolidation of a new economic vision and increased opportunities for import-substitution industrialization. The depression also impelled British imperial proconsuls and business managers to negotiate new political and economic arrangements with colonial politicians and businessmen. The abolition of the capitulations in 1937 encouraged Egyptian business elites to aspire to a larger share of power relative to foreign capital. Their intimate ties to the newly reorganized state facilitated, to a considerable degree, realization of these aspirations. By the 1940s, a clear tendency toward Egyptianization of capital and the skilled labor force was evident. Nonetheless, with the exception of the cotton manufacturing and export sectors, Muslims and Copts were significantly underrepresented at the commanding heights of the economy, especially the financial sector.

Was the Misr group an incipient national bourgeoisie? Reading Eric Davis's study of Talʿat Harb and Bank Misr against the grain to emphasize Davis's own point that "Harb and his colleagues probably never thought" of themselves as seeking "to challenge fundamentally foreign capital's domination of the Egyptian economy," Robert Vitalis argues that the Misr group sought collaboration with foreign capital and did not seek autocentric capitalist development.[31] In 1924, Talʿat Harb joined the board of the Crédit Foncier Egyptien, one of the most powerful foreign-controlled financial institutions in Egypt. The next year he joined the board of the Egyptian Federation of Industry, the bastion of foreign and *mutamassir* capital. In 1927, foreigners were admitted as directors of four new enterprises established by Bank Misr. In 1929, Bank Misr and German cotton magnate Hugo Lindemann jointly established the Misr Cotton Export Company—Misr's first collaboration with a foreign firm and one of its most profitable enterprises. An even more conspicuous departure from Misr's nationalist image was the negotiation of several joint ventures with British firms in the 1930s: Misr Air and Air Work Ltd. in 1931, Misr Insurance Company and C. T. Bowring and Company of Lloyd's in 1933, and Misr Travel and Cox and Kings Ltd. in 1935. The most substantial Misr-British joint venture established two new textile mills—Misr Fine Spinning and Weaving Company and Misr Bayda Dyers Company—at Kafr al-Dawwar in 1938.[32] Bradford Dyers, a large but declining firm, sought an Egyptian partner to avoid the tariff on imported cotton goods enacted in 1930, and Misr was anxious to offset the advantage of La Filature Nationale, its largest local rival in the textile sector, which had established a joint venture with another British firm, Calico Printers, in 1934.[33] All these joint ventures were undertaken while Tal'at Harb was still the director of BankMisr, and they did not diminish the bank's nationalist image or Harb's nationalist rhetoric.

Vitalis builds on Robert Tignor's work, which argues that foreign capital made positive contributions to industrial development in Egypt.[34] Tignor is primarily concerned with providing an empirical refutation of dependency theory, which he does quite effectively. But his focus on that objective leads him to avoid asking whether any forms of foreign investment were exploitative, based on colonial privilege, or hindered the development of the Egyptian economy. Consequently, his approach tends to eliminate the category of imperialism altogether. Vitalis usefully emphasizes the distinction between investors with an international horizon who had no particular interest in or commitment to Egypt per se, such as Sir Ernest Cassel, a business partner of the brother of Lord Cromer, the British viceroy in Egypt from 1883 to 1907, and investors, regardless of their citizenship, culture, or religion, who lived in Egypt, saw Egypt as their field of activity, and whose business success depended primarily on its future.[35]

This latter group developed into a local bourgeoisie with interests distinct from those of metropolitan capital, though not necessarily in fundamental contradiction to it. This local bourgeoisie had close links to

both Egyptian large landowners and foreign capital; it was not particularly democratic; and it often opposed the leading nationalist party, the
Wafd, which cultivated a populist image. Nonetheless, one of the leading representatives of this local bourgeoisie, Ahmad ʿAbbud, was a major financial backer of the Wafd until Mustafa al-Nahhas became party
leader in 1927 and again in 1950–52. ʿAbbud and others who came to
be designated as compradors during the high tide of Nasserist Arab socialism in the 1960s, including the Jewish business elite, were key figures
in the development of industrial capitalism and transferring the ownership of firms originally established with foreign capital into the hands of
Egyptians—Muslims, Copts, and resident minorities.

There is nothing unusual about the absence of a national bourgeoisie
seeking autochthonous industrial development in Egypt. In Chile and
Brazil, for example, industrial development was the result of a similar
mix of landed and industrial interests, local and foreign capital, and the
state.[36] Working from African cases, Gavin Kitching argues that late
capitalist development strategies "never involve the total exclusion of
foreign capital" and that "genuinely transformatory capitalist development . . . *may be possible without the need of a national bourgeoisie*,"
though it may occur "under the hegemony of international capital and
in alliance with dominant sections of a local ruling class (an alliance not
without its contradictions and tensions)."[37] As in many former colonial
and semicolonial countries, economic development in Egypt was neither
a function of nationalist political rhetoric nor directed toward serving
the interests of the subaltern strata.

There are few examples of a bourgeoisie taking private risks in the interests of the nation in the formerly colonized and semicolonized world.
This is not because this class is somehow defective, but because late developing capitalism has little choice but to rely on state intervention in
the economy and to collaborate with the existing structures of the international market in which it can have only a subordinate position.
Moreover, the propensity of entrepreneurs to seek private gain rather
than national development is not peculiar to non-Europeans. As Immanuel Wallerstein has argued, the image of a risk-taking, individualis-
tic bourgeoisie is a reification. Investors have always preferred rent over
profit and sought to appropriate public resources for their private gain
when they had the political influence to do so.[38]

This conception does not make the bourgeoisie—Jewish or otherwise—the unqualified hero of Egyptian industrial development. Karl
Marx proposed that the historical development of capitalism should be

understood as a simultaneous process of construction and destruction, and Fredric Jameson reminds us that "the lapse from this austere dialectical imperative into the more comfortable stance of taking moral positions is inveterate and all too human."[39] Capitalist development in Egypt has increased productivity, promoted a limited industrialization, expanded the ranks of the urban wage-labor force, and improved the standards of living of many workers and their families. At the same time, the Egyptian economy has remained in a subordinate position in the international economy, maintained a highly unequal division of the national income, and failed to provide adequately for the needs of a majority of the population. Nationalist approaches to the economic history of the Jewish community seek to explain the exploitation, human pain, and highly uneven results of the development of capitalism in Egypt as something unnatural or unusual, attributable to the economic or ethnic deficiencies of Egypt's capitalists. It is much less satisfying, and at the end of the twentieth century perhaps also less hopeful, to argue that this is in the nature of capitalism. As an illustration of the operation and developments of colonial capitalism in Egypt, I offer the following brief business history of the La Société Générale des Sucreries et de la Raffinerie d'Egypte (Egyptian Sugar Company), a firm in which the Jewish business group composed of the Suarès-Qattawi-Rolo-Menasce families was the leading local actor.

THE EGYPTIAN SUGAR COMPANY

The Suarèses, Spanish Jews with Italian citizenship who arrived in Egypt via Italy in the early nineteenth century, were among the wealthiest Egyptian Jewish families in the late nineteenth and early twentieth centuries.[40] Building on the ruins of the state-owned sugar company established by Khedive Isma'il to diversify Egypt's agroindustrial sector, Raphael Suarès (1846–1902) and two other resident foreigners built a new sugar refinery in 1881 at Hawamdiyya, about twenty-five kilometers south of Cairo.[41] In 1893, the Suarès family bank contributed two-thirds of the capital to a new sugar partnership with the French Raffinerie C. Say to form the Sucrerie Raffinerie d'Egypte. In 1897, this enterprise merged with La Société Générale des Sucreries de la Haute Egypte to form La Société Générale des Sucreries et de la Raffinerie d'Egypte. In 1902, the Egyptian Sugar Company bought nine cane crushing mills in upper Egypt from the firm originally established by Khedive Isma'il, now the Daira Saniyeh Sugar Company owned by an Anglo-

Egyptian group led by the German-English investor Sir Ernest Cassel. Consequently, the Egyptian Sugar Company became heavily indebted to Cassel, and he secured a role in its management. This enterprise soon established a near monopoly over Egyptian sugar production.

Rapid expansion and the heavy debt to the Cassel group led to the firm's bankruptcy in 1905. The company was reorganized, and a new management team was installed, led by a Belgian, Henri Naus, and Sir Victor Harari Pasha, a Jew born in Lebanon, a British citizen, and a former high official in the Egyptian Ministry of Finance. Harari served as Ernest Cassel's local agent. Naus managed the Egyptian Sugar Company until his death in 1938.

In addition to their major investment in the Egyptian Sugar Company, the Suarès-Qattawi-Rolo-Menasce business group, in collaboration with French interests and Ernest Cassel, held an extensive complex of interests in agricultural land, irrigation, financing, and sugar production in upper Egypt centered on the sugar producing region of Kom Ombo. Thus, at the beginning of the twentieth century, the sugar industry was a colonial economic enterprise with origins connected to lands acquired by foreigners as a result of Egypt's foreign debt and bankruptcy in 1876. The Suarès family was the link between European capital and Egypt's agricultural resources. Even in this period it would be incorrect to see the Suarèses as blind tools of European interests. Though they were certainly local allies of European capital, the Suarèses operated only in Egypt, unlike Ernest Cassel or the French Say interests, who had worldwide ambitions. By World War I, the Qattawis eclipsed the Suarèses in economic and political influence, becoming the most prominent Jewish family in Egypt and the major local investors in the Egyptian Sugar Company. After several decades, the character of the ownership and management of the company changed significantly. The new relations among foreign capital, resident Jewish capital, and Egyptian Muslim capital in the Egyptian Sugar Company from the late 1930s to the mid-1950s are comparable to developments in other firms during this period.

In the late 1930s, the French shareholders, who had always exercised loose control over the firm, became even less significant in its management.[42] When Henri Naus died, the French Embassy in Egypt tried to encourage the French shareholders, who then held 30 percent of the Egyptian Sugar Company's stock, to exert their power in determining the direction of the firm. But they could not do so. Effective control had shifted into the hands of Belgians (Henri Naus), Egyptian Jews (Qattawi and Harari), and Egyptian Greeks (a group led by the Cozzika family).

In 1942, after a brief period of Cozzika preeminence, Ahmad 'Abbud Pasha was elected to the board of directors and became managing director of the Egyptian Sugar Company. In 1948, his takeover of the firm was completed by his election as chairman of the board. During the 1940s, two Jews—René Qattawi Bey and Col. Ralph A. Harari, the son of Victor Harari,—sat on the board with 'Abbud Pasha and several other prominent Muslim Egyptians—Sharif Sabri Pasha, Husayn Sirri Pasha, Muhammad Mahmud Khalil Bey, 'Abd al-Hamid Badawi Pasha, Hasan Mazlum Pasha, and Sir Mahmud Shakir Muhammad Pasha. The only representative of the French interests that began the firm with the Suarès family was Baron Louis de Benoist, who was also the agent-supérieur of the Suez Canal Company resident in Egypt. Thus, in 1948, the board was composed of eight Egyptian citizens, of whom one was Jewish (Qattawi), and two foreign nationals, of whom one was Jewish (Harari).

'Abbud Pasha began Egyptianizing the staff when he took over the management of the sugar company. By 1947, the firm had 954 administrative and technical employees, of whom 725 (76 percent) were Egyptian and 38 were *mutamassirun*. Another 34 claimed to be Egyptian but had no documentary proof.[43] Less than 30 (0.3 percent) of the 9,000 laborers were foreigners in 1947, but they were more skilled (or at least management considered them to be so), better paid, and received better benefits than the Egyptians. These figures exceeded the minimum quotas for employment of Egyptians established by the 1947 Company Law, and no changes were required to comply with this legislation. At the top echelon of the firm, ten of thirteen members of the Managerial Committee were still foreigners in 1947. But by 1952, ten of fourteen members were Egyptians. This change probably resulted as much from 'Abbud's desire to assert control through his own appointees as from pressure to Egyptianize. After 1947, the number of Egyptian employees and laborers in all capacities rose gradually.

The composition of the firm's capital also changed in the 1940s and 1950s. By 1955, only 26 percent of the shares of the Egyptian Sugar Company were held in France.[44] The Qattawi family continued to maintain a substantial interest in the firm. The remnants of the Jewish Suarès-Qattawi-Rolo-Menasce interests, who had originally served as intermediaries for colonial-style direct foreign investment by Sir Ernest Cassel and the French Say firm, had become willing collaborators with Ahmad 'Abbud, Egypt's most dynamic and successful Muslim entrepreneur.

Despite what appeared to be the successful Egyptianization of the firm, on August 24, 1955, the Egyptian Sugar Company was placed in

the custody of the Ministry of Finance because of a dispute between ʿAbbud and the new regime over taxes and prices (a protective tariff had
guaranteed the company's profits and market share since 1931). The government sequestered the firm and in 1956 liquidated it. After the
Suez/Sinai War, it became a state-owned enterprise. The Egyptian Sugar
Company was nationalized not because the government was concerned
about foreign economic domination, but because ʿAbbud, an autocratic
and imperious personality, would not bow to the government's economic
policy demands. The Qattawis were forced to abandon their interest in
the Egyptian Sugar Company when they left Egypt after the 1956 war,
but their role in the firm had little to do with why it became one of the
first firms of Egypt's public sector.

   None of these shifts in the ethnic composition of the shareholders,
management, and work force is noted by Anis Mustafa Kamil, Nabil
ʿAbd al-Hamid Sayyid Ahmad, or ʿArfa ʿAbduh ʿAli in their discussions
of the Egyptian Sugar Company.[45] All of them regard the firm simply as
a foreign/Jewish colonial enterprise. Their accounts suggest that the
firm's character was forever determined by its beginnings, resulting in
ahistorical accounts of the sugar company (and many other firms they
discuss as well) in which the normal activity of capitalist competition
and the rise and fall of rival groups of investors are absent from the analysis. This permits them to represent "Jewish capitalism" or the "Jewish
bourgeoisie" as a monolithic bloc. All of them, in various ways, accuse
the Jewish business elite of Zionist sympathies.

   In the case of the sugar company, Kamil notes that the firm "continued until 1948 to be the basic source of sugar for the Zionists of Tel
Aviv."[46] This sounds very incriminating for an audience that may not
know that there were many commercial ties between Egypt and Palestine
until 1948 and that exporting sugar to Palestine (some of which was undoubtedly consumed by the Arab majority of the population) was both
legal and beneficial for Egypt's balance of foreign trade. Moreover, the
Qattawis, the leading Jewish family in the firm, were the most outspo-
ken anti-Zionists in the Jewish community (except perhaps the communists). Their motive for exporting sugar to Palestine—most likely, simply
the opportunity for profit—was certainly not sympathy with Zionism.

WAS THERE A JEWISH BOURGEOISIE?

Can a conception of a unified bloc of Jewish capital with Zionist political sympathies exercising a dominant role in the Egyptian economy

TABLE I

JEWISH DIRECTORS OF EGYPTIAN JOINT
STOCK COMPANIES

	Directors		Directorships	
Year	Total	Jews	Total	Jews
1943	728	112 (15.4%)	1,626	262 (16%)
1947–48	1,103	140 (12.7%)	2,411	305 (12.6%)
1951	1,248	111 (8.9%)	2,749	264 (9.6%)
1960	1,399	7 (0.5%)	1,886	8 (0.4%)
1961–62	950			

SOURCE: Thomas Philipp, *The Syrians in Egypt, 1725–1975* (Stuttgart: Franz Steiner Verlag, 1985), p. 137, based on computations from *The Stock Exchange Year-Book of Egypt.* (The 1951 date may refer to the volume for 1950–51 or 1951–52; these are the title dates for those years.)

before 1948 be sustained by historical evidence? Statistics compiled by Thomas Philipp (see Table I) indicate that in the 1940s, when Jews made up less than 0.5 percent of the Egyptian population, they occupied between 12.6 and 16 percent of all the directorships of Egyptian joint stock companies. Although this is a highly disproportionate overrepresentation, Philipp's figures demonstrate that Jews were a small and declining minority of the entire business elite even before the first Arab-Israeli war.

Although some Jewish directors left Egypt as a result of that war, a significant number remained in the country and continued to manage their businesses in the early 1950s, an expression of their lack of Zionist commitment, their desire to continue to make profits in Egypt, and their hope that their lives could be restored to normalcy. A broader measure of the weight of prominent and wealthy Jews in Egyptian society in the early 1950s can be obtained from the listing of names in *Le Mondain égyptien: L'Annuaire de l'élite d'Egypte (The Egyptian Who's Who).* In the 1954 edition, there were 715 Jewish names out of a total of 4,632 entries.[47] By this indicator, Jews made up over 15.4 percent of the Egyptian elite in 1954.

Some Jewish families—Aghion, Menasce, Nahman, Pinto, Qattawi, Rolo, and Suarès—served as links between European capital and Egypt during the period of direct colonial rule, when many of the business relationships that shaped the modern economy were formed. After World War I, when Muslim Egyptians began to enter commerce and industry in larger numbers, many of these Jews eventually became willing collaborators with them and lent their experience and capital to the project of shifting control of what Tignor terms the "loosely administered firms" like the Egyptian Sugar Company and the Salt and Soda Company from Europe to Egypt.[48] Egyptian Jews were generally not involved at the highest levels in what Tignor calls "tightly controlled companies"—the Suez Canal Company, Anglo-Egyptian Oilfields Ltd. (Royal Dutch-Shell), and Barclays Bank.[49] These are the firms most clearly connected to British and French political and economic influence in Egypt. At the same time, other Jews, including very wealthy families like the Curiels and Cicurels, had a much narrower range of business contacts and operated their firms as family enterprises employing a high percentage of Jews and other minorities. Consequently, in terms of the categories of political economy, there was not a unified bloc of Jewish capital or a Jewish bourgeoisie with a common set of economic interests.

All businessmen in Egypt from 1880 to 1960—Jews as well as Muslims, Copts, Greeks, Italians, Armenians, Syrian Christians, and resident Europeans—adopted a similar investment strategy.[50] They collaborated with foreign capital; they relied on the state to secure their markets and ease their access to public resources; and they diversified their operations across several economic sectors. They participated in the construction of many new industrial enterprises and by the 1940s assumed a major share of control over many enterprises established with foreign capital. There were no significant differences between the economic strategies of the leading Jewish and Muslim elements of the Egyptian haute bourgeoisie; indeed, they were often partners in the same enterprises.

Anis Mustafa Kamil regards any collaboration of Jews with other Egyptians as an ominous indicator of Jewish intention to control the Egyptian economy. For example, describing the participation of Yusuf 'Aslan Qattawi and Yusuf Cicurel in the board of directors of Bank Misr, he concludes regretfully, "[T]he only Egyptian bank did not escape the Jewish presence which had consolidated its grip over the world of finance."[51] But Tal'at Harb's business alliances with Jews were not unique and certainly not evidence of a Jewish conspiracy to dominate Bank Misr. Qattawi and Cicurel considered themselves Egyptian patriots, and Harb collaborated with them on that basis.

The volumes of *The Stock Exchange Year-Book of Egypt* for the 1940s and 1950s document a thick network of prominent Muslims and Copts who collaborated with Jews in many joint stock companies in every sector of the economy. The names that appear most often in such partnerships are Hasan Mazlum Pasha, Tawfiq Duss Pasha, Muhammad Ahmad 'Abbud Pasha, Isma'il Sidqi Pasha, 'Abd al-Hamid Sulayman Pasha, Husayn Sirri Pasha, 'Ata 'Afifi Bey, Muhammad Ahmad Farghali

Pasha, ʿAli Amin Yahya Pasha, Muhammad Mahmud Khalil Bey, and Dr. Hafiz ʿAfifi Pasha. This list includes prominent politicians, cabinet members, prime ministers, and the leaders of every major business group in Egypt under the monarchy, including what was regarded as the citadel of economic nationalism, Bank Misr.

There is little evidence of competition along rigid ethnoreligious lines among members of this group, although, of course, the interests of individuals and particular business alliances coalesced or clashed according to circumstances, and ethnoreligious affiliation remained a prominent element of personal identity. Some of the Muslims in the group were quite close to their Jewish business allies. The president of the senate, Muhammad Mahmud Khalil Bey, was affectionately known by his friends as Mahmud Mosseri because of his close ties with the wealthy Jewish Mosseri family.[52] Isaac G. Levi was the secretary-general of the Egyptian Federation of Industries and editor of its journal, *Egypte Industrielle.* He and Ismaʿil Sidqi were the most energetic promoters of the federation's program to diversify the Egyptian economy through reliance on the local bourgeoisie, regardless of its citizenship.[53] Elie Politi, another Jewish publicist for bourgeois interests, immigrated to Egypt from Izmir as a young boy in 1906. He established a weekly commercial newspaper, *L'Informateur Financier et Commercial,* in 1929. Its first subscribers were Ismaʿil Sidqi and Amin Yahya.[54]

Uncommonly among the Jewish business elite, Politi was a Zionist. Nonetheless, he seems to have identified himself as an Egyptian and endeavored to promote Egyptian economic interests as he understood them. He tried to persuade the Belgian entrepreneur Baron Edouard Empain, one of the largest foreign investors in Egypt, to add Egyptians who had become major stockholders to the board of directors of his Cairo Electric Railways and Heliopolis Oasis Company. Empain refused Politi's "national considerations" in terms suggesting that, for Empain, Politi and his partners—Muslims, Copts, or resident minorities—were all Egyptians, unlike himself.[55] This is the same dismissive arrogance that motivated Uncle Cicurel's hatred of Europeans and desire to continue living in Africa in Ronit Matalon's novel, *Zeh ʿim ha-panim eleynu* (see Chapter 8). On these grounds, Politi could feel a community of interests with his Muslim and Coptic class peers despite his enjoyment of class and colonial privileges that distinguished him from the vast majority of Egyptians.

The Arab-Israeli conflict was an important factor in the collapse of the entire Egyptian Jewish community, but it alone is insufficient as an explanation for the fate of the Egyptian Jewish business elite. Other diasporic *mutamassir* communities—Greeks, Italians, Armenians, Syrian Christians—played a similar economic and cultural role as the Jews. Like the Jews, most members of these communities left Egypt after 1956, and the bourgeois elements lost their property. Moreover, many of the Muslim and Coptic collaborators with Jewish and other *mutamassir* investors, as well as those who bought out Jewish business interests at bargain prices after the 1956 war, were also expropriated in the 1960s as part of the Nasserist Arab socialist project. The government and its supporters justified these expropriations with the argument that these businessmen were compradors who had collaborated with foreign capital and imperialism. They had not undertaken the task presumed to be the charge of an entrepreneurial national bourgeoisie: to develop an advanced industrial economy independent of foreign capital. Rather, it was argued, their economic activities had contributed to continuing Egypt's domination by European capital. Developing the data and arguments presented by Robert Tignor and Robert Vitalis, I have proposed that the behavior of the haut bourgeois elements of the Jewish community was not a function of their real or imagined cultural attributes and certainly not of their Zionist sympathies. It was circumscribed by the possibilities of capitalism in Egypt.

CONTENTION AND DIALOGUE ACROSS THE BORDERS

Since 1979, Egyptian Jews residing in Israel, Europe, and North America have actively begun to revalorize their relationship with Egypt in both literary and historical texts. But to fully transcend the limits of nationalist discourse or nostalgia, this process requires an active dialogue with Egyptian interlocutors. The intransigent policies of Israel's governments toward the Arab world despite (some would argue enabled by) the 1979 Egyptian-Israeli peace treaty have not been conducive to such a dialogue. However, it must also be acknowledged that the anti-Semitic character of much of what the Egyptian intelligentsia has recently written about Jews has also obstructed dialogue. Most of what has been written about the modern history of the Jews of Egypt by Egyptian intellectuals since 1979 has been in the genre of "know your enemy," a phrase actually used by the editor of *al-Ahram al-Iqtisadi*, Lutfi ʿAbd al-ʿAzim, in his introduction to Anis Mustafa Kamil's series of articles.[56]

Because I did not want to appear to be joining the vocal chorus of Westerners who have been abusively critical of Egypt, Arabs, and Islam,

it was only after overcoming considerable reluctance that I resolved to
include a chapter on Egyptian representations of Egyptian Jews in this
book. When Anis Mustafa Kamil's articles on Jewish capitalism appeared in *al-Ahram al-Iqtisadi,* I was living in Cairo and researching the
history of the Egyptian labor movement. I sympathized with my Egyptian colleagues who opposed normalizing relations with Israel before a
just resolution of the Palestinian-Israeli conflict was achieved and shared
their concern about the inequities of the open door policy. I was also uncomfortable with Kamil's anti-Semitic tone. There seemed to be no constructive way to open a discussion of this issue, and so I avoided it, hoping that more open-minded Egyptian colleagues would take on the task
in their own time and manner.

In the same period, an astute and politically active Egyptian friend remarked to me that he foresaw a difficult future for people like us, who
supported peaceful resolution of the Arab-Israeli conflict based on recognition of the national rights of both Israel and the Palestinian Arabs, but
who opposed the particular terms of the Egyptian-Israeli peace treaty because it left the question of Palestine unresolved. He was uncomfortable
about opposing the treaty in a tacit alliance with pan-Arab nationalists
and radical Islamists who opposed *any* peace with Israel. He predicted
that these elements would resort to anti-Semitic portrayals of Israel and
Jews, attack the government with demagogic rhetoric, delegitimize the
concept of peace with Israel, and discredit progressive and internationalist perspectives in Egyptian politics and culture. Unfortunately, this
proved to be a prescient prediction.

Recent political currents and the canons of Egyptian nationalist historiography have therefore unwittingly converged with the main lines of
Zionist historiography in portraying Jews as an inherently alien community whose members sojourned in Egypt only until they could emigrate to Israel. Egyptians who still remember their personal experience
with Jews often know that this is an inadequate characterization. But despite the proliferation of books, articles, and even references to Jews in
films and television programs, there has been little significant public debate challenging the dominant representations of Egyptian Jews as exemplified by the texts I have examined here.

There are some faint signs that a direct dialogue has begun, though it
remains circumscribed by the still unresolved political tensions between
Israel and its Arab neighbors. I noted previously Nabil 'Abd al-Hamid
Sayyid Ahmad's weak effort to refute the claim of Ada Aharoni's *The*

Second Exodus that eligible Jews could not obtain Egyptian citizenship. 'Ali Shalash's extended rejoinder to Aharoni's novel has already been discussed in Chapter 8.

In a similar vein, Tawhid Magdi responded to Yoram Meital's guide to Jewish sites in Egypt, *Atarim yehudiyim be-mitzrayim*.[57] Meital's main audience is Israeli tourists who wish to visit places of Jewish interest in Egypt. He provides descriptions of synagogues, communal buildings, and cemeteries in Cairo, Alexandria, Ma'adi, Hilwan, and Damanhur, with brief historical sketches of those Jewish communities. The volume was produced with the assistance of several establishment Israeli institutions, including the Kaplan Chair for the History of Egypt and Israel at Tel Aviv University and the Israeli Academic Center in Cairo. The cover features an endorsement by Shimon Shamir, who has served as Israel's ambassador to both Egypt and Jordan in addition to his academic positions as holder of the Kaplan Chair and former director of the Dayan Center for Middle East Studies at Tel Aviv University. Consequently, Magdi sees Meital's guidebook as "a new maneuver against Egypt."[58] He is convinced that Meital has prepared a survey of Jewish property that will serve as the basis for establishing an Israeli claim to ownership of these sites.[59] Magdi is especially concerned that Meital includes a description of the Israeli Academic Center in Cairo, housed in a rented apartment located in a building owned by an Egyptian and over which Israel could have no rightful claim.[60] Meital's scholarship is actually quite critical of official Israeli policies toward Egypt. He has collaborated with the Institute for Peace Research at Giv'at Haviva directed by Ilan Pappé, one of the boldest of the Israeli "new historians." So he is very unlikely to advocate the objectives Magdi attributes to him. Moreover, Egyptian Jews living in Israel who have tried to convince the government to press their property claims against Egypt since the 1950s are convinced that it has no intention of doing so because this would open the door to Egyptian counterclaims (see Chapter 8).

Ruz al-Yusuf, the weekly that published Magdi's article, is no longer the serious and respectable political journal it was for many years. It now regularly features yellow sensationalism and rumor mongering. Thus, it would be easy to dismiss Magdi's response to Meital's book as merely another expression of anti-Semitism. But I would argue that one of the effects of publishing Magdi's profusely illustrated, lengthy article in a popular weekly is to remind readers that there was a substantial Jewish community in Egypt. And even if Magdi is alarmed by Meital's survey of its communal sites, he has responded to a Hebrew book written by an Israeli that would otherwise have received no notice in Egypt. Moreover, Meital was immediately aware of Magdi's review of his book. Though Shalash and Magdi both consider Israel and Jews as enemies, they nonetheless felt compelled to respond directly, however polemically, to representations of Egyptian Jewish life published by Israelis.

There is a small number of signs of more productive dialogue, though their significance should not be overestimated. Anis Mansur's memoir of Anwar al-Sadat's era serialized in *Uktubir* relates that when Israeli President Yitzhak Navon visited Egypt in 1980, he brought, as a personal present for al-Sadat, a copy of the story of Joseph from the Hebrew Bible as first translated into Arabic by an Egyptian rabbi, Sa'adya ben Yosef al-Fayyumi (882–942). The text was beautifully rendered in Farsi-style Arabic calligraphy by an Egyptian Jew then living in Bat Yam, Israel, described by Mansur as "the colleague Yusuf Wahba, who used to work as a calligrapher at *Akhbar al-Yawm*."[61] Yusuf Wahba had emigrated from Egypt after the 1956 war. He was thrilled that Anis Mansur remembered him from the days when they both worked at *Akhbar al-Yawm* and publicly acknowledged him as a "colleague" (*zamil*). Preferring to conduct our conversation in Arabic rather than Hebrew, Wahba fondly recalled his life in Egypt, proudly displayed examples of his Arabic calligraphy, and spoke warmly of the many Palestinian Arabs he had trained in the art before he retired.[62]

Samir W. Raafat has published a chronicle of Ma'adi, a suburb of Cairo built by Jewish investors, which offers many fond remembrances of the Jews unencumbered by the ideological agenda of most of the works examined in this chapter.[63] Raafat also regularly contributes a column to the Saturday *Egyptian Mail* and occasionally other English newspapers in which he has often written about Jewish business families, their enterprises, their homes, and other topics touching on Egyptian Jews.[64] One of his articles asking why there is no tree at Israel's Yad Vashem Holocaust memorial honoring the Egyptians who gave refuge to Jewish survivors of the Nazi persecutions was translated and reprinted in the Saturday supplement of *ha-Aretz*.[65]

Raafat's broader project is to revalorize the era of the monarchy by highlighting its architectural monuments, economic accomplishments, and social life, an objective regarded with suspicion by many contemporary Egyptians. He has so far operated primarily outside the circuits of Arabo-Egyptian intellectual life. And because his work has appeared only in English, it has had limited influence.

These meager indications of a positive reassessment of the history of the Jewish community by Egyptian intellectuals are disappointing for those who hoped that the Egyptian-Israeli peace treaty would open a new era. It seems that hostility and suspicion toward Jews has actually increased in Egypt since the signing of that agreement. The deep dissatisfaction of important sectors of the Egyptian intelligentsia with the partial diplomatic peace with Israel and Israel's continuing exercise of its overwhelming military power to guarantee its regional hegemony have prevented the broader cultural peace that many eagerly anticipated from materializing.

Egyptian Jews have become historical subjects once again since 1979. But they remain fiercely contested by Zionist and Egyptian nationalist historiographies committed to establishing and defending the authenticity of their national communities and their cultures. This contention is likely to persist even if a more just and comprehensive Arab-Israeli peace is achieved, though such a peace would probably contribute substantially to making it a more civil and constructive debate.

Interview with Jacques Hassoun

"I am Jewish because I am Egyptian.
I am Egyptian because I am Jewish."

Jacques Hassoun was born in 1936 and educated at the Lycée de l'Union Juive pour L'Enseignement in Alexandria, where the dominant intellectual orientation was Marxism. As a teenager, he joined the Dror Marxist-Zionist youth organization affiliated with the Le-Ahdut ha-ʿAvodah faction of MAPAM in Israel. In 1952, Dror's leaders in Egypt decided that Marxism and Zionism were incompatible and dissolved the organization. Hassoun then joined HADETU, the largest of the illegal Egyptian communist organizations. In 1954, after being arrested as a communist, he was expelled from Egypt.

Upon resettling in France, Hassoun joined the Egyptian Jewish emigres who formed the Rome Group—a cell of HADETU in exile under the leadership of Henri Curiel. He remained active with Curiel's group until 1968. In 1979, Hassoun, several other Jews who had formerly been active in the French branch of HADETU, and others initiated the Association to Safeguard the Cultural Patrimony of the Jews of Egypt. The association sponsored the publication of two books, which Hassoun edited, *Juifs du nil* (Paris: Le Sycomore, 1981) and *Histoire des Juifs du nil* (Paris: Minerve, 1990), as well as an elegant collaboratively produced photo essay, Gilbert Cabasso et al. (eds.), *Juifs d'Egypte: Images et textes* (Paris: Editions du Scribe, 1984). It also published a journal, *Nahar Misraïm* (The Nile River), from 1981 to 1986.

Paula Jacques and Edmond Jabès, who are discussed briefly in the interview, are perhaps the best-known Egyptian Jews who resettled in France. Jacques was born in Cairo in 1949 and left Egypt with her family in 1957. She is the author of four novels that depict the Egyptian Jewish community in Cairo and France. Jabès, a philosopher and literary critic, also arrived in France after the 1956 war.

Q: How did you feel as a Jew, as a member of a minority community, in Egypt before 1948?

A: I was born a Jew. I was from a completely Jewish family, religiously observant, Arabic speaking (even if my mother spoke French). Being Jewish was part of my identity. It posed no problem. It is certainly true that in . . . 1946, 1947, 1948, we sensed a growing hatred toward Zionism, which was often expressed as a hatred of Jews. However, this hatred in no way detracted from the legitimacy of our existence

Q: Why were a relatively large number of Egyptian Jews attracted to the left, to Marxist organizations, in the 1940s?

A: Apart from some exceptions who, before the Second World War, were part of the nationalist movement or at least members of the Wafd, Egyptian Jews, after the establishment of the state of Israel, did not have the possibility of becoming Egyptian nationalists, close to the Egyptian people, etcetera. . . . The only possibility for them was to take part in the communist movement, that is to say, a movement which at that time was not anti-Semitic and [from late 1947 on] favored the creation of the state of Israel. It was also very internationalist—with all of the ideology of that time. In other words, the triumph of communism would liberate the Jews from their situation, etcetera. Communism and Marxism provided a coherent vision, a theoretically coherent possibility of being Jewish and Egyptian at the same time without any major contradiction, at least until the 1950s.

Q: Does that mean that being communist meant the same thing as being Egyptian?

A: From that perspective, it seemed that to be a conscientious Egyptian, nationalistic, in favor of independence, and—to use the political terminology of the era, "a patriotic Egyptian"—was the only solution for the Jews.

Q: Were there social differences between those Jews who became Marxists and those who became Zionists?

A: There was, it seems, a cell of communist Jews in *harat-al-yahud* (the Jewish quarter of Cairo). But in general, the Jews that became communists were either from the middle class, or even the upper class. Very few poor Jews became communists. Zionists, on the other hand, were never from the upper class. They came from the middle or lower classes.

Q: When you arrived in France, why did you continue to engage actively in politics as an Egyptian?

A: You must remember, I was not expelled from Egypt because I was a Jew but because I was a communist—that is a very different situation. It was before the great expulsion of Jews following the 1956 war. I believed that if a socialist government came to power in Egypt, I would return to the country with full rights. I completely identified with the struggle of the Egyptian people. I considered myself completely Egyptian; I even had an expression for a very long time, which I repeated as recently as ten years ago: "I am Jewish because I am Egyptian. I am Egyptian because I am Jewish."

Q: France has a very strong secular tradition as well as a very strong tradition of nationalism. Did this combination resolve for you the identity problems that you had confronted being Jewish in Egypt?

A: Resolve? No. I think that [being in France] actually complicated things; it did not resolve them.

Q: How?

A: It complicated things because after 1956–1957, I realized, even if I did not necessarily want to believe it . . . that I would never return to Egypt. The desire to be Egyptian, Jewish, communist, and French at the same time was really too much. For me it was a very long process. I had to practically reconstruct for myself the category of Egyptian Jews, I had to create associations with others, and I had to finish with this story of the Egyptian Jew in order to finally see all the different aspects of my identity reconciled. For a nonreligious Egyptian Jew like myself, resigning oneself to live permanently in France is extremely difficult. Though I was not religious, I was Jewish. I called myself "Juif d'Egypte" [an Egyptian Jew] even though I knew I would never return to Egypt. This was really a significant collection of contradictions for me. I think that politics, in other words, the ability to remain a communist, and then almost immediately to become a Trotskyist, allowed me to resolve all of this because the internationalist ideology permitted a certain marriage of these contradictions.

Q: Why did Egyptian Jews in France begin to form a collective identity in 1980?

A: I think that there are two reasons. The first is that it seems that the members of a persecuted group need twenty or thirty years before they can reappropriate their story. For example, look at what happened to the Jews in Europe. . . . It wasn't until 1975–1980 that there was discussion once again about the Holocaust, the extermination camps, etcetera. In addition, at the end of the 1970s and the beginning of the 1980s in France, it was the other order of the day to reconsider questions of identity. Moreover, several of us returned to visit Egypt between 1977 and 1979. Ibram Gabbai, André Cohen, Emile Gabbay, and I decided at that moment that we had to preserve the traces of a history that we feared was going to disappear.

Q: What was the French public reaction at that time toward this project of recuperating Egyptian Jewish identity, the publication of books, etcetera?

A: I was very surprised. There were of course write-ups in the Jewish newspapers. There were also write-ups in French newspapers, a significant amount in *Le Monde* (where there is rarely coverage of this sort of thing), in *Liberation,* on *France Culture* [a radio program]. There was a whole series of very interesting reactions. It seemed that people were curious. In particular, it appeared that French Jews were very curious about who the Egyptian Jews were. No one had ever talked about it before. They did not know that Egyptian Jews existed.

Q: If the Egyptian Jews have a certain repute in France, does that mean that someone like the novelist Paula Jacques is very well known?

A: Paula Jacques became famous late, very late. Paula Jacques published her first book [*Lumière de l'oeil*] in 1980. But Paula Jacques, despite the quality of her book, which I would say is very high, is not at all liked by the Jews of Egypt. In fact, they dislike her.

Q: Why?

A: The Egyptian Jews think that she tells nonfiction stories even though she writes novels. These stories present Egyptian Jewry as ridiculous, composed of crooks, the impoverished, etcetera. The Egyptian Jews don't want to identify with this depiction. They don't like her. There was also Edmond Jabès. But Edmond Jabès waited until one or two years before his death before admitting publicly, in an interview that I did with him and Carole Naggar, that he was from a very old Egyptian family—that his grandfather, his father, his great grandfather, were *gabais* (sextons) of the synagogue of *harat al-yahud* and that he had continued, until his expulsion from Egypt [in 1957], to go once a year to the synagogue, of which he was still, in principle, the *gabai,* on the evening of Yom Kipur for Kol Nidre.

Q: So the most famous Egyptian Jews in France are not known as Egyptian Jews but as French Jews?

A: As French Jews, exactly. But even Paula Jacques knows very well, I can say very frankly, that she could not have published her book without the work that we did in the journal *Nahar Misraïm* and in the association. We introduced her to the characters she used in her first novel. I am sure, and I told her this, and I say it publicly, that she would not have existed if we had not done this work. She would have written something else. She would have written it another way. But we cleared the path for her.

Q: How does the French public feel about the setting of Paula Jacques's novels?

A: It amuses them. They find it very funny. They think it is a bizarre diaspora because they know only the diaspora of Eastern Europe or the North African diaspora. They find it extravagant, a little strange, but nothing more.

Q: The fear of Islam is so strong in France now. Has it affected the Jewish community or you personally with your experience of being a resident and citizen of France of Middle Eastern origin?

A: It touches me not as Jew, but personally right now, as a French citizen. The big danger, the thing which would affect me, is that the Islamists threaten to transform an integrated, republican state, into a multi-ethnic state. I am for a republican, centralized, and integrated state.

Q: So you believe that the ideas of the French Revolution are still valid.

A: For me, as a Jew, yes. Perhaps it is different for American Jews. But in Europe and in France, the only way that the Jews can live in peace is to live in an integrated state. Personally, I am against the public manifestation of the Jewish religion. I am against the wearing of the *yarmulke* [skull cap]. Not at all because I am secular, but because I believe that we shouldn't openly flaunt ourselves as Jews. I am against the fact that, each year during Hanukah, the Hasidim light a *menorah* on the Champs de Mars, the most important place in Paris, while shouting about the Messiah coming, etcetera. . . . I think it is dangerous because, if there are different communities, [this type of demonstration] would create, given the latent atmosphere in France and in Europe, a pretext for anti-Semitism.

Palo Alto, California
November 2, 1995
Transcribed and translated from French
by Mara Kronenfeld

Notes

ABBREVIATIONS USED IN THE NOTES

AJC/FAD   American Jewish Committee Records (Record Group 347)/ Foreign Affairs Division (YIVO Institute for Jewish Research, New York)

CZA   Central Zionist Archives (Jerusalem)

    S6 Jewish Agency, Immigration Department

    S20 Jewish Agency, Department for Middle Eastern Jewry

    S25 Jewish Agency, Political Department

    S41 Jewish Agency, Berl Locker's Office

    Z6 Nahum Goldman's Office

FO   Great Britain Foreign Office Archives (Public Records Office, London)

HH   Arkhion ha-Shomer ha-Tzaʿir, Yad Yaʿari, ha-Merkaz le-Teʿud ve-Heker shel ha-Shomer ha-Tzaʿir (Givʿat Haviva, Israel)

JLMC   Jamie Lehmann Memorial Collection, Records of the Jewish Community of Cairo 1886–1961 (Yeshiva University Archives, New York)

MHT   ha-Makhon le-Heker ha-Tfuzot, Tel Aviv University (Ramat Aviv, Israel)

USNA   United States National Archives (College Park, Maryland)

WJC   World Jewish Congress (New York)

YT   Arkhion ha-Kibutz ha-Me'uhad, Yad Tabenkin (Efal, Israel)

YTM   ha-Makhon le-Heker ha-Tnu'ah ha-Tzionit ve-ha-Halutzit be-Artzot ha-Mizrah, Yad Tabenkin (Efal, Israel)

1. INTRODUCTION

1. Gudrun Krämer, *The Jews in Modern Egypt, 1914–1952* (Seattle: University of Washington Press, 1989), pp. 234–35.

2. For comprehensive modern histories of the Karaite Jews of Egypt, see Mourad El-Kodsi, *The Karaite Jews of Egypt, 1882–1986* (Lyons, NY: Wilprint, 1987); Yosef Algamil, *Ha-yahadut ha-kara'it be-mitzrayim be-'et he-hadashah* (Ramlah: ha-Mo'etzah ha-Artzit shel ha-Yehudim ha-Kara'im be-Yisra'el, 1985). In 1996, the last formally affiliated male member of the Karaite community living in Cairo, Yusuf al-Qudsi, died.

3. For a popular exposition of the tensions around these issues, see Alexander Lesser, "Don't Call Us Jews," *The Jerusalem Report,* June 18, 1992, pp. 36–38.

4. Yosef Algamil, "Ha-hakham tuvia simha levi babovitch: aharon hakhmei kehilat ha-kara'im be-mitzrayim," *Pe'amim* 32 (1987):49; Tzvi Zohar, "Bayn nikur le-ahavah: nisu'im bayn kara'im le-rabanim 'al pnei hakhmei yisra'el be-mitzrayim be-me'ah ha-'esrim," *Pe'amim* 32 (1987):32.

5. Shlomo Barad, "ha-Pe'ilut ha-tzionit be-mitzrayim, 1917–1952," *Shorashim ba-mizrah* 2 (1989):115.

6. Leonard Praeger, "Yiddish Theater in Cairo," *Bulletin of the Israeli Academic Center in Cairo* no. 16 (May 1992):24–30.

7. Ahmad Sadiq Sa'd (Isadore Salvator Saltiel), conversation, Cairo, May 1986.

8. On the Jews of Syria and their diaspora community in Brooklyn, see Joseph A. D. Sutton, *Magic Carpet: Aleppo in Flatbush, the Story of a Unique Ethnic Jewish Community* (New York: Thayer-Jacoby, 1979); Joseph A. D. Sutton, *Aleppo Chronicles: The Story of the Unique Sephardeem of the Ancient Near East—in Their Own Words* (New York: Thayer-Jacoby, 1988).

9. Dipesh Chakrabarty, "The Death of History? Historical Consciousness and the Culture of Late Capitalism," *Public Culture* 4 (no. 2, 1992):57.

10. James Clifford, "Identity in Mashpee," in *The Predicament of Culture* (Cambridge: Harvard University Press, 1988), p. 317.

11. Salman Rushdie, *Imaginary Homelands: Essays and Criticism, 1981–1991* (London: Granta Books in association with Penguin Books, 1991), pp. 10, 12.

12. Edward W. Said, *Culture and Imperialism* (New York: Knopf, 1993), especially pp. 191–281; Edward W. Said, "The Mind of Winter: Reflections on Life in Exile," *Harper's,* Sept. 1984, pp. 49–55.

13. Paul Gilroy, *There Ain't No Black in the Union Jack* (Chicago: University of Chicago Press, 1991); Paul Gilroy, *The Black Atlantic: Modernity and Double Consciousness* (Cambridge: Harvard University Press, 1993).

14. Gilroy, *The Black Atlantic,* pp. 211, 212.

15. Ibid., pp. 22, 217.

16. Assia Djebar, *Fantasia: An Algerian Cavalcade* (Portsmouth, N.H.: Heinemann, 1993); Yael Zerubavel, *Recovered Roots: Collective Memory and the Making of Israeli National Tradition* (Chicago: University of Chicago Press, 1995).

17. Chakrabarty, "The Death of History?" p. 57.

18. Gilles Deleuze and Félix Guattari, *A Thousand Plateaus: Capitalism and Schizophrenia* (Minneapolis: University of Minnesota Press, 1987), p. 23.

19. Ibid., p. 21.

20. Ronit Matalon, *Zeh 'im ha-panim eleynu* (Tel Aviv: 'Am 'Oved, 1995), pp. 294–95.

21. Carol A. Breckinridge and Arjun Appadurai, "Moving Targets," *Public Culture* 2 (no. 1, 1989):i.

22. Rushdie, *Imaginary Homelands,* pp. 13, 14.

23. Mark R. Cohen, "The Neo-Lachrymose Conception of Jewish-Arab History," *Tikkun* 6 (May–June 1991):55–60. A revised version of this essay, with the force of its argument somewhat moderated, appears as the first chapter of Mark R. Cohen, *Under Crescent and Cross: The Jews in the Middle Ages* (Princeton: Princeton University Press, 1994).

24. Yahudiya Misriya (an earlier pseudonym of Giselle Littman), *Les juifs en Egypte: Aperçu sur 3000 ans d'histoire* (Geneva: Editions de l'Avenir, 1971).

25. Bat-Ye'or, *Yehudei mitzrayim* (Tel Aviv: Sifriat Ma'ariv ve-ha-Kongres ha-Yehudi ha-'Olami be-Yozmat Misrad ha-Hinukh ve-ha-Tarbut be-Hishtatfut ha-Mahlakah la-Kehilot ha-sfaradiyot shel ha-Histadrut ha-Tziyonit, 1974).

26. Many scholars are more nuanced and careful in their judgments than Bat-Ye'or. Nonetheless, her general approach has been embraced by prominent figures in Anglo-American intellectual life. Martin Gilbert explicitly adopts Bat-Ye'or's perspective in arguing that from 750 to 1900, "Despite many decades of prosperity, influence, trade and toleration, the Jews living in the Arab and Muslim World faced the continual danger of anti-Jewish discrimination, violence and persecution": *The Jews of Arab Lands: Their History in Maps* (London: World Organization of Jews from Arab Countries and Board of Deputies of British Jews, 1976), Map 4. She is recognized in Gilbert's acknowledgments. Gilbert lists random acts of discrimination and persecution against Jews with no reference to historical context or sources. His text contains errors, inflated numbers, and tendentious "facts." It is, in fact, a propaganda tract rather than a piece of scholarship, but it is remarkable that a widely acclaimed historian was not embarrassed to put his name on such a work. Norman A. Stillman's reply to Mark Cohen, "Myth, Countermyth, and Distortion," *Tikkun* 6 (May–June 1991):60–64, puts a certain distance between himself and Bat-Ye'or, but his books *The Jews of Arab Lands* (Philadelphia: Jewish Publication Society, 1979) and *The Jews of Arab Lands in Modern Times* (Philadelphia: Jewish Publication Society, 1991), though less crude, embrace a similar perspective. Likewise,

Bernard Lewis's *The Jews of Islam* (Princeton: Princeton University Press, 1984) adopts a judicious stance, which nonetheless tends to degenerate into neo-lachrymosity in the final chapter on the modern period. Written for a popular audience, Lewis's *Semites and Anti-Semites: An Inquiry into Conflict and Prejudice* (New York: Norton, 1986) indulges in vulgar characterizations of Arab-Jewish relations. See my review in *Middle East Report* no. 147 (July–Aug. 1987):43–45.

27. This is the implication of Gilbert, *The Jews of Arab Lands,* Map 13.

28. Anonymous bystander at the July 1987 demonstration. For details see Joel Beinin, "From Land Day to Equality Day," in Zachary Lockman and Joel Beinin (eds.), *Intifada: The Palestinian Uprising against Israeli Occupation* (Boston: South End Press, 1989), p. 214.

29. Yehoshafat Harkabi, *Arab Attitudes to Israel* (Jerusalem: Keter, 1972). Harkabi's work from the 1980s until his death substantially repudiates the arguments of this book. However, Harkabi never admitted that he changed his mind about the Arabs; he always argued that it was the Arabs who changed their mind about Israel.

30. Egypt, Ministry of Information, *The Story of Zionist Espionage in Egypt* (Cairo: Ministry of Information [1955]), p. 5. The copy I examined is in USNA RG 84 Cairo Embassy General Records (1955) Box 264, 400.1, Israeli Spies in Egypt.

31. The French novel by Karmona's daughter, Marcelle Fisher, *Armando* (Tel Aviv: Yeda Sela, 1982), presents a fictionalized account of his fate.

32. This possibility is insinuated by Avri El-Ad (Avraham Seidenwerg/Paul Frank) in his memoir, *Decline of Honor* (Chicago: Henry Regnery, 1976). Stephen Green, *Taking Sides: America's Secret Relations with a Militant Israel* (New York: William Morrow, 1984), pp. 110–14, presents a circumstantial case for this possibility. In a 1982 interview, El-Ad told Green that he believed the Mosad intentionally exposed him and his group.

33. Despite these limitations, Shabtai Teveth compiled such a political history, *'Onat ha-gez: Kitat yorim be-vayt jan, Kalaba"n* (Tel Aviv: Ish Dor, 1992), abridged English edition: *Ben Gurion's Spy: The Story of the Political Scandal That Shaped Modern Israel* (New York: Columbia University Press, 1996). Teveth presents a systematic apology for Ben-Gurion. He does not deign to engage and refute arguments that differ from his own. Therefore, Teveth should be used with great caution despite his access to many documents unavailable to others.

34. In addition to Teveth, *'Onat ha-gez,* see Eliyahu Hasin and Dan Hurvitz, *ha-Parasha* (Tel Aviv: 'Am ha-Sefer, 1961); David Ben-Gurion, *Dvarim ke-hevyatam* (Tel Aviv: 'Am ha-Sefer, 1965); Hagai Eshed, *Mi natan et ha-hora'ah? "ha-'esek ha-bish," parashat lavon ve-hitpatrut ben-gurion* (Jerusalem: 'Edanim, 1979); Iser Harel, *Kam ish 'al ahiv: ha-nituah ha-musmakh ve-ha-mematzeh shel "parashat lavon"* (Jerusalem: Keter, 1982); Yehoshafat Harkabi, *'Edut ishit: ha-parashah mi-nekudat re'uti* (Tel Aviv: Ramot, 1994).

35. Itamar Rabinovich, *The Road Not Taken: Early Arab-Israeli Negotiations* (New York: Oxford University Press, 1991), and Benny Morris, *Israel's Border Wars, 1949–1956* (Oxford: Oxford University Press, 1993), offer divergent assessments of the extent of Israeli responsibility for the "second round" in 1956.

36. Eric Davis, *Challenging Colonialism: Bank Misr and Egyptian Industrialization, 1920–1941* (Princeton: Princeton University Press, 1983), p. 116.

37. Quoted in Nabil ʿAbd al-Hamid Sayyid Ahmad, *al-Hayat al-iqtisadiyya waʾl-ijtimaʿiyya liʾl-yahud fi misr, 1947–1956* (Cairo: Maktabat Madbuli, 1991), p. 39.

38. On the Yemenis, see Gershon Shafir, *Land, Labour and the Origins of the Israeli-Palestinian Conflict, 1882–1904* (Cambridge: Cambridge University Press, 1989), pp. 91–122.

39. Ella Shohat, "Sephardim in Israel: Zionism from the Standpoint of Its Jewish Victims," *Social Text* nos. 19–20 (1988):1–35; Shlomo Swirski, *Israel: The Oriental Majority* (London: Zed Books, 1989); Gideon N. Giladi, *Discord in Zion* (London: Scorpion Publishing, 1990); Raphael Cohen-Almagor, "Cultural Pluralism and the Israeli Nation-Building Ideology," *International Journal of Middle East Studies* 27 (no. 4, 1995):461–84.

40. This is the only instance in this book where I have altered a name and identifying details to protect the identity of someone who has spoken with me.

2. COMMUNITARIANISMS, NATIONALISMS, NOSTALGIAS

1. Aviezer Golan, as told by Marcelle Ninio, Victor Levy, Robert Dassa, and Philip Natanson, *Operation Susannah* (New York: Harper & Row, 1978), original Hebrew version: *Mivtza ʿsuzanah* (Jerusalem: ʿEdanim, 1976).

2. Ibid., pp. 5–6.

3. *al-Ahram*, Oct. 6, 1954, p. 1.

4. Egypt, Ministry of Information, *The Story of Zionist Espionage in Egypt* (Cairo: Ministry of Information [1955]), pp. 25, 61.

5. Foreign Broadcast Information Service, Jan. 6, 1955, quoted in Don Peretz, "Egyptian Jews Today" (a report compiled for the AJC, Committee on Israel, Jan. 1956), pp. 35–36, AJC/FAD-1/Box 15.

6. *al-Musawwar*, Oct. 15, Oct. 29, Dec. 17, 1954; especially Hasan al-Husayni, "Maʿa jawasis israʾil fi al-sijn," Jan. 7, 1955.

7. Maurice Fargeon (ed.), *Annuaire des Juifs d'Egypte et du proche-orient, 1942* (Cairo: La Société des Editions Historiques Juives d'Egypte, 1943), p. 117.

8. Ibid., p. 118.

9. Maurice Fargeon (ed.), *Annuaire des Juifs d'Egypte et du proche-orient, 5706/1945–1946* (Cairo: La Société des Editions Historiques Juives d'Egypte [1945]), pp. 80–86.

10. Ernest Renan, *Qu'est-ce qu'une nation?* (Paris: Pierre Bordas et Fils, 1991), p. 34.

11. Albert D. Mosseri, "L'espoir d'un vieux sioniste," *Israël* 6 (no. 12, Mar. 20, 1925):1, quoted in Michael M. Laskier, *The Jews of Egypt, 1920–1970: In the Midst of Zionism, Anti-Semitism, and the Middle East Conflict* (New York: New York University Press, 1992), p. 51.

12. Maurice Mizrahi, *L'Egypte et ses Juifs: Le temps révolu, xix$_e$ et xx$_e$ siècles* (Geneva: Imprimerie Avenir, 1977), pp. 37–44; Gudrun Krämer, *The Jews*

of Modern Egypt, 1914–1952 (Seattle: University of Washington Press, 1989), pp. 126, 128.

13. Shlomo Kohen-Tzidon, *Dramah be-aleksandriah ve-shnei harugei malkhut: mehandes sh. ʿazar ve-doktor m. marzuk* (Tel Aviv: Sgiʿal, 1965).

14. For more detail on the issues in this paragraph, see Chapter 3.

15. Laskier, *The Jews in Egypt*, p. 187.

16. "Rapport presenté à l'Agence Juive Department du Moyen Orient sur la situation actuelle des Juifs en Egypte par un Juif d'Egypte ayant quitté l'Egypte vers la fin de l'année 1949," p. 13, Matzav ha-yehudim be-mitzrayim, 1948–1952/no subdivision, CZA S20/552.

17. Haim Shaʾul le-mahleket ha-mizrah ha-tikhon, Cairo, Mar. 12, 1950, CZA S20/552/851/71/28754.

18. Felix Benzakein, "A History in Search of a Historian," *The Candlestick* (monthly publication of Congregation Sons of Israel, Newburgh, New York), reprinted in *Goshen: alon moreshet yahadut mitzrayim* no. 7 (Dec. 1988):11.

19. For an elaboration of the points in this paragraph, see Aron Rodrigue, "Difference and Tolerance in the Ottoman Empire" (interview with Nancy Reyonolds), *Stanford Humanities Review* 5 (no. 1, 1995):80–90.

20. For a survey of these orientations, see Israel Gershoni and James P. Jankowski, *Beyond the Nile Valley: Redefining the Egyptian Nation, 1930–1945* (Cambridge: Cambridge University Press, 1995).

21. Shimon Shamir, "The Evolution of the Egyptian Nationality Laws and Their Application to the Jews in the Monarchy Period," in Shimon Shamir (ed.), *The Jews of Egypt: A Mediterranean Society in Modern Times* (Boulder: Westview Press, 1987), pp. 41, 58.

22. Ibid., p. 34.

23. "Peʿulot ha-haganah be-mitzrayim, 1947," Avigdor (Levi Avrahami) le-ha-ramah, Sept. 1, 1947, Arkhion ha-Haganah (Tel Aviv) 14/1024.

24. There are no statistics available, but the testimony of Egyptian Jews is nearly unanimous on this point.

25. *al-Kalim*, Apr. 1, 1945, p. 2; Apr. 1, 1950, pp. 2–3.

26. In a discussion with Maurice Farid Musa (Maurice Shammas), Chief Rabbi Haim Nahum noted that in Turkish, *milla* means "a people" and not a religious community and that for this reason the Rabbanite Jews called their communal council *al-majlis al-taʾifi*. See *al-Kalim*, June 16, 1950, p. 6. Regardless of its etymology, the phrase used by the Karaite community could not but invoke the late Ottoman millet conception.

27. *al-Kalim*, Apr. 1, 1945, p. 2.

28. *al-Kalim*, Sept. 1, 1945, p. 10. A more secular formulation might have offered condolences to the Muslim *umma* or to Egyptian Muslims.

29. *al-Kalim*, Nov. 16, 1945, p. 6.

30. *al-Kalim*, Jan. 1, 1946, p. 6.

31. Matatya Ibrahim Rassun, "al-Qaraʾun fi al-ʿasr al-islami," *al-Kalim*, Dec. 1, 1945, p. 5; "al-Qaraʾun fi misr," ibid., June 1, 1948, p. 2.

32. Yusuf Zaki Marzuq, "Samaʿtu . . . walakin lam usaddiq," *al-Kalim*, June 1, 1948, p. 5. The observations of this article were confirmed by Maurice Shammas, interview, Jerusalem, May 5, 1994.

33. For example, the editor of *al-Kalim* interviewed five young women during a trip to Maʿadi sponsored by the YKJA and printed their pictures in the paper. He considered this a bold step because of the many conservative ideas and social restrictions on women prevalent in the community; *al-Kalim*, June 1, 1945, pp. 6–7.

34. *al-Kalim*, Nov. 16, 1946, p. 12. See also the introduction to Tuvia ben Simha Levi Babovitch, *In lam asʿa li-nafsi fa-man yasʿa liyya* (Cairo: Jamʿiyyat al-Ikhwan al-Qaraʾin, 1946).

35. Eli Amin Lishaʿ, "Makanat taʾifat al-qaraʾin fi misr," *al-Kalim,* Jan. 1, 1947, p. 3.

36. Rassun, "al-Qaraʾun fi al-ʿasr al-islami."

37. *al-Kalim*, Mar. 1, 1947, p. 1; Rassun, "al-Qaraʾun fi al-ʿasr al-islami"; "al-Qaraʾun fi misr," ibid., June 1, 1948, p. 2.

38. See Joel Beinin, "Writing Class: Workers and Modern Egyptian Colloquial Poetry (*Zajal*)," *Poetics Today* 15 (no. 2, 1994):191–215.

39. "al-Qaraʾun fi misr," *al-Kalim*, June 1, 1948, p. 2.

40. *al-Kalim*, Dec. 1, 1945, p. 3; ibid., Jan. 1, 1951, pp. 4–5; ibid., Dec. 16, 1953, p. 2; ibid., Dec. 16, 1954, pp. 2–3; ibid., Dec. 16, 1955, p. 6.

41. Rassun, "al-Qaraʾun fi al-ʿasr al-islami"; "al-Qaraʾun fi misr," ibid., June 1, 1948, p. 2.

42. Eli Amin Lishaʿ, "al-Qaraʾun fi misr," *al-Kalim,* June 16, 1946, p. 8.

43. Ahmad Safwat basha al-muhammi, "Qudaʾ al-tawaʾif al-milliyya watashih khataʾ shaʾiʿ ʿanhi," *al-Kalim,* Nov. 16, 1950, pp. 4, 14. Nonetheless, when communal courts were abolished in 1955, the community publicly supported the decision. See Abu Yaʿqub, "Tawhid al-qudaʾ," ibid., Nov. 1, 1955, p. 2.

44. Y[usuf] K[amal], "al-Jinsiyya al-misriyya wa-aʿdaʾ al-majlis al-milli," *al-Kalim,* Mar. 1, 1950, p. 6.

45. Lishaʿ, "al-Qaraʾun fi misr."

46. *al-Kalim*, Aug. 16, 1947; ibid., Oct 15, 1949; ibid., May 16, 1951; ibid., July 16, 1951; ibid., Feb. 1, 1952; ibid., Oct. 1, 1952.

47. The only reference to anything that could be considered Zionism in *al-Kalim* between 1945 and May 15, 1948, a period when Zionist activity was legal in Egypt, is a letter to the editor by Lieto Ibrahim Nunu on July 1, 1945, p. 11. He encouraged Karaite youth to settle in Jerusalem because only one Karaite currently resided there, and he could not perform his religious obligations alone. This proposal was framed entirely in religious communal terms and did not use the vocabulary of political Zionism. Nunu was neither a regular contributor to *al-Kalim* nor a recognized leader of the community. Krämer, *The Jews in Modern Egypt*, p. 214, refers to this as a call for ʿaliyah. Because Krämer does not appear to have read *al-Kalim,* I suspect she relied on the opinion of Siham Nassar, *al-Yahud al-misriyyun bayna al-misriyya waʾl-sahyuniyya* (Beirut: Dar al-Wahda, 1979), p. 75. For a critique of Nassar, see Chapter 9.

48. Testimony of Lazare Bianco (interviewed by Shlomo Barad, Mar. 6, 1985), YTM.

49. Ibid.; Nelly Masliah, interview, San Francisco, May 8, 1992; Maurice Shammas, interview, Jerusalem, May 5, 1994.

50. Yosef Marzuk, interview, Tel Aviv, conducted by Shlomo Barad, July 17, 1985. (Shlomo Barad kindly gave me the tape recording of this interview.)

51. Ibid.

52. On the biography of Yusuf 'Aslan Qattawi, see Krämer, *The Jews in Modern Egypt,* pp. 94–101; Eric Davis, *Challenging Colonialism: Bank Misr and Egyptian Industrialization, 1920–1941,* (Princeton: Princeton University Press, 1983), pp. 93–97; Fargeon, *L'Annuaire des Juifs d'Egypte et du proche-orient, 1942,* p. 248.

53. Davis, *Challenging Colonialism,* pp. 91–97.

54. Krämer, *The Jews in Modern Egypt,* pp. 95, 195.

55. *Israël,* Nov. 18, 1937, quoted in Bat Ye'or, "Zionism in Islamic Lands: The Case of Egypt," *Wiener Library Bulletin* 30, n.s. (nos. 43–44, 1977):27.

56. Krämer, *The Jews in Modern Egypt,* pp. 101–102.

57. R. Cattaoui and E. N. Goar, "Le point de vue des communautés Juives d'Egypte: Note sur la question juive," CZA S25/5218.

58. Krämer, *The Jews in Modern,* pp. 201–202.

59. See Edna Bonacich and John Modell, *The Economic Basis of Ethnic Solidarity* (Berkeley: University of California Press, 1980), p. 110.

60. On the Cicurel family and the early history of the store, see Krämer, *The Jews in Modern Egypt,* pp. 44–45, 101, 107, 213; Robert L. Tignor, *State, Private Enterprise, and Economic Change in Egypt, 1918–1952* (Princeton: Princeton University Press, 1983), pp. 60, 66, 102; Mizrahi, *L'Egypte et ses Juifs,* pp. 64–65; Fargeon, *L'Annuaire des Juifs d'Egypte et du proche-orient, 1942,* p. 250; Nabil 'Abd al-Hamid Sayyid Ahmad, *al-Hayat al-iqtisadiyya wa'l-ijtima'iyya li'l-yahud fi misr, 1947–1956* (Cairo: Maktabat Madbuli, 1991), pp. 38–40.

61. Krämer, *The Jews in Modern Egypt,* p. 107.

62. E. J. Blattner (ed.), *Le Mondain égyptien: L'Annuaire de l'élite d'Egypte (The Egyptian Who's Who)* [title varies] (Cairo: Imprimairie Française, 1947, 1952, 1954, 1956, 1959). A less comprehensive demographic analysis was performed by Ethel Carasso, "La communauté Juive d'Egypte de 1948 à 1957" (Maîtrise d'Histoire Contemporaine, Université de Paris X, 1982), pp. 31 ff.

63. Aron Rodrigue, *French Jews, Turkish Jews: The Alliance Israélite Universelle and the Politics of Jewish Schooling in Turkey, 1860–1925* (Bloomington: Indiana University Press, 1990).

64. Victor D. Sanua, "A Jewish Childhood in Cairo," in Victor D. Sanua (ed.), *Fields of Offerings: Studies in Honor of Raphael Patai* (Rutherford, NJ: Farleigh Dickinson University Press, 1983), p. 283.

65. Jacqueline Kahanoff, *Mi-mizrah shemesh* (Tel Aviv: Yariv-Hadar, 1978), p. 17. The English version of this essay, "Childhood in Egypt," appeared in *The Jerusalem Quarterly* no. 36 (Summer 1985):31–41. I have corrected the omission of a critical word in *The Jerusalem Quarterly* version that changed a meaning entirely.

66. For the political history of ha-Shomer ha-Tza'ir and MAPAM, see Joel Beinin, *Was the Red Flag Flying There? Marxist Politics and the Arab-Israeli Conflict in Egypt and Israel, 1948–1965* (Berkeley: University of California Press, 1990).

67. Jacques Hassoun, interview, Paris, May 30, 1994.

68. Ibid.; "Hitkatvuyot shel va'adat hu"l 'im shlihim ve-'im snifim," especially "Du"ah 'al ha-tnu'ah be-mitzrayim ve-hisulah," July 9, 1952, YTM, Hativa 2-Hu"l. Mekhal 1. Tik 2 and "Hitkatvuyot shel pe'ilim 'im ha-merkaz ba-aretz," Hativa 2-Hu"l. Mekhal 1. Tik 3.

69. Laskier, *The Jews of Egypt,* p. 155, cites an anonymous report from the Office of the Advisor for Special Tasks of the Israeli Foreign Ministry (which I located in CZA S41/449/bet/1/851/71, June 20, 1951) claiming that in June 1951 thirty senior members were expelled from ha-Shomer ha-Tza'ir because they considered their primary loyalty to be to the Soviet Union and Marxism rather than to Zionism and the state of Israel. Several movement leaders, including Albert 'Amar, Ninette Piciotto Braunstein, and Benny Aharon, who were on the spot, emphatically denied this in an interview in Tel Aviv on Apr. 28, 1994. Laskier's source may have been a report composed to impugn the reputation of MAPAM.

70. Before she became a spy for Israel, Marcelle Ninio had been a member (according to some accounts only a supporter) of ha-Shomer ha-Tza'ir. Her brother, Isaac, was a communist. Aharon Costi (Keshet), the leader of the ha-Shomer ha-Tza'ir branch in Dahir, was interned at Huckstep on May 15, 1948. His brother, Ralph, was a communist. Aimée Setton Beressi, was a member of the Central Committee of the communist Democratic Movement for National Liberation. Her brother-in-law, Victor Beressi, was the secretary of ha-Shomer ha-Tza'ir in Egypt in 1950–51, and another of her relatives owned a travel agency that was critical in organizing illegal immigration to Israel. Avraham Matalon, a leader of he-Halutz, was interned as a Zionist in 1948. His cousin, Joe Matalon, was a communist.

71. Rahel Maccabi, *Mitzrayim sheli* (Tel Aviv: Sifriat ha-Po'alim, 1968), p. 90.

72. Ibid., p. 9.

73. Ibid., p. 30.

74. Ibid., 10, 60, 83, 84–86.

75. Rahel Maccabi, "Mitzrayim sheli," *Hotam,* Aug. 14, 1968, p. 12.

76. Kahanoff, *Mi-mizrah shemesh,* p. 17.

77. Ibid., p. 29.

78. Ibid.

79. Ibid., p. 31.

80. Jacqueline [Kahanoff] Shohet, *Jacob's Ladder* (London: Harvill Press, 1951).

81. Rivka Gorfin, "Ashlayot poriot," *'Al ha-mishmar,* Nov. 20, 1959, p. 6.

82. Ya'irah Ginosar, "'Otzmat ha-kfilut," *'Iton 77* (nos. 8–9, May–June 1978):14.

83. Yitzhaq Gormezano-Goren, *Kayitz aleksandroni* (Tel Aviv: 'Am 'Oved, 1978), p. 9.

84. Ibid., p.134.

85. Ibid., p. 136.

86. Shulamit Kori'anski, "Kmo shahar she-nirdam," *Maznayim* nun (no. 1, 1979):151–52; Yisra'el Bramah, "Aleksandriah, hazarnu elayikh shenit," *Akhshav* 39–40 (Spring–Summer 1979):341–44. Gershon Shaked adopts a similar

attitude, explicitly consigning *Kayitz aleksandroni* and other novels of the same genre to the "margins of literary life" by designating it as "nostalgic-folkloric" in his authoritative history of Hebrew fiction, *ha-Siporet ha-'ivrit, 1880–1980*, vol. 4 (Tel Aviv: ha-Kibutz ha-Me'uhad and Keter, 1993), pp. 173, 187.

87. Izah Perlis, "Sipurah shel aleksandriah," *'Al ha-mishmar*, Dec. 29, 1978.

88. Ester Etinger, review of *Kayitz aleksandroni, Yerushalayim* 13 (no. 3, taf shin lamed tet):92.

89. Yitzhaq Gormezano-Goren, *Blanche* (Tel Aviv: 'Am 'Oved, 1987), pp. 80, 81.

90. Dan Miron, "Ha-genrah ha-yam-tikhoni ha-yehudi ba-safrut ha-yisra'elit, *Ha-'olam ha-zeh*, Apr. 8, 1987. Miron also discusses Amnon Shamosh's novel, *Mishel 'azra safra u-vanav*, set in Aleppo.

91. Tamar Wolf, "Kitsh aleksandroni," *'Iton 77* (no. 87, Apr. 1987):7.

92. Anat Levit, interview with Yitzhaq Gormezano-Goren, *Ma'ariv*, Feb. 6, 1987.

93. Robert Dassa, *Be-hazarah le-kahir* (Tel Aviv: Misrad ha-Bitahon, 1992).

94. Ibid. p. 7.

95. Ibid., pp. 18, 30.

96. Ibid., p. 14.

97. Ibid., pp. 11, 12.

98. Ibid., p. 13.

99. Ibid., p. 15.

100. Ibid., pp. 100, 102, 105, 106.

101. Ibid., p. 8.

102. Ibid., p. 10.

103. Ibid., p. 111.

3.   CITIZENS, *DHIMMIS,* AND SUBVERSIVES

1. "Unitary Palestine Fails in Committee," *New York Times*, Nov. 25, 1947, p. 9.

2. For example, AJC, *A Report on the Situation in Egypt* (Jan. 1949), AJC/FAD-1, Box 12, Foreign Countries, Egypt, 1948–49; WJC, *The Treatment of Jews in Egypt and Iraq* (1948), MHT A-1/92.12; Nehemiah Robinson [for WJC], *The Arab Countries of the Near East and Their Jewish Communities* (1951), MHT A-1/33.9; American Jewish Congress, *The Black Record: Nasser's Persecution of Egyptian Jewry* (New York: American Jewish Congress, 1957). Don Peretz, "Egyptian Jews Today" (New York, AJC, 1956, mimeographed) and S. Landshut, *Jewish Communities in the Muslim Countries of the Middle East: A Survey* (London: Jewish Chronicle Association, 1950), prepared for AJC and the Anglo-Jewish Association, are far more judicious than the typical publications of this era.

3. Ian Lustick, *Arabs in the Jewish State: Israel's Control of a National Minority* (Austin: University of Texas Press, 1980).

4. This definition of the conflict in material terms is based on Gershon Shafir, *Land, Labour and the Origins of the Israeli-Palestinian Conflict, 1882–1904* (Cambridge: Cambridge University Press, 1989).

5. *al-Siyasa al-ʿusbuʿiyya,* Nov. 5, 1938, pp. 3–4.

6. Information in the next three paragraphs is drawn from James P. Jankowski, "Egyptian Responses to the Palestine Problem in the Interwar Period," *International Journal of Middle East Studies* 12 (no. 1, 1980):1–38; James P. Jankowski, "Zionism and the Jews in Egyptian National Opinion, 1920–1939," in Amnon Cohen and Gabriel Baer (eds.), *Egypt and Palestine: A Millennium of Association (868–1948)* (Jerusalem: Ben Zvi Institute for the Study of Jewish Communities in the East, 1984), pp. 314–31.

7. *al-Ahram,* Sept. 29, 1929, p. 1.

8. Information in the next two paragraphs is drawn from Thomas Mayer, *Egypt and the Palestine Question, 1936–1945* (Berlin: Klaus, Schwarz Verlag, 1983), pp. 298 ff; Michael M. Laskier, *The Jews of Egypt, 1920–1970* (New York: New York University Press, 1992), pp. 84–93.

9. Rifʿat al-Saʿid, interview, Cairo, May 22, 1986.

10. A French translation of the letter, apparently made by British intelligence, appears in "Matzav ha-yehudim be-mitzrayim, 1938–1948," CZA S25/5218.

11. Maurice Fargeon (ed.), *Annuaire des Juifs d'Egypte et du proche-orient, 1944* (Cairo: Societé des Editions Historiques des Juives d'Egypte, 1944), p. 111.

12. Excerpt from letter (no names given) of Feb. 16, 1948, CZA S25/9034/899/71.

13. Maurice Mizrahi, *L'Egypte et ses Juifs: Le temps revolu, xixe et xxe siècles* (Geneva: Imprimerie Avenir, 1977) p. 120.

14. For example, Gibraʾil Duʿayq, "al-Daʿaya al-sahyuniyya," *al-Ahram,* July 18, 1948.

15. Anonymous letter of a Jewish prisoner in El-Tor (where conditions were much worse than in Huckstep or Abu Qir) to Jewish prisoners in Huckstep asking them to help free them, "Mitzrim, El Tor, Huckstep," YTM. Other sources state that as many as 1,000 Jews were interned, but this figure usually includes Jewish communists and a certain inflation due to distance from the spot.

16. Gudrun Krämer, *The Jews in Modern Egypt, 1914–1952* (Seattle: University of Washington Press, 1989), p. 212.

17. Efraim S. "Skirah ktzarah ʿal matzav ha-ʿaliyah mi-mitzrayim," July 24, 1949, CZA S20/552 (no subdivision indicated).

18. AJC, *A Report on the Jewish Situation in Egypt,* pp. 10–11; Laskier, *The Jews of Egypt,* pp. 127–29.

19. Mario Perez, interview, Paris, June 2, 1994.

20. *al-Ahram,* June 21, 1948, p. 3; *al-Kalim,* July 1, 1948; Laskier, *The Jews of Egypt,* p. 133.

21. Rabbi Avraham Gabr, interview, Ramlah, Jan. 11, 1993.

22. *al-Kalim,* July 1, 16, Aug. 1, 1948. The paper did not appear at all on Aug. 16, Sept. 1, and Sept. 16; Maurice Shammas, interview, Jerusalem, May 5, 1994.

23. *al-Ahram,* July 16, 1948; AJC, *A Report on the Jewish Situation in Egypt,* p. 24–32.

24. *al-Ahram,* July 20, Sept. 23, 1948; Richard P. Mitchell, *The Society of the Muslim Brothers* (New York: Oxford University Press, 1993), pp. 63–64.

25. Mitchell, *The Society of the Muslim Brothers,* pp. 58–79.

26. Ibid., p. 71.

27. Campbell to Bevin, Oct. 4, 1948, Great Britain, FO 371/69250.

28. Ben Ya'akov le-menahel mahleket ha-mizrah ha-tikhon, Apr. 17, 1949, "Matzav ha-yehudim be-mitzrayim, 1948–1952," CZA S20/552/851/71/9776.

29. Vaena was the leading exporter of onions, Egypt's third largest source of foreign currency. In 1965, the Nasser regime sequestered his assets, and he immigrated to France. Months later, unable to market its onion crop, the government invited Vaena to return and resume his commercial activity. He did so but was disappointed by his reception and treatment and died soon after his return to Egypt. See Maurice Mizrahi, "The Role of Jews in Economic Development," in Shimon Shamir (ed.), *The Jews of Egypt: A Mediterranean Society in Modern Times* (Boulder: Westview Press, 1987), pp. 92–93.

30. Laskier, *The Jews of Egypt*, p. 187. The Israeli census of 1961 records 14,895 immigrants from Egypt and Sudan who arrived in Israel from 1948 to 1951, and 15,872 for 1948–54. These figures are somewhat lower than those presented by Laskier, who relies largely on Jewish Agency records and makes no effort to resolve any of the inconsistencies in his sources. Part of the discrepancy is probably due to those who died or left Israel. All the emigration figures presented in this chapter are approximations based on my interpretation of those presented by Laskier and other sources.

31. Ibid.

32. This estimate is based on a collation of conflicting figures. Others whose estimates are similar include Krämer, *The Jews in Modern Egypt*, p. 221, and Institute of Jewish Affairs, WJC, "Egypt in September, 1957" (New York, Sept. 30, 1957), p. 3, MHT D-6/51.5.

33. Dr. Isaac I. Schwartzbart, "Toward Unity between Sephardim and Ashkenazim" and "Comparative Chart of the Sephardim in the World Jewish Population, 1950–54" (New York, WJC Organization Department, Apr. 1954), p. 4, CZA Z6/852.

34. Laskier, *The Jews of Egypt*, pp. 164–98; Shlomo Barad, "ha-Pe'ilut ha-tzionit be-mitzrayim, 1917–1952," *Shorashim ba-mizrah* 2 (1989): 65–127; Shlomo Barad et al. (eds.), *Haganah yehudit be-artzot ha-mizrah: rav-siah shlishi, ha-ha'apalah be-mitzrayim, 25 februar 1985* (Efal: Yad Tabenkin, ha-Mahon le-Heker ha-Tnu'ah ha-Tzionit ve-ha-Halutzit be-Artzot ha-Mizrah, ha-Mahon le-Heker Koah ha-Magen, 1986), especially the testimony of David Harel.

35. David Harel and Benny Aharon, interview, Tel Aviv, Mar. 25, 1993; Laskier, *The Jews of Egypt*, pp. 183–85.

36. Ben Ya'akov le-menahel mahleket ha-mizrah ha-tikhon, Apr. 17, 1949, "Matzav ha-yehudim be-mitzrayim, 1948–1952," CZA S20/552/851/71/9776.

37. Amin Lisha', "al-Isra'iliyun wa'l-jinsiyya al-misriyya," *al-Kalim*, Nov. 15, 1949, p. 2.

38. "al-Bulis al-siyasi fi qafas al-ittiham." *al-Musawwar*, Oct. 5, 1951, p. 28.

39. *al-Ahram*, Dec. 1, 1949.

40. Ibrahim Husni, "Nazaltu al-hara, tala'tu al-'abassiyya," *al-Kalim*, May 16, 1946, p. 4; May 1, 1947, p. 2.

41. *al-Ahram*, Aug. 3, 1952.

42. On this aspect of Rabbi Nahum's career, see Esther Benbassa (ed.), *Haim Nahum: A Sephardic Chief Rabbi in Politics, 1892–1923* (Tuscaloosa: University of Alabama Press, 1995).

43. *al-Ahram,* Aug. 9, 1952.

44. *al-Kalim,* Oct. 1, 16, 1952.

45. El-Kodsi, *The Karaite Jews of Egypt,* p. 61.

46. Ibid., pp. 88–90; *al-Balagh,* Oct. 25, 1952; *Journal d'Egypte,* Oct. 26, 1952.

47. Lettres Expediés, janvier–juin 1953, nos. 99, 105, 106, 123, 124, 161, JLMC, Box 2, General Correspondence, 1926–57, Folder 7.

48. Ibid., no. 157, E. Goar and S. Cicurel to the governor of the National Bank of Egypt, Apr. 25, 1953.

49. Ibid., Box 2, Folder 8, Lettres Expediés, juillet–décembre 1953, nos. 321, 324, 325.

50. *al-Ahram,* Feb. 9, 1953.

51. Lettres Expediés, janvier–juin 1953, no. 55, JLMC, Box 2, General Correspondence, 1926–57, Folder 7.

52. Mizrahi, *L'Egypte et ses Juifs,* p. 57.

53. Albert Mizrahi, "Kalam eh al-faragh da ya si salah ya salim," *al-Tas'ira,* Mar. 22, 1954, p. 4.

54. *Jerusalem Post,* Sept. 27, 1955.

55. Eric Rouleau, interview, Paris, May 25, 1994.

56. *Jewish Chronicle,* July 6, 1951, quoted in Nehemiah Robinson, *The Arab Countries of the Near East and Their Jewish Communities* (New York: WJC, Institute for Jewish Affairs, 1951), p. 74, MHT A-1/33.9.

57. *al-Saraha,* Dec. 8, 25, 1952.

58. Sasson Somekh, "Participation of Egyptian Jews in Modern Arabic Culture, and the Case of Murad Faraj," in Shimon Shamir (ed.), *The Jews of Egypt: A Mediterranean Society in Modern Times* (Boulder: Westview Press, 1987), p. 133.

59. Nehemiah Robinson, "Persecution in Egypt," *Congress Weekly,* Nov. 17, 1954 (reprinted by the American Jewish Congress, Office of Jewish Information), MHT D-61/151.6, 1.

60. Adel M. Sabet, *A King Betrayed: The Ill-Fated Reign of Farouk of Egypt* (London: Quartet Books, 1989), p. 217.

61. "Rapport presenté à l'Agence Juive Department du Moyen Orient sur la situation actuelle des Juifs en Egypt par un Juif d'Egypte ayant quitté l'Egypte vers la fin de l'année 1949" [no author, but apparently the president of the Zionist Organization of Cairo from internal evidence, no date], "Matzav ha-yehudim be-mitzrayim, 1948–1952," CZA S20/552.

62. Michael Stern, *Farouk* (New York: Bantam, 1965), pp. 195–98.

63. Robinson, *The Arab Countries of the Near East,* p. 74.

64. Reported in *al-Kalim,* Dec. 15, 1949.

65. *Akhir sa'a,* July 11, 1951; reprinted in *al-Kalim,* July 16, 1951, p. 6.

66. *al-Kalim,* Dec. 16, 1952, p. 8.

67. *al-Kalim,* Dec. 1, 1953. p. 8; Dec. 16, 1955, p. 6.

68. "Ya'qub sannu' . . . al-musawi al-misri al-muslim," *al-Musawwar,* Feb. 18, 1955.

69. *al-Saraha,* May 12, 1951, p. 1.

70. Somekh, "Participation of Egyptian Jews in Modern Arabic Culture, and the Case of Murad Faraj," p. 132.

71. Layla Murad's biography is based on the following obituary notices and articles that appeared after her death: Amjad Mustafa, "Layla murad, 77 'amman min al-'ata'," *al-Wafd,* Nov. 23, 1995, p. 8; "Misr: ghiyab layla murad," *al-Hayat,* Nov. 23, 1995, p. 24; 'Adil Disuqi, "Rahalat layla murad, sindarila al-shasha al-misriyya wa-sahibat al-sawt al-dhabi," *al-Hayat,* Nov. 25, 1995, p. 24; Fatemah Farag, "Farewell to the Last Artist of Integrity," *Middle East Times,* Dec. 3–9, 1995, p. 17. Salih Mursi's instant biography, *Layla Murad* (Cairo: Dar al-Hilal, 1995), Dar al-Hilal's featured book the month immediately after Layla Murad's death, avoids all the controversial aspects of her career and barely acknowledges her Jewish origins (see p. 11).

72. "Layla murad," *al-Ahram,* Sept. 12, 1952, p. 6; "Layla murad tukadhdhib tabarru'aha li-isra'il 50 alf junayh," *al-Ahram,* Sept. 13, 1952, p. 7; 'Adil Hasanayn, *Layla murad: ya musafir wa-nas hawak* (Cairo: Amadu, 1993), pp. 85 ff; 'Adil 'Abd al-'Alim, "Watha'iq tuthbit bara'at layla murad min tuhmat ziyarat isra'il," *al-Hayat,* July 4, 1993, p. 1.

73. "Layla murad tukadhdhib tabarru'aha li-isra'il 50 alf junayh."

74. Hasanayn, *Layla murad,* p. 89.

75. *Ruz al-yusuf,* Nov. 8, 1954, p. 34; Layla Murad, "Ta'alamtu wa-ta'adhabtu fi sabil ikhlasi," *Ruz al-yusuf,* Dec. 6, 1954, p. 33.

76. Disuqi, "Rahalat Layla Murad."

77. "Kharaju min dinihim fi sabil al-hubb," *Ruz al-yusuf,* Feb. 7, 1955, p. 40.

78. "Cairo's Jews: Uneasy Friendship," *Jerusalem Post,* Feb. 16, 1955.

79. Unless otherwise noted, the next two paragraphs are based on AJC, "The Situation of the Jews in Egypt at the Beginning of 1957" (New York, Jan. 7, 1957), MHT A1/969. Laskier, *The Jews of Egypt,* pp. 253–64, relies extensively on the same source.

80. Institute of Jewish Affairs, WJC, "Egypt in September, 1957."

81. WJC, *The Persecution of Jews in Egypt: The Facts* (Apr. 1957), p. 7, MHT A1/22–19.

82. For precise figures, see the table in Laskier, *The Jews of Egypt,* p. 273.

83. Gilbert Cabasso et al, *Juifs d'Egypte: Images et textes* (Paris: Editions du Scribe 1984), p. 42, estimates that the numbers of Egyptian Jewish emigrants to destinations other than Israel were 15,000 to Brazil, 10,000 to France, 9,000 to the United States, 9,000 to Argentina, and 4,000 to the United Kingdom, with smaller numbers in Canada, Italy, and Australia. This total of 47,000 cannot be reconciled with the Jewish Agency's figures for *'aliyah* without assuming a Jewish community of at least 85,000 before 1948, a larger figure than most estimates. It is more easily reconcilable with the Israeli census figures (see note 30 in this chapter). The same source claims that only one-third of all Egyptian Jews emigrated to Israel. A certain number of Jews who went to Israel because that was the only available destination immediately after the 1948 and 1956 wars ultimately settled elsewhere, and this may account for part of the discrepancy. The available statistics are incomplete and to some extent politically designed.

84. Dina Monet, "Absorption of Egypt's Aliya in Good Hands," *Jerusalem Post,* Dec. 31, 1955.

4. NAZIS AND SPIES: THE DISCOURSE
OF OPERATION SUSANNAH

1. See Boaz Evron, "Holocaust: The Uses of Disaster," *Radical America* 17 (no. 4, 1983):7–21; Tom Segev, *The Seventh Million: The Israelis and the Holocaust* (New York: Hill and Wang, 1993).

2. Israel, Ministry of Foreign Affairs, Press and Information Division, "The Position of Jews in Egypt," Nov. 8, 1948, enclosed in USNA RG 84 Cairo Embassy General Records (1948), 840.1.

3. *Palestine Post,* Nov. 14, 1948.

4. Max Isenburgh (AJC, Paris) to Dr. John Slawson (executive vice-president, AJC, New York) Oct. 1, 1948, AJC/FAD-1, Box 12, Foreign Countries, Egypt, 1948–49.

5. Dr. Alfred Wiener, "Report on Conditions in Egypt," Oct. 26, 1948, AJC/FAD-1, Box 12, Foreign Countries, Egypt, 1948–49.

6. Joseph M. Levy to Dr. John Slawson, May 10, 1949, AJC/FAD-1, Box 12, Foreign Countries, Egypt, 1948–49.

7. John Roy Carlson, "Pogrom Promoters of Egypt" (a report obtained by the AJC London office via the Wiener Library and forwarded to New York), Nov. 15, 1948, AJC/FAD-1, Box 12, Foreign Countries, Egypt, 1948–49.

8. Ibid.

9. AJC, *A Report on the Jewish Situation in Egypt* (Jan. 1949), AJC/FAD-1, Box 12, Foreign Countries, Egypt, 1948–49.

10. "Meeting with Mr. Securel [i.e., Cicurel] of Cairo, Egypt," Oct. 28, 1948, AJC/FAD-1, Box 12, Foreign Countries, Egypt, 1948–49. Among those present was AJC Executive Vice-President John Slawson.

11. S. Landshut, *Jewish Communities in the Muslim Countries of the Middle East: A Survey* (London: Jewish Chronicle Association, 1950), pp. 29, 40. The first quote is from AJC, *A Report on the Jewish Situation in Egypt.*

12. *Jerusalem Post,* Oct. 15, 1954, p. 1.

13. Ibid., Oct. 17, 1954, p. 1.

14. Among the credible accounts of the activities of former Nazis in Egypt are Reinhard Gehlen, *The Service: The Memoirs of General Reinhard Gehlen* (New York: World Publishing, 1972), p. 260; Burton Hersh, *The Old Boys: The American Elite and the Origins of the CIA* (New York: Scribner's, 1992), pp. 331–32. They note the role of the CIA in supplying former Wehrmacht and SS officers to staff the Egyptian State Security Service but do not indicate that these officers operated in any policy-making capacity. See also the report of Don Peretz in note 63 of this chapter. Perhaps the *Jerusalem Post* referred to the "National Guard," an auxiliary military unit with a function similar to that of the U.S. military units bearing the same name.

15. *Manchester Guardian,* Dec. 24, 1954, p. 1.

16. *Herut,* Dec. 12, 1954, p. 2.

17. Ibid., Dec. 22 1954, pp. 1, 2.

18. *Davar,* Dec. 12, 1954, p. 1.

19. Haim Sar-Avi, "Natzim germanim 'omdim be-rosh 'mahlakah yehudit'be-memshelet mitzrayim. Hem biyemu mishpat ha-13 u-mekhinim mishpatim nosafim," ibid., Dec.17, 1954, p. 1.

20. Ibid., Feb. 1, 1955, p. 1.

21. Nehemiah Robinson, "Persecution in Egypt" (New York, American Jewish Congress, Office of Jewish Information, Nov. 17, 1954), MHT D-61/151.6, 1.

22. *ha-Aretz,* Dec. 14, 1954, p. 1.

23. "Text of a Not for Attribution Background Talk by Ambassador Eban," Feb. 1, 1955, AJC/FAD-1, Box 14, Espionage Trial, Egypt, 1954–60.

24. Hevesi to Slawson Feb. 7, 1955, ibid.

25. *Jerusalem Post,* Feb. 9, 1955, p. 1.

26. *al-Jumhuriyya* and *al-Ahram,* Sept. 3, 1954, p. 1.

27. "al-Qissa al-kamila li'l-shuyu'iyya . . . fi misr," *al-Musawwar,* Dec. 24, 1954, pp. 16 ff.

28. "al-Sahyuniyya allati lam tastati' al-intihar . . . wa-la al-harb ila isra'il," *al-Musawwar,* Oct. 29, 1954, p. 14.

29. *al-Ahram,* Dec. 12, 1954, p. 1.

30. Ibid., Dec. 14, 1954, p. 1.

31. Ibid., Dec. 11, 1954, p. 11, for the quote; ibid., Dec. 12, 13, 17, 1954, for the photographs.

32. "al-Sahyuniyya allati lam tastati' al-intihar . . . wa-la al-harb ila isra'il," ibid., p. 9.

33. Ibid., p. 16.

34. "Kayfa tutbukh isra'il 'umala'aha fi misr," *al-Musawwar,* Dec. 17, 1954, p. 22.

35. Ibid., p. 20.

36. Hasan Husayni, "Ma'a jasus isra'il fi al-sijn," *al-Musawwar,* Jan. 7, 1955, pp. 14 ff.

37. FO 371/108548/JE1571 (1954).

38. Michael M. Laskier, "A Document on Anglo-Jewry's Intervention on Behalf of Egyptian Jews on Trial for Espionage and Sabotage, December 1954," *Michael* 10 (1986):143–53.

39. Caffery to State, Apr. 21, 1954, USNA RG 84 Cairo Embassy General Records (1954) Box 258, 350.21. See also "Little Discrimination against Jews in Egypt," Caffery to State, June 5, 1954, ibid., 570.1.

40. This assertion is based on my examination of the State Department central files and the post records from Cairo that were available in 1992 and 1995 (USNA RG 59 and RG 84). Using the Freedom of Information Act, Stephen Green obtained a perfunctory and incomplete preliminary report by Ambassador Caffery passing on information received from the Egyptian police. For a facsimile, see Stephen Green, *Taking Sides: America's Secret Relations with a Militant Israel* (New York: William Morrow, 1984), pp. 324–26.

41. Caffery to the secretary of state, Jan. 10, 1955, USNA RG 84 Cairo Embassy General Records (1955) Box 264, 400.1, "Israeli Spies in Egypt."

42. Simon Segal to John Slawson, Jan. 17, 1955, enclosing Baldwin's memos to Segal from Cairo, especially Baldwin to Segal, Jan. 8, 1955, AJC/FAD-1, Box 14, Espionage Trial, Egypt, 1954–60.

43. International League for the Rights of Man, press release, Feb. 3, 1955, ibid.

44. *London Observer,* Dec. 26, 1954.

45. *The New York Times,* Jan. 28, 1955.

46. *The New York Herald Tribune,* Feb. 2, 1955.

47. Quoted in the *Jerusalem Post,* Dec. 24, 1954, p. 1.

48. *Washington Post,* Dec. 22, 1954; Simon Segal to John Slawson, Jan. 17, 1955, AJC/FAD-1, Box 14, Espionage Trial, Egypt, 1954–60.

49. *Washington Star,* Feb. 2, 1955.

50. Egypt, Ministry of Information, *The Story of Zionist Espionage in Egypt,* (Cairo: Ministry of Information [1955]) p. 3.

51. Ibid., p. 57.

52. AJC flyer, "Anti-Semitic Propaganda Distributed by Egyptian Embassy," Apr. 4, 1955, AJC/FAD-1 Box 12, Egypt, 1950–55.

53. Jones to State, Jan. 31, 1955, USNA RG 84 Cairo Embassy General Records(1955) Box 264, 400.1.

54. Documents 105 and 106 in the appendix to Muhammad Hasanayn Haykal, *Milaffat al-suways: harb al-thalathin sana* (Cairo: al-Ahram, 1989), pp. 763–66. These are the only available official Egyptian documents relating to the case, so the conclusion based on them most be considered provisional.

55. Ali Rowghani, "The Portrayal of Nasser by the *New York Times*" (unpublished manuscript, Stanford University, Department of History, Mar. 1994).

56. As reported in the *New York Times,* Nov. 29, 1956.

57. "Statement on Situation of Egyptian Jewry Issued by International Conference of Representatives of Major Jewish Organizations," Waldorf Astoria Hotel, New York, Jan. 22, 1957, AJC/FAD-1, Box 12, Egypt, 1956.

58. Press release, Jan. 15, 1957, AJC/FAD-1, Box 13, Jewish Agencies, B'nai B'rith.

59. Zachariah Shuster to Eugene Hevesi Feb. 13, 1957, ibid.

60. "The Plight of the Jews of Egypt: A Fact Sheet from the American Jewish Committee," AJC/FAD-1, Box 12, Egypt, 1957.

61. Nathaniel H. Goodrich to Edwin J. Lukas, Mar. 25, 1957, AJC/FAD-1, Box 13, AJC Fact Sheet, Egypt, 1957; *Congressional Record,* Mar. 21, 1957, p. 3676.

62. Don Peretz to John Slawson, July 1, 1957, AJC/FAD-1, Box 13, AJC Fact Sheet, Egypt, 1957.

63. Unsigned, untitled report, Aug. 1957, AJC/FAD-1 Box 12, Egypt, 1956; *Frankfurter Allgemeine Zeitung,* July 25, 1957.

64. Don Peretz, "Egyptian Jews Today" (New York, AJC, Committee on Israel, Jan. 1956), AJC/FAD-1, Box 12, Egypt, 1956.

65. Karl Marx, *The Eighteenth Brumaire of Louis Bonaparte,* in Lewis S. Feuer (ed.), *Karl Marx and Friedrich Engels: Basic Writings on Politics and Philosophy* (Garden City, NY: Anchor Books, 1959), p. 320.

66. Tzenzura rashit le-ʿitonut ve-radyo le-menahel mahleket ha-ʿaliya, ha-sokhnut ha-yehudit, Jerusalem, Oct. 18, 1955, CZA S6/7241, "Mahleket ha-ʿaliya—1953–55."

67. Aviezer Golan, *Operation Susannah* (New York: Harper & Row, 1978), pp. 245–46; Robert Dassa, *Be-hazarah le-kahir* (Tel Aviv: Misrad ha-Bitahon, 1992), p. 69.

68. Dassa, *Be-hazarah le-kahir,* p. 69. This charge was first made in their 1975 television appearance, see below.

69. Hagai Eshed, *Mi natan et ha-hora'a? "ha-'esek ha-bish," parashat lavon, ve-hitpatrut ben-gurion* (Jerusalem: 'Edanim, 1979).

70. Eliyahu Hasin and Dan Hurvitz, *ha-Parashah* (Tel Aviv: 'Am ha-Sefer: 1961), p. 92.

71. Ibid., pp. 15–16, 92.

72. Shlomo Kohen-Tzidon, *Dramah be-aleksandriah ve-shnei harugei malkhut: mehandes sh. 'azar ve-doktor m. marzuk* (Tel Aviv: Sgi'al, 1965), pp. 63–65. An intended second volume memorializing Moshe Marzuq was apparently never published.

73. Felix Harari, "Mishpatei kahir 1954," *Yedi'ot aharonot,* Dec. 13, 1964, reproduced in ibid., p. 89.

74. Kohen-Tzidon, *Dramah be-aleksandriah ve-shnei harugei malkhut,* p. 112.

75. Ze'ev Schiff, "'Eser shanim le-mishpat ha-rigul," *ha-Aretz,* Dec. 11, 1964, reproduced in ibid., pp. 96–99. The quote from *The New Statesman and Nation,* Feb. 5, 1955, first appeared in *ha-Aretz,* Feb. 18, 1955.

76. Israeli Television, "Yoman yom shishi," report by Eitan Oren, Mar. 14, 1975. I viewed a film of the original broadcast at the archive of Israeli Television, Jerusalem.

77. Golan, *Operation Susannah,* p. 146.

78. Ibid., p. xii.

5. THE GRADUATES OF HA-SHOMER
   HA-TZA'IR IN ISRAEL

1. Gudrun Krämer, "Zionism in Egypt, 1917–1948," in Amnon Cohen and Gabriel Baer (eds.), *Egypt and Palestine: A Millennium of Association (868–1948)* (Jerusalem: Ben Zvi Institute for the Study of Jewish Communities in the East, 1984), p. 354.

2. Shlomo Barad, "ha-Pe'ilut ha-tzionit be-mitzrayim, 1917–1952," *Shorashim ba-mizrah* 2 (1989):105.

3. Ibid., pp. 94–95.

4. Biographical information on Ezra Talmor and all the quotes are taken from interviews conducted on Feb. 22 and Mar. 16, 1993, at Kibutz Nahshonim.

5. Barad, "ha-Pe'ilut ha-tzionit be-mitzrayim," p. 84.

6. Mitzrayim, tnu'at ha-shomer ha-tza'ir, HH 18–2.1(4) "Nahshonim—Erev zikaron le-aharon keshet za"l be-30 le-moto, 1983"[same as 97.10 (5 'ayin)].

7. Testimony of Ezra Talmor (interviewed by Shlomo Barad, Sept. 14, 1983) gives the date as 1940: YTM, Chativa 25/'ayin. Mekhal 7. Tik 1. When I spoke to Ezra Talmor in 1993, he dated this incident to 1938. This is, in fact, the more likely date.

8. Lazare Guetta [Givʿati], Mazkirut hanhagah ʿironit aleksandriah la-hanhagah ha-ʿelyonah, May 27, 1947, "Hanhagah ʿelyonah yisraʾel, mitzrayim, 1944–1947," HH 31.78(1), vol. 1.

9. Ha-ʿivri ha-tzaʿir, kvutzat birya, aleksandriah, *Iton Birya,* [1940s], MHT, T-12.2.

10. See Joel Beinin, *Was the Red Flag Flying There? Marxist Politics and the Arab-Israeli Conflict in Egypt and Israel, 1948–1965* (Berkeley: University of California Press, 1990).

11. Barad, "ha-Peʿilut ha-tzionit be-mitzrayim," pp. 103–104, gives the figure of 200 immigrants, but Michael M. Laskier, *The Jews of Egypt, 1920–1970: In the Midst of Zionism, Anti-Semitism, and the Middle East Conflict* (New York: New York University Press, 1992), p. 115, presents credible evidence to support the lower figure.

12. "35 be-Nahshonim: alon hag ha-35" (1984) and a brief history of the kibutz in French, source not indicated, HH 101.55.1—Nahshonim, (2) and (4).

13. Ezra [Talmor], "Kibutz ʿedot-mizrah ve-yiʿudav," *ha-Shavuʿa ba-kibutz ha-artzi,*" Oct. 16, 1964, p. 11.

14. Lazare Givʿati, interview, Nahshonim, Feb. 26, 1993.

15. Sami Shemtov, interview, Herzliah, Feb. 27, 1993.

16. Haim Shaʾul, interview, Nahshonim, Mar. 16, 1993.

17. Hanhagah rashit be-mitzrayim, la-hanhagah ha-ʿelyonah, Jan. 13, 1950, and Hanhagah rashit, ha-shomer ha-tzaʿir la-hanhagah ha-ʿelyonah, Paris, Jan. 31, 1950, HH 31.78(1) Hanhagah ʿelyonah, mitzrayim, 1948–50, vol. 2.

18. Peleg le-mazkirut ha-hanhagah ha-ʿelyonah shel ha-shomer ha-tzaʿir u-le-mazkirut ha-kibutz ha-artzi, July 4, 1950, Ha-makhlakah le-ʿinyanei ha-yehudim be-mizrakh ha-tikhon, Paris, Eli Peleg (1950–51), vol. 2., HH 31.82(5).

19. On the antagonism between Brakha and Shaʾul, see Hanhagah rashit be-mitzrayim, la-hanhagah ha-ʿelyonah, Jan. 13, 1950, and Hanhagah rashit, ha-shomer ha-tzaʿir la-hanhagah ha-ʿelyonah, Paris, Jan. 31, 1950, Hanhagah ʿelyonah, mitzrayim, 1948–50, vol. 2., HH 31.78(1). On Eli Peleg's complaints about anti-MAPAM sentiment, see Peleg le-mazkirut ha-hanhagah ha-ʿelyonah shel ha-shomer ha-tzaʿir u-le-mazkirut ha-kibutz ha-artzi, July 4, 1950, Ha-makhlakah le-ʿinyanei ha-yehudim be-mizrakh ha-tikhon, Paris, Eli Peleg (1950–51), vol. 2., HH 31.82(5). MAPAI decided to form ha-Bonim as a result of le-Ahdut ha-ʿAvodah joining MAPAM. He-halutz had sent members to kibutzim of ha-Kibutz ha-Meʾuhad, which was affiliated with le-Ahdut ha-ʿAvodah. Now that this movement was part of MAPAM (albeit only briefly until 1954), MAPAI wanted to establish a new youth movement loyal to itself.

20. "Din ve-heshbon ʿal ha-tnuʿah be-mitzrayim," hanhagah ha-rashit shel ha-shomer ha-tzaʿir, mitzrayim, no date, received in Jewish Agency on Jan. 23, 1950, CZA S20/112/230/71/18394.

21. Nurit Burlas (Jeanette Salama), interview, Kibutz ʿEin Shemer, Mar. 4, 1993.

22. David Harel, interviewed by ʿEinav Grosman, Oct. 31, 1988, "Parashat sneh ve-hishtakfutah be-kibutz ʿein-shemer," (Mevoʾot ʿEiron High School, Bagrut project, Jan. 1988), p. 27.

23. Perla Cohen, interview, Kibutz ʿEin-Shemer, Mar. 4, 1993.

24. Shlomo Burlas, Nurit Burlas, Perla Cohen, and Yitzhak Danon, interview, Kibutz ʿEin-Shemer, Mar. 4, 1993.

25. David Harel, interviewed by Grosman, *Parashat sneh,* p. 26.

26. Nurit Burlas, interview, Kibutz ʿEin-Shemer, Mar. 4, 1993. Others who expressed similar opinions were ʿAda and Haim Aharoni, interview, Haifa, Mar. 5, 1993; Ninette Piciotto Braunstein, interview, Tel Aviv, Mar.8, 1993; Zvi and Regine Cohen, interview, Tel Aviv, June 4 1993.

27. Ninette Piciotto Braunstein, interview, Tel Aviv, Mar. 8, 1993; Regine Cohen and others, interview, Tel Aviv, June 4, 1993.

28. Miyetek Zilbertal, interviewed by Grosman, *Parashat sneh,* pp. 20, 22.

29. Benny Aharon and David Harel, interview, Tel Aviv, Mar. 25, 1993.

30. Ninette Piciotto Braunstein, interview, Tel Aviv, Mar. 8, 1993.

31. Ibid.

32. Ibid.

33. Braunstein, interview, Tel Aviv, June 4, 1993.

34. Braunstein, interview, Mar. 8, 1993.

35. Haim Aharon, interview, Haifa, Mar. 5, 1993.

36. See Beinin, *Was the Red Flag Flying There?* pp. 130–34.

37. "Yeshivot ha-vaʿadah ha-politit ve-ha-medinit," Nov. 23, 1952, HH 90.66 bet (8).

38. The results of the vote and the total number of expulsions are based on Eli Tzur, "Parashat prag: ha-hanhagah ve-ha-opozitziah ba-kbhˮa," *Meʾasef* 18 (June 1988):51–52. Tzur's figures are drawn from the Yaʿakov Hazan papers, which were not available when I was conducting research for *Was the Red Flag Flying There?* Based on partial and different documentation, I estimated that over 20 percent of the members of ha-Kibutz ha-Artzi voted against clause one and over 200 members were expelled for political opposition: *Was the Red Flag Flying There?* pp. 132–33. Grosman, *Parashat sneh,* p. 18, cites the same article by Tzur but incorrectly quotes him as saying that between 160 and 200 individuals left their kibutzim. This understatement, perhaps a Freudian error, expresses a persistent tendency to minimize the significance of this entire affair among ha-Shomer ha-Tzaʿir loyalists. All the published numbers underestimate the strength of the left opposition in ha-Kibutz ha-Artzi because they are based on public votes, and many quiet sympathizers may not have expressed themselves if they were unable to contemplate leaving their kibutz for economic or other reasons.

39. Grosman, *Parashat sneh,* p, 23.

40. Ibid.

41. David Harel, interviewed by Grosman, *Parashat sneh,* pp. 28–29.

42. Two notes from Eliʿezer Beʾeri to Miyetek Zilbertal, Feb. 5, 1953, facsimiles in Grosman, *Parashat sneh,* appendix 12, p. 57; Eliʿezer beʾeri la-vaʿadah ha-politit, ʿein-shemer, Feb. 15, 1953, facsimile in Grosman, *Parashat sneh,* appendix 11, p. 56.

43. Correspondence between Natan Peled, mazkirut ha-kibutz ha-artzi and mazkirut of ʿEin-Shemer, Mar. 12, 1953, and between Natan Peled and Miyetek Zilbertal, Mar. 12, 1953, facsimiles in Grosman, *Parashat sneh,* appendix 6, p. 51.

44. These events were reported extensively in the Israeli press. See, for example, *ha-Shavuʻah ba-kibutz ha-artzi,* Apr. 9, 1953; *ʻAl ha-mishmar, Maʻariv,* and *Yediʻot aharonot,* Mar. 29, 1953; *Kol ha-ʻAm,* Apr. 7, 1953.

45. Facsimile in Grosman, *Parashat sneh,* appendix 10, p. 55.

46. Mazkirut Kibutz Mesilot, "Haʼemet ʻal ha-meʼoraʻot be-kibutz mesilot," *ha-Shavuʻa ba-kibutz ha-artzi,* June 12, 1953; "30 shanah le-kibutz mesilot, 1938–1968," *Ba-bayit,* no. 339, Jan.17, 1969, HH 101.47.1—K. Mesilot, Toldot.

47. Esty Comay, interview, Tel Aviv, Mar. 21, 1993.

48. Nelly and Benny Aharon, Susie and Albert ʻAmar, Ninette Piciotto Braunstein, Regine and Tzvi Cohen, Esty Comay, Ruby and Eli Danon, Bertha Kastel, Pninah and Izzy Mizrahi, interview, Tel Aviv, June 4, 1993.

6. THE COMMUNIST EMIGRES IN FRANCE

1. For further details and documentation about the communist movement in Egypt during this period, see Joel Beinin, *Was the Red Flag Flying There? Marxist Politics and the Arab-Israeli Conflict in Egypt and Israel, 1948–1965* (Berkeley: University of California Press, 1990).

2. Henri Curiel, *Pages autobiographiques* (1977, typescript), p. 54 and appendix, "Les principales étapes de la lutte intérieur qui s'ést déroulée autour du MDLN durant l'année Mai 1947–Juin 1948, dite année de l'unité" (rapport addressé par Henri Curiel à ses camarades du MDLN à la fin de 1955), p. 7.

3. Gilles Perrault, *Un homme à part* (Paris: Bernard Barrault, 1984), p. 195. *A Man Apart* (London: Zed Books, 1987) is an abridged English translation of the first part of the book but omits the passage referred to in this note.

4. Marcel Israel, letter to Gilles Perrault (n.d., typescript response to *Un homme à part*).

5. Perrault, *Un homme à part,* p. 195; English edition, p. 146.

6. This organization adopted several different names: New Dawn, Popular Vanguard for Liberation, Popular Democracy, Workers' Vanguard, and, finally, in 1957 the Workers' and Peasants' Communist Party.

7. Hilmi Yasin, interview, Cairo, May 25, 1986.

8. Fuʼad Mursi, interview, Cairo, May 19, 1986.

9. Perrault, *Un homme à part,* p. 199; English edition, p. 149.

10. Saʻd Zahran, *Fi usul al-siyyasa al-misriyya: maqal tahlili naqdi fi al-taʼrikh al-siyyasi* (Cairo: Dar al-Mustaqbal al-ʻArabi, 1985), p. 139.

11. Quoted in Selma Botman, *The Rise of Egyptian Communism, 1939–70* (Syracuse: Syracuse University Press, 1988), pp. 94–95

12. Mohamed Sid-Ahmed, interview, Cairo, June 22, 1992.

13. Curiel explained why HADETU supported the partition of Palestine in an interview in Rifʻat al-Saʻid, *al-Yasar al-misri waʼl-qadiyya al-filastiniyya* (Beirut: Dar al-Farabi, 1974), p. 284. The introductions by Raʼuf ʻAbbas and ʻIzzat Riyad to Raʼuf ʻAbbas (ed.), *Awraq hinri kuriyal waʼl-haraka al-shuyuʻiyya al-misriyya* (Cairo: Sina liʼl-Nashr, 1988) and Ibrahim Fathi, *Hinri kuriyal didda al-haraka al-shuyuʻiyya al-ʻarabiyya: al-qadiyya al-filastiniyya* (Cairo: Dar al-Nadim, 1989) crudely reproduce charges of Curiel's Zionist sympathies without critically evaluating the evidence.

14. Curiel, *Pages autobiographiques,* p. 57.

15. Arrest warrant quoted in Perrault, *Un homme à part,* p. 213.

16. Ibid., p. 220.

17. The total contribution of the members of the Rome Group to their comrades in Egypt was fifteen million (old) francs according to Yusuf Hazan, ibid., p. 274.

18. Ibid., p. 215.

19. Ibid., p. 263; English edition, p. 193.

20. Gilles Deleuze and Félix Guattari, *A Thousand Plateaus: Capitalism and Schizophrenia* (Minneapolis: University of Minnesota Press, 1987), p. 508.

21. Jonathan Boyarin, *Polish Jews in Paris: The Ethnography of Memory* (Bloomington: Indiana University Press, 1991).

22. *Bulletin d'études et d'information sur l'Egypte et le Soudan* no. 17 (Aug. 1952), Henri Curiel Papers.

23. "The Anglo-Egyptian Treaty, an Alienation of Egypt's National Sovereignty, a Danger for Asia's and World Security" (n.d., mimeographed) and "To the Conference of African and Asian Countries" (Apr. 18, 1955, mimeographed), both in Henri Curiel Papers.

24. For details, see Beinin, *Was the Red Flag Flying There?* pp. 153–59.

25. Ahmad Hamrush, interview, Cairo, Jan. 14, 1996. Perrault, *Un homme à part,* p. 271, relates the same story with somewhat different details.

26. Rifʿat al-Saʿid, *Ta'rikh al-haraka al-shuyuʿiyya al-misriyya: al-wahda, al-inqisam, al-hall, 1957–1965* (Cairo: Dar al-Thaqafa al-Jadida, 1986), p. 88.

27. "Khitab ila al-maktab al-siyasi," Jan. 12, 1958, Henri Curiel Papers.

28. Edward W. Said, "The Mind of Winter: Reflections on Life in Exile" *Harper's,* Sept. 1984, p. 51.

29. For an example of the kind of information on the political prisoners in Egypt provided to the European public, see Adel Montasser, "La répression anti-democratique en Egypte," *Les Temps Modernes* 16 (Aug.–Sept. 1960):418–41.

30. Quoted in Perrault, *Un homme á part,* p. 287.

31. Didar Rossano-Fawzy, interview, Paris, June 22, 1994.

32. Perrault, *Un homme à part,* p. 299.

33. Ibid., p. 351.

34. Ibid., pp. 352–53.

35. Ibid., p. 370.

36. Ibid., p. 365.

37. Georges Suffert, "Le patron des résaux d'aide aux terroristes," *Le Point,* June 21, 1976, pp. 52–57. For a point-by-point refutation, see Perrault, *Un homme à part,* pp 546–48.

38. Suffert, "Le patron des résaux d'aide aux terroristes," p. 57.

39. Quoted in Perrault, *Un homme à part,* p. 351.

40. Said, "The Mind of Winter," p. 53.

41. Raymond Aghion, interview, Paris, May 11, 1994.

42. Pierre Mendès-France, "Au Moyen-Orient, comme au Viêt-nam, la paix est un devoir," *Le Nouvel Observateur,* Apr. 24–30, 1968, p. 24.

43. Raymond Aghion, interview, Paris, May 23, 1994. Aghion also showed me copies of the correspondence between himself and Pierre Mendès-France.

44. Perrault, *Un homme à part,* pp. 533–35; Uri Avnery, *My Friend, the Enemy* (Westport, Conn.: Lawrence & Hill, 1986), p. 30.

45. Henri Curiel, "Note aux camarades égyptiens sur la nécessité de la poursuite de la lutte pour la paix," in *Pour une paix juste au proche-orient* (Paris: n.p., 1980), pp. 111–12. Hebrew edition: 'Al mizbeah ha-shalom (Jerusalem: Mifras, 1982).

46. This argument is developed in detail in Beinin, *Was the Red Flag Flying There?*

47. Hamrush, interview. Perrault, *Un homme à part,* pp. 535–36, presents a slightly different version of these events.

48. Hamrush, interview.

49. For example, *New York Times,* Apr. 6, 8, 1970.

50. Eric Rouleau, interview, Paris, May 15, 1994.

51. Abu Iyad with Eric Rouleau, *My Home, My Land: A Narrative of the Palestinian Struggle* (New York: Times Books, 1981). French edition: *Palestinien sans patrie* (Paris: Fayolle, 1978).

52. Hamrush, interview.

53. Perrault, *Un homme à part,* p. 552.

54. Hamrush, interview.

55. Perrault, *Un homme à part,* pp. 537–38; Curiel, 'Al mizbeah ha-shalom, p. 15.

56. Curiel, "Pour un 'second Bologne,'" in *Pour une paix juste au proche-orient,* pp. 152–55.

57. Mahmoud Hussein, letter to the editor of *Nouvel Observateur,* Oct. 22, 1973.

58. Saul Friedländer and Mahmoud Hussein, moderated by Jean Lacouture, *Arabs & Israelis: A Dialogue* (New York: Holmes & Meir, 1975).

59. See Fathi, *Hinri kuriyal didda al-haraka al-shuyu'iyya al-'arabiyya.*

60. Mahmoud Hussein, *The Class Struggle in Egypt, 1945–1970* (New York: Monthly Review Press, 1973).

61. Mohamed Sid-Ahmed, *After the Guns Fall Silent: Peace or Armageddon in the Middle East* (London: Croom Helm, 1976). Arabic edition: *Ba'da an tasquta al-madafi'* (Beirut: Dar al-Qadaya, 1975).

62. Ilan Halevi, interview, Paris, June 24, 1993. Benny Lévy is today the head of a *yeshiva* (religious seminary) in Strasbourg.

63. *The Times,* Nov. 16, Dec. 17, 1973.

64. Quoted in Alain Gresh, *The PLO: The Struggle within: towards an Independent Palestine* (London: Zed Books, 1985), p. 168. Gresh does a fine job of recounting the debates leading to this formulation in this book dedicated "To Issam Sartawi and Henri Curiel who died that the Palestinian and Israeli peoples might live in peace." Yusuf Hazan is also mentioned in the acknowledgments.

65. Avnery, *My Friend, the Enemy,* pp. 53–55.

66. Ibid., pp. 40–55, 71–73, 92–96, 119.

67. Ibid., p. 119–21; Perrault, *Un homme à part,* pp. 542–44.

68. Gresh, *The PLO: The Struggle Within,* p. 197.

69. *Ma'ariv,* Dec. 5, 1976.

70. Gresh, *The PLO: The Struggle Within,* p. 197; Perrault, *Un homme à part,* p.567. Perrrault's dates are Sept. 1976 to Mar. 1977. Because Gresh was much closer to the participants and his political analysis is superior to Perrault's, I have chosen his version.

71. Perrault, *Un homme à part,* p. 568; Avnery, *My Friend, the Enemy,* pp. 153–56.

72. Avnery, *My Friend, the Enemy.* p. 160.

73. Quoted in Gresh, *The PLO: The Struggle Within,* p. 199.

74. Ibid.

75. Didar Rossano-Fawzy, interview.

7. THE KARAITES OF THE SAN FRANCISCO BAY AREA

1. Joel Beinin, *Was the Red Flag Flying There? Marxist Politics and the Arab-Israeli Conflict in Egypt and Israel, 1948–1965* (Berkeley: University of California Press, 1990), pp. 185–88.

2. For example, Gudrun Krämer, *The Jews in Modern Egypt, 1914–1952* (Seattle: University of Washington Press, 1989) and Michael M. Laskier, *The Jews of Egypt, 1920–1970: In the Midst of Zionism, Anti-Semitism, and the Middle East Conflict* (New York: New York University Press, 1992) mention the Karaites only briefly.

3. Meron Benvenisti, *City of Stone: The Hidden History of Jerusalem* (Berkeley: University of California Press, 1996), p. 170.

4. Rabbi Avraham Gabr, interview, Ramlah, Jan. 11, 1993.

5. Mourad El-Kodsi, *The Karaite Jews of Egypt, 1882–1986* (Lyons, NY: Wilprint, 1987), p. 296.

6. Maurice Shammas, interview, Jerusalem, May 5, 1994.

7. Yosefa Nunu, interview, Ramlah, Mar. 7, 1993.

8. The lower figure is that of Nathan Schur, *History of the Karaites* (Frankfurt am Main: Peter Lang, 1992). p. 142. The higher figure is the one usually given by Karaite spokespersons. Schur's work is informed by traditional anti-Karaite biases and is not particularly perceptive or reliable.

9. Sumi Colligan, "Religion, Nationalism and Ethnicity in Israel: The Case of the Karaite Jews" (Ph.D. thesis, Princeton University, 1980), pp. 296–97.

10. Shlomo Barad, "ha-Pe'ilut ha-tzionit be-mitzrayim, 1917–1952," *Shorashim ba-mizrah* 2 (1989):118. Barad offers no documentary evidence in this article to support this rather harsh allegation, so I went to interview him at his home in Kibutz Karmia on Jan. 3, 1996, to hear how he had come to this conclusion. Barad was a member of ha-Shomer ha-Tza'ir in Tunisia, and his *gar'in* was training at the movement's farm at La Roche, France. The Tunisians were to have completed their training and emigrated to Israel, but they could not leave La Roche until a new group of trainees arrived to replace them. Their departure was delayed because of the late arrival of members of the Egyptian *gar'in* from Egypt headed toward 'Ein-Shemer. The Egyptians told him that they had delayed their departure and halted all immigration from Egypt as a protest against the Jewish Agency's policy of excluding Karaites from immigration to Israel. They resumed recruitment and processing of immigrants and

they themselves departed only after receiving assurances that this policy had been reversed.

11. Colligan, "Religion, Nationalism and Ethnicity in Israel," pp. 234–35; Y. Bitsur, *Ma'ariv,* June 30, 1961.

12. El-Kodsi, *The Karaite Jews of Egypt,* p. 99–100.

13. Ibid., pp. 62, 296.

14. Joe Pessah, interview, Mountain View, California, June 12, 1992.

15. Jehoash Hirshberg, "Musikah ke-gorem le-likud ha-kehilah ha-kara'it be-san frantzisko," *Pe'amim* 32 (1988):73.

16. Information about the Masliah family is based on my long friendship with Yusuf Darwish and many meetings with Jacob and Nelly Masliah, especially formal interviews in their home in San Francisco on May 8 and 16, 1992 (the second with the participation of their daughter, Nadia Hartmann).

17. Number of professionals as estimated by Maurice Shammas, interview, Jerusalem, May 5, 1994.

18. Nadia Hartmann, interview, San Francisco, May 16, 1992.

19. Henry and Doris Mourad, interview, Los Altos Hills, California, June 10, 1992.

20. Ibid.

21. Joe and Remy Pessah, interview, Mountain View, June 12, 1992.

22. "Egyptian Love Story Leads to Altar Here," *San Francisco Jewish Bulletin,* Jan. 29, 1971, p. 1.

23. Henry and Doris Mourad, interview.

24. Hirshberg, "Musikah ke-gorem le-likud ha-kehilah ha-kara'it be-san frantzisko," p. 70.

25. Information in this section is based on articles in various issues of the *KJA Bulletin,* confirmed and elaborated by discussion with members of the community.

26. *Northern California Jewish Bulletin,* Sept. 9, 1994.

27. Jehoash Hirshberg, "Musical Tradition as a Cohesive Force in a Community in Transition: The Case of the Karaites," *Asian Music* 17 (no. 2, 1986):46–68; Hirshberg, "Musikah ke-gorem le-likud ha-kehilah ha-kara'it be-san frantzisko," pp. 66–81.

28. Conversation with Elie Nounou, Congregation B'nai Israel, Daly City, California, Feb. 16, 1996.

29. Elaine Laporte, "Karaite Grandmother Celebrates Bat Mitzvah—at 70," *Northern California Jewish Bulletin,* Sept. 23, 1994, reprinted in *KJA Bulletin,* Mar. 1995, pp. 15–16.

30. Deborah Kalb, *The Jewish Monthly,* Mar. 1992, reprinted in *KJA Bulletin,* Sept. 1992, p. 6.

31. Rabbi Haim Levy, interview, San Francisco, July 13, 1993.

32. Rabbi Avraham Gabr, interview.

33. Sumi Colligan, personal communication, September 14, 1994.

8. THE RECOVERY OF EGYPTIAN JEWISH IDENTITY

1. Israel, Central Bureau of Statistics, Population and Housing Census, 1961, Publication No. 13, *Demographic Characteristics of the Population, Part*

III (Jerusalem, 1963), Table G, pp. xxx-xxxi. This figure does not include Egyptians who reached Israel but died before 1961 or Israeli-born children of Egyptians. Hence, the size of the Egyptian Jewish community and the total number of those who immigrated to Israel are somewhat larger. The Sudanese component of this figure is quite small, and some Sudanese Jews were of Egyptian origins.

2. Shlomo Kohen-Tzidon, "Kehilat yehudei kahir," *Mahanayim* 114 (Adar bet 5727/1967):44.

3. Ibid.

4. Ibid.

5. Shlomo Kohen-Tzidon, *Dramah be-aleksandriah ve-shnei harugei malkhut: mehandes sh. 'azar ve-doktor m. marzuk* (Tel Aviv: Sgi'al, 1965), jacket copy, p. 13.

6. Information about Sami 'Atiyah and his political activities is based on my interview with his son, Eliyahu 'Atiyah, and daughter, Sarah 'Atiyah Rayten, Holon, Jan. 12, 1993, and the following texts: Irgun Nifga'ei ha-Redifot ha-Anti-Yehudiot be-Mitzrayim, *Du"ah le-shnat 1971* (Holon: [ha-Irgun], 1972), MHT D-11/69.2; *Irgun nifga'ei ha-redifot ha-anti-yehudiot be-mitzrayim (1958–1978): 20 shanah shel pe'ilut mevurakhat shel ha-yo"r sami 'atiyah ve-haverei ha-mo'etza* (Holon: [ha-Irgun], 1978); Ronen Bergman, "Kamah haviyot neft shavah mishpahat qattawi," *Musaf ha-aretz,* Dec. 15, 1996, pp. 52–53.

7. *Irgun nifga'ei ha-redifot ha-anti-yehudiot be-mitzrayim (1958–1978),* pp. 20–21.

8. Bergman, "Kamah haviyot neft shavah mishpahat qattawi," p. 54.

9. Ibid.

10. Shlomo Barad et al. (eds.), *Haganah yehudit be-artzot ha-mizrah: rav siah shlishi, ha-ha'apalah ve-ha-haganah be-mitzrayim, 25 be-februar 1985* (Efal: Yad Tabenkin, ha-Makhon le-Heker ha-Tnu'ah ha-Tzionit ve-ha-Halutzit be-Artzot ha-Mizrah, ha-Makhon le-Heker Koah ha-Magen, 1986).

11. Shlomo Barad, interview, Kibutz Karmiah, Jan. 3, 1996.

12. Shlomo Barad, "ha-Pe'ilut ha-tzionit be-mitzrayim, 1917–1952," *Shorashim ba-mizrah* 2 (1989):65–127; Michael M. Laskier, *The Jews of Egypt, 1920–1970: In the Midst of Zionism, Anti-Semitism, and the Middle East Conflict* (New York: New York University Press, 1992) largely follows and elaborates on Barad's narrative.

13. Barad, "ha-Pe'ilut ha-tzionit be-mitzrayim," pp. 115–16.

14. Ada Aharoni, "Ha-tzionut lo yuva le-mitrayim—hi haytah sham," in Barad et al. (eds.), *Haganah yehudit be-artzot ha-mizrah,* pp. 20–21.

15. David Harel, "Ha-shomer ha-tza'ir be-mitzrayim," in Barad et al. (eds.), *Haganah yehudit be-artzot ha-mizrah,* pp. 44–48.

16. Judith Sudilovsky, "The 3,500-Year Exodus," *Jerusalem Post,* Passover supplement, Mar. 25, 1994, p. 10. David Harel reiterated and expanded on this point in interviews with me in Tel Aviv on Mar. 18 and 25, 1993.

17. *Irgun nifga'ei ha-redifot ha-anti-yehudiot be-mitzrayim (1958–1978),* pp. 28–29.

18. *al-Ahram,* Nov. 21, 1977, facsimile in ibid., p. 101.

19. Levana Zamir, *Ma'akhalim me-eretz ha-nilus (kasher)* (Tel Aviv: ha-Kibutz ha-Me'uhad, 1982), p. 9.

20. Ibid., p. 7.

21. Eleven issues appeared from Sept. 1985 to May 1993.

22. "A la rencontre des Juifs d'Egypte," *Le Monde*, Dec. 3, 1978.

23. "Retour aux sources en Egypt," *Nahar Misraïm* nos. 4–5 (Nov. 1981):28–40.

24. Paula Jacques, *Lumière de l'oeil* (Paris: Mercure de France, 1980), *Un Baiser froid comme la lune* (Paris: Mercure de France, 1983), *L'Héritage de tante Carlotta* (Paris: Gallimard, 1990), *Déborah et les anges dissipés* (Paris: Mercure de France, 1991).

25. Jacques Hassoun, interview, Paris, May 30, 1994.

26. Jacques Hassoun (ed.), *Juifs du nil* (Paris: Le Sycomore, 1981). Second edition, revised and expanded: *Histoire des Juifs du nil* (Paris: Minerve, 1990).

27. Hassoun, interview.

28. Ibid.; R. Stambouli, "Mémoire des juifs d'Egypte," *Information Juive*, July 1991, p. 11.

29. Victor D. Sanua, "A Jewish Childhood in Cairo," in Victor D. Sanua (ed.), *Fields of Offerings: Studies in Honor of Raphael Patai* (Rutherford, N.J.: Farleigh Dickinson University Press, 1983); Victor D. Sanua, "Emigration of the Sephardic Jews from Egypt after the Arab-Israeli Wars," *Proceedings of the Eleventh World Congress of Jewish Studies*, vol. 3 (Jerusalem: World Union of Jewish Studies, 1994), pp. 215–22; Mary Halawani (director and producer), *I Miss the Sun* (Sphinx Productions, 26 min., 1983).

30. Thirteenth World Congress of Poets [program], Haifa, Sept. 7–10, 1992; Thirteenth World Congress of Poets, *The International Shin Shalom Peace Poem Competition—a Selection* (Haifa, 1992, mimeographed).

31. The research project was carried out under the auspices of the Shmu'el Neaman Institute of the Technion. Ada Aharoni showed me copies of the questionnaire. Preliminary results of Haifa and Jerusalem respondents were reported by Uri Sharon, "80% me-ha-yehudim yotzei mitzrayim mukhanim levater 'al shtahim kedei liftor ha-ba'ayah ha-falestinit," *Davar*, Apr. 7, 1993.

32. Ada Aharoni, "The Image of Jewish Life in Egypt in the Writings of Egyptian Jewish Authors in Israel and Abroad," in Shimon Shamir (ed.), *The Jews of Egypt: A Mediterranean Society in Modern Times* (Boulder: Westview Press, 1987), p. 197. This essay brought many of the works discussed in this chapter to my attention.

33. Ada Aharoni, "ha-Shalom ve-ha-sfinks," in *Me-ha-piramidot la-karmel; Matehet ve-sigaliyot* (Tel Aviv: 'Eked, 1978), p. 38 (my translation from the Hebrew based on the English version of the poem). Freedom Square should more properly be rendered as Liberation Square, but I have retained this minor error so that the terminology of my translation of the poem coincides with that of the Hebrew version.

34. Ada Aharoni, "What Is Peace to Me?" in *From the Pyramids to the Carmel* (Tel Aviv: 'Eked, 1979), pp. 26–27.

35. Ada Aharoni, "Me-haifa le-kahir be-ahavah," *Musaf ha-aretz*, June 20, 1975, p. 28. Reprinted in *Me-ha-piramidot la-karmel*, pp. 75–80. English version: "Letter to Kadreya: From Haifa to Cairo with Love," in *From the Pyramids to the Carmel*, pp. 149–58. The letter was originally composed in English.

36. Ada Aharoni, *The Second Exodus: A Historical Novel* (Bryn Mawr: Dorrance, 1983). *Me-ha-nilus la-yarden* [From the Nile to the Jordan] (Tel Aviv: Tammuz, 1992) is a slightly expanded and revised version of the original English text. In the Hebrew version, the names of the characters have been changed. I refer to and quote from the English version.

37. Aharoni, *The Second Exodus*, p. 36.

38. Ibid., p. 54.

39. Ibid., pp. 54, 55, 56.

40. Ibid., p. 27.

41. Ibid., p. ix

42. Ibid., p. 60.

43. Aharoni, *From the Pyramids to the Carmel*, p. 149.

44. ʿAli Shalash, *al-Yahud waʾl-masun fi misr: dirasa taʾrikhiyya* (Cairo: al-Zahraʾ liʾl-Iʿlam al-ʿArabi, 1986). The original articles appeared in *al-Majalla* in the issues of July 17–23 through Aug. 28–Sept. 3, 1985.

45. Biographical details about Anda Harel-Dagan are drawn from an interview I conducted with her at Kibutz Hatzor, Mar. 9, 1993.

46. Anda Harel-Dagan, *Avraham hayah* (Tel Aviv: "Traklin" le-yad ʿEked, 1974), p. 9.

47. Harel-Dagan, interview.

48. Ibid.

49. My translation from the Hebrew. The reference is to Amos 9:13. The Israeli song is "Etz ha-rimon natan rayho" (The pomegranate tree gives forth its fruit), words by Y. Orland, music based on a Bukharan folk song.

50. My translation. The phrase *al tira* appears in Genesis 15:1, Genesis 26:25, Isaiah 44:2, and elsewhere.

51. Harel-Dagan, interview.

52. Maurice Shammas, *Shaykh shabtay wa-hikayat min harat al-yahud* (Shafa ʿAmr: al-Mashriq, 1979), pp. 6–7.

53. Maurice Shammas, interview, Jerusalem, May 5, 1994.

54. Shammas, *Shaykh shabtay wa-hikayat min harat al-yahud*, p. 49.

55. Ibid., p. 52.

56. Ibid., p. 78.

57. Ronit Matalon, *Zeh ʿim ha-panim eleynu* (Tel Aviv: ʿAm ʿOved, 1995).

58. The literary traces of this movement have been collected for the first time in any language in Ammiel Alcalay (ed.), *Keys to the Garden: New Israeli Writing* (San Francisco: City Lights Books, 1996).

59. The most extensive review that I have seen is Nisim Kalderon, "Lo ha-kol sipur ehad: ʿal ʿzeh ʿim ha-panim eleynuʾ shel ronit matalon," *Rehov* 2 (Aug. 1995):48–58. See also the interview with Ronit Matalon in *Davar* in note 73 in this chapter and the references there to positive reviews in *Maʿariv* and *ha-Aretz*.

60. Matalon, *Zeh ʿim ha-panim eleynu*, p. 22.

61. Ibid., pp. 254–55.

62. Ibid., p. 28.

63. Ibid., pp. 28, 29.

64. Ibid., p. 266.

65. Ibid., p. 157.

66. Ibid., p. 232.

67. Ibid., p. 261.

68. Ibid., p. 241.

69. Ibid., p. 225.

70. Ibid., pp. 268–69.

71. Ibid., p. 290.

72. Ibid., pp. 294–95.

73. Yitzhak Levtov, "Kismah shel ha-optziah ha-levantinit," *Davar,* Apr. 28, 1995, p. 13.

74. For example, Rif'at Sayyid Ahmad, *Wasf misr bi'l-'ibri: tafasil al-ikhtiraq al-isra'ili li'l-'aql al misri* (Cairo: Sina li'l-Nashr, 1989); 'Arfa 'Abduh 'Ali, *Gitu isra'ili fi al-qahira* (Cairo: Maktabat Madbuli, 1990).

75. Yosef Algazi, "Gam ha-gvul shelanu sagur," *ha-Aretz,* Mar. 17, 1996.

76. Ibid.

9. OPPOSING CAMP DAVID AND REMEMBERING THE JEWS OF EGYPT

1. For example, D. F. Green (ed.), *Arab Theologians on Jews and Israel* (Geneva: Editions de l'Avenir, 1971); Yehoshafat Harkabi, "On Arab Anti-semitism Once More," in Shmuel Almog (ed.), *Antisemitism through the Ages* (Oxford: Pergamon Press, 1988), pp. 227–39.

2. Rivka Yadlin, *An Arrogant and Oppressive Spirit: Anti-Zionism as Anti-Judaism in Egypt* (Oxford: Pergamon Press, 1989), pp. 96, 100.

3. For example, Qasim 'Abduh Qasim, *al-Yahud fi misr* (Cairo: Dar al-Shuruq, 1993); Ahmad 'Uthman, *Ta'rikh al-yahud,* vol. 1 (Cairo: Maktabat al-Shuruq, 1994).

4. Ahmad Muhammad Ghunaym and Ahmad Abu Kaff, *al-Yahud wa'l-haraka al-siyasiyya fi misr, 1897–1948* (Cairo: Dar al-Hilal [1969]).

5. Siham Nassar, *al-Yahud al-misriyyun bayna al-misriyya wa'l-sahyuniyya* (Beirut: Dar al-Wahda, 1979), pp. 8, 31. Egyptian reprint edition: *al-Yahud al-misriyyun: suhufuhum wa-majallatuhum, 1877–1950* (Cairo: al-'Arabi li'l-Nashr wa'l-Tawzi' [1980]). This work is based on the author's M.A. thesis granted by Cairo University's College of Communications in 1974. Nassar expanded her research into a doctoral thesis published as *al-Sahafa al-isra'iliyya wa'l-da'aya al-sahyuniyya fi misr* (Cairo: al-Zahra' li'l-I'lam al-'Arabi, 1991), which has a more Islamist tone than her earlier work.

6. 'Awatif 'Abd al-Rahman, *al-Sahafa al-sahyuniyya fi misr, 1897–1954: dirasa tahliliyya* (Cairo: Dar al-Thaqafa al-Jadida [1979]), pp. 11–12, 58–59, 120.

7. Nassar, *al-Yahud al-misriyyun bayna al-misriyya wa'l-sahyuniyya,* pp. 103–105.

8. See Victor Nahmias, "al-Shams: 'iton yehudi be-mitzrayim, 1934–1948," *Pe'amim* 16 (1983):128–41, especially pp. 140–41, for a critique of 'Awatif 'Abd al-Rahman's treatment of *al-Shams.*

9. Nassar, *al-Yahud al-misriyyun bayna al-misriyya wa'l-sahyuniyya,* p. 75. The reference is to a letter from Lieto Ibrahim Nunu, *al-Kalim,* July 1, 1945, p. 11. See Chapter 2, note 47, for further details.

10. Nassar, *al-Yahud al-misriyyun bayna al-misriyya wa'l-sahyuniyya,* p. 139.

11. Ibid., p. 82; ʿAbd al-Rahman, *al-Sahafa al-sahyuniyya fi misr,* pp. 47–48.

12. ʿAbd al-Rahman, *al-Sahafa al-sahyuniyya fi misr,* p. 116.

13. ʿArfa ʿAbduh ʿAli, *Malaff al-yahud fi misr al-haditha* (Cairo: Maktabat Madbuli, 1993); Saʿida Muhammad Husni, *al-Yahud fi misr, 1882–1948* (Cairo: al-Hayʾa al-Misriyya al-ʿAmma liʾl-Kitab, 1993).

14. Nabil ʿAbd al-Hamid Sayyid Ahmad, *al-Yahud fi misr: bayna qiyam israʾil waʾl-ʿudwan al-thulathi, 1948–1956* (Cairo: al-Hayʾa al-Misriyya al-ʿAmma liʾl-Kitab, 1991), pp. 42–43.

15. Ibid., p. 51.

16. Shihata Harun, *Yahudi fi al-qahira* (Cairo: Dar al-Thaqafa al-Haditha, 1987), p. 39.

17. Anis Mustafa Kamil, "al-Raʾsmaliyya al-yahudiyya fi misr," *al-Ahram al-iqtisadi* nos. 636–42 (Mar. 23–May 4, 1981).

18. Ibid., no. 636 (Mar. 23, 1981), p. 18.

19. Ibid., p. 19.

20. Ibid., no. 642 (May 4, 1981), p. 23.

21. Nabil ʿAbd al-Hamid Sayyid Ahmad, *al-Nashat al-iqtisadi liʾl-ajanib wa-atharuhu fi al-mujtamaʿ al-misri min sanat 1922 ila sanat 1952* (Cairo: al-Hayʾa al-Misriyya al-ʿAmma liʾl-Kitab, 1982); Nabil ʿAbd al-Hamid Sayyid Ahmad, *al-Hayat al-iqtisadiyya waʾl-ijtimaʿiyya liʾl-yahud fi misr, 1947–1956* (Cairo: Maktabat Madbuli, 1991); Ahmad, *al-Yahud fi misr.*

22. Ahmad, *al-Yahud fi misr,* pp. 5–6.

23. Ibid., pp. 7–8.

24. Ahmad, *al-Hayat al-iqtisadiyya waʾl-ijtimaʿiyya liʾl-yahud fi misr,* p. 21, n. 1.

25. Shimon Shamir, "The Evolution of Egyptian Nationality Laws and Their Application to the Jews in the Monarchy Period," in Shimon Shamir (ed.), *The Jews of Egypt: A Mediterranean Society in Modern Times* (Boulder: Westview Press, 1987), pp. 55 ff.

26. Ahmad, *al-Hayat al-iqtisadiyya waʾl-ijtimaʿiyya liʾl-yahud fi misr,* p. 44.

27. Ibid., pp. 48, 49.

28. Ibid., p. 11.

29. ʿAsim Disuqi, *Nahwa fahm taʾrikh misr al-iqtisadi al-ijtimaʿi* (Cairo: Dar al-Kitab al-Jamiʿi, 1981); Eric Davis, *Challenging Colonialism: Bank Misr and Egyptian Industrialization, 1920–1941* (Princeton: Princeton University Press, 1983). The following three paragraphs are based on my essay, "Economy and Society, 1923–1952," in M. W. Daly and Carl Petry (eds.), *Cambridge History of Egypt* (Cambridge: Cambridge University Press, forthcoming).

30. Anouar Abdel-Malek, *Idéologie et renaissance nationale* (Paris: Editions Anthropos, 1969), p. 112; Roger Owen, "The Development of Agricultural Production in Nineteenth Century Egypt: Capitalism of What Type?" in A. L. Udovitch (ed.), *The Islamic Middle East, 700–1900: Studies in Economic and Social History* (Princeton: Darwin Press, 1981), pp. 521–46.

31. Davis, *Challenging Colonialism,* p. 199; Robert Vitalis, *When Capitalists Collide: Business Conflict and the End of Empire in Egypt* (Berkeley: University of California Press, 1995), p. 10; Robert Vitalis, "On the Theory

and Practice of Compradors: The Role of 'Abbud Pasha in the Egyptian Political Economy," *International Journal of Middle East Studies* 22 (no. 3, 1990):291–315, especially n. 73, pp. 314–15.

32. Robert L. Tignor, "Bank Misr and Foreign Capitalism," *International Journal of Middle East Studies* 8 (no. 2, 1977):170–74, 177–78.

33. Robert L. Tignor, *Egyptian Textiles and British Capital, 1930–1956* (Cairo: American University in Cairo Press, 1989), pp. 23–42.

34. Ibid.; Robert L. Tignor, *State, Private Enterprise, and Economic Change in Egypt, 1918–1952* (Princeton: Princeton University Press, 1984).

35. Vitalis, *When Capitalists Collide*, pp. 12–15.

36. Maurice Zeitlin and Richard Earl Ratcliff, *Landlords & Capitalists: The Dominant Class of Chile* (Princeton: Princeton University Press, 1988); Peter Evans, *Dependent Development: The Alliance of Multinational, State, and Local Capital in Brazil* (Princeton: Princeton University Press, 1979).

37. Gavin Kitching, "The Role of the National Bourgeoisie in the Current Phase of Capitalist Development: Some Reflections," in Paul M. Lubeck (ed.), *The African Bourgeoisie: Capitalist Development in Nigeria, Kenya, and the Ivory Coast* (Boulder: Westview Press, 1987), p. 50.

38. Immanuel Wallerstein, "The Bourgeois(ie) as Concept and Reality," *New Left Review* no. 167 (Jan.–Feb. 1988):91–106. See also Robert Vitalis, "Ra'smaliyyun fi al-khayal: iydiyulujiyat al-tabaqa wa'l-zabun fi al-iqtisad al-siyasi al-misri," *Jadal* 1 (Aug. 1991):54–83.

39. Fredric Jameson, *Postmodernism, or the Cultural Logic of Late Capitalism* (Durham: Duke University Press, 1991), p. 47.

40. On the Suarès family, see Gudrun Krämer, *The Jews in Modern Egypt, 1914–1952* (Seattle: University of Washington Press, 1989), pp. 39–41.

41. On the Suarès family and the sugar industry, see Floresca Karanasou, "Egyptianisation: The 1947 Company Law and the Foreign Communities in Egypt" (D. Phil., St. Antony's College, Oxford University, 1992), pp. 161 ff; Tignor, *Egyptian Textiles and British Capital*, pp. 87–89.

42. Information in this paragraph is based on Karanasou, "Egyptianisation," pp. 165–66; Tignor, *Egyptian Textiles and British Capital*, pp. 87–89; annual volumes of Clément Levy (comp.), *The Stock Exchange Year-Book of Egypt* (Cairo: Stock Exchange Year-Book of Egypt, 1937–59) from 1947–48 to 1954–55.

43. Karanasou, "Egyptianisation," pp. 171–86.

44. Tignor, *Egyptian Textiles and British Capital*, p. 89.

45. Kamil, "al-Ra'smaliyya al-yahudiyya fi misr," *al-Ahram al-iqtisadi* no. 641 (Apr. 27, 1981):30; Ahmad, *al-Nashat al-iqtisadi li'l-ajanib*, pp. 196–98; 'Ali, *Malaff al-yahud fi misr al-haditha*, p. 98.

46. Kamil, "al-Ra'smaliyya al-yahudiyya fi misr," *al-Ahram al-iqtisadi* no. 641 (Apr. 27, 1981):30.

47. Ethel Carasso, "La Communauté Juive d'Egypte de 1948 à 1957" (Maîtrise d'Histoire Contemporaine, Université de Paris X, 1982), p. 34.

48. Tignor, *Egyptian Textiles and British Capital*, pp. 84 ff.

49. Ibid., pp. 91 ff. The chairman of the board of Anglo-Egyptian Oilfields from 1947 to February 1950 was a Jew, Sir Robert Waley Cohen, but he had no other connection to Egypt.

50. The following argument is based on Vitalis, *When Capitalists Collide.*

51. Kamil, "al-Ra'smaliyya al-yahudiyya fi misr," *al-Ahram al-iqtisadi* no. 640 (Apr. 20, 1981):11.

52. E. I. Politi, *L'Egypte de 1914 à Suez* (Paris: Presses de la Cité, 1965), p. 122.

53. Robert L. Tignor, "The Economic Activities of Foreigners in Egypt, 1920–1980: From Millet to Haute Bourgeoisie," *Comparative Studies in Society and History* 22 (1980):437–39.

54. Politi, *L'Egypte de 1914 à Suez,* pp. 117–18.

55. Ibid., p. 99.

56. Lutfi ʿAbd al-ʿAzim, "Ta'rikh al-yahud fi misr . . . li-madha," *al-Ahram al-iqtisadi* no. 636 (Mar. 23, 1981):16.

57. Yoram Meital, *Atarim yehudiyim be-mitzrayim* (Jerusalem: Makhon Ben-Tzvi le-Heker Kehilot Yisra'el ba-Mizrah, 1995); Tawhid Magdi, "Amlak al-yahud fi misr," *Ruz al-yusuf,* Dec. 18, 1995, pp. 39–45.

58. Magdi, "Amlak al-yahud fi misr," p. 40.

59. Ibid., pp. 41, 46.

60. Ibid., p. 40.

61. Anis Mansur, "Hadiyya li'l-sadat: Ikhtaraha yusuf wa-katabaha yusuf ʿan hayat yusuf," *Uktubir,* Feb. 2, 1992, p. 13. Wahba was responsible for calligraphic production of the headlines of the newspaper because headliners were not then used in Egypt.

62. Yusuf Wahba, interview, Bat Yam, Mar. 3, 1993.

63. Samir W. Raafat, *Maadi, 1904–1962: Society and History in a Cairo Suburb* (Cairo: Palm Press, 1994).

64. Samir W. Raafat, "Dynasty: The House of Yacoub Cattaui," *Egyptian Mail,* Apr. 2, 1994, p. 3; "Mr. Rabin, Where's Our Tree?" *Egyptian Mail,* Feb. 18, 1995; "The House Suares Built and How it Became the Mohamed Mahmoud Khalil Museum," *Egyptian Mail,* May 6, 1995; "The Hassan Sabri Street Murders Revisited," *Egyptian Mail,* Dec. 9, 1995, p. 3; "The National Bank of Egypt, 1898–1956," *Egyptian Mail,* May 11 and 25, 1996; "The House of Cicurel, *Al Ahram Weekly,* Dec. 15, 1994.

65. Raafat, "Mr. Rabin, Where's Our Tree?"; "Mar rabin, ayfo ha-etz shelanu," *Musaf ha-aretz,* Nov. 3, 1995, pp. 14–16.

Bibliography

ARCHIVAL COLLECTIONS

American Jewish Committee Records (YIVO Institute for Jewish Research, New York)
Arkhion ha-Haganah (Tel Aviv, Israel)
Arkhion ha-Kibutz ha-Me'uhad, Yad Tabenkin (Efal, Israel)
Arkhion ha-Shomer ha-Tza'ir, Yad Ya'ari, ha-Merkaz le-Te'ud ve-Heker shel ha-Shomer ha-Tza'ir (Giv'at Haviva, Israel)
Central Zionist Archives (Jerusalem, Israel)
Great Britain Foreign Office Archives, FO 371 (Public Records Office, London)
Henri Curiel Papers (Paris and International Institute of Social History, Amsterdam)
Jamie Lehmann Memorial Collection: Records of the Jewish Community of Cairo, 1886–1961 (Yeshiva University Archives, New York)
ha-Makhon le-Heker ha-Tfutzot, (Tel Aviv University, Ramat Aviv, Israel)
ha-Makhon le-Heker ha-Tnu'ah ha-Tzionit ve-ha-Halutzit be-Artzot ha-Mizrah, Yad Tabenkin (Efal, Israel)
United States National Archives (College Park, Maryland)

UNPUBLISHED WORKS

Arba'im shana la-gar'in ha-mitzri (Tel Aviv, Supergraf, 1979).
Carasso, Ethel, "La communauté Juive d'Egypte de 1948 à 1957," (Maîtrise d'Histoire Contemporaine, Université de Paris X, 1982).
Colligan, Sumi, "Religion, Nationalism and Ethnicity in Israel: The Case of the Karaite Jews" (Ph.D. dissertation, Princeton University, 1980).
Curiel, Henri, Pages autobiographiques (1977, typescript).

Gottesman, Lois, "Israel in Egypt: The Jewish Community in Egypt, 1922–1957" (M.A. thesis, Princeton University, 1982).

Grosman, 'Einav, "Parashat sneh ve-hishtakfutah be-kibutz 'ein-shemer" (Mevo'ot 'Eiron High School, Bagrut project, Jan. 1988).

Israel, Marcel, letter to Gilles Perrault (undated, typescript).

Karanasou, Floresca, "Egyptianisation: The 1947 Company Law and the Foreign Communities in Egypt" (D. Phil., St. Anthony's College, Oxford University, 1992).

Laniado, Asaf, "Kehilat yehudei mitzrayim, ha-perek ha-aharon be-sipurah shel kehilah 'atikat yomin: Korot kehilot kahir ve-aleksandriah bayn ha-shanim 1914–1950" (Gimnasia Rehavia, 'Avodat gemer, Jan. 1991).

Peretz, Don, "Egyptian Jews Today" (New York, American Jewish Committee, 1956, mimeographed).

Rowghani, Ali, "The Portrayal of Nasser by the *New York Times*" (typescript, Stanford University, Department of History, Mar. 1994).

Sanua, Victor D., "A Return to the Vanished World of Egyptian Jewry" (1993, typescript).

Thirteenth World Congress of Poets [program], Haifa, Sept. 7–10, 1992.

—, *The International Shin Shalom Peace Poem Competition—a Selection* (Haifa, 1992, mimeographed).

UNPUBLISHED INTERVIEWS

Raymond Aghion, Paris, May 11, May 23, 1994 (French)

Benny Aharon, Albert 'Amar, and Ninette Piciotto Braunstein, Tel Aviv, Apr. 28, 1994 (Hebrew)

Nelly and Benny Aharon, Suzy and Albert 'Amar, Ninette Piciotto Braunstein, Regine and Tzvi Cohen, Esty Comay, Ruby and Eli Danon, Bertha Kastel, Pninah and Izzy Mizrahi, (all except Esty Comay and Pninah Mizrahi were members of the Egyptian *gar'in* of 'Ein Shemer), Tel Aviv, June 4, 1993 (Hebrew)

Ada and Haim Aharoni, Haifa, Mar. 5, 1993 (Hebrew)

Mohamed Sid-Ahmed, Cairo, June 22, 1992 (English)

Albert 'Amar, Kfar Saba, Apr. 7, 1993 (Hebrew)

Eliyahu 'Atiyah and Sarah 'Atiyah Rayten, Holon, Jan. 12, 1993 (Hebrew)

Shlomo Barad, Karmiah, Jan. 3, 1996 (Hebrew)

Ninette Piciotto Braunstein, Tel Aviv, Mar. 8, 1993 (Hebrew)

Nurit and Shlomo Burlas, 'Ein-Shemer, Mar. 4, 1993 (Hebrew)

Perla Cohen and Yitzhak Danon, 'Ein-Shemer, Mar. 4, 1993 (Hebrew)

Esty Comay, Ramat Aviv, Mar. 21, 1993 (Hebrew)

Ralph Costi, Paris, May 27, 1994 (French and Arabic)

Rabbi Avraham Gabr, Ramlah, Jan. 11, 1993 (Hebrew)

Lazare Giv'ati (Guetta), Nahshonim, Feb. 26, 1993 (Hebrew)

Ilan Halevi, Paris, June 24, 1993 (English)

Ahmad Hamrush, Cairo, Jan. 14, 1996 (Arabic)

David Harel (Wahba), Tel Aviv, Mar. 18, 1993 (Hebrew)

David Harel and Benny Aharon, Tel Aviv, Mar. 25, 1993 (Hebrew)

Anda Harel-Dagan, Hatzor, Mar. 9, 1993 (Hebrew)
Nadia Hartmann, San Francisco, May 16, 1992 (English)
Jacques Hassoun, Paris, May 30, 1994, Palo Alto, California, Nov. 2, 1995 (French)
Rabbi Haim Levy, San Francisco, July 13, 1993 (Hebrew)
Yosef Marzuk, Tel Aviv, July 17, 1985 (Hebrew, interviewed by Shlomo Barad)
Nelly and Jacob Masliah, San Francisco, May 8 and May 16, 1992 (English)
Doris and Henry Mourad, Los Altos Hills, California, June 10, 1992 (English)
Fu'ad Mursi, Cairo, May 19, 1986 (Arabic)
Elie Nounou, Daly City, California, Feb. 16, 1996 (English)
Yosefa Nunu, Ramlah, Mar. 7, 1993 (Hebrew)
Albert Oudiz, Paris, May 26, 1994 (French)
Mario Perez, Paris, June 2, 1994 (French and English)
Remy and Joe Pessah, Mountain View, California, June 12, 1992 (English)
Raymond Pinto, Paris, May 14, 1994 (French)
Yusuf al-Qudsi, Cairo, May 19, 1993 (Arabic)
Didar Rossano-Fawzy, Paris, June 22, 1994 (French and English)
Eric Rouleau, Paris, May 25, 1994 (French and English)
Rif'at al-Sa'id, Cairo, May 22, 1986 (Arabic)
Maurice Shammas, Jerusalem, May 5, 1994 (Hebrew)
Haim Sha'ul, Nahshonim, Mar. 16, 1993 (Hebrew)
Sami Shemtov, Herzliah, Feb. 27, 1993 (Hebrew)
Raymond Stambouli, Paris, May 20, 1994 (French)
Ezra Talmor (Zanona), Nahshonim, Feb. 23 and Mar. 16, 1993 (Hebrew)
Yusuf Wahba, Bat Yam, Mar. 3, 1993 (Arabic)
Hilmi Yasin, Cairo, May 25, 1986 (Arabic)

PUBLISHED DOCUMENTS

American Jewish Congress, *The Black Record: Nasser's Persecution of Egyptian Jewry* (New York: American Jewish Congress, 1957).
Le Comité pour la restauration de l'autoriteé du Grand Rabbinat d'Alexandrie, *La Verité sur la démission de S. Em. Dr. Moise Ventura, Grand-Rabbin d'Alexandrie* (Alexandria: La Comité, Mar. 1948).
Communauté Israelite du Caire, *Assemblé Générale Ordinaire, Mars 1954* [text in French and Arabic] (Cairo: Imprimerie La Patrie [1954]).
—, *Novembre 1960* [text in French and Arabic] ([Cairo]: mimeographed [1960]).
Egypt, Ministry of Information, *The Story of Zionist Espionage in Egypt* (Cairo: Ministry of Information [1955]).
Irgun nifga'ei ha-redifot ha-anti yehudiot be-mitzrayim, *Du"ah le-shnat 1971* (Holon: [ha-Irgun], 1972).
Irgun nifga'ei ha-redifot ha-anti-yehudiot be-mitzrayim (1958–1978): 20 shanah shel pe'ilut mevurakhat shel ha-yo"r sami 'atiyah ve-haverei ha-mo'etza (Holon: [ha-Irgun], 1978).
Israel, Central Bureau of Statistics, Population and Housing Census, 1961, Publication No. 13, *Demographic Characteristics of the Population, Part III* (Jerusalem, 1963).

PERIODICALS

al-Ahram
Al Ahram Weekly
'Al ha-mishmar
ha-Aretz
al-Balagh
Bnai mikra'
ha-Boker
Davar
Egyptian Mail
Goshen: alon moreshet yahadut mitzrayim
al-Hayat
Herut
Jerusalem Post
Journal d'Egypte
al-Jumhuriyya
al-Kalim
KJA Bulletin
Kol ha-'Am
Ma'ariv
Manchester Guardian
la-Merhav
Middle East Times
al-Musawwar
Nahar Misraïm
New York Times
Northern California Jewish Bulletin
Revue de l'histoire juive en Egypte
Ruz al-yusuf
al-Saraha
ha-Shavu'a ba-kibutz ha-artzi
al-Siyasa al-usbu'iyya
al-Tas'ira
The Times (London)
al-Wafd
Yedi'ot aharonot

BOOKS, ARTICLES, FILMS, TELEVISION PROGRAMS

'Abbas, Ra'uf (ed.), *Awraq hinri kuriyal wa'l-haraka al-shuyu'iyya al-misriyya* (Cairo: Sina li'l-Nashr, 1988).

'Abbas, Ra'uf, "Hinri kuriyal bayna al-ustura wa'l-waqi' al-ta'rikhi," *al-Hilal* 66 (no. 11, Nov. 1988).

'Abd al-'Azim, Lutfi, "Ta'rikh al-yahud fi misr ... li-madha," *al-Ahram al-iqtisadi* no. 636 (Mar. 23, 1981):16.

'Abd al-Rahman, 'Awatif, *al-Sihafa al-sahyuniyya fi misr, 1897–1954* (Cairo: Dar al-Thaqafa al-Jadida [1979]).

Abdel-Malek, Anouar, *Idéologie et renaissance nationale* (Paris: Editions Anthropos, 1969).

Abu Iyad, with Eric Rouleau, *My Home, My Land* (New York: Times Books, 1981).

Abu Kaff, Ahmad, *al-Yahud al-misriyyun fi al-fikr wa'l-waqi' al-misri* (Cairo: Jam'iyyat Khariji Kulliyat al-Iqtisad wa'l-'Ulum al-Siyasiyya [1980?]).

Aciman, André, *Out of Egypt* (New York: Farrar Straus Giroux, 1994).

Aghion, Raoul, and I[sadore?] R. Feldman, *Les Actes de Montreux: Abolition des Capitulations en Egypte* (Paris: Editions Jos. Vermaut, 1937).

Aharoni, Ada, *From the Pyramids to the Carmel* ([Tel Aviv]: 'Eked, 1979).

—, "The Image of Jewish Life in Egypt in the Writings of Egyptian Jewish Authors in Israel and Abroad," in Shimon Shamir (ed.), *The Jews of Egypt: A Mediterranean Society in Modern Times* (Boulder: Westview Press, 1987), pp. 192–98.

—, *Me-ha-nilus la-yarden* (Tel Aviv: Tammuz, 1992).

—, *Me-ha-piramidot la-karmel; Matehet ve-sigaliyot* (Tel Aviv: 'Eked, 1978).

—, *The Second Exodus: A Historical Novel* (Bryn Mawr: Dorrance, 1983).

Ahmad, Nabil 'Abd al-Hamid Savyid, *al-Hayat al-iqtisadiyya wa'l- ijtima'iyya li'l-yahud fi misr, 1947–1956* (Cairo: Maktabat Madbuli, 1991).

—, *al-Nashat al-iqtisadi li'l-ajanib wa-atharuhu fi al-mujtama' al-misri, min sanat 1922 ila sanat 1952* (Cairo: al-Hay'a al-Misriyya al-'Amma li'l-Kitab, 1982).

—, *al-Yahud fi misr: bayna qiyam isra'il wa'l-'udwan al-thulathi, 1948–1956* (Cairo: al-Hay'a al-Misriyya al-'Amma li'l-Kitab, 1991).

Ahmad, Rif'at Sayyid, *Wasf misr bi'l-'ibri: tafasil al-ikhtiraq al-isra'ili li'l-'aql al misri* (Cairo: Sina li'l-Nashr, 1989).

Alcalay, Ammiel, *After Jews and Arabs: Remaking Levantine Culture* (Minneapolis: University of Minnesota Press, 1993).

—(ed.), *Keys to the Garden: New Israeli Writing* (San Francisco: City Lights Books, 1996).

Algamil, Yosef, "Ha-hakham tuvia simha levi babovitch: aharon hakhmei kehilat ha-kara'im be-mitzrayim," *Pe'amim* 32 (1987):40–59.

—, *Toldot ha-yahadut ha-kara'it: korot hayei ha-kehilah ha-kara'it be-galut u-ve-eretz yisra'el,* vol.1 (Ramlah: ha-Mo'etzah ha-Artzit shel ha-Yehudim ha-Kara'im be-Yisra'el, 1979), vol 2 (Ramlah: Author, 1981).

—, *ha-Yahadut ha-kara'it be-mitzrayim be'et hehadashah* (Ramlah: ha-Mo'etzah ha-Artzit shel ha-Yehudim ha-Kara'im be-Yisra'el, 1985).

'Ali, 'Arfa 'Abduh, *Gitu isra'ili fi al-qahira* (Cairo: Maktabat Madbuli, 1990).

—, *Malaff al-yahud fi misr al-haditha* (Cairo: Maktabat Madbuli, 1993).

Avnery, Uri, *My Friend, the Enemy* (Westport, Conn.: Lawrence & Hill, 1986).

Babovitch, Tuvia ben Simha Levi, *In lam as'a li-nafsi fa-man yas'a liyya* (Cairo: Jam'iyyat al-Ikhwan al-Qara'in, 1946).

Barad, Shlomo, "ha-Pe'ilut ha-tzionit be-mitzrayim, 1917–1952," *Shorashim ba-mizrah* 2 (1989):65–127.

—, et al. (eds.), *Haganah yehudit be-artzot ha-mizrah: rav-siah shlishi, ha-ha'apalah be-mitzrayim, 25 februar 1985* (Efal: Yad Tabenkin, ha-Makhon le-Heker ha-Tnu'ah ha-Tzionit ve-ha-Halutzit be-Artzot ha-Mizrah, ha-Makhon le-Heker Koah ha-Magen, 1986).

Barth, Frederick, *Ethnic Groups and Boundaries: The Social Origins of Cultural Difference* (Bergen: Scandinavian University Books, 1969).

Bat Ye'or [Giselle Littman], *The Dhimmi: Jews and Christians under Islam* (Rutherford, N.J.: Farleigh Dickinson University Press, 1985).

—, "Islam and the Dhimmis," *Jerusalem Quarterly* no. 42 (Spring 1987):83–88.

—, *Yehudei mitzrayim* (Tel Aviv: Sifriat Ma'ariv ve-ha-Kongres ha-Yehudi ha-'Olami be-Yozmat Misrad ha-Hinukh ve-ha-Tarbut be-hishtatfut ha-Mahlakah la-Kehilot ha-Sfaradiyot shel ha-Histadrut ha-Tziyonit, 1974).

—, "Zionism in Islamic Lands: The Case of Egypt," *Wiener Library Bulletin* 30, n.s. (nos. 43–44, 1977):16–29.

Beinin, Joel, "Bernard Lewis's Anti-Semites," *Middle East Report* no. 147 (July–Aug. 1987):43–45.

—, "Economy and Society, 1923–1952," in M. W. Daly and Carl Petry (eds.), *Cambridge History of Egypt* (Cambridge: Cambridge University Press, forthcoming).

—, "From Land Day to Equality Day," in Zachary Lockman and Joel Beinin (eds.), *Intifada: The Palestinian Uprising against Israeli Occupation* (Boston: South End Press, 1989), pp. 205–16.

—, *Was the Red Flag Flying There? Marxist Politics and the Arab-Israeli Conflict in Egypt and Israel, 1948–1965* (Berkeley: University of California Press, 1990).

—, "Writing Class: Workers and Modern Egyptian Colloquial Poetry (*Zajal*)," *Poetics Today* 15 (no. 2, 1994):191–215.

Benbassa, Esther (ed.), *Haim Nahum: A Sephardic Chief Rabbi in Politics, 1892–1923* (Tuscaloosa: University of Alabama Press, 1995).

Ben-Gurion, David, *Dvarim ke-hevyatam* (Tel Aviv: 'Am ha-Sefer, 1965).

Bensimon, Doris, *Les Juifs de France et leurs relations avec Israël, 1945–1988* (Paris: L'Harmattan, 1989).

Benvenisti, Meron, *City of Stone: The Hidden History of Jerusalem* (Berkeley: University of California Press, 1996).

Berg, Nancy E., *Exile from Exile: Israeli Writers from Iraq* (Albany: State University of New York Press, 1996).

Biton, Erez, *Mabat le-mitzrayim* (Ramat Gan: Apirion, 1989).

Blackbourn, David, and Geoff Eley, *The Peculiarities of German History* (Oxford: Oxford University Press, 1984).

Blattner, E. J. (ed.), *Le Mondain égyptien: L'Annuaire de l'élite d'Egypte (The Egyptian Who's Who)* [title varies](Cairo: Imprimairie Française, 1947, 1952, 1954, 1956, 1959).

Bonacich, Edna and John Modell, *The Economic Basis of Ethnic Solidarity* (Berkeley: University of California Press, 1980).

Botman, Selma, *The Rise of Egyptian Communism, 1939–70* (Syracuse: Syracuse University Press, 1988).

Boyarin, Jonathan, *Polish Jews in Paris: The Ethnography of Memory* (Bloomington: Indiana University Press, 1991).

Bramah, Yisra'el, "Aleksandriah, hazarnu elayikh shenit," *Akhshav* 39–40 (Spring–Summer 1979):341–44.

Breckinridge, Carol A., and Arjun Appadurai, "Moving Targets," *Public Culture* 2 (no. 1, 1989):i–iv.

Cabasso, Gilbert, et al., *Juifs d'Egypte: Images et textes* (Paris: Editions du Scribe, 1984).

Carasso, Ethel, "La stuation economique des Juifs d'Egypte," *Nahar Misraïm* no. 7 (June 1982):15–20.

Chakrabarty, Dipesh, "The Death of History? Historical Consciousness and the Culture of Late Capitalism," *Public Culture* 4 (no. 2, 1992):47–65.

Chatterjee, Partha, *The Nation and its Fragments* (Princeton: Princeton University Press, 1993).

Clifford, James, *The Predicament of Culture* (Cambridge: Harvard University Press, 1988).

Cohen, Hayyim J., *The Jews of the Middle East, 1860–1972* (New York: Wiley, 1973).

Cohen, Mark R., "Islam and the Jews: Myth, Counter-Myth, History," *Jerusalem Quarterly* no. 38 (Spring 1986):125–37.

—, Letter to the Editor, *Tikkun* 6 (July–Aug. 1991):96.

—, "The Neo-Lachrymose Conception of Jewish-Arab History," *Tikkun* 6 (May–June 1991):55–60.

—, *Under Crescent and Cross: The Jews in the Middle Ages* (Princeton: Princeton University Press, 1994).

Cohen-Almagor, Raphael, "Cultural Pluralism and the Israeli Nation-Building Ideology," *International Journal of Middle East Studies* 27 (no. 4, 1995):461–84.

Curiel, Henri, *Pour une paix juste au proche-orient* (Paris: n.p.,1980); Hebrew edition: *'Al mizbeah ha-shalom* (Jerusalem: Mifras, 1982).

Danon, Hilda, and Ilios Yannakakis, "Le sujet local citoyen d'Egypte," in Maurice Olender and Pierre Birnbaum (eds.), *Le racisme, le mythe et science* (Brussels: Complexe, 1981), pp. 247–55.

Dassa, Robert, *Be-hazarah le-kahir* (Tel Aviv: Misrad ha-Bitahon, 1992).

Davis, Eric, *Challenging Colonialism: Bank Misr and Egyptian Industrialization, 1920–1941* (Princeton: Princeton University Press, 1983).

Deeb, Marius, "The Socioeconomic Role of the Local Foreign Minorities in Modern Egypt, 1805–1961," *International Journal of Middle East Studies* 9 (no. 1, 1978):11–22.

Deleuze, Gilles, and Félix Guattari, *A Thousand Plateaus: Capitalism and Schizophrenia* (Minneapolis: University of Minnesota Press, 1987).

Didier, Monciaud, "Mémoire, politique et passions: Perceptions égyptiens d'Henri Curiel," *Egypte/Monde Arabe* no. 20 (1994):91–105.

Disuqi, 'Asim, *Misr al-mu'asira fi dirasat al-mu'arikhin al-misriyyin* (Cairo: Dar al-Hurriya, 1978).

—, *Nahwa fahm ta'rikh misr al-iqtisadi al-ijtima'i* (Cairo: Dar al-Kitab al-Jami'i, 1981).

Djebar, Assia, *Fantasia: An Algerian Cavalcade* (Portsmouth, NH: Heinemann, 1993).

El-Ad, Avri, *Decline of Honor* (Chicago: Henry Regnery, 1976).

El-Kodsi, Mourad, *The Karaite Jews of Egypt, 1882–1986* (Lyons, NY: Wilprint, 1987).

Eshed, Hagai, *Mi natan et ha-hora'ah? "ha-'esek ha-bish," parashat lavon, ve-hitpatrut ben-gurion* (Jerusalem: 'Edanim, 1979).

Eskandarany, Ya'acoub Daoud, "Egyptian Jewry: Why It Declined," *Khamsin* 5 (1978):27–34.

Etinger, Ester, review of *Kayitz aleksandroni, Yerushalayim* 13 (no. 3, taf shin lamed tet):90–92.

Evans, Peter, *Dependent Development: The Alliance of Multinational, State, and Local Capital in Brazil* (Princeton: Princeton University Press, 1979).

Evron, Boaz, "Holocaust: The Uses of Disaster," *Radical America* 17 (no. 4, 1983):7–21.

Farag, Murad, *al-Qudsiyyat* (Cairo: Matba'at al-I'timad, 1923).

Fargeon, Maurice, *Les Juifs en Egypte: Depuis les origines jusqu'a ce jour* (Cairo: Paul Barbey, 1938).

—, *Médecins et avocats Juifs au service de l'Egypte* (Cairo: Imprimerie Lencioni, 1939).

—, (ed.), *Annuaire des Juifs d'Egypte et du proche-orient, 1942* (Cairo: La Société des Editions Historiques Juives d'Egypte, 1943).

—, (ed.), *Annuaire des Juifs d'Egypte et du proche-orient, 5706/1945–1946* (Cairo: La Société des Editions Historiques Juives d'Egypte [1945]).

Fathi, Ibrahim, *Hinri kuriyal didda al-haraka al-shuyu'iyya al-'arabiyya: al-qadiyya al-filastiniyya* (Cairo: Dar al-Nadim, 1989).

Fau, Jean Francois, and Frédéric Abecassis, "Les Karaites: une communaute cairote a l'heure de l'état nation," *Egypte/Monde Arabe* no. 11 (1992):47–58.

Fisher, Marcelle, *Armando* (Tel Aviv: Yeda Sela, 1982).

—, *Les Khamsins d'antan: La Petite histoire des Juifs d'Egypte* (Tel Aviv: M. Rachlin Ltd., 1990).

Friedländer, Saul, and Mahmoud Hussein, moderated by Jean Lacouture, *Arabs & Israelis: A Dialogue* (New York: Holmes & Meir, 1975).

Gehlen, Reinhard, *The Service: The Memoirs of General Reinhard Gehlen* (New York: World Publishing, 1972).

Gendzier, Irene, *The Practical Visions of Ya'qub Sanu'* (Cambridge: Center for Middle Eastern Studies, Harvard University, 1966).

Gershoni, Israel, and James P. Jankowski, *Beyond the Nile Valley: Redefining the Egyptian Nation, 1930–1945* (Cambridge: Cambridge University Press, 1995).

Ghunaym, Ahmad Muhammad, and Ahmad Abu Kaff, *al-Yahud wa'l-haraka al-sahyuniyya fi misr, 1897–1947* (Cairo: Dar al-Hilal [1969]).

Giladi, Gideon N., *Discord in Zion* (London: Scorpion, 1990).

Gilbert, Martin, *The Jews of Arab Lands: Their History in Maps* (London: World Organization of Jews from Arab Countries and Board of Deputies of British Jews, 1976).

Gilroy, Paul, *The Black Atlantic: Modernity and Double Consciousness* (Cambridge: Harvard University Press, 1993).

—, *There Ain't No Black in the Union Jack* (Chicago: University of Chicago Press, 1991).

Ginosar, Ya'irah, "'Otzmat ha-kfilut," *'Iton 77* (nos. 8–9, May–June 1978):14.

Golan, Aviezer, *Mivtza' suzanah* (Jerusalem: 'Edanim, 1976); English translation: *Operation Susannah* (New York: Harper & Row, 1978).

Gormezano-Goren, Yitzhaq, *Blanche* (Tel Aviv: 'Am 'Oved, 1987).

—, *Kayitz aleksandroni* (Tel Aviv: 'Am Oved, 1978).

Green D. F. (ed.), *Arab Theologians on Jews and Israel* (Geneva: Editions de l'Avenir, 1971).

Green, Stephen, *Taking Sides: America's Secret Relations with a Militant Israel* (New York: William Morrow, 1984).

Gresh, Alain, *The PLO: The Struggle Within, Towards an Independent Palestine* (London: Zed Books, 1985).

Gupta, Akhil, "The Song of the Nonaligned World: Transnational Identities and the Reinscription of Space in Late Capitalism," *Cultural Anthropology* 7 (no. 1, 1992):63–79.

—, and James Ferguson, "Beyond 'Culture': Space, Identity, and the Politics of Difference," *Cultural Anthropology* 7 (no. 1, 1992):6–23.

Halawani, Mary (director and producer), "I Miss the Sun" (Sphinx Productions, 26 min., 1983).

Halbwachs, Maurice, *On Collective Memory* (Chicago: University of Chicago Press, 1992).

Halevi, Ilan, *A History of the Jews: Ancient and Modern* (London: Zed Books, 1987).

Hall, Stuart, "Cultural Identity and Diaspora," in Jonathan Rutherford (ed.), *Identity, Community, Culture, Difference* (London: Lawrence & Wishart, 1990), pp. 222–37.

Hamuda, 'Adil, *'Amaliyyat suzana: al-malaff al-kamil li-qadiyat lafun* (Cairo: Maktabat Madbuli, 1988).

Harel, Iser, *Bitahon ve-demokratiah* (Tel Aviv: 'Edanim, 1989).

—, *Kam ish 'al ahiv: ha-nituah ha-musmakh ve-ha-mematzeh shel "parashat lavon"* (Jerusalem: Keter, 1982).

Harel-Dagan, Anda, *Avraham hayah* (Tel Aviv: "Traklin" le-yad 'Eked, 1974).

—, *Po'emah kahirit* (Tel Aviv: 'Eked, 1981).

Harkabi, Yehoshafat, *Arab Attitudes to Israel* (Jerusalem: Keter, 1972).

—, *'Edut ishit: ha-parashah mi-nekudat re'uti* (Tel Aviv: Ramot, 1994).

—, "On Arab Antisemitism Once More," in Shmuel Almog (ed.), *Antisemitism through the Ages* (Oxford: Pergamon Press, 1988), pp. 227–39.

Harun, Shihata, *Yahudi fi al-qahira* (Cairo: Dar al-Thaqafa al-Haditha, 1987).

Hasanayn, 'Adil, *Layla murad: ya musafir wa-nas hawak* (Cairo: Amadu, 1993).

Hasin, Eliyahu, and Dan Hurvitz, *ha-Parasha* (Tel Aviv: 'Am ha-Sefer, 1961).

Hassoun, Jacques, "De l'Egypte et de quelques Juifs Egyptiens . . . ," in Liliane Abensour et al. (eds.), *Cultures Juives méditerranéennes et orientales* (Paris: Syros, 1982), pp. 221–31.

—, "I Am Jewish Because I Am Egyptian, I Am Egyptian Because I Am Jewish" (interview by Joel Beinin), *MERIP Newsletter*, Winter 1997, pp. 2–3.

—, "The Traditional Jewry of the Hara," in Shimon Shamir (ed.), *The Jews of Egypt: A Mediterranean Society in Modern Times* (Boulder: Westview Press, 1987), pp. 169–73.

—(ed.), *Juifs du nil* (Paris: Le Sycomore, 1981); 2d edition: *Histoire des Juifs du nil* (Paris: Minerve, 1990).

Haykal, Muhammad Hasanayn, *Milaffat al-suways: harb al-thalathin sana* (Cairo: al-Ahram, 1989).

Hersh, Burton, *The Old Boys: The American Elite and the Origins of the CIA* (New York: Scribner's, 1992).

Hirshberg, Jehoash, "Musical Tradition as a Cohesive Force in a Community in Transition: The Case of the Karaites," *Asian Music* 17 (no. 2, 1986):46–68.

—, "Musikah ke-gorem le-likud ha-kehilah ha-kara'it be-san frantzisko," *Pe'amim* 32 (1988):66–81.

Husni, Sa'ida Muhammad, *al-Yahud fi misr, 1882–1948* (Cairo: al- Hay'a al-Misriyya al-'Amma li'l-Kitab, 1993).

Hussein, Mahmoud, *The Class Struggle in Egypt, 1945–1970* (New York: Monthly Review Press, 1973).

—, Letter to the Editor, *Nouvel Observateur*, Oct. 22, 1973.

Ilbert, Robert, with Jacques Hassoun (eds.), *Alexandrie, 1860–1960* (Paris: Editions Autrement, 1992).

Issawi, Charles, *Egypt in Revolution: An Economic Analysis* (London: Oxford University Press, 1963).

Jacques, Paula, *Un Baiser froid comme la lune* (Paris: Mercure de France, 1983).

—, *Déborah et les anges dissipés* (Paris: Mercure de France, 1991).

—, *L'Héritage de tante Carlotta* (Paris: Gallimard, 1990).

—, *Lumière de l'oeil* (Paris: Mercure de France, 1980).

Jameson, Fredric, *Postmodernism, or the Cultural Logic of Late Capitalism* (Durham: Duke University Press, 1991).

Jankowski, James P., "Egyptian Responses to the Palestine Problem in the Interwar Period," *International Journal of Middle East Studies* 12 (no. 1, 1980):1–38.

—, "Zionism and the Jews in Egyptian National Opinion, 1920–1939," in Amnon Cohen and Gabriel Baer (eds.), *Egypt and Palestine: A Millennium of Association (868–1948)* (Jerusalem: Ben Zvi Institute for the Study of Jewish Communities in the East, 1984), pp. 314–31.

Kahanoff, Jacqueline, "Childhood in Egypt," *Jerusalem Quarterly* no. 36 (Summer 1985):31–41.

—, *Mi-mizrah shemesh* (Tel Aviv: Yariv-Hadar, 1978).

Kalderon, Nisim, "Lo ha-kol sipur ehad: 'al 'zeh 'im ha-panim eleynu' shel ronit matalon," *Rehov* 2 (Aug. 1995):48–58.

Kamil, Anis Mustafa, "Ta'rikh al-ra'smaliyya al-yahudiyya fi misr," *al-Ahram al-iqtisadi* nos. 636–42 (Mar. 23–May 4, 1981).

Kitching, Gavin, "The Role of the National Bourgeoisie in the Current Phase of Capitalist Development: Some Reflections," in Paul M. Lubeck (ed.), *The African Bourgeoisie: Capitalist Development in Nigeria, Kenya, and the Ivory Coast* (Boulder: Westview Press, 1987), pp. 27–55.

Kohen-Tzidon, Shlomo, *Dramah be-aleksandriah ve-shnei harugei malkhut: mehandes sh. 'azar ve-doktor m. marzuk* (Tel Aviv: Sgi'al, 1965).

—, "Kehilat yehudei kahir," *Mahanayim* 114 (Adar bet 5727/1967):38–45.

Koriansky, Shulamit, "Kemo shahar she-nirdam," *Moznayim* Nun (no. 1, 1979):151–52.

Krämer, Gudrun, "'Aliyatah ve-shkiy'atah shel kehilat kahir," *Pe'amim* 7 (1981):4–30.

—, *The Jews in Modern Egypt, 1914–1952* (Seattle: University of Washington Press, 1989).

—, "Political Participation of the Jews in Egypt between World War I and the 1952 Revolution," in Shimon Shamir (ed.), *The Jews of Egypt: A Mediterranean Society in Modern Times* (Boulder: Westview Press, 1987), pp. 68–81.

—, "Radical Nationalists, Fundamentalists, and the Jews of Egypt or, Who Is a Real Egyptian?" in Gabriel R. Warburg and Uri M. Kupferschmidt (eds.), *Islam, Nationalism, and Radicalism in Egypt and the Sudan* (New York: Praeger, 1983).

—, "Zionism in Egypt, 1917–1948," in Amnon Cohen and Gabriel Baer (eds.), *Egypt and Palestine: A Millennium of Association (868–1948)* (Jerusalem: Ben Zvi Institute for the Study of Jewish Communities in the East, 1984), pp. 348–66.

Landau, Jacob M., "The Confused Image: Egypt as Perceived by Jewish Emigrants," in Amnon Cohen and Gabriel Baer (eds.), *Egypt and Palestine: A Millennium of Association (868–1948)* (Jerusalem: Ben Zvi Institute for the Study of Jewish Communities in the East, 1984), pp. 367–75.

—, *Jews in Nineteenth Century Egypt* (New York: New York University Press: 1969).

—, *Studies in the Arab Theater and Cinema* (Philadelphia: University of Pennsylvania Press, 1958).

Landshut, S., *Jewish Communities in the Muslim Countries of the Middle East: A Survey* (London: Jewish Chronicle Association, 1950).

Laskier, Michael M., "A Document on Anglo-Jewry's Intervention on Behalf of Egyptian Jews on Trial for Espionage and Sabotage, December 1954," *Michael* 10 (1986):143–53.

—, "Egyptian Jewry Under the Nasser Regime, 1956–1970," *Middle Eastern Studies* 31 (no. 3, 1995):573–619.

—, "Egypt's Jewry in the Post–World War II Period: 1945–1948," *Revue des Etudes Juives* 148 (July–Dec. 1989):337–60.

—, "From War to War: The Jews of Egypt from 1948 to 1970," *Studies in Zionism* 7 (no. 1, 1986):111–47.

—, *The Jews of Egypt, 1920–1970: In the Midst of Zionism, Anti-Semitism, and the Middle East Conflict* (New York: New York University Press, 1992).

Lesser, Alexander, "Don't Call Us Jews," *The Jerusalem Report,* June 18, 1992, pp. 36–38.

Levy, Clement (comp.), *The Stock Exchange Year-Book of Egypt* (Cairo: Stock Exchange Year-Book of Egypt, 1937–59).

Lewis, Bernard, *The Jews of Islam* (Princeton: Princeton University Press, 1984).

—, *Semites and Anti-Semites: An Inquiry into Conflict and Prejudice* (New York: Norton, 1986).

Lustick, Ian, *Arabs in the Jewish State: Israel's Control of a National Minority* (Austin: University of Texas Press, 1980).

Maccabi, Rahel, *Mitzrayim sheli* (Tel Aviv: Sifriat ha-Poʿalim, 1968).

Magdi, Tawhid, "Amlak al-yahud fi misr," *Ruz al-yusuf,* Dec. 18, 1995, pp. 39–45.

Malkki, Liisa, "National Geographic: The Rooting of Peoples and the Territorialization of National Identity among Scholars and Refugees," *Cultural Anthropology* 7 (no. 1, 1992):24–44.

Mansur, Anis, "Hadiyya li'l-sadat: ikhtaraha yusuf wa-katabaha yusuf ʿan hayat yusuf," *Uktubir,* Feb. 2, 1992, pp. 11–13.

Marx, Karl, *The Eighteenth Brumaire of Louis Bonaparte,* in Lewis S. Feuer (ed.), *Karl Marx and Friedrich Engels: Basic Writings on Politics and Philosophy* (Garden City, NY: Anchor Books, 1959).

Matalon, Ronit, *Zeh ʿim ha-panim eleynu* (Tel Aviv: ʿAm ʿOved, 1995).

Mayer, Thomas, *Egypt and the Palestine Question, 1936–1945* (Berlin: Klaus Schwarz Verlag, 1983).

Meital, Yoram, *Atarim yehudiyim be-mitzrayim* (Jerusalem: Makhon Ben-Tzvi le-Heker Kehilot Yisra'el ba-Mizrah, 1995).

Menasche, Rosy, *Couleurs du temps: Hymne à la paix* (Haifa: Dora Barkai, 1992).

Mendès-France, Pierre, "Au Moyen-Orient, comme au Viêt-nam, la paix est un devoir," *Le Nouvel Observateur,* Apr. 24–30, 1968, p. 24.

Miron, Dan, "Ha-genrah ha-yam-tikhoni ha-yehudi ba-safrut ha-yisra'elit, *Ha-ʿolam ha-zeh,* Apr. 8, 1987.

Mitchell, Richard P., *The Society of the Muslim Brothers* (New York: Oxford University Press, 1993).

Mizrahi, Maurice, *L'Egypte et ses Juifs: Le Temps révolu, xixe et xxe siècles* (Geneva: Imprimerie Avenir, 1977).

—, "The Role of Jews in Economic Development," in Shimon Shamir (ed.), *The Jews of Egypt: A Mediterranean Society in Modern Times* (Boulder: Westview Press, 1987), pp. 85–93.

Monet, Dina, "The Jewish Community of Egypt," *New Outlook* 1 (July 1957):25–28.

Montasser, Adel, "La répression anti-démocratique en Egypte," *Les Temps Modernes* 16 (Aug.–Sept. 1960):418–41.

Morris, Benny, *Israel's Border Wars, 1949–1956* (Oxford: Oxford University Press, 1993).

Murad, Mahmud, *Man kana yahkum misr? shahadat watha'iqiyya* (Cairo: Maktabat Madbuli, 1975).

Mursi, Salih, *Layla murad* (Cairo: Dar al-Hilal, 1995).

Nahmias, Victor, "al-Shams: iton yehudi bemitzrayim, 1934–1948," *Peʿamim* 16 (1983):128–41.

Nassar, Siham, *al-Sahafa al-isra'iliyya wa'l-diʿayya al-sahyuniyya fi misr* (Cairo: al-Zahra' li'l-Iʿlam al-ʿArabi, 1991).

—, *al-Yahud al-misriyyun bayna al-misriyya wa'l-sahyuniyya* (Beirut: Dar al-Wahda, 1979); Egyptian edition: *al-Yahud al-misriyyun: suhufuhum wa-majallatuhum, 1877–1950* (Cairo: al-ʿArabi li'l-Nashr wa'l-Tawziʿ [1980?]).

Nemoy, Leon, "A Modern Karaite-Arabic Poet: Mourad Farag," *Jewish Quarterly Review* 70 (1979–80):195–209.

Oren, Eitan, "Yoman yom shishi," Israeli Television, Mar. 14, 1975.

Oren, Michael B., "Secret Egypt-Israel Peace Initiatives Prior to the Suez Campaign," *Middle Eastern Studies* 26 (no. 1, 1990):351–70.

Owen, Roger, "The Development of Agricultural Production in Nineteenth Century Egypt: Capitalism of What Type?" in A. L. Udovitch (ed.), *The Islamic Middle East, 700–1900: Studies in Economic and Social History* (Princeton: Darwin Press, 1981), pp. 521–46.

Perrault, Gilles, *Un homme à part* (Paris: Bernard Barrault, 1984); abridged English edition: *A Man Apart* (London, Zed Books, 1987).

Philipp, Thomas, "Nation State and Religious Community," *Welt des Islams* 29 (1988):379–91.

—, *The Syrians in Egypt, 1725–1975* (Stuttgart: Franz Steiner Verlag, 1985).

Politi, E. I., *L'Egypte de 1914 à Suez* (Paris: Presses de la Cité, 1965).

Praeger, Leonard, "Yiddish Theater in Cairo," *Bulletin of the Israeli Academic Center in Cairo* no. 16 (May 1992):24–30.

Qasim, Qasim ʿAbduh, *al-Yahud fi misr* (Cairo: Dar al-Shuruq, 1993).

—, *al-Yahud fi misr min al-fath al-ʿarabi hatta al-ghazw al-ʿuthmani* (Cairo: Dar al-Fikr, 1987).

Raafat, Samir W., *Maʿadi 1902–1962: Society and History in a Cairo Suburb* (Cairo: Palm Press, 1994).

Rabinovitch, Itamar, *The Road Not Taken: Early Arab-Israeli Negotiations* (New York: Oxford University Press, 1991).

Raymond, André, *Le Caire* (Paris: Fayard, 1993).

Renan, Ernest, *Qu'est-ce qu'une nation?* (Paris: Pierre Bordas et fils, 1991).

Rodinson, Maxime, *Cult, Ghetto, and State: The Persistence of the Jewish Question* (London: Al Saqi Books, 1983).

Rodrigue, Aron, "Difference and Tolerance in the Ottoman Empire" (interview with Nancy Reyonolds), *Stanford Humanities Review* 5 (no. 1, 1995):80–90.

—, "L'Exportation du paradigme révolutionnaire: Son influence sur le judaisme sépharade et oriental," in Pierre Birnbaum (ed.), *Histoire politique des Juifs de France: Entre universalisme et particularisme* (Paris: Presses de la Fondation Nationale des Sciences Politiques, 1990), pp. 182–95.

—, *French Jews, Turkish Jews: The Alliance Israélite Universelle and the Politics of Jewish Schooling in Turkey, 1860–1925* (Bloomington: Indiana University Press, 1990).

Roshwald, Mordecai, "Marginal Jewish Sects in Israel," part I, *International Journal of Middle East Studies* 4 (no. 2, 1973):219–37.

Rushdie, Salman, *Imaginary Homelands: Essays and Criticism, 1981–1991* (London: Granta Books in association with Penguin Books, 1991).

Rutherford, Jonathan, "A Place Called Home: Identity and the Politics of Cultural Difference," in Jonathan Rutherford (ed.), *Identity, Community, Culture, Difference* (London: Lawrence & Wishart, 1990), pp. 9–27.

Sabet, Adel M., *A King Betrayed: The Ill-Fated Reign of Farouk of Egypt* (London: Quartet Books, 1989).

Said, Edward W., *Culture and Imperialism* (New York: Knopf, 1993).

—, "The Mind of Winter: Reflections on Life in Exile," *Harper's,* Sept. 1984, pp. 49–55.

al-Saʿid, Rifʿat, *Taʾrikh al-haraka al-shuyuʿiyya al-misriyya: al-wahda, al-inqisam, al-hall, 1957–1965* (Cairo: Dar al-Thaqafa al-Jadida, 1986).

—, *al-Yasar al-misri waʾl-qadiyya al-filastiniyya* (Beirut: Dar al-Farabi, 1974).

Sanua, Victor D., "Emigration of the Sephardic Jews from Egypt after the Arab-Israeli Wars," *Proceedings of the Eleventh World Congress of Jewish Studies,* vol. 3 (Jerusalem: World Union of Jewish Studies, 1994), pp. 215–22.

—, "A Jewish Childhood in Cairo," in Victor D. Sanua (ed.), *Fields of Offerings: Studies in Honor of Raphael Patai* (Rutherford, N.J.: Farleigh Dickinson University Press, 1983), pp. 283–95.

Schur, Nathan, *History of the Karaites* (Frankfurt am Main: Peter Lang, 1992).

Segev, Tom, *The Seventh Million: The Israelis and the Holocaust* (New York: Hill and Wang, 1993).

Shafir, Gershon, *Land, Labour and the Origins of the Israeli-Palestinian Conflict, 1882–1904* (Cambridge: Cambridge University Press, 1989).

Shaked, Gershon, *ha-Siporet ha-ʿivrit, 1880–1980,* vol. 4 (Tel Aviv: ha-Kibutz ha-Meʾuhad and Keter, 1993).

Shalash, ʿAli, "Malaff al-yahud fi misr," *al-Majalla* no. 284, July 17–23, through no. 290, Aug. 28–Sept. 3, 1985.

—, *al-Yahud waʾl-masun fi misr: dirasa taʾrikhiyya* (Cairo: al-Zahraʾ liʾl-Iʿlam al-ʿArabi, 1986).

Shamir, Shimon, "The Evolution of the Egyptian Nationality Laws and Their Application to the Jews in the Monarchy Period," in Shimon Shamir (ed.), *The Jews of Egypt: A Mediterranean Society in Modern Times* (Boulder: Westview Press, 1987), pp. 33–67.

Shammas, Maurice, "The Scholar and Poet Murad Bey Farag: A Brief Review of his Life and Works," *Bulletin of the Israeli Academic Center in Cairo* no. 13 (July 1990):26–29.

—, "Shakhsiyyat yahudiyya fi ʿalam al-fikr waʾl-iqtisad anjabatha misr fi al-qarn al-ʿishrin," *Bulletin of the Israeli Academic Center in Cairo* no. 10 (July 1988):31–34.

—, *al-Shaykh shabtay wa-hikayat min harat al-yahud* (Shafa ʿAmr: al-Mashriq, 1979).

Shohat, Ella, "Notes on the "Post-Colonial," *Social Text* nos. 31–32 (1992):99–113.

—, "Sephardim in Israel: Zionism from the Standpoint of Its Jewish Victims," *Social Text* nos. 19–20 (1988):1–35.

Shohet, Jacqueline [Kahanoff], *Jacob's Ladder* (London: Harvill Press, 1951).

Sid-Ahmed, Mohamed [Muhammad Sayyid-Ahmad], *After the Guns Fall Silent: Peace or Armageddon in the Middle East* (London: Croom Helm, 1976); Arabic edition: *Baʿda an tasquta al-madafiʿ* (Beirut: Dar al-Qadaya, 1975).

Somekh, Sasson, "Participation of Egyptian Jews in Modern Arabic Culture and the Case of Murad Faraj," in Shimon Shamir (ed.), *The Jews of Egypt: A Mediterranean Society in Modern Times* (Boulder: Westview Press, 1987), pp. 130–40.

Stambouli, R., "Mémoire des juifs d'Egypte," *Information Juive,* July 1991, p. 11.

Sterling, Claire, *The Terror Network: The Secret War of International Terrorism* (New York: Holt, Rinehart & Winston, 1981).

Stern, Michael, *Farouk* (New York: Bantam, 1965).

Stillman, Norman A., *The Jews of Arab Lands* (Philadelphia: Jewish Publication Society, 1979).

—, *The Jews of Arab Lands in Modern Times* (Philadelphia: Jewish Publication Society, 1991).

—, Letter to the Editor, *Tikkun* 6 (July–Aug. 1991):97.

—, "Myth, Countermyth, and Distortion," *Tikkun* 6 (May–June 1991):60–64.

Stoler, Laura Ann, "Rethinking Colonial Categories: European Communities and the Boundaries of Rule," *Comparative Studies in Society and History* 31 (no. 1, 1989):134–61.

Suffert, Georges, "Le patron des réseaux d'aide aux terroristes," *Le Point,* June 21, 1976, pp. 52–57.

Sutton, David, "Yehudei suriyah be-nyu york" *ha-Do'ar,* Aug. 18, 1972, pp. 590–91.

Sutton, Joseph A. D., *Aleppo Chronicles: The Story of the Unique Sephardeem of the Ancient Near East—in Their Own Words* (New York: Thayer-Jacoby, 1988).

—, *Magic Carpet: Aleppo in Flatbush, the Story of a Unique Ethnic Jewish Community* (New York: Thayer-Jacoby, 1979).

Swirski, Shlomo, *Israel: The Oriental Majority* (London: Zed Books, 1989).

Tawil, Muhammad, *al-Yahud fi barlaman misr* (Cairo: Dar al-Sha'b, 1988).

Teveth, Shabtai, *'Onat ha-gez: Kitat yorim be-vayt jan, Kalaba"n* (Tel Aviv: Ish Dor, 1992); abridged English edition: *Ben-Gurion's Spy: The Story of the Political Scandal That Shaped Modern Israel* (New York: Columbia University Press, 1996).

Tignor, Robert L., "Bank Misr and Foreign Capitalism," *International Journal of Middle East Studies* 8 (no. 2, 1977):161–81.

—, "Decolonization and Business: The Case of Egypt," *Journal of Modern History* 59 (Sept. 1987):479–505.

—, "The Economic Activities of Foreigners in Egypt:. 1920–1950: From Millet to Haute Bourgeoisie," *Comparative Studies in Society and History* 22 (Jan. 1980):416–49.

—, "Egyptian Jewry, Communal Tension, and Zionism," in Amnon Cohen and Gabriel Baer (eds.), *Egypt and Palestine: A Millennium of Association (868–1948)* (Jerusalem: Ben Zvi Institute for the Study of Jewish Communities in the East, 1984), pp. 332–47.

—, *Egyptian Textiles and British Capital, 1930–1956* (Cairo: American University of Cairo Press, 1989).

—, *State, Private Enterprise, and Economic Change in Egypt, 1918–1952* (Princeton: Princeton University Press, 1984).

—, "The Suez Crisis of 1956 and Egypt's Foreign Private Sector," *Journal of Imperial & and Commonwealth History* 20 (no. 2, 1992):274–97.

Tzur, Eli, "Parashat prag: ha-hanhagah ve-ha-opozitziah ba-kbh"a," *Me'asef* 18 (June 1988):30–61.

'Uthman, Ahmad, *Ta'rikh al-yahud,* vol. 1 (Cairo: Maktabat al-Shuruq, 1994).

Valensi, Lucette, and Nathan Wachtel, *Jewish Memories* (Berkeley: University of California Press, 1990).

Vidal, Esther Mosseri, *L'Etreinte du Passé* (Giv'atayim: Editions Ma'amtan [1992?]).

Vitalis, Robert, "On the Theory and Practice of Compradors: The Role of 'Abbud Pasha in the Egyptian Political Economy," *International Journal of Middle East Studies* 22 (no. 3, 1990):291–315.

—, "Ra'smaliyyun fi al-khayal: iydiyulujiyat al-tabaqa wa'l-zabun fi al-iqtisad al-siyasi al-misri," *Jadal* 1 (Aug. 1991):54–83.

—, *When Capitalists Collide: Business Conflict and the End of Empire in Egypt* (Berkeley: University of California, Press, 1995).

Wallerstein, Immanuel, "The Bourgeois(ie) as Concept and Reality," *New Left Review,* no. 167 (Jan.–Feb. 1988):91–106.

Watts, Michael J., "Space for Everything (a Commentary)," *Cultural Anthropology* 7 (no. 1, 1992):115–27.

Wolf, Tamar, "Kitsh aleksandroni," *'Iton 77* (no. 87, Apr. 1987):7.

Yadlin, Rivka, *An Arrogant and Oppressive Spirit: Anti-Zionism as Anti-Judaism in Egypt* (Oxford: Pergamon Press, 1989).

Yahudiya Misriya [Giselle Littman], *Les juifs en Egypte: Aperçu sur 3000 ans d'histoire* (Geneva: Editions de l'Avenir, 1971).

Zahran, Sa'd, *Fi usul al-siyyasa al-misriyya: maqal tahlili naqdi fi al-ta'rikh al-siyyasi* (Cairo: Dar al-Mustaqbal al-'Arabi, 1985).

Zamir, Levana, *Ma'akhalim me-eretz ha-nilus (kasher)* (Tel Aviv: ha-Kibutz ha-Me'uhad, 1982).

Zeitlin, Maurice, and Richard Earl Ratcliff, *Landlords & Capitalists: The Dominant Class of Chile* (Princeton: Princeton University Press, 1988).

Zerubavel, Yael, *Recovered Roots: Collective Memory and the Making of Israeli National Tradition* (Chicago: University of Chicago Press, 1995).

Zohar, Tzvi, "Bayn nikur le-ahvah: nisu'im beyn kara'im le-rabanim 'al-pnei hakhmei yisra'el be-mitzrayim be-me'ah ha-'esrim." *Pe'amim* 32 (1987):21–38.

Index

Abaza, Fikri, 73
'Abbud, Ahmad, 255, 258–59, 261
'Abd Allah, Isma'il Sabri, 144, 157, 165
'Abd al-'Azim, 263
'Abd al-Hadi, Ibrahim, 35, 70, 91
'Abd al-Rahman, 'Awatif, 245–47, 251
'Abd al-Wahhab, Muhammad, 83
Abdel Malek, Anouar, 145, 146,
    147, 253
Abdel Nasser, Gamal, 18, 20, 37, 78, 79,
    84, 86, 99, 101, 103, 107, 114, 152,
    155, 156, 158, 165, 168, 169, 209,
    214, 236, 248
Abraham Btesh Jewish Community
    School, 123
Abu Faysal, 176
Abu 'Iyad (Salah Khalaf), 169–70
Abu Mazin, 176
Abu Nidal, 178
Abu Ya'qub, 41
activism, 112
Adjiman, Salvator, 80
'Afifi, 'Ata, 261
'Afifi, Hafiz, 262
Aghion, Raymond, 148, 164–65, 174
Aharon, Benny, 130, 139
Aharon, Haim, 139, 220
Aharoni, 'Ada, 139, 213, 220–27, 232,
    250, 264–65
Le-Ahdut ha-'Avodah, 22, 97, 126, 140,
    212, 269
Ahmad, Nabil 'Abd al-Hamid Sayyid,
    247, 249–51, 259, 264
Aide et Amitié (Aid and friendship), 162

'Ali, 'Arfa 'Abduh, 247, 259
'aliyah. *See* emigration
Alliance Israelite Universelle, 6, 49
American Jewish Committee, 60, 91,
    92–93, 104–05, 108–09
American Jewish Congress, 108
American University in Cairo, 25, 26, 27
Amir, Aharon, 54
Amit, Daniel, 176
Amitai, Yossi, 170, 175, 176
'Anan ben David, 2, 40
Angel, Aaron, 87–88
Anglo-Egyptian Oilfields Ltd., 261
Anglo-Jewish Association, 103
anti-Semitism, 16, 17, 27, 58, 61, 62, 64,
    70, 90, 91–99, 100, 103–04, 106, 107,
    116–17, 136, 146, 152, 169, 208, 209,
    227, 241–42, 244, 249, 263, 264, 265,
    270, 274
Arab-Israeli War: 1948, 1, 18, 35, 43,
    48, 60, 62, 66–70, 77, 81, 85–86,
    91–93, 99, 106, 127, 130, 145, 147,
    181; 1967, 16, 27, 89, 165, 166, 191,
    236, 248; 1973, 166, 171, 174, 179,
    188, 214, 220
Arab nationalism. *See* pan-Arab
    nationalism
Arab socialism, 12, 19, 159, 172, 185,
    187, 189, 214, 243, 255, 263
'Arafat, Yasir, 177, 178
Arnon, Ya'akov, 176
Ashkenazim, 4–5, 15, 16, 22, 23, 59, 64,
    65, 71, 115, 121, 128, 129, 207, 208,
    209, 211, 216, 226, 236, 238

Designer: Nola Burger
Compositor: BookMasters, Inc.
Text: 10/13 Sabon
Display: Sabon
Printer and Binder: Braun-Brumfield